MW00772411

"The goals of this preaching seri point to what God must do in Christ from every book of the Bible, and to include expositions that are rich in pastoral illustrations and theologically driven applications—make this work of Platt, Mason, and Shaddix a treasure of gospel insights, theological precision, and pastoral aid."

Bryan Chapell, pastor, author of *Christ-Centered Preaching*

"In John 4, Jesus tells the Samaritan woman that she is worshiping what she does not know, revealing that the Father seeks those who worship him in spirit and truth. What better way to inspire and inform our congregations about our corporate responsibilities in worship than to preach the great worship texts of Psalms. The tool you have in your hands will assist any preacher in that pursuit. Thank you, Jim Shaddix, Matt Mason, and David Platt, for giving pastors this great resource to put the exaltation of God in our mouths and the double-edged sword in our hands (Ps 148:6). God's people will be helped by this work."

Mike Harland, director, LifeWay Worship Resources

"We know God feels our infirmities (Heb 4:15). Sometimes though, in our secret place, we want to know humans have felt our infirmities, our fear, our desperation and have survived to tell of God's deliverance. In this excellent exposition of Psalms 51–100, David Platt, Matt Mason, and Jim Shaddix bring the reality of anguish, thrill of exuberance, paralyzing fear, and other emotions felt by psalmists and apply them to our realm of understanding through the lens of Christ. The authors lift lessons, encouragement, and warnings applicable for believers who want to walk with our Messiah in every season of life confident in their faith and in our God. The pages of this book will meet you wherever you are and help you find the path to where you need to go."

Dr. Robert Smith Jr., Charles T. Carter Baptist Chair of Divinity, Beeson Divinity School, Samford University

CHRIST-CENTERED

Exposition

AUTHOR **David Platt, Jim Shaddix, and Matt Mason**

SERIES EDITORS **David Platt, Daniel L. Akin, and Tony Merida**

CHRIST-CENTERED

Exposition

EXALTING JESUS IN

PSALMS 51–100

HOLMAN®

REFERENCE

NASHVILLE, TENNESSEE

SERIES DEDICATION

Dedicated to Adrian Rogers and John Piper. They have taught us to love the gospel of Jesus Christ, to preach the Bible as the inerrant Word of God, to pastor the church for which our Savior died, and to have a passion to see all nations gladly worship the Lamb.

—David Platt, Tony Merida, and Danny Akin
March 2013

TABLE OF CONTENTS

DP = David Platt
JS = Jim Shaddix
MM = Matt Mason

ACKNOWLEDGMENTS

This commentary is the fruit of God's grace in the lives of many brothers and sisters. I am grateful to God for David Burnette's diligent and wise editing in taking these sermons that I have preached and turning them into chapters for this commentary. I am also grateful for Chris Hunsberger and the entire Radical team, who are serving the church in so many ways around the world with God's Word. I am continually grateful to God for Heather as well as Caleb, Joshua, Mara Ruth, and Isaiah; I am blessed beyond measure with the family he has entrusted to me. I am deeply grateful to God for The Church at Brook Hills, a church family I love deeply composed of brothers and sisters who heard me preach many of these sermons. Further, I thank God for McLean Bible Church, the church family I now have the joy and privilege of shepherding with God's Word. What a joy it is for us to have God's Word! And to know, enjoy, worship, and walk with him according to it! As the overflow of God's grace in many people, I pray that this commentary serves as an instrument in God's hands for the spread of his glory among all peoples, particularly among those who don't yet have his Word. In the words of Psalm 67:3, "Let the peoples praise you, God; let all the peoples praise you!"

—David Platt

Thank you, David Platt and Matt Mason, for allowing me the privilege of co-laboring with you in the preaching of God's Word. Thank you, Keith Myatt and Forrest Moss, for keeping me from hurting myself by carefully editing my work in this study. Thank you, faith families of The Church at Brook Hills and the First Baptist Church of Charlotte, North Carolina, for eagerly receiving these messages from God's Word and applying them to your lives.

— Jim Shaddix

First of all, I would not be contributing to this volume were it not for
David Platt and Jim Shaddix. You've been chief encouragers and dear
friends. Thank you for making room for me in ministry. Thanks to Jenny
Riddle for helping tidy up early manuscripts. To my faith family—the
Church at Brook Hills. What a joy it is to sing to the Lord and declare
his glory among the nations with you! Thanks, Dennis Blythe—my close
companion in ministry whose prayers and encouragement have often
kept my head above water. I thank God for my parents, through whom
the Spirit principally worked to fill up my heart with love for Jesus. And
finally, my greatest earthly joys: Paula, my wife, and our three children,
Hunter, Will, and Ellie. May the Lord be our portion all our days until,
together, we know pleasures evermore!

—Matt Mason

SERIES INTRODUCTION

Augustine said, "Where Scripture speaks, God speaks." The editors of the Christ-Centered Exposition Commentary series believe that where God speaks, the pastor must speak. God speaks through His written Word. We must speak from that Word. We believe the Bible is God breathed, authoritative, inerrant, sufficient, understandable, necessary, and timeless. We also affirm that the Bible is a Christ-centered book; that is, it contains a unified story of redemptive history of which Jesus is the hero. Because of this Christ-centered trajectory that runs from Genesis 1 through Revelation 22, we believe the Bible has a corresponding global-missions thrust. From beginning to end, we see God's mission as one of making worshipers of Christ from every tribe and tongue worked out through this redemptive drama in Scripture. To that end we must preach the Word.

In addition to these distinct convictions, the Christ-Centered Exposition Commentary series has some distinguishing characteristics. First, this series seeks to display exegetical accuracy. What the Bible says is what we want to say. While not every volume in the series will be a verse-by-verse commentary, we nevertheless desire to handle the text carefully and explain it rightly. Those who teach and preach bear the heavy responsibility of saying what God has said in His Word and declaring what God has done in Christ. We desire to handle God's Word faithfully, knowing that we must give an account for how we have fulfilled this holy calling (Jas 3:1).

Second, the Christ-Centered Exposition Commentary series has pastors in view. While we hope others will read this series, such as parents, teachers, small-group leaders, and student ministers, we desire to provide a commentary busy pastors will use for weekly preparation of biblically faithful and gospel-saturated sermons. This series is not academic in nature. Our aim is to present a readable and pastoral style of commentaries. We believe this aim will serve the church of the Lord Jesus Christ.

Third, we want the Christ-Centered Exposition Commentary series to be known for the inclusion of helpful illustrations and theologically driven applications. Many commentaries offer no help in illustrations, and few offer any kind of help in application. Often those that do offer illustrative material and application unfortunately give little serious attention to the text. While giving ourselves primarily to explanation, we also hope to serve readers by providing inspiring and illuminating illustrations coupled with timely and timeless application.

Finally, as the name suggests, the editors seek to exalt Jesus from every book of the Bible. In saying this, we are not commending wild allegory or fanciful typology. We certainly believe we must be constrained to the meaning intended by the divine Author himself, the Holy Spirit of God. However, we also believe the Bible has a messianic focus, and our hope is that the individual authors will exalt Christ from particular texts. Luke 24:25-27,44-47 and John 5:39,46 inform both our hermeneutics and our homiletics. Not every author will do this the same way or have the same degree of Christ-centered emphasis. That is fine with us. We believe faithful exposition that is Christ centered is not monolithic. We do believe, however, that we must read the whole Bible as Christian Scripture. Therefore, our aim is both to honor the historical particularity of each biblical passage and to highlight its intrinsic connection to the Redeemer.

The editors are indebted to the contributors of each volume. The reader will detect a unique style from each writer, and we celebrate these unique gifts and traits. While distinctive in their approaches, the authors share a common characteristic in that they are pastoral theologians. They love the church, and they regularly preach and teach God's Word to God's people. Further, many of these contributors are younger voices. We think these new, fresh voices can serve the church well, especially among a rising generation that has the task of proclaiming the Word of Christ and the Christ of the Word to the lost world.

We hope and pray this series will serve the body of Christ well in these ways until our Savior returns in glory. If it does, we will have succeeded in our assignment.

David Platt
Daniel L. Akin
Tony Merida
Series Editors
February 2013

Psalms 51–100

The Confession of Man and the Compassion of God

PSALM 51

Main Idea: Sin is an infinitely serious offense against God, but by his grace and mercy we can be forgiven and restored to God through honest and humble confession.

I. **Sin Is Serious.**
   - A. Sin is offensive.
     1. Sin defies God.
     2. Sin destroys man.
   - B. Sin is comprehensive.
   - C. Sin is pervasive.
     1. Sin appears so subtly.
     2. Sin harms so deeply.
     3. Sin controls so quickly.
     4. Sin devastates so painfully.
II. **God Is Gracious.**
   - A. His cleansing is costly.
   - B. His forgiveness is free.
III. **Confession Is the Connection.**
   - A. Confession involves honesty.
   - B. Confession involves humility.
IV. **Restoration Is the Result.**
   - A. God re-creates our heart.
   - B. God reestablishes our joy.
   - C. We walk with him.
   - D. We witness for him.
   - E. We worship him.

Psalm 51 is one of the most well-known, humbling, convicting, and encouraging psalms in the whole Bible. In the words of Charles Spurgeon, "Such a psalm may be wept over, absorbed into the soul, and exhaled again in devotion; but, commented on—ah! where is he who having attempted it can do other than blush at his defeat?" (*Spurgeon on*

3

the Psalms, 3). As we make our way through this psalm, we should do so
humbly, pondering its meaning along the way and allowing its truth to
penetrate our hearts.

In order to understand what this psalm is saying and how it applies
to our lives, we need to start by reading its superscription. The events
of 2 Samuel 11:1–12:23, instrumental for understanding the psalm's
message, are the psalm's historical background. Apart from this story of
David's sin, we won't feel the weight of Psalm 51.

David committed adultery with Bathsheba then arranged for her
husband to be put to death. This tragic story is not merely there to
provide historical information. We have much to learn in our own lives
and in the church by looking not only at the triumphs but also at the
failures of those who have gone before us. These failures should serve
as a warning. Thankfully, we can also learn from David's response to his
failure in Psalm 51.

Amid the various ways this psalm teaches and shapes us, there are
four simple yet significant truths we need to grasp.

Sin Is Serious

David uses words like "rebellion" (vv. 1,3), "guilt" (vv. 2,5,9), and "evil"
(v. 4) throughout this psalm, reminding us that **sin is offensive**. The
word *rebellion*, sometimes translated as "transgression" (ESV), refers to
going against divine law. We see the nature of sin here in two ways.

First, *sin defies God* (v. 4). We may think the most serious consequence of our sin is the harm we bring to someone else—a spouse, children, parents, or friends. In our narcissistic age, we may even think the
worst consequence of our sin is what happens to us. But that's not a
biblical view of sin.

The worst consequence—and the primary problem—of our sin is
that we have defied the infinitely holy God of the universe. Think about
the transition that has come about in David at this point: he has gone
from asking, "How do I cover up my sin?" to "How could I do this to
God?" This is the place we all need to come to. We need to see our sin
for what it is—outright defiance of God himself.

In addition to defying God, *sin destroys man*. The effect of David's
sin with Bathsheba carried beyond David to the murder of Uriah, which
also means a wife lost her husband. And, tragically, the child of David
and Bathsheba died in the process. Never underestimate the power of
sin in your life to cause pain in others' lives.

Sin is comprehensive. David doesn't just say he messed up a few times. No, he has a much more comprehensive understanding of sin. He knows sin goes back to the moment he was born (v. 5). That's not a reference to an immoral relationship David's mother had, nor is it a reference to the specific circumstances surrounding David's birth. It's a reference to the reality that affects every one of us from the moment we are born. We are born into sin. We are born with hearts that are prone to defy God and destroy others. I've seen in my youngest children a nature that is sweet, cute, and cuddly at one moment and in the next defiant and uncontrollable. This is true of all of us—we don't just *occasionally* sin. We are comprehensive sinners, possessing a nature that is prone to disobey.

Sin is pervasive (v. 3). Like David, we too can say "my sin is always before me" (v. 3). Even in my best deeds and on my best days, when I am doing what would seem to be the most noble things, I am still prone to do those things for selfish reasons. Even in my clearest displays of Christlike actions on the outside, I can harbor some of the most evil thoughts on the inside. I am a sinner, through and through.

David's life is a reminder that *sin appears so subtly*. It all started with a walk outside and a glance across the roof. This is why Jesus says in Matthew 5:29, "If your right eye causes you to sin, gouge it out and throw it away. For it is better that you lose one of the parts of your body than for your whole body to be thrown into hell." Jesus's words may at first sound extreme, but they make sense given the consequences of sin. If David only knew the disastrous effects that would spring from this glance—a glance that would wreck the rest of his life—if only he had the chance to do it all over again, he would have preferred to gouge out his own eye. That's the point of what Jesus is saying: take radical measures to guard yourself against pervasive sin that appears so subtly.

Also, *sin harms so deeply*. A lustful look leads to adultery, adultery to lying, lying to murder, and murder to the death of a child. And beyond this episode, David's oldest son, Amnon, repeats the sin of his father, except he rapes his half sister. We're reminded that *sin controls so quickly*. David's sin permeated his household throughout the rest of 2 Samuel. Within two years his son Absalom murdered his brother Amnon and rebelled against his father (see 2 Sam 13–15). *Sin devastates so painfully*. David's reign as king eventually ends with strife between the men of Judah in the south and the men of Israel in the north, strife that would one day lead to a divided kingdom. This devastation started with one look on one day, and it resulted in David's crying out because his joy was gone and his bones had been "crushed" (v. 8).

Psalm 51 reminds us of the gravity of sin. You and I may think our sin is small, but it is extremely serious. What we perceive to be the slightest sin is infinitely serious before God. It's a defiance of God, and it destroys you and others. That is not an overstatement; recall that, according to Genesis 3, sin and death entered the world through one sin. A piece of fruit was eaten, and condemnation came to all men (see Rom 5:12-21). All the effects of sin in the world—murders and rapes and holocausts and world wars and slavery and sex trafficking and thousands of other evils—trace back to that one sin in the garden.

We see the seriousness of sin throughout Scripture. To take a small snapshot, Numbers 14–16 recounts several instances of God's judgment against sin. God's people sinned at the edge of the promised land in Numbers 14, and God said that none of them (except Joshua and Caleb) would see the land that he swore to give to their fathers (Num 14:22-23). Then, in the next chapter, we read of the following incident:

> While the Israelites were in the wilderness, they found a man gathering wood on the Sabbath day. Those who found him gathering wood brought him to Moses, Aaron, and the entire community. They placed him in custody because it had not been decided what should be done to him. Then the Lord told Moses, "The man is to be put to death. The entire community is to stone him outside the camp." So the entire community brought him outside the camp and stoned him to death, as the Lord had commanded Moses. (Num 15:32-36)

Stoned for picking up sticks on the Sabbath! Finally, in Numbers 16, Korah and others rebelled against Moses, and ultimately against God. This rebellion elicited the following reaction from God:

> Just as he finished speaking all these words, the ground beneath them split open. The earth opened its mouth and swallowed them and their households, all Korah's people, and all their possessions. They went down alive into Sheol with all that belonged to them. The earth closed over them, and they vanished from the assembly. (Num 16:31-33)

These stories are written down for a reason. To a world and a culture and a church that are prone to treat sin lightly, God is repeatedly telling us how serious sin is. It destroys us.

God Is Gracious

Just as David uses different words to describe his sin, he also uses different words to describe God's grace. From the very beginning of the psalm, David appeals to God's "faithful love" and "abundant compassion" as he cries out for God to be "gracious" (v. 1). Then he asks that God would "un-sin" him, that is, remove his iniquity from him (v. 2) (Tate, *Psalms 51–100*, 21). Talk about a bold request!

David knows there is no basis in himself to warrant God's grace. David knows he has committed two sins for which the law of Moses provided no forgiveness: adultery and murder (Campbell, *From Grace to Glory*, 95–96). The penalty for these sins was death (Exod 21:12; Lev 20:10). David had nothing in himself to appeal to, so his first words are a cry for mercy. He appeals to the grace of God, an attribute God has revealed about himself in the history of his dealings with his people. To Moses God revealed himself as Yahweh, who is "a compassionate and gracious God, slow to anger and abounding in faithful love and truth, maintaining faithful love to a thousand generations, forgiving iniquity, rebellion, and sin" (Exod 34:6b-7). This is the God who had said, "I will be gracious to whom I will be gracious, and I will have compassion on whom I will have compassion" (Exod 33:19). David appeals, therefore, to the one who freely bestows his grace and mercy on the undeserving.

David knows that **his cleansing is costly**. It involves sacrifice. This need for a costly sacrifice leads to what James Boice (*Psalms 42–106*, 429) called the "most important" yet "least understood" words in Psalm 51:7: "Purify me with hyssop." Hyssop was a small plant shaped in such a way that it could be used as a brush. The priests used hyssop to brush, or sprinkle, blood over a sacrifice or offering. For example, the prescriptions for the Passover sacrifice included, "Take a cluster of hyssop, dip it in the blood that is in the basin, and brush the lintel and the two doorposts with some of the blood in the basin" (Exod 12:22a). In Leviticus and Numbers hyssop was used to sprinkle blood on people or sacrifices in cleansing ceremonies. So when David asks God to purify him with hyssop, he is referring to the process of sacrifice, specifically the sprinkling of blood.

David knows that the penalty for his sin is death. Therefore, in order for his sin to be removed from him, the penalty for sin must be paid by something (and, ultimately, someone) besides him. God cannot simply overlook sin as if it did not happen. Knowing God's justice, David uses the language of sacrifice. The author of Hebrews highlights this need for sacrifice and the shedding of blood under the old covenant:

> *For when every command had been proclaimed by Moses to all the people according to the law, he took the blood of calves and goats, along with water, scarlet wool, and hyssop, and sprinkled the scroll itself and all the people, saying, This is the blood of the covenant that God has ordained for you. In the same way, he sprinkled the tabernacle and all the articles of worship with blood. According to the law almost everything is purified with blood, and without the shedding of blood there is no forgiveness.* (Heb 9:19-22)

The author of Hebrews also tells us how this need for sacrifices in the Old Testament is fulfilled in the New Testament by our great high priest, Jesus Christ, who "has appeared one time . . . for the removal of sin by the sacrifice of himself" (Heb 9:26). Only on this basis can we come before a holy God:

> *Therefore, brothers and sisters, since we have boldness to enter the sanctuary through the blood of Jesus—he has inaugurated for us a new and living way through the curtain (that is, through his flesh)— and since we have a great high priest over the house of God, let us draw near with a true heart in full assurance of faith, with our hearts sprinkled clean from an evil conscience and our bodies washed in pure water.* (Heb 10:19-22)

In our sin we can only approach God through the sacrifice of another. We must rely on Christ, who died in *our* place and for *our* sin. And it is only because of God's costly sacrifice that **his forgiveness is free** for you and me. This is the wonder of God's grace. We stand before God guilty in our sin, and he is justified in his judgment against us. But in his mercy—in his "abundant compassion" (Ps 51:1)—he makes a way for you and me to be cleansed of all our sin, to be washed whiter than snow (Isa 1:18).

Confession Is the Connection

How do we receive this grace? How can you and I be clean before God? How can our sins—in all of their comprehensiveness and pervasiveness—be wiped away completely? Confession is the connection. That's what this whole psalm is about—acknowledgment of sin alongside pleading for forgiveness. David asks God to "purify" him and to "wash" him (v. 7). He pleads, "Turn your face away from my sins and blot out all my guilt" (v. 9).

This kind of **confession involves honesty**. David is completely transparent before God. He does not try to cover over his sin, for he knows he cannot do that; and he does not try to blame other people or his circumstances for his sin, something we often do. We talk about how we were tired or how someone else did something to us or how we were put in a certain situation. We are prone to do exactly what our sinful ancestors did in the very beginning. God confronted Adam in his sin, and Adam essentially said, "It was her fault" (Gen 3:12). Then God confronted Eve, and she claimed it was the serpent's fault (Gen 3:13). Eventually, we try to blame God.

David took a different approach (vv. 16-17). He knew sacrifice was an outward ritual that must reflect an inward reality. He could not deal with his sin simply by offering a burnt offering, as if the outward act would take care of everything. David was not demeaning the sacrificial system, but he knew that in order for confession to be genuine, something had to happen on the inside, in his heart.

If we are not careful, religion can become one of the biggest cover-ups for our sin. We can live in sin, particularly secret sin, and still gather together regularly and convince ourselves that we're OK. Sadly, we can participate in outward ritual while covering up the inward reality of sin in our lives. May God help us not to sing songs and listen to sermons while bypassing brokenness over our sin. The path to the grace of God is paved with honesty before God.

In addition to honesty, **confession involves humility**. David humbles himself before God and admits his wrongdoing (v. 4a). David knows he can't escape his sin and that he needs God to take it away. This humble confession that we need God's grace and mercy is one of the realities that sets Christianity apart from other religions.

There is nothing we can do to make cleansing and forgiveness possible. Our sins are not removed by reciting prayers, reading holy books, chanting mantras, spinning prayer wheels, fasting, taking pilgrimages, going to certain buildings, or performing certain rituals. Forgiveness comes through honestly and humbly asking God to do what we cannot do—make us clean (v. 2). And when we come before him like this and ask for his cleansing, we find that he is gracious. "If we confess our sins, he is faithful and righteous to forgive us our sins and to cleanse us from all unrighteousness" (1 John 1:9). This is the greatest news in all the world: you can be made right with God, not by doing a list of good works to try to cover up the evil and uncleanness in your heart but by trusting in divine grace and confessing your need for God.

Restoration Is the Result

David doesn't just want a clean slate; he wants a clean heart. He wants a new start. And he knows he can't make this happen on his own, so he prays (v. 10). There's an emphasis on inner transformation. David knows his heart is sinful, and he knows he needs God to create a change at the core of his being. David knows he doesn't just need to try harder; he knows he needs a new heart—a radically new start—and this is exactly what God gives.

In response to our confession, God doesn't only wipe the slate clean, washing our sins away. No, the good news of God's grace gets even better, for **God re-creates our heart**. Just as God created a sun and a moon, light and darkness, the earth and the seas, so he has the power to create a new heart in you and me. This is exactly what God does for us in Christ. Second Corinthians 5:17 says, "Therefore, if anyone is in Christ, he is a new creation; the old has passed away, and see, the new has come."

God reestablishes our joy (v. 12). Again, only God can do this. It's *God's* salvation, not David's. God brings "crushed" bones to rejoice (v. 8). When we sin and defy God, we offend him and hinder our fellowship with him. Sin and its devastating effects steal our joy. But in confession, when we come honestly and humbly before God in our sin, he restores our relationship with him, and in the process he reestablishes our joy before him.

David had tried to conceal his sin, and that didn't work. Concealment of sin is the pathway to misery, but confession of sin is the pathway to joy.

A quick word of caution: When we talk about being restored to God and experiencing joy again, this doesn't mean all the consequences of sin go away. Remember, David's sin had disastrous effects, not just in his life but in the life of his family and in all of Israel for generations to come. Likewise, when we sin, there will be consequences in our lives and in the lives of others. Sometimes people wonder why, after confessing their sin, they would still have to pay for their sin years later. However, the effects of sin don't just disappear. But praise God that the ultimate effect of sin—death (Rom 6:23)—has been paid for by Christ!

We are absolutely looking forward to the day when Christ returns, the day when sin and its effects will be removed from the world. We will dwell with God in a new heaven and a new earth (Rev 21:1-4). But until that day, past sin can cause present pain. Yet, even amid the pain, you can know that in Christ, because of his sacrifice, you have been restored to God. You can know that when God looks at your life, he does not see your sin. Instead, he sees the righteousness of Christ (2 Cor 5:21).

I was recently asked on a radio interview about some of my biggest regrets in life, and so many things came to my mind. There are things I wish I had never done or thought or desired. And when I think about those things, I can feel so dirty, so unclean, so regretful. I'm guessing I'm not alone in this. Even as Christians, those who have been forgiven and cleansed by God, we tend to beat ourselves up over past sin. So what do you do with these feelings of filth and regret? You go running to the reality that when the God of the universe—the only one whose opinion ultimately matters—looks at you, he doesn't see the sin and filth and regret. His abundant mercy and faithful love in Christ have wiped those things away. We can find deep, abiding, eternal joy in that reality.

When God re-creates our heart and reestablishes our joy, by his enabling **we walk with him**. David goes from cleansing *from* God to communion *with* God. It is not only that his sins are washed away; he is now willing to follow God wherever and however God leads, according to his Spirit. This is what we most need in the world—a clean heart before God and a steadfast spirit to walk with him daily.

In addition to walking with God, **we witness for him** (v. 13). David is compelled by God's grace to proclaim God's grace. We have the greatest news in the world, and we should be proclaiming it in our own neighborhoods and to unreached peoples around the world. We should be telling people that Christ alone can make them clean if they will simply trust in him.

Finally, as a result of our confession to God and his cleansing, **we worship him** (vv. 14-15). When you realize that you have sinned against God, and that, in his grace, he has wiped away all your sins through the sacrifice of his Son on a cross, then worship is the natural (or supernatural!) overflow. We sing . . . *loudly*. We declare praise. And not just in each of our lives individually, for this psalm closes with a corporate cry for all the people of God (vv. 18-19). David wants the grace he has found in God to be applied across the entire community of Israel. He wants all of

God's people to worship him rightly, honestly, humbly, and truly. May it be so among you and me and our churches.

Reflect and Discuss

1. What are some ways we try to hide or justify our sin?
2. Respond to this statement: "Sin is terrible because it keeps you from reaching your potential."
3. How would you describe David's view of sin in Psalm 51? What does this tell us about David's view of God, and what is the connection between these two things?
4. What are some ways our sin affects others? Give some specific examples.
5. What does Scripture mean when it says God is merciful and gracious? How is this different from God's simply overlooking sin?
6. Is it presumptuous to ask God for mercy when we sin? Why?
7. How does Christ's death help us understand how God can be both holy and merciful?
8. Why is it important that we be honest and specific in our confession before God?
9. How does honest confession, which we too often avoid, actually lead to joy?
10. In addition to being forgiven, what are the results of genuine confession before God?

The Faithful Love of God's Adoption

PSALM 52

Main Idea: People can trust God to love orphans faithfully, adopt them compassionately, and stand by them permanently.

I.   **The Rejection of God's Faithful Love (52:1-4)**
II. **The Vindication of God's Faithful Love (52:5-7)**
III. **The Application of God's Faithful Love (52:8-9)**
    A.   We flourish in God's presence.
    B.   We trust in God's nature.
    C.   We give thanks because of God's grace.
    D.   We live differently because of God's goodness.

My heart is always so encouraged and inspired when I run across families who have adopted children, mothers and families who courageously have chosen life by placing a child for adoption instead of choosing abortion, and children who have been placed for adoption by parents who either preceded them in death or for whatever reason didn't feel like they could care for them adequately. One of the reasons those stories bless me so much is that—while I'm confident those journeys are accompanied by feelings of abandonment, fear, loneliness, and anxiety on the parts of both parents and children—the adoption journey is a beautiful picture of how God addresses those feelings when he lovingly adopts us into his family and cares for us. Adoption is such a beautiful picture of the gospel of God's faithful love in Christ.

I think we see that picture here. Psalm 52 is rooted in one of David's most bitter experiences on his way to becoming king of Israel. In 1 Samuel 21–22—while running for his life from King Saul—he ducked in to see a priest named Ahimelech and asked for a few provisions and a sword. When Saul found out about it, he ordered the massacre of Ahimelech, his family, and his entire community. One of Ahimelech's sons, Abiathar, somehow escaped the merciless slaughter. When David heard about it, he extended a gracious invitation to the orphaned and defenseless son: "Stay with me. Don't be afraid, for the one who wants to take my life wants to take your life. You will be safe

13

with me" (1 Sam 22:23). In Psalm 52 David unpacks the nature of this compassionate offer.

To understand David's offer we need to see two themes that prop up this psalm. First, **this psalm is about God's character**. The repeated phrase *God's faithful love* bookends this song in verses 1 and 8. "Faithful love" is loving-kindness, or love that is loyal and steadfast. That's God's character—he loves with a love that never shrinks back, gives up, cops out, or lets down. It can be trusted. Second, **this psalm is about our choice**.

We can choose to reject or accept God's faithful love. Rejection is reflected in the guy who's described in verse 7. Acceptance is reflected in the author of this psalm in verse 8.

What we find in this psalm is an offer for all spiritual orphans—people who have been abandoned, who are afraid, who feel alone, who are anxious about the future—to trust a heavenly Father who loves them faithfully, adopts them compassionately, and stands by them permanently, just as David promised to do for Abiathar. This psalm is about our choice either to trust God's faithful love that will never fail and reaps glorious benefits or to trust in our own capacity that lasts a short time and has grave eternal consequences. David develops this choice in three major segments.

The Rejection of God's Faithful Love
PSALM 52:1-4

The informant and executioner who orchestrated Saul's massacre was an Edomite named Doeg. In verses 1-4 David takes this murderous snitch as his case study of one who rejects God's faithful love. The psalmist calls him out as "evil" and immediately offers the superior alternative. The meaning of the phrase *faithful love* and its context indicate "constant" means eternity. So David's question here implies the utter foolishness of choosing evil in this brief life when Doeg could have God's faithful love forever! To further magnify Doeg's folly, David sarcastically refers to him as a "hero," as if he earned the title by his exploit in butchery. The once modest shepherd of Saul's sheep (1 Sam 21:7) became the mighty executioner of Saul's enemies (1 Sam 22:18).

Doeg obviously took great pride in his loyalty to Saul and his obedience to carry out his diabolical orders. These verses indicate he wasn't at all shy about publicizing his self-perceived status and newfound fame.

The clear theme of these first few verses is the proud speech that flows from Doeg's wicked heart. Terms sprinkled through the verses like "tongue" (vv. 2,4), "lying" (v. 3), "speaking" (v. 3), and "words" (v. 4) describe the oral vehicles that exploited his wickedness. Every time he spoke, he revealed the depths of his evil boasts (v. 1), destructive plots (v. 2), lacerating deceit (v. 2), preference for evil over good and false-hood over truth (v. 3), and devouring motives (v. 4). And the phrase repeated in verses 3-4—*You love*—suggests Doeg not only was attracted to these sins, but he intentionally chose them as the course of his life.

Doeg's egotistical swagger is no different from that of any human being. What we find in him is a fairly good picture of what we find in ourselves outside of God's faithful love. Jesus said, "The mouth speaks from the overflow of the heart" (Matt 12:34), and, "What comes out of the mouth comes from the heart" (Matt 15:18). Our self-exaltation reflects the wickedness that corrodes our hearts, including our love for self and sin. And our love for self and sin is rejection of God's loving-kindness. We can't have both. The two are mutually exclusive and can't coexist. So the psalmist starts with an example of the poor choice of rejecting God's faithful love—a clear portrayal of us all.

The Vindication of God's Faithful Love
PSALM 52:5-7

God is characterized not only by faithful love but also by justice. And jus-tice can't allow something as good as God's everlasting loving-kindness to be trampled forever. So the psalmist announces that Doeg's self-exal-tation will be relatively short-lived. God will vindicate himself and his children by condemning those who reject his faithful love. Doeg con-sciously chose to trust himself—his fleeting power, position, and posses-sions—for his security ("refuge"), as opposed to God's faithful love. This foolish choice is amplified by a string of strong verbs graphically pictur-ing God's future judgment on Doeg's rebellion. This judgment will be violent ("bring down . . . take . . . uproot"), permanent ("forever"), swift and unexpected ("ripping"), and ultimately resulting in eternal death ("from the land of the living").

The horrible nature of this judgment can only be understood rightly in juxtaposition with the celebrative worship of the righteous. Their response to the judgment is one of both awe ("see and fear") and ridicule ("derisively"). This language may at first surprise us when we read it on this side of the cross. It seems to advocate an attitude in which the righteous rub victory in the face of those facing judgment, contrary to the Christian ethic. After all, the New Testament is clear that Christians are to love their enemies and pray for their persecutors (Matt 5:44; Rom 12:14; 1 Pet 3:9). We should not assume an attitude of malicious and vindictive contempt (Job 31:29; Prov 24:17).

So what do we make of this laughter that's coming on the day of God's justice? First, on that day the forgiveness of sin will inspire greater worship. Right now we are only conscious of our forgiveness by faith; but when we see our forgiveness in contrast to the literal judgment against the unforgiven, and we fully and functionally realize we've escaped God's wrath, it will prompt outbursts of jubilation like this one. Second, on that day the judgment against sin will involve greater consequences. Right now it seems as if the unrighteous always prosper and the righteous always get kicked in the teeth! However, the final judgment against sin will be so horrible that it can only be described rightly in contrast to the hyperbolic language of the laughter of the righteous (cf. Luke 14:26), with whom the unrighteous will be forced to switch places (Luke 16:19-31).

The Application of God's Faithful Love
PSALM 52:8-9

The little conjunction *but* indicates a sharp contrast between the testimony of the psalmist and that of Doeg. David gives witness, not as one who rejects God's loving-kindness but as one who receives it and extends it to others, just as he did to the orphan Abiathar. It's here we see the gospel, God's gracious adoption of us into his family. And we see its implications for our lives, not just in the future but right now while we wait in faith for God to vindicate his faithful love, and while there's often nothing to laugh about. In the midst of our abandonment, loneliness, fear, and anxiety, we find joy and security in the good news of God's loving-kindness. Our lives have four characteristics when we embrace the faithful love of God.

We Flourish in God's Presence

The psalmist likens himself to an olive plant in verse 8, one of the longest living and most resilient of all trees. It was invaluable to the Hebrews not only as a sign of security and well-being but also as a source of food, medicine, and ointments (Wilson, Vol. 1, 788). It's no wonder they often domesticated it, bringing it into their homes and nurturing it as we do potted plants. However, this olive plant isn't growing in your average Hebrew house. It's "in the house of God"—the sacred court-yard—where it's sure to get the best nourishment and protection. What a difference from the fate of the wicked who will be snatched away, torn from his tent, and uprooted from nourishing soil! We who trust in God's faithful love will be planted deep in the life-giving soil of his dwelling, flourishing with abundant life (Wilson, Vol. 1, 787).

In the Old Testament the *house of God* was first the tabernacle and later the temple, both representing where God dwelled. But when Jesus came, God stopped living in houses made by people and started living *with* people (John 1:14). God's life-giving, eternal presence with his people through Jesus Christ is the ultimate expression of these Old Testament houses of worship (John 2:18-22; 1 Cor 3:16-17; Eph 2:19-22; Rev 21:22). So we flourish forever in God's presence through Jesus! This truth informs our responsibility as believers to bear fruit as well as our assurance of eternal security (John 10:10; 15:7). We flourish and bear fruit wherever we are because of Jesus, and we are secure for all of eternity because we are in relationship with him!

We Trust in God's Nature

The psalmist expresses "trust" (v. 8). To trust in something is to depend on it, rest in it, hope in it, put confidence in it, bank everything on it. David was completely reliant on God's faithful love in a way that stood in pointed contrast to Doeg, who trusted in "riches" and "destructive behavior" (v. 7). And David said he would trust God's love "forever and ever." How could he be sure? Because—by definition—God's faithful love is eternal! Doeg's trust was in something tangible yet transient. So his trust would peter out. David's trust was in something unseen yet eternal. So his trust would last forever! The trust of God's children is forever because the object of their trust is eternal—his faithful love!

And why would anyone trust in anything else, especially when they see God's nature from this side of the cross? The New Testament indicates that God ultimately has manifested himself in his Son, Jesus Christ (John 1:1,14). The repeated references to Jesus being the very nature of God all associate that nature with the gospel (see 2 Cor 4:1-6; Col 1:15-20; Heb 1:1-4). Above everything, the divine nature is reflected in the one who came to incur God's wrath and die for our sins that we might be reconciled to him. This is the gospel: God in faithful love pursued us in our sin and did everything necessary to bring us into his household. I appeal to you, if you've yet to trust Jesus, to cry out to God now in repentance and faith that you might be saved! Trust in the nature of God to be your refuge.

We Give Thanks Because of God's Grace

Verse 9 straightforwardly mentions what God has "done." David's "I" statements in verses 8-9 ("am . . . trust . . . praise . . . put my hope") are in such direct contrast with Doeg's "you" statements in verses 1-4 ("boast . . . devises destruction . . . love evil . . . love any words that destroy"). What makes the difference? It's the "this is why God" statement that opens verse 5! The unrighteous are exalted right now, but God—in due time—will do what's necessary as the righteous Judge to levy justice and to vindicate his faithful love and his children. He loves us, assures us of justice, and promises us safekeeping and care. And nowhere in this text do you find any reference to the merit or capacity of the psalmist. It's all God's grace, and it merits the loudest and longest of thanksgivings!

On our side of the cross, thanksgiving remains the natural response to God's unmerited actions and favor toward us. When God became flesh in Jesus Christ, we saw his glory "full of grace and truth" and "received grace upon grace" (John 1:14,16). In John's Gospel the phrase *grace and truth* parallels the Old Testament ideas of *faithful love and truth*, which together convey the same idea of God's grace that we find in Psalm 52 (cf. Exod 33:18-19; 34:6-7). While God's grace is evident in Psalm 52 and throughout the whole Old Testament, the *greatness* of his grace is seen only in the person of Jesus Christ! So if God's grace is fully manifest in Christ, then our thanksgiving should be fully rooted in Christ as well. And that means thanksgiving must permeate all we do (Col 3:15-17).

We Live Differently Because of God's Goodness

There's some debate about what the psalmist says he will do in the last part of verse 9. Some translations read, "I will wait," indicating hope and trust in something. Others render it, "I will proclaim," suggesting a verbal witness. Anytime this uncertainty happens it's always best for us to start with what we know. Whatever David says he will do, it will be invested in God's name, inspired by God's goodness, and intended for God's people. When we get that right, the first part is easily reconciled: people who trust in God's faithful love live differently, in both word and action, as a witness to the truth that God is good!

And so it must be among the people of God on this side of the cross. In James's letter he identifies God as the only and unchanging source of goodness (Jas 1:17). Then he describes God's supreme act of goodness in all of history: "By his own choice, he gave us birth by the word of truth so that we would be a kind of firstfruits of his creatures" (Jas 1:18). He was referring to God's glorious gift of salvation in Jesus. And immediately he launches into five chapters calling on believers to live out their faith before one another in tangible ways, including caring for widows and orphans, taming their tongues, speaking well of one another, suffering patiently, and praying a lot. God's goodness in Christ demands we live differently, and that the difference is seen in the covenant community through the demonstration of our faith by our works.

Conclusion

Life can be fairly complex sometimes. Sin opens a Pandora's box of messy variables. There are lots of gray areas. But in all of its complexity, life does have simple choices. Some things are black-and-white, a matter of two simple options. Psalm 52 presents one of those situations. One choice is to trust in God's faithful love in Jesus Christ. It will never fail, and it reaps glorious benefits. The other choice is to trust in yourself. That lasts a short time and has grave eternal consequences. Hear our Lord's gracious, compassionate offer in this psalm to give you rest in his presence: "Stay with me. Don't be afraid. You will be safe with me." Be careful to choose wisely.

Reflect and Discuss

1. In verse 1 David speaks of evil in the context of eternity ("constant"). How does a right view of eternity affect our avoidance of sin? How does it affect our pursuit of holiness?

2. In what ways does David's description of Doeg reflect the natural human heart? In what ways can it even reflect a regenerate heart?

3. The Bible's witness, as expressed explicitly in this psalm, proclaims that God is just. Why, though, does God not judge immediately? How can we have peace in God when his justice seems delayed?

4. David envisions a day when the righteous will laugh at the unrighteous while they are facing judgment by God. What are we to make
of this? Is this an un-Christian attitude?

5. How should a vision of God's future judgment press us toward
mission?

6. What Hebraic symbolism stands behind the olive tree? What could
be a similar metaphor that we use today?

7. To be in God's house was comfort and peace in David's day. As
Christians, what is our relationship to the "house of God"?

8. David trusts "in God's faithful love forever and ever." Could you
characterize your life as one that trusts in God? At what moments in
life do you still trust in self?

9. David says in verse 9, "I will praise you forever for what you have
done." What has God done? How do we, in the new covenant, have
an even greater understanding of God's having done it?

10. How does the goodness of God's name change the way we, his children, live?

Human History Set to Music

PSALM 53

Main Idea: If you live as though God doesn't exist, you will face judgment.

I.   **Fools Reject God (53:1-3).**
II. **Fools Oppress His People (53:4).**
III. **God Rejects Fools (53:5).**
IV. **God Restores His People (53:6).**

Born and raised in former Yugoslavia, Miroslav Volf currently serves as professor of theology at Yale Divinity School. Volf describes his journey in considering God's judgment.

> I used to think that wrath was unworthy of God. Isn't God love? Shouldn't divine love be beyond wrath? God is love, and God loves every person and every creature. That's exactly why God is wrathful against some of them. My last resistance to the idea of God's wrath was a casualty of the war in former Yugoslavia, the region from which I come. According to some estimates, 200,000 people were killed and over 3,000,000 were displaced. My villages and cities were destroyed, my people shelled day in and day out, some of them brutalized beyond imagination, and I could not imagine God not being angry. Or think of Rwanda in the last decade of the past century, where 800,000 people were hacked to death in one hundred days! How did God react to the carnage? By doting on the perpetrators in a grandparently fashion? By refusing to condemn the bloodbath but instead affirming the perpetrators' basic goodness? Wasn't God fiercely angry with them? Though I used to complain about the indecency of the idea of God's wrath, I came to think that I would have to rebel against a God who wasn't wrathful at the sight of the world's evil. God isn't wrathful in spite of being love. God is wrathful because God is love. (Volf, *Free of Charge*, 138–39)

Our culture sneers at the idea of God's judgment. Were this psalm set to music, it wouldn't likely be played on popular radio stations. The outcry would be severe: "God scattering the bones of atheists? God rejecting people? That's not the God we believe in." Friends, this is why it is so good that we have God's own Word. God himself has given us these sixty-six books of Scripture. In the Bible, God, our Creator, tells us about himself. He tells us about who we are. He tells us why everything feels off—not only in the world around us but in our own hearts. He tells us how the wrong is made right.

Every person reading this and every person you encounter today has a developing narrative of how the world works. We're trying to make sense of it. In Scripture God tells us, "This is how it is." God's self-revealing Word is a means by which reality, if you will, walks up, taps us on the shoulder, and invites us in.

Psalm 53 is a shoulder-tapping passage. It's the story of human history since the fall, and God wants us to understand what this story has to do with our lives now. If God, your Creator, stooped to tell you about life, to tell you where the dangers are, to point the way to a happy ending, would you be interested? Here's a spoiler: We need more than for God to just point the way, but we'll come back to that later.

The song about human history develops in four stages in Psalm 53.

Fools Reject God
PSALM 53:1-3

The Bible doesn't use the word *fool* in a cavalier way. A fool isn't merely someone who is unintelligent. A fool isn't a person who goofs off all the time and can't be taken seriously. A fool is someone who says in his heart, "There's no God" (v. 1).

The psalmist isn't limiting this description to the card-carrying atheist. The emphasis is on functional or practical atheism. The fool in verse 1 has a God-denying *heart*. Regardless of what this person may say with his mouth, his heart—the controlling center of his life—screams, "There's no God."

Since our actions flow from the heart, this God-denying heart produces a God-denying life. The psalmist talks about corruption and vile deeds. He talks about wisdom or, in this case, the lack of wisdom. Wisdom, like foolishness, is defined in terms of how we live in relation to God. In verse 2 wisdom is related to one practice—seeking God.

The wise person seeks the Lord. The wise person lives in the awareness that God is Creator and King, that God is good and wise. In the Old Testament the fear of the Lord is the beginning of wisdom (Prov 9:10). Wisdom is found in pursuing the knowledge of God—his character, his commands, his promises, his workings in history. Scripture can't conceive of someone being wise apart from knowing God and living in accordance with reality as God defines it.

Tragically, since the fall in Genesis 3, foolishness is our natural-born condition. When Adam and Eve bit the fruit, the juice of foolishness ran down *our* chins. The story of humanity from that point forward is described in verse 3. Left to ourselves, the only thing that happens in this fallen world is corruption. We are born with foolish, God-neglecting hearts. We come of age, and our hands and feet and words express our God-neglecting hearts. No one has to teach children to lie. No one takes a class on envy and unforgiveness. We don't have to learn the ways of foolishness.

Friends, this is why the gospel of Jesus Christ is unavoidably confrontational. Paul says the message about salvation through faith in what Jesus did on the cross—the message that displays God's manifold wisdom—is considered by unregenerate people to be foolishness.

> For the word of the cross is foolishness to those who are perishing, but it is the power of God to us who are being saved. For it is written, I will destroy the wisdom of the wise, and I will set aside the intelligence of the intelligent.
>
> Where is the one who is wise? Where is the teacher of the law? Where is the debater of this age? Hasn't God made the world's wisdom foolish? For since, in God's wisdom, the world did not know God through wisdom, God was pleased to save those who believe through the foolishness of what is preached. For the Jews ask for signs and the Greeks seek wisdom, but we preach Christ crucified, a stumbling block to the Jews and foolishness to the Gentiles. Yet to those who are called, both Jews and Greeks, Christ is the power of God and the wisdom of God, because God's foolishness is wiser than human wisdom, and God's weakness is stronger than human strength. (1 Cor 1:18-25)

Once we've read the whole Bible, we discover that God's wisdom is seen in its highest expression in the cross of Jesus Christ. God's wisdom exposes the foolishness of humanity. In our God-neglecting life, if we thought God didn't see our sin or that he isn't bothered by it, the cross says otherwise. If we thought wisdom is found in books and philosophy, rhetoric, technology, and cultural sophistication, the cross of Jesus Christ shouts, "No!" The wisdom of God—the wisdom this world calls foolishness—is the proclamation that Jesus Christ, God's Son, came into this world, lived a perfect life, was crucified in our place, bearing the judgment against our God-neglecting lives in his body on the tree, then rose again with new life for all who believe.

According to these words from Paul, at our stage in history—on this side of the cross—we can't study foolishness and wisdom without reference to what God did, in the fullness of time, when he sent his Son to be our Redeemer.

You want wisdom? The wisdom of the ages begins its lesson here. Embrace Jesus Christ as Lord. Believe that what he did on the cross was enough to cover every God-dismissive, God-neglecting word, thought, and deed.

What an unbelieving world needs is not more proof of the existence of God. Scripture makes clear that every person in the world knows—at the core of his being—there is a God (Rom 1:18-22).

The foolishness that instinctively pushes God aside—the foolishness that says, "There's no God"—lives in the heart. Our passage announces this as a universal reality (Ps 53:3). Paul, in Romans 1, says the primary work of this innate, God-neglecting foolishness is to suppress the truth that we know about God. The card-carrying atheist and the practical atheist are motivated by the same desire: I don't want to serve a God; I want to serve myself. I want to live by my own dictates. I want to define my existence, to live for my own pleasures. I'll distract myself away from the truth God has revealed. I'll close my ears to creation as it declares God's "handiwork" (Ps 19:1 ESV). I'll twist the evidence to rid my world of God.

Here's the sobering reality: there comes a point when God stops speaking. Go read the rest of Romans 1. There comes a point when we've worked so hard to suppress the truth that God gives us over to foolishness. It becomes baked in. At first the atheist closed his ears to God's glory-revealing symphony in creation. Once hardened, he removes his hands, and he doesn't hear the trees of the field clapping their hands and the mountains singing for joy. They're just trees and mountains.

Psalm 53's portrait of the fool, however, isn't limited to a functional rejection of God.

Fools Oppress His People
PSALM 53:4

Again the focus here is not so much on a formal, conceptually developed atheism. In a way this psalm, like Psalm 1, divides humanity into two categories of people—the ones who are with God and the ones who aren't. The former group are "my people" (v. 4), "you" (v. 5), "his people . . . Jacob . . . Israel" (v. 6). They are, by implication, those who *do* seek God (contrast of v. 2) and who *do* "call on God" (contrast of v. 4).

In wisdom psalms the contrasts are absolute. The world is full of two kinds of people: the righteous and the unrighteous. The righteous live this way; the unrighteous do exactly the opposite. Psalm 53 has elements of a wisdom psalm. The way the fool treats God (v. 1) carries over in his hostility toward God's people (v. 4). It's a kind of hatred by association. So the people who "do not call on God" are the same people who "consume my people as they consume bread." The curse that fell in Genesis 3 included a promise that there would be enmity between the seed of the woman and the seed of the serpent. That is to say, world history is a battle of light and darkness.

Christian friend, if we think we will have an easy road in this life, we have not yet understood what it means to live as children of light in a world of darkness. Jesus told his disciples he was sending them out as sheep among wolves (Matt 10:16). Notice how binary that is. Jesus, in that moment taking up the rhetorical tools of the wisdom tradition, divided the world in two. There are sheep, and there are wolves. What did he mean? He meant, don't expect this to be easy. He told them, they hated me; they'll hate you as well because you're with me.

This is why Paul said, "For our struggle is not against flesh and blood, but against the rulers, against the authorities, against the cosmic powers of this darkness, against evil, spiritual forces in the heavens" (Eph 6:12). And this is why you hear, for example, Paul speak this way:

> But Elymas the sorcerer (that is the meaning of his name) opposed them and tried to turn the proconsul away from the faith.
>
> But Saul—also called Paul—filled with the Holy Spirit, stared straight at Elymas and said, "You are full of all kinds of deceit and trickery, you son of the devil and enemy of all that is right. Won't you ever stop perverting the straight paths of the Lord?" (Acts 13:8-10)

It's almost as though Paul is looking not just at Elymas but through him to invisible realities that operate behind flesh and blood, seeking to keep the world in darkness.

The serpent who wants nothing more than to seek, kill, and destroy (John 10:10) has workers (John 13:27; Acts 13:8-10; 1 Tim 1:19-20). The King who came to give life and that abundantly (John 10:10) has workers as well (Matt 9:38; Phil 2:15; Rev 12:11).

This means, church, we are not living in peacetime. The kingdom of God advances through bold witness and light-bearing holiness. We will not march unimpeded. There is an enemy who will oppose Christ's glory in your life and your witness to Christ in the world. He wants to distract you, to discourage you. Some he'll attack with spiritual pride and self-righteousness. Others will be drawn in with the bait of different sins. Others, perhaps many Christians in our culture, he'll simply distract with a materialism and busyness that, in effect, takes us off the field of kingdom action. This world's God-rejecting foolishness notwithstanding, our call is forward!

We are counted as fools in this world, but God is the one who defines the terms, and in the end reality will win out. God's wisdom will prevail. The foolishness of God will be wiser than the God-neglecting "wisdom" of this world. This is where history is heading. Whose side are you on? Are you with God and with his Christ?

God Rejects Fools
PSALM 53:5

Verse 5 is sobering. Remember, this isn't just a song. And, since we have New Testament revelation throwing its light back into the Old Testament, we also know verse 5 isn't just ancient history. Verse 5 is prophecy. Verse 5 is coming.

Dread will fall on those who have foolishly pushed God aside and opposed the progress of his kingdom through his people. Conceptual, card-carrying atheists and practical, God-patronizing dabblers—all will fall before him when God the Judge appears in glory.

This verse paints a picture of where this world's God-denying "wisdom" is headed. Bones scattered. Rejected by God. The ones who consumed God's people (v. 4) are consumed.

God's judgment is righteous. No one is wrongly punished. If human history seems to be one unending tale of injustice and oppression, that story will end. All wrongs will be made right. A world that has desired to live without God—outside the light of his love, out from under his rule and blessing and provision—will have what they desire. Jesus said they will be cast into outer darkness (Matt 22:13).

God Restores His People
PSALM 53:6

If humanity is divided into two categories, verse 5 tells us what happens to the fools. Verse 6 tells us what happens to those who belong to God— the ones who *have* called on his name, the ones who were evildoers but, by grace, stand righteous in his sight because of the work of Jesus Christ.

Look at the concepts that collect around God's people in verse 6: Deliverance. Restoration. Fortune. Rejoicing. Gladness. This is the salvation the psalmist is praying for. Apparently there was some experience that felt like verse 4. They were being consumed like bread. They were not strong enough to fight off their adversaries. The psalmist announces that the adversaries of God's people will be put to shame, and what remains for the people of God will be joy. Peter calls it "inexpressible and glorious joy" (1 Pet 1:8). King David calls it "eternal pleasures" at God's right hand (Ps 16:11).

The story of the world is seen in this psalm through what God is doing. He looks for one who does good. He finds no one seeking him; all have turned away. The New Testament tells us what God does about this. He sends Messiah to rescue us from our sin and God-neglecting foolishness. Then, in the end, God scatters and rejects a world of fools who have suppressed the truth in unrighteousness, and he restores and saves and gladdens the hearts of his people forever.

Where are you in the story?

Reflect and Discuss

1. Do you agree that our culture sneers at God's judgment? How do you see this play out?
2. What would you say to someone who believes God's judgment is more of an Old Testament thing and not something anyone needs to worry about today?
3. How would you help someone see the cross as revealing both God's mercy and his righteous judgment? Where might you go in Scripture to help explain this?

4. As a Christian, how are you pursuing wisdom? How are you cultivating your relationship with God and pursuing obedience to him in all things?

5. Do you catch yourself complaining as if life was supposed to become easy when you became a Christ follower? How does it change the way we live in this world if we expect persecution and pushback?

6. How does the future hope of the believer impact the way we live now? What difference do you think it makes if Christians stop thinking about what God has in store for us when this short life is through?

7. How can you cultivate thankfulness today that God sought you when you weren't seeking him and opened your eyes to the wisdom and power of the gospel?

What's in a Name?

PSALM 54

Main Idea: The gospel compels believers to trust in God's character when friends betray us and enemies attack us.

I. **Our Desperation for God (54:1-3)**
   A. The reason (54:3)
   B. The request (54:1-2)
II. **Our Dependence on God (54:4-5)**
   A. Who God is (54:4)
   B. What God will do (54:5)
III. **Our Devotion to God (54:6-7)**
   A. What we do (54:6)
   B. Why we do it (54:7)

A rose by any other name would smell as sweet" is a familiar reference from William Shakespeare's *Romeo and Juliet*. Juliet appears to be arguing that it doesn't matter that Romeo bears the name "Montague," her family's rival house. The reference is often used to suggest that a person's name doesn't affect who they really are. While this may be true in some cases, nothing could be farther from the truth when it comes to God's name. God's name tells us everything about him and gives us great confidence in him.

The superscription of the psalm reveals its backdrop. Although they're referred to as "strangers" in the song itself (v. 3), these Ziphites actually were fellow Israelites, not foreigners (Josh 15:24). David had even rescued a nearby city from the Philistines (1 Sam 23), so he assumed them to be allies. However, now they've done a one-eighty on him and ratted him out to King Saul. It was one thing to have been betrayed by Doeg the Edomite (Ps 52; 1 Sam 22:22), but now David finds himself the target of men he thought to be on his side (1 Sam 23:19; 26:1). So with Saul in hot pursuit, David is not only disillusioned from being betrayed, but his life is in danger (Kidner, *Psalms 1–72*, 215). Psalm 54 is the prayer of a desperate man when his heart is hurting, his faith is fainting, and his safety is suspect.

So, what exactly does David do? He does what we should do in desperate times: he calls on the name of his God. This prayer is bookended by references to God's "name," which is the object of his hope for deliverance (vv. 1,6; cf. 52:9). And in the middle is the psalm's major theme that unpacks the nature of that divine name: "helper" and "sustainer" (v. 4; Wilson, *Psalms*, 797). Prophetically, this psalm demonstrates how the gospel compels us to trust in God's character when friends betray us and enemies attack us. Moreover, it compels us to look to Jesus Christ as the ultimate expression of God's name and glory. Paul said,

> For this reason God highly exalted him and gave him the name that is above every name, so that at the name of Jesus every knee will bow—in heaven and on earth and under the earth—and every tongue will confess that Jesus Christ is Lord, to the glory of God the Father. (Phil 2:9-11)

So as we travel through this psalm, we're ultimately talking about the name of Jesus.

The term *choir director* in the heading refers to some liturgical officiant or worship leader. Along with the reference to "stringed instruments," this psalm evidently was intended to be part of the corporate worship of God's people. But it also was intended to be educational. The term *Maskil* is well known in wisdom literature and often meant "to instruct" or "make perceptive" (Wilson, *Psalms*, 545). The word *Selah* is inserted at the end of verse 3. While its exact meaning is unknown, it's generally thought to indicate a pause or interlude in a musical presentation of the psalm. The term often corresponds to structural divisions within a text and can help us understand the various components of a poem (Wilson, *Psalms*, 128). These terms show us that David thinks his words—especially his confidence in God's name—are important enough to put to music and be rehearsed by the people of God.

So let's explore how our God delivers and vindicates us when we cry out to his great name. Consider how our desperation for God leads to our dependence on God and results in our devotion to God.

Our Desperation for God
PSALM 54:1-3

Psalm 54 begins with a desperate request for God's help, followed by the reason for that desperation. Let's look at the reason first—which is found in verse 3—before we look at the actual request in verses 1-2.

The Reason (54:3)

One of the most traumatic and disillusioning experiences I've ever had in ministry came during my first pastorate. One of my deacons, who was a close friend, had a middle-school daughter in our student ministry. One year as we were preparing to go to summer camp, this young lady made it known to the other students that she was planning a series of pranks while we were at camp. As other parents began to express concern, I decided I needed to have a conversation with her dad. I made an appointment with him and shared my concerns. It was like flipping a switch. This brother—who had been my biggest supporter and one of my closest confidants—immediately turned against me. It's hard to describe the degree of bitterness he harbored. After a number of attempts at reconciliation, I went to his house one morning to plead with him one more time. He opened his door, and without saying a word, threw a cup of hot coffee in my face and slammed the door. I turned and went back to my vehicle, drenched in coffee . . . and tears.

We expect to be ridiculed, maligned, and attacked by our enemies. But what catches us by surprise—and usually hurts the most—is when we're stabbed in the back by those within our own ranks. When people we thought were for us suddenly and surprisingly turn against us, we find ourselves in a painful and precarious position. That's what was happening in this psalm. The word *For* at the beginning of verse 3 flags the reason for David's dire predicament in verses 1-2. The stakes are high in this text. David's desperation is highlighted and intensified as he describes his circumstances as life-threatening! These were violent men who had betrayed him, ones who wanted him dead. The word *violent* can be translated as "awe-inspiring, terror-striking" (BDB, s.v. *'arits*).

However, probably the most frightening description here is not that David's enemies are described as "violent" but that they are called "strangers." While this word often refers to foreigners, such couldn't be the case here. The Ziphites were fellow countrymen! Here it has to be referring to someone or something "foreign" to the community or its standards. The word is used for the "unauthorized fire" that Nadab and Abihu burned on the altar in Leviticus 10:1. It wasn't pagan incense but simply fire other than what they were authorized to use. It shows up again in Proverbs 5:3, where the "forbidden woman" isn't characterized as a foreigner but as the unchaste wife of another man (Ross, *Psalms*, vol. 2, 231–32).

No, these "strangers" weren't foreigners to David's national family. However, they were foreigners to his faith family. These were people who were *geographically* and *genetically* associated with the kingdom, but they weren't *genuinely* associated with it. They were part of Israel but not the true Israel (cf. Rom 2:28-29; 9:6-8; Gal 3:7-9).

In the New Testament Jesus said such hypocrisy will be prevalent in the kingdom of God until he returns for his people, his *true* people. The parable of the sower (Matt 13:1-23) and the parable of the weeds (Matt 13:24-30), as well as the analogy of the separation of the sheep and goats (Matt 25:31-46), all suggest that the earthly kingdom will have people in it who put on the face of kingdom citizenship but who aren't genuinely children of the King. Paul even suggests that these frauds—like the "strangers" in Psalm 54—will persecute true believers: "In fact, all who want to live a godly life in Christ Jesus will be persecuted. Evil people and impostors will become worse, deceiving and being deceived" (2 Tim 3:12-13).

The church today is filled with such phonies. They join our churches, attend our worship gatherings, participate in our programs, sing our music, listen to our sermons, give their money, and sometimes even live moral lives. Yet they've never truly experienced the life-transforming, heart-regenerating power of the gospel. They are geographically affiliated with the kingdom because they're in our midst. They are genetically affiliated with the kingdom because they're often related to us by bloodline. But they're not genuinely affiliated with the kingdom because they don't know Christ.

Jesus is clear that at his coming a distinction will be made between genuine believers and these pretenders:

> *Not everyone who says to me, "Lord, Lord," will enter the kingdom of heaven, but only the one who does the will of my Father in heaven. On that day many will say to me, "Lord, Lord, didn't we prophesy in your name, drive out demons in your name, and do many miracles in your name?" Then I will announce to them, "I never knew you. Depart from me, you lawbreakers!"* (Matt 7:21-23)

No, none of these charlatans will sneak into the eternal kingdom. Our Lord's avowal concerning the clear distinction that awaits is truly haunting: "Let both grow together until the harvest. At harvest time I'll tell the reapers: Gather the weeds first and tie them in bundles to burn them, but collect the wheat in my barn" (Matt 13:30). True and false believers may coexist in the kingdom on earth, but they won't in heaven.

The end of verse 3 confirms such a commentary on the spiritual condition of these "strangers." The reason for their hypocrisy is simple: "They do not let God guide them." Like the "fool" who "says in his heart, 'There's no God'" (53:1), they reject God's authority over their lives. Wilson says that when letting God guide you, you keep your eyes fixed on the one out in front—the leader—in order to know the right way. These attackers didn't do that but instead chose to follow their own ruthless devices (Wilson, *Psalms*, 799). They had no regard for God's authority.

One can be guilty of this rebellion, even passively. I travel quite a bit as part of my ministry, so I'm on a lot of airplanes. Most of the time I don't think much about the pilots who fly the planes, other than to greet them and say, "Thank you," as I'm deplaning. However, every once in a while, the plane in which I'm flying hits some turbulence that jerks the big vessel around a bit. Whenever that happens, I start thinking things like, *I wonder how many flight hours this pilot has*, and, *I hope he's had some experience flying through stuff like this*. I can be kind of passive about airplane pilots until I hit some rough air. And passivity can be a manifestation of rebellion. God wants me to set him before my eyes constantly, not just when there's turbulence in my life. Otherwise—like David's detractors—I'm not much different from the fool who says that there is no God.

The Request (54:1-2)

Now that we understand David's circumstances, we have a context for appreciating the intensity of the request he makes in these verses. The psalmist makes his plea through two pairs of parallel ideas. The first pair is the words *save* and *vindicate*, which express David's urgent need for God to deliver him both physically and justly. The word *vindicate* is a judicial term that suggests an acquittal. David knew such a verdict would have to be levied through saving deeds, not words. The slander on his character was that he was a traitor against Saul, the king of Israel (Kidner, *Psalms 1–72*, 215). He knew the only way for his reputation to be reestablished would be as a direct result of God's saving his life. So he was asking for his life to be spared and his name to be cleared.

The agent of David's petitioned deliverance is expressed in the words *name* and *might*, the second of the two pairs of parallel thoughts. He knew he was in a situation he couldn't solve. He was going to need something beyond himself, and that something was God's strength expressed in his name. The children of Israel believed God was present on earth in his name, which represented his essential character and nature. His name referred to "the whole of the divine manifestation, the character of God as revealed in his relationship and dealings with his people" (Ross, *Psalms*, vol. 2, 231).

At least part of God's character and nature is his power and authority as demonstrated through his might. So basically David is crying out to God to deliver him from his enemies by means of his glorious attributes. That's an expression of faith. Faith isn't believing something hard enough that it comes to pass. Neither is it a leap in the dark. Faith is actually a leap in the light: responding to and acting on what God says and reveals about himself. David is confident God will be his deliverer and vindicator because that's who God has revealed himself to be. That is faith prompted by the revealed nature and character of God. And that faith will win out every time!

Verse 2 also begins by addressing David's deliverer. The name *God* is emphasized by its position at the beginning of each verse. The psalmist is acknowledging that no one else is able to save him. So he pleads that God will "hear" him and "listen" to him. The language in these two verbs conveys attempts to gain access to a judge in order to hear the plaintiff's case (Wilson, *Psalms*, 799). David wants God to hear his plea and respond favorably on his behalf. The picture is of a man on trial for his life desperately pleading with the judge to hear his side of the story.

I remember when my daughter was little and needed something from me while my mind was on other things. She would crawl up in my lap while I was watching a ball game or reading and begin to ask me for what she needed. When she noticed that my attention was given to something other than her, she would grab both of my cheeks with her two little hands, turn my head in her direction, and plead, "Daddy, listen to me!" That's what the psalmist is doing. He's grabbing hold of God's face and saying, "God, listen to me!" But when those words roll off of his lips, they're not directed at one who is distracted and busy with other matters. They're finding a hearing with a good Father who desires his children to seek his face and appeal to his strength. What Father doesn't take delight in his children's dependence on him?

Our heavenly Father wants us to pray with this kind of abandon. He wants us to plead our case to him when we find ourselves betrayed by people we thought were for us. He wants us to appeal to him when our safety and our character are on the line. He wants us to cry out to him and ask him to come to our aid and to show himself strong for us. God is both blessed and glorified when his children express their utter desperation for and dependence on him. And he delights in giving to us out of the abundance of his goodness. Jesus teaches his followers to pray this way (Luke 11:1-13). He tells us to be like the friend at midnight, who pleaded with his neighbor with annoying relentlessness to open his door and give him some bread. He said for us to ask and keep on asking, to seek and keep on seeking, to knock and keep on knocking. And he said to pray this way, knowing that God is a good Father who wants to give his presence to those who ask in this way.

Our Dependence on God
PSALM 54:4-5

One of the great mysteries of the earthy praying that God desires from his children is the way desperation *for* him seems to always breed dependence *on* him. In verses 1-3 David passionately brought himself and his enemies to God's attention. Now, in verses 4-5, he abruptly turns his own attention toward God. Somehow God has wired prayer to work this way. If you and I can bring ourselves sincerely to cry out to God when we're distressed, it will drive us to the doorstep of dependence on him. There we will find our confidence in his great name and all that it represents. Here the psalmist acknowledges God as the one who helps, sustains, and props up his children. Then he declares what God will do to bring justice to their plight.

Who God Is (54:4)

Psalm 54:4 appears to betray a sudden mood swing in the author's disposition. This verse houses the big idea of the whole psalm—confidence in the God who shows himself strong to his children (Ross, Vol. 2, 233). David addresses the congregation, reminding them of the fundamental principle by which God's people resolve to live their lives. David is acknowledging that God is the one who does for his children what they can't do for themselves.

The next line of the song strengthens the claim. The Hebrew here seems to number God merely *among* the psalmist's sustainers, an idea that seems unsettling to several modern translators. However, Kidner believes such a translation doesn't belittle God but demonstrates his hand through human help (cf. 1 Sam 23:13; 2 Sam 23:8-39), an aspect of his faithfulness that served as David's support and delight (Kidner, *Psalms 1–72*, 216). God is the helper and upholder of his children, even when he chooses to levy it through human instruments!

Here we find one of the beautiful pictures of the gospel in the Psalms. We're reminded that Jesus Christ is our helper and upholder and that our gaze remains fixed on him. To do otherwise is to be overwhelmed by the cares and burdens of this life. Peter learned this lesson painfully. When he saw the one who had power over creation walking on the water, he wanted to go meet him by doing the same thing. As he miraculously made his way toward our Lord, everything was peachy until he started looking at the elements on which he was treading instead of looking at Jesus. That's when he started to sink! So, like the psalmist, "he cried out, 'Lord, save me!' Immediately Jesus reached out his hand, caught hold of him, and said to him, 'You of little faith, why did you doubt?'" (Matt 14:30-31). Jesus helps and upholds us when we cry out to him.

Hypocrites don't do this, but God's true children keep their eyes on the one who has saved them, trusting in his name and all that it represents. When we do, the stormy seas and tumultuous circumstances of our lives fade into the background as lesser concerns. When friends betray us (cf. 55:12-14), when our leaders fall (cf. 146:3-5), and when family members abandon or abuse us (cf. 27:7-10), Jesus helps us and holds us up (Wilson, Vol. 1, 802-3). So the old gospel hymn got it right: "Turn your eyes upon Jesus, / Look full on His wonderful face, / And the things of earth will grow strangely dim, / In the light of His glory and grace" (Lemmel, "Turn Your Eyes upon Jesus," 1922).

When people set their eyes on someone or something other than the Lord Jesus Christ, they don't see the "glory and grace" of God as it is revealed in his Son. When Jesus came, "The Word became flesh and dwelt among us. We observed his glory, the glory as the one and only Son from the Father, full of grace and truth" (John 1:14). Keeping our gaze on him changes how we look at everything else in the universe. When we look at Jesus, we see a God of justice and equity; we see the righteous one who takes no pleasure in evil; we see the Creator God who cares for all of creation. When we look at God in Christ, we can't take lightly his power and glory, and we can't take a pass on being involved in his mission in the world (Wilson, *Psalms*, 803). The name of God as revealed in Christ compels us to reflect his character, nature, and values in this world.

What God Will Do (54:5)

God's name suggests that he always acts according to his character, not only on behalf of his children but also toward those who oppose them. The psalmist acknowledges as much when he says that God "will repay my adversaries." He knows that God's nature is to right wrongs, and that includes rendering justice to his people's enemies. Basically, David is confidently claiming here that God will cause his enemies' plans to backfire on them.

The fate of these slanderers is specified as the psalmist speaks directly to God in the parallel statement of the Hebrew poetry. God will annihilate them, destroy their lives. The preposition at the beginning of this clause indicates a cause: "on the basis of what your faithfulness demands." God's faithfulness is the truth that characterizes him. On the basis of God's truth, the psalmist prays that his enemies would be exterminated (Ross, Vol. 2, 234). He's asking God to act according to his name, his character.

Praying for God to act according to his character is always right and good. And it's the most potent praying we can do because we're always appealing to what is true, to what God has revealed about himself. John said, "This is the confidence we have before him: If we ask anything according to his will, he hears us. And if we know that he hears whatever we ask, we know that we have what we have asked of him" (1 John 5:14-15). This is the assurance we have whenever we pray according to God's will, and God's will always issues forth from his character.

But let's admit, it does seem a bit awkward for us to ask God to obliterate our enemies. If we're honest, some of the prayers we find in the Psalms bother us a bit. After all, didn't Jesus say, "Love your enemies and pray for those who persecute you, so that you may be children of your Father in heaven" (Matt 5:44-45)? And Paul seems to advocate the same sentiment: "Bless those who persecute you; bless and do not curse" (Rom 12:14). As Christ followers, don't we reflect the character of God by doing the *opposite* of what David is doing in Psalm 54? The gospel of Christ does seem to constrain us not to respond in anger toward our enemies or desire revenge for what they do to us but to forgive them, love them, bless them, and respond to their evil intentions with good (Matt 5:43-48; Rom 12:14-21).

However, the kind of praying the psalmist does here isn't actually out of harmony with the gospel. First, this prayer lifts the lid off of our own hearts and reveals our need for the gospel. We really need to press pause before we start feeling too high and mighty and think that David was a lesser human being than us because he lived during Old Testament times. Think about the last time you heard of someone abducting a child, raping a woman, or walking into a public building and gunning down a mass of innocent people. Reflect for a moment on the most recent news report of a terrorist bombing a Christian church building in some part of the world or even the threat of a dictator to launch a nuclear missile. Consider how you felt—including the outcome you desired—as you followed the latest high-profile trial of a mass murderer. Ponder for a moment what you were feeling when you first read the testimonies of Nazi Holocaust prisoners, victims of apartheid in South Africa, or survivors of the killing fields of Cambodia (Wilson, Vol. 1, 803). Didn't your heart long for justice? And what about the last time someone unjustly attacked you, whether physically or otherwise? Wasn't there a part of you that wanted them to get what they deserved?

This is why I love the earthiness of the Psalms and the prayers that fill them. They are so *me*! While it's easy for me to feel superior to the people of God who lived on the other side of the cross, I often hate those who hurt me and want them to get their due. The emotion of the psalmist in this prayer causes me to see myself and acknowledge the wickedness of my own heart. It causes me to see my desperate need for the gospel. Additionally, the heart cry of David always reminds me of the people in our world who are suffering to the point that they, too, want to pray this way. Bible prayers like this can actually raise our awareness of our own hearts and the hearts of others in seasons of suffering. And when we see our own wickedness, we see our need for the gospel.

This kind of praying is gospel praying for another reason. We should pray like this, not because it's right for us to hate our enemies and desire their demise but because God wants us to be honest and intimate with him. The psalmist had such a genuine relationship with God that he could express his deepest feelings, even those that didn't necessarily reflect citizenship in the kingdom that was to come. And guess what—God can handle that! He knows we live in a world infected by sin, and he knows the pain this world can prompt in us. As a good Father, he wants us to crawl up in his lap and express the deepest groaning of our heart, even if in the moment it's the desire for our enemies to be zapped! When we are willing to come to God and pray this way, he always welcomes us and loves us, just as a father does with a child. And as we commune with him in such unguarded honesty, he responds to us with the gospel. And that gospel refines and tweaks and redeems our childish passions, motives, and desires.

Another reason Psalm 54:5 is gospel praying is because the God of both the Old Testament and the New Testament is actually a God of justice and judgment. We know God ultimately is going to set things right, vindicate the righteous, and punish the wicked. He wasn't kidding when he said all that stuff about fire and brimstone, eternal condemnation, and the wicked being damned to hell. So any time you pray for his kingdom to come and his will to be done, you're actually praying for him to destroy the wicked. Wilson insightfully points out that

> it is a bit naive of us to believe in a holy and righteous God who is incompatible with evil and to ask him to enter our world decisively in order to end the effects of evil, and to ignore the fact that such a clean-up would have negative consequences for anyone and everything infected by wickedness. (Wilson, *Psalms*, 803–4)

If that's true, then the flip side is equally valid. Whenever we pray for God to destroy the wicked, as the psalmist is doing here, we're praying for him to act justly, stop evil, make things right, and vindicate the righteous.

Finally, praying for God to destroy our enemies is gospel praying *if* we trust him with it. Vindication is never our assignment. David was clear: "Because of *your* faithfulness, [*you*] annihilate them" (emphasis added). He wasn't asking to do it himself, and neither should we. Vindication is never our assignment or responsibility. It's God's. Jesus said, "You have heard that it was said, Love your neighbor and hate your enemy. But I tell you, love your enemies and pray for those who persecute you, so that you may be children of your Father in heaven" (Matt 5:43-45). Paul agreed:

> *Do not repay anyone evil for evil. Give careful thought to do what is honorable in everyone's eyes. If possible, as far as it depends on you, live at peace with everyone. Friends, do not avenge yourselves; instead, leave room for God's wrath, because it is written, "Vengeance belongs to me; I will repay," says the Lord. "But If your enemy is hungry, feed him. If he is thirsty, give him something to drink. For in so doing you will be heaping fiery coals on his head."*
>
> *Do not be conquered by evil, but conquer evil with good.* (Rom 12:17-21)

When we cry out to God and ask him to vindicate us, we trust him to do it, to do it his way, and to do it in his time. And we follow our prayer for such justice with gospel-driven actions that involve loving our enemies, praying for them, blessing them, living peaceably with them, and doing good deeds for them. That's what Jesus did (Luke 23:34), and that's what the gospel demands of us.

Our Devotion to God
PSALM 54:6-7

Our trust in and dependence on God is the seedbed for worship. The demonstration of confidence in his great name issues forth into uninhibited devotion to him. The progression in this psalm is astounding. The distressed servant of the Most High pours out his heart in desperation. That desperation ushers him right to the confident assurance of God's strong help. And the reminder and awareness of that help compels him to worship this one in whose name he trusts. As is the case with many of the laments in the psalms, this one concludes with sacrifice and praise. David describes what we do in response to God's great name and then why we do it.

What We Do (54:6)

In response to God's strong name and the anticipation of his vindication, the psalmist spontaneously promises to worship him. He vows to make a sacrifice of praise when his God comes through with deliverance. David's intended worship provides a worthy model for us as we respond to God's faithfulness and the confidence that he will deliver us. Consider three applications.

First, **our worship should be shared**. The kind of sacrifice referenced here was to be offered in the sanctuary and accompanied by a peace offering. They opened the door to God's presence through atonement, expressed the love of the worshiper, and assembled the congregation so they could hear the story of God's work (cf. Deut 12:6-14). David knew that God's deliverance was intended to inspire praise from those he helped and to build up the faith of everyone else who heard the report of his actions. We frequently ask people to join us in praying for God's help with some crisis in our lives, but too often we forget to circle back around and report when he comes through for us. God's deliverance is something to be shared with our brothers and sisters so they can join in worshiping him.

Second, **our worship should be sincere**. The word *freewill* indicates the psalmist would make this sacrifice willingly, not under compulsion or obligation. This would be no religious routine to follow or lame liturgical box to check off. It would be a heartfelt response of public praise that acknowledged what God had done. Our worship of the God who delivers must be the natural outflow of hearts moved by his actions on behalf of his people. We can't afford to get caught up in the routine of weekly worship and never have our affections stirred by God's gracious work for us.

Third, **our worship should be substantive**. David vows to worship God's name, a name he describes as "good." This theme now comes full circle in the psalm and features God's identity as helper and upholder. The psalmist's worship would be prompted by the character and nature of his God who is for him, the one who is good because he protects and provides for the life of his people. God's name—his divine character and very person—is good. So, like the psalmist, we need to vow never to hoard the celebration of the demonstration of God's good name but to share it willingly with the community of faith.

Why We Do It (54:7)

Why do we worship as a natural response to God's deliverance in time of trouble? The little word *For* flags the reason. When we find ourselves in the midst of struggle, it's important for us to remember and acknowledge God's track record of all the times he's delivered us in the past. That should lead us to praise him because we know he will be consistent and comprehensive in his help—past, present, and future.

The verb tense used in the phrase *he has rescued* appears to support this understanding. The construction is common in vows of praise and likely indicates the anticipation of an outcome as opposed to the reflection on a completed act. Perowne says, "The [perfect verb tenses] in this verse denote not that the deliverance is already accomplished, but the confidence of faith that it will be, and give the reason for the thanksgiving of the preceding verse" (Perowne, *Psalms*, 434). So the psalmist worships, not just because God has delivered him in the past but because he has complete confidence that he will deliver him in the future as well. We worship our God with such an assurance of his faithfulness that we actually view what we anticipate he will do in the future as an accomplished fact! It's as good as done!

The psalmist finishes his prayer with a declaration of victory. The Hebrew places "my enemies" at the front. Why? Because this is his reason for praying in the first place: to ask God to do something about his enemies. And the verb tense is the same as above, confidently anticipating a victory. The psalmist will take great delight when he sees his enemies ultimately overcome. This won't be exultation over their misfortune but the celebration that God's righteous judgment has been administered and the satisfaction that his good name has been vindicated (*Gesenius'*, 380). Anticipating the defeat of the wicked is actually an anticipation of our vindication as those who trust in God. Whenever that happens, it always calls attention to and prompts praise for his great name!

Conclusion

What do we draw from this psalm? I offer two takeaways, one for believers and one for unbelievers. For believers, let's learn that we can pray with confidence in Jesus's name for deliverance that will vindicate our faith when people threaten and attack us. Satan always will work through ungodly people to undermine the gospel and those who embrace it, but we can rest in the assurance that God promises he ultimately will crush the threats and deliver his children. Sometimes his deliverance will be immediate (e.g., Acts 12:1-19; 16:16-40). Sometimes it will be delayed (e.g., Acts 21:27–28:31), even until the other side of death (e.g., Acts 7:54-60). Regardless of the timing, Jesus taught us to keep praying, "Deliver us from the evil one" (Matt 6:13). And when we do, we can pray confidently in his name (John 14:13-14) because we know that one day God ultimately and finally will end the threat of evil people and give eternal victory to his children.

For unbelievers, Psalm 54 is such a beautiful and simple picture of the gospel of Jesus Christ and the salvation we find only in him. We are all in a desperate situation because of our sin. The assault of our enemy, the evil one, has left us in a situation we can't do anything about. We can't save ourselves. That's why God left heaven and came to earth in the form of a man, Jesus Christ. He came to live a life we couldn't live and to die a death we should have died. And he overcame that death by rising again and defeating our enemy. Now he stands ready to deliver us and give us back the life we were created to have. So, what do we do? We cry out to his strong name—the name of Jesus—to save us, to help us, to uphold us. After all, "there is salvation in no one else, for there is no other name under heaven given to people by which we must be saved" (Acts 4:12; cf. 10:43; Matt 1:21). In repentance and faith, we express our desperation for him to do for us what we can't do. And we trust him and depend on him to do it. And he does! In return, we give him our devoted lives as a sacrifice of praise to his great name.

What's in a name? Well, if it's Jesus's name, there is help for all who are desperate for him, who depend on him, and who are devoted to him.

Reflect and Discuss

1. How does knowing the context of this psalm help us understand David's plight?
2. Knowing that one can be so close to the kingdom of God, yet be a stranger to it, what reaction should that stir within us?
3. That there might be false believers in our churches—is this a concern for church leaders?
4. In verse 2 David uses the words "hear my prayer" and "listen." How should David's example shape our own prayer lives?
5. How does God use desperate circumstances in our lives to draw us to him?
6. What are some examples of distractions in our lives that could draw our eyes away from God, our helper and upholder?
7. How is praying for God's justice on your and his enemies in line with the gospel? What dangers do we need to avoid as we pray for God's judgment against our enemies?
8. What are some practical ways we can share in worship with others?
9. What are some stumbling blocks that cause insincere worship? How can we avoid those stumbling blocks?
10. How does God's track record of delivering "from every trouble" affect our confidence in his faithfulness?

How Faith Talks

PSALM 55

Main Idea: Faithful Christians can acknowledge hardship while trusting the Lord.

I.   **I Need Help (55:1-5).**
II. **This Is Hard (55:6-15).**
III. **I Believe (55:16-23).**

The Psalms are full of pain. They speak from a range of difficult experiences: inside problems like sin, guilt, and shame; outside problems like injustice, military threats, or one of the acute experiences here—betrayal.

We don't know what experience prompted this psalm. It could be pointing to the story in 2 Samuel 15, when David's counselor, Ahithophel, betrayed David and helped Absalom lead a revolt to overthrow David. Sadly, David experienced more than one betrayal, so it's hard to pin down.

Though betrayal is the acute experience of suffering in this psalm, it's not the only experience of hardship here. Ultimately, I hope we see God's glory shining out in ways that strengthen our faith.

The question isn't, Will you have problems as you live in this world? Of course you will! The question is, How do we, as people who trust in Jesus Christ, respond to hardship? Where do we turn? Will we allow our instincts to be trained by the truth of God's Word?

There is a vocabulary of faith in this passage—three things people of faith are invited to say.

I Need Help
PSALM 55:1-5

You hear that request underneath every verse in this chapter. I need help.

Verse 1 contains a classic example of Hebrew poetry:

Listen to
    my prayer.
Do not hide from
    my plea for help.

This is two ways of saying the same thing. But look at the light it throws on what prayer is: "my plea for help." That's not everything the Bible says about prayer, but it is what Psalm 55:1 says about prayer.

Have you ever bumped into the prayer police? Someone gives you the impression that your prayers, if they're really spiritual, aren't concerned about your own life. "If you want to really pray, you won't even think about yourself; you'll only be focused on God's glory."

We might respond this way. "Well, yes, God's glory matters more than anything in the universe. I would never want to dispute that. But where did we get the idea that God's glory and our good are mutually exclusive?"

This reminds me of what you see when you watch little boys play battle with little army figures. When the battle reaches a fever pitch, you know it. Because one of the army guys is being hammered down on top of the other figure. Similarly, Christians can take one group of Bible passages and use them to smash another group of Bible passages. Friends, there is a better way! And as it relates to the relationship between God's glory and our good, according to John Piper, the beauty of the Christian faith is, "God is most glorified in us when we are most satisfied in him." In other words, God gets glory by being a refuge, a rock, a shelter for his people.

The psalmist isn't afraid of the prayer police. He uses "I, me, my" language twenty-seven times in thirteen verses. He relates eleven hard experiences in eight verses. I hope this liberates us to run to God in prayer! Paul Miller says, "Prayer is a moment of incarnation—God with us. God involved in the details of my life" (*A Praying Life*, 125). See those descriptions in verses 4-5: "My heart shudders within me; terrors of death sweep over me. Fear and trembling grip me; horror has overwhelmed me."

Prayer is what happens at the intersection of real life and an all-sufficient God who hears when we call to him. One of the reasons I love the Psalms is you hear God telling you in no uncertain terms, "You can say verse 4 kind of stuff, and those can be words of faith." David's requests carry the force of imperatives: *listen, do not hide, pay attention, answer.*

This Is Hard
PSALM 55:6-15

We get to overhear David's anguish—restlessness, turmoil, pressure, pain. It's all here. And he's bringing it all, his real life, into God's presence. David isn't too proud to plead. What is he after? It becomes clear in verses 6-8: rest and shelter.

Think about this in your personal experience. Have you ever found yourself reaching for something God's Word says is a good thing, but you can't get your hands on it? It's a frustrating and painful place to be.

This is where David is in verses 6-8. We move from what David feels to what David sees: "violence and strife" (v. 9). This reminds me of something an Old Testament leader named Nehemiah faced as he led the effort to rebuild the protective wall around the city. Nehemiah discovered that there wasn't just danger from the outside, but there was opposition on the inside. And here you see phrases telling that story: "in the city . . . on its walls . . . within it . . . inside it . . . its marketplace" (vv. 9-11).

And all that trouble seems to be connected to a source, which happened to be one of David's closest friends (vv. 12-14,20-21). No wonder the Bible goes to such great lengths to work on how we as believers treat one another. No wonder there's so much instruction about forgiveness and reconciliation and peacemaking. The fellowship we share in the body of Christ is not a fellowship of men and women who are models of perfect contentment, selflessness, and humility. James asks, "What is the source of wars and fights among you?" (Jas 4:1). And his answer is that we want things too much. We want something we're not getting, so we try to force people to give it to us. We want peace, but instead we have children, and they, on any given night, don't seem interested in the "peace" thing. So we blow up. We want to be worshiped (of course, we don't just come out and say that!), but instead someone thinks to criticize us.

Our fellowship, even as believers in whom God is working, is fellowship with fellow sinners. However, this is not a reason for apathy. God wants to work precisely here. So, for example, in New Testament books like Ephesians, Romans, Philippians, and 1 Peter, there's a clear connection between our vertical worship and our horizontal relationships, between knowing God has forgiven us in Christ and forgiving others, between the story of Jesus humbling himself and becoming a servant and the exhortation to esteem others more highly than ourselves.

No one should have a clearer understanding of how to lower the heat in our relationships and pursue peace than Christians. No one should demonstrate better what a real apology sounds like than Christians. And no one should be more eager to put a stop to abuse and injustice than Christians. That, by the way, is what's behind verses like verse 15. The so-called imprecatory prayers are basically prayers asking God to make it stop. Stop the violence in the city (vv. 9-10). Stop the oppression and deceit (v. 11).

As it relates to us, is it OK, for example, to pray that the acts of those committing domestic violence would come to light and be brought to justice? Or are we only supposed to pray for the salvation of the guy who is hitting his family members? It's a false dilemma. We can pray for both. As a matter of fact, we can pray while we pick up the phone to call the police.

The imprecatory psalms teach us something critical. They remind us that the instinct to pray (and, for that matter, to work) against injustice and oppression is not only permitted; it's commanded. It's a vital way we reflect God's image and display his character.

Think about this in your own life. Do you talk to God about what you're feeling (v. 2), saying (v. 6), and seeing (v. 9)? The psalmist models the vocabulary of faith.

I Believe

PSALM 55:16-23

There's this beautiful progression of first-person statements: "I am" (v. 2). "I said" (v. 6). "I see" (v. 9). "I call" (v. 16). "I will trust in you" (v. 23).

It is hard to read the Psalms and get the impression that God wants us to speak to him as if nothing is wrong in our lives—as if the sole purpose of prayer is to review the finer points of theology in his presence.

> We know that to become a Christian we shouldn't try to fix ourselves up, but when it comes to praying we completely forget that. We'll sing the old gospel hymn, "Just as I Am," but when it comes to praying, we don't come just as we are. We try, like adults, to fix ourselves up. Private, personal prayer is one of the last great bastions of legalism. In order to pray like a child, you might need to unlearn the nonpersonal, nonreal praying that you've been taught. (Miller, *A Praying Life*, 32)

If you want to fall out of the practice of prayer, start by nurturing the idea that God doesn't want to help you. Think of prayer as a field full of land mines, trip wires everywhere. Or think of prayer as paperwork with pages and pages of fine print. Rules that, if broken, ruin the whole thing. "Oh, that's an infraction. You got too honest." Or, "Oh no. You asked for help too soon. That's a breach of prayer protocol. You need at least a paragraph of adoration before you're allowed to sound like you're dying."

Christian friend, if that's how your prayer life died, Psalm 55 welcomes you back to try this again. And this time, don't pray in a way that forgets the gospel. Here's our story: We sinned against the God who made us. It separated us from him. As sinful people we don't deserve answers to our prayers. We deserve condemnation, not blessings. And instead of condemning us, which he could've done and been perfectly righteous, he sent his Son to reconcile us to him—to die for our sins. And in rising from the dead, the living, resurrected Jesus addresses every man, woman, and child here and offers you salvation. He calls us to trust in his perfect and finished work, to humble ourselves before him and receive the mercy we so desperately need and he is so eager to give. We turn from sin and trust in Christ, and we are then reconciled to God forever.

As it relates to prayer, once that happens, there isn't a moment in your life, even on your worst day, when God isn't utterly, completely, and irreversibly for you. And that's the reality David is finding here! "I call to God" (v. 16). And he's preaching truth to his soul: "and the Lord will save me" (v. 16). "I complain and groan . . . and he hears my voice" (v. 17). I'm not talking to the ceiling. I'm not godforsaken. He's listening. "Though many are against me, he will redeem me" (v. 18).

Now he reviews theology, not out of protocol but prompted by genuine faith. God—the one enthroned from long ago—*that* God will hear and will humiliate them (v. 19). God will right the wrongs in his time.

Does your faith talk like this? Do you pray as to a God who is enthroned? So often, when our ancestors in faith are groaning, the truths about God that rush in like first responders are the truths about how big God is: his sovereignty, his omniscience. At one point in history, his great love for us displayed in Jesus Christ. The God who hears our prayers is the sovereign Ruler and reigning King, and the gospel tells us that God is for us.

David doesn't yet have the full picture of what we know on this side of the cross, yet what he has is fortifying his soul in the face of hardship, so much so that he not only looks upward but outward. He calls in fellow brothers and sisters to exhort them. And what's the first thing he says when this passage, if you will, goes churchwide? "Cast your burden on the LORD" (v. 22). And the first promise he extends to the community of faith is, "He will sustain you; he will never allow the righteous to be shaken." You might say, "But I feel shaken." Here again, note the parallelism: "He will sustain you." In other words, by "shaken" he means to say, "God will never allow the righteous to be beyond recovery, beyond redemption." This is why we may grieve—grieve deeply, in this fallen world—but we do not grieve as those who have no hope.

I wonder if any of you have seen God's grace come full circle like it did for David—where God sustains and strengthens you to such a point that you, in turn, strengthen others? Have you ever experienced comfort from God only to discover that you are able and desirous to minister comfort to others? That's God's beautiful way of multiplying his grace through real human contact in the life of the church.

Psalm 55 invites us into not only faith but faith that works through love. It invites us up (to God) and out (to one another). Its invitation is, don't just cast your burdens on him; offer God's promise of grace to others. In one sense no one would blame David in verse 1 for *not* saying, "Cast your burden on the LORD" (v. 22). But here's the thing. From verse 1, that was where God was taking him: up and (eventually) out.

I could name members of this church who have walked through hardship, and the suffering comes full circle when, in God's timing, they steward that pain for the consolation of others. That doesn't mean the loss is any less real, but we begin to see how God is redeeming it. And here in Psalm 55, after exhorting his brothers and sisters, David looks directly at God (v. 23) and says, God, you will bring them down. You will right the wrongs. He closes with the resolution that demonstrates the sustaining grace of God: "But I will trust in you" (v. 23).

In other words, David says, God, you do the saving, the redeeming (v. 18). You bring down the proud in your timing as you see fit (v. 23). Here's what I'll do: I'll keep my eyes on you.

There is welcome realism. The truth is, an unshaken soul (sustained by grace) is not necessarily saying, "Everything is awesome." If you want to see a soul that is held in the strong grip of God's grace, it's the person who may feel totally weak, unable to sleep, vulnerable in the raging storm of affliction, but nevertheless saying, "I will trust in you." That's faith.

We can express this full range of the vocabulary of faith that we see at each critical turning point in this psalm: I need help, this is hard, but I believe. And we turn to one another and outward to the world, and we say, "Cast your burden on the Lord. There is a Redeemer who saves. There is a God who is enthroned, and he sustains us in this present darkness."

May this truth both steady our hearts and send us out. Our world is without rest and without shelter. And we can show them what it looks like, and we can tell them where it's found. It's all found in knowing Jesus. Church, keep your eyes on Jesus. Upward and outward—that's how God makes us stronger.

Reflect and Discuss

1. What is the difference between pouring our hearts out to God and praying a self-focused prayer?
2. What is your instinct when responding to hardship and suffering? To whom do you turn first?
3. What is your instinct when talking to God in the midst of hardship and suffering? What does that reveal about your view of God? (Think back to the last trial you faced.)
4. How will you incorporate other elements in your prayers to God this week—by not being afraid to pour out to him but to also focus on other biblically necessary aspects of prayer such as confession, praise, praying for the lost, etc.?
5. How did David bring his real life into his conversation with God? How can we, like David, have faith while still admitting that life is hard?
6. Why is it OK to ask that sins be exposed and justice be brought at the same time we pray for salvation and offer forgiveness? What is the danger of seeing them as mutually exclusive?
7. What does it look like for us to steward our pain for the consolation of others?

From Fear to Faith

PSALM 56

Main Idea: When we are fearful or suffering in any way, we can trust in God's character, rely on his Word, and hope in his Son.

I.   **Identifying with the Psalmist**
   A.   Have you ever felt overwhelmed?
   B.   Have you ever been opposed?
   C.   Have you ever felt alone?
   D.   Have you ever been afraid?
II. **Three Implications for Our Lives**
   A.   Put your trust in the character of God.
   B.   Lift your heart to the Word of God.
   C.   Place your hope in the Son of God.

Once again the superscript adds to our understanding of the historical setting: "When the Philistines seized him in Gath." Saul, the king of Israel, had determined to kill David (1 Sam 20), so David had gone to wherever Saul least likely suspected him to be. Remember that Gath was the home of Goliath, the giant whom David had killed in 1 Samuel 17. David was certainly not expecting a welcome party when he arrived; and to add insult to injury, David had walked into the hometown of Goliath with Goliath's old sword in his hand—talk about desperation! When David arrived in Gath, the people recognized him and seized him. Fearing that he might be killed, David pretended to be insane, which apparently worked!

Identifying with the Psalmist

David was not having a good day, which makes this psalm so relevant to our experience. Sure, you may not have been forced to run for your life by a king, and it is likely you have not been seized in the hometown of a giant you once killed. Yet you can probably identify with what David felt.

Have You Ever Felt Overwhelmed?

Knowing the background of 1 Samuel 20–21, think about Psalm 56:1-2 and 3-6. This psalm describes a man under unremitting pressure. David describes how men are trampling on him, oppressing him, and injuring him, and he says this happens "all day" (vv. 1,2,5). It's as if he's saying, "I can't take a breath. First it's Saul; now it's the Philistines. It's one thing after another."

Have you ever felt like that—like you just can't get out from under it? One thing drives you to despair, and in your attempt to deal with that, something else comes along and drives you into deeper despair. You just want to be able to take a breath or for something good to happen, or even just a moment to rest. Maybe it is something big, or perhaps it is just a bunch of little things, but you're left feeling overwhelmed.

Have You Ever Been Opposed?

David uses the language of opposition in this psalm. He says people are "trampling" on him; the enemy "fights" and "oppresses" him (v. 1); he faces "adversaries" (v. 2); their thoughts against him are "evil" (v. 5). Some of this is military language, and while there may not be a physical attack against David at this point, there are verbal battles and plots against him. Maybe you can relate to David when he says, "They twist my words" (v. 5).

Have you ever been slandered? This is a difficult form of opposition, particularly when you've done nothing wrong. David had done nothing wrong, yet Saul and others opposed him in 1 Samuel. Have you ever been opposed for doing something right? Have you ever been unjustly attacked by others? Has someone ever plotted strife against you?

Have You Ever Felt Alone?

David has *no one* around him at this point. What about you—have you ever felt alone? Maybe you were literally alone, in a physical sense, or maybe you just *felt* alone. Even when you are surrounded by people, you can sometimes feel alone. It's as if no one else understands what you are going through; they can't step inside your shoes.

Have You Ever Been Afraid?

They key word in Psalm 56 is *afraid* (vv. 3,4,11). It's the same word used in 1 Samuel 21:12 to describe how David feared King Achish in Gath.

Where this word *afraid* shows up, David asks essentially the same question: What can mere "mortals" (v. 4), or "humans" (v. 11), do to me?

Those are rhetorical questions, with "nothing" being the implied answer. However, it seems like man can do a lot to you. Man can attack, oppose, injure, threaten, and even kill you. David expresses his fear of these dangers with honesty, which is what I appreciate about this psalm. This is not some superficial religiosity that ignores life's realities. David is running for his life. Enemies pursue him on one side and surround him on the other, and he is afraid.

We're all familiar with fear. After all, it's frightening to think about what people can do to you. They can slander you, ruin your reputation, or fire you from your job. Your spouse can be unfaithful to you or abandon you. People you love can abuse you, harm you, and hurt you. And it's not only people who make us afraid but also circumstances. The threat of a tornado, terrorism, or cancer can leave us paralyzed with fear. Like David we fear the unknown. Even with little things we can become so worried and anxious.

In Psalm 56 David is experiencing his worst nightmare. The question for us is, How does David deal with real fear in this world, the kind of fear we're all familiar with? The answer to that question comes in the most poignant part of this psalm, and it's really the crux of the song.

David begins with "When I am afraid" in verse 3, but he ends up saying, "I will not be afraid," in verse 4. So how do you go from being afraid to not being afraid in a matter of one verse? How do you go from a frightening sense of what man can do to you to confidently asking the (rhetorical) question, "What can mere mortals do to me?" The answer is right in the middle: "I will trust in you. In God, whose word I praise, in God I trust."

Three Implications for Our Lives

So, how do you move from fear to faith? What do you do when you're overwhelmed, when you are wrongfully opposed, or when you feel alone or afraid?

Put Your Trust in the Character of God

What is the first thing David does? He looks to God and cries out to him. This must also be our first reaction when we are overwhelmed, opposed, alone, or afraid. Our approach should not be, "When all else fails, pray." Prayer is not a last resort; it is a first resort.

It is so easy to focus on what is overwhelming us, and the more we focus on it, the more overwhelming it gets. For instance, the more we think about those who oppose us, the more oppressive they can be; the more we dwell on our loneliness, the lonelier we feel; the more we contemplate our fears, the more afraid we become. So, what is the antidote? Instead of looking at *them*, look at *him*. Put your trust in the character of God and see your circumstances in light of him.

The object of your faith is so important. We're not talking about moving from fear to faith in general, as if the object of your faith doesn't matter. That's how the world often tries to cope with fear—by telling us to put faith in ourselves, in our circumstances, or in other people. But that's not where David puts his faith. He puts his faith, his trust, in the character of God. So, what about God's character should compel us to trust him? Consider what Psalm 56, as well as the rest of Scripture, reveals about God's character:

He is the omnipotent God. Four different times David refers to God in this psalm by using the Hebrew term *Elohim*. This is the most common word for "God" in Scripture, and it often carries with it the idea of God's authority and power as Creator and Sustainer of everything in the world. Confidence in this God leads David to say, "In God I trust; . . . What can mere mortals do to me?" We've already seen that people can do a lot to us. However, what *people* can do *to* you must be put in light of what *God* can do *for* you. The same goes for the world in general. The basis for fear is what people (or this world) can do to you, and the basis for faith is what God can and will do for you. What David says here fits with what Paul says in Romans 8:31: "If God is for us, who is against us?" Likewise, when Jesus sends his disciples "like sheep among wolves" (Matt 10:16), he tells them three times not to be afraid (vv. 26,28,31). The reason they do not need to be afraid is that, though people can do a lot of things to them, even kill them, God alone has the power and authority to save their souls (v. 28). He is omnipotent over all.

He is the merciful God. The omnipotent God is merciful to us in our time of need. So David cries from the first verse, "Be gracious to me, God." David knows God delights in showing mercy to the overwhelmed and the opposed, the alone and the afraid, so he cries out for grace, for unmerited, much-needed mercy. The omnipotent God of the universe is an endless source of grace to those who trust in him, to those who cry out to him. He is the merciful God who tells his people to cast their cares on him, because "he cares about you" (1 Pet 5:7).

He is the God who judges sin. In verses 5-7 the psalmist calls down God's judgment against his enemies. Such passages leave some Christians feeling confused because we're not accustomed to praying for the punishment of others.

David is referring to unjust men who are wrongfully opposing him and sinfully plotting to take his life, so he cries out for God to show his justice. And David is also calling for judgment against "the nations" (v. 7). This reference to the nations gives us a larger picture of sinful peoples and armies that are unjustly attacking and opposing David and others who are part of God's people. David finds comfort and hope in the fact that God will indeed judge sin.

This kind of prayer in the psalms really hit home when I spent time in the Himalayas recently. I saw the face of human trafficking and the villages where little girls were taken, and I walked past the brothels they were taken to. I found myself praying (with tears) not only for those girls but also for the men (and women) who were trafficking them and running these brothels. On the one hand, I prayed for God to save those men and women. If, on the other hand, that was not God's plan, then I found myself praying for God to smite them, to shut them down, to stop this injustice. And I find myself praying this way every week when I pray for the oppressed and the enslaved. I find comfort in the fact that God's justice will prevail. Those who traffic boys and girls will not ultimately get away with their sin. God's justice brings hope and stabilizes faith in a world of heinous evil.

It's worth noting briefly that sometimes we are overwhelmed, opposed, alone, or afraid as a result of *our* sin. For instance, if you are unrepentant and experiencing church discipline, then you may feel overwhelmed by those approaching you and calling you back to Christ. And if you've spurned those attempts to bring about your repentance, then you may feel opposed or alone. The last thing Scripture is calling you to do in this situation is to take comfort in God. No, Scripture is calling you to come back to God. Until you repent, you have reason to be afraid. You need to put your trust in God's character. The one who takes sin seriously is the one who desires to show you mercy and unmerited grace.

He is the God who sees, hears, knows, and remembers suffering. Psalm 56:8 may be the most beautiful verse in this psalm. David knows the character of the one to whom he is praying.

David recognizes that God has "recorded my wanderings," and he asks God to "put my tears in your bottle" (v. 8). Because they lived in

arid climates, ancient Israelites would preserve precious liquids such
as water or wine or milk in special containers. David was asking God to
store his tears like that. He knew his tears were precious to God, every
single one of them, and that they were in God's "book" (v. 8).

Suffering friend, overwhelmed and opposed, alone or afraid, the
God of the universe knows every time you've tossed back and forth in
the bed. He sees and counts every tear you shed; he hears every single
cry; he records and remembers. He never forgets any of these things.
The omnipotent God is not indifferent toward you. He sees, hears,
knows, remembers, and cares for you in *all* your suffering.

He is the God who delivers from darkness and death. After hearing
about God's compassion, you might be tempted to say, "That's nice, but
what good is it if God can't do anything about my suffering?" This is
the beauty of verses 9-11, where David reaffirms his confidence in God.
Then, in faith, David mentions vows and future offerings in verses 12-13.

Keep in mind, David says this while he's still in the fearful throes
of Gath with King Saul and his army on his heels. Yet David promises to
render "thank offerings" to God (v. 12) because he knows that he's praying to the God who "rescued me from death" and kept "my feet from
stumbling" (v. 13). Although enemies may assail your steps, and trouble
may pack your path, God has the power to keep your feet from faltering.

He is the God who gives light to life. In this psalm that begins with
such a bleak picture of being overwhelmed and overtaken by trouble,
David ends by saying he was rescued in order to "walk before God in the
light of life" (v. 13). God takes us from death to life, from darkness to
light. Instead of stumbling, we walk by faith in the God who saves.

So to return to our original question, What do you do when you're
overwhelmed or opposed, alone or afraid, or all of the above? The first
thing to do is to put your trust in the character of God. The second
thing flows directly from the first.

Lift Your Heart to the Word of God

Three times in this psalm David praises the Word of God (vv. 4,10).
Clearly, then, God's Word has a fundamental place in moving from fear
to faith. And David is not just *reading* God's Word, or *knowing* God's
Word, but *praising* God's Word. Consider three reasons we ought to
praise God's Word.

His Word is supreme. Some people might be uncomfortable with
the language of praising the Word of God, as if we're making the Word

out to be an idol. However, God is OK with viewing his Word like this. After all, this is his Word giving us this picture (in a positive light). And this isn't the only place we read this kind of language about God's Word—his commands and promises. Consider the following verses:

I will lift up my hands to your commands, which I love, and will meditate on your statutes. (Ps 119:48)

I will bow down toward your holy temple and give thanks to your name for your constant love and truth. You have exalted your name and your promise above everything else. (Ps 138:2)

God puts his name on the same plane as he puts his Word (cf. Rev 3:8). So praising God's name is similar, at least in some sense, to praising his Word. Therefore, trusting God in the midst of despair must mean trusting his Word.

His Word is sure. Many commentators believe David's reference to the word of God here is not just a general reference to God's Word as a whole but a specific reference to God's promises about making David king. Back in 1 Samuel 16, David was anointed king by the decree (the word) of God. So now when David is forced to flee King Saul, fearing for his life, he remembers the word, God's declaration, and he praises it. If that word is true, David has hope. If that word is true, then he knows he will be delivered from darkness and death and walk in the light of life.

Of course, you and I don't have this specific word of promise given to David. However, we have something better. We have sixty-six books that are the written, revealed Word of God on which we can bank our lives. These sixty-six books are filled with countless promises that God is with us and for us, promises of peace and comfort, guidance and grace, promises to love and lead us, promises worthy of our praise and delight (e.g., Rom 8:31-39).

His Word is sufficient. Regardless of what we're going through, God's Word is what we need. In a real sense it's *all* we need. Oh, if only we would believe this! There's a good illustration in Numbers 13–14 of the role of the Word as it relates to fear and faith. God's people came to the edge of the promised land and sent spies in to scout it out, and most of those spies returned afraid. They feared they couldn't take the land because the people there were too large. Unfortunately, those spies won the day; they convinced the people that the land God had promised them for centuries was impossible to take.

But then Caleb and Joshua stood up and said, "We can take this land." They became models of faith, but what they had was really pretty simple. They trusted in the character of God, and they praised the word of God. God had spoken. He had said this land was theirs. It was that simple for Joshua and Caleb. For if God had spoken, then the issue was settled. This was also true for David in Psalm 56.

When we face cancer, fear, or any other difficulty, we must trust that God's Word is sufficient. However, we cannot lift our hearts to his Word if we don't know his Word. This is why we should regularly read and meditate on the Bible. Certainly there are days when we wonder how a particular passage or chapter applies to our life. Perhaps God is using our reading of the Word on a particular day to prepare us for something coming in the future. Let us join Caleb and Joshua and David, and scores of brothers and sisters who have gone before us, believing that God's Word is supreme, sure, and sufficient.

This psalm does not end in verse 13, for it points to something greater. More specifically, along with all of Scripture, it points to *someone* greater.

Place Your Hope in the Son of God

Jesus Christ is the center of the Bible, and he is the center of this hymnbook known as Psalms. Therefore, the ultimate exhortation in Psalm 56, when seen in light of the entirety of Scripture, is this: when you are overwhelmed or opposed, alone or afraid, place your hope in the Son of God.

Jesus Christ, the Son of God, encapsulates the first two exhortations above. **He is the fullness of God's character.** All of the attributes of God we've see in Psalm 56—his omnipotence and mercy, his justice and kindness—are revealed in the person of Christ. And so the call to put your trust in the character of God is a call to put your trust in Christ. He is the one who delivers us from darkness and death, for he has taken the judgment due our sin. Jesus has died on a cross in our place, and he has risen from the grave in victory over death so that you and I might walk with God in the light of life.

Just as David said in Psalm 56:9, "This I know: God is for me," so Paul says of those who are in Christ: "If God is for us, who is against us?" (Rom 8:31). Such faith is grounded in the work of Christ for us. If God, through Christ, has saved you from sin, death, hell, and the devil, then in what circumstance in this world can you not trust him? What can man do to you? You can trust God amid overwhelming opposition, loneliness, and fear. He has taken on sin and death on your behalf, so you now have nothing to fear.

Finally, we can put our faith in the Son of God because **he is the Word made flesh.** David praises God's word because it brings light to his life. Jesus says,

> *"I am the light of the world. Anyone who follows me will never walk in the darkness but will have the light of life. . . . A thief comes only to steal and kill and destroy. I have come so that they may have life and have it in abundance."* (John 8:12; 10:10)

Christ, the Word of God made flesh, is the light of life. Fix your gaze on the face of Christ, and you will find yourself moving from fear to faith. Like David you will find yourself saying, "In God I trust; I will not be afraid. What can mere humans do to me?" (Ps 56:11).

Reflect and Discuss

1. In what ways can you identify with the psalmist? When have you recently felt overwhelmed, opposed, alone, or afraid?
2. What is your typical reaction when you feel afraid or overwhelmed? Based on Psalm 56, what is spiritually unhealthy about your typical reaction?
3. Some people wrongly claim that true Christians should never feel depressed. How does this psalm speak to this issue?
4. How would you use Psalm 56 to respond to someone who says, "The Bible doesn't speak into the struggles of everyday life"?
5. What aspects of God's character would you point to in order to encourage someone who is being opposed for their faith in Christ?
6. Why is it so critical that we believe in the authority of God's Word?
7. What are some ways we demonstrate that we do not believe in the sufficiency of God's Word?
8. What promises from God's Word do you rely on when you are afraid? Make a list. (If you can't list any, then select a few verses to memorize.)
9. In what ways does Psalm 56 witness to the person of Christ?
10. How does this psalm undermine an attitude of self-sufficiency?

How Do I Glorify God?

PSALM 57

Main Idea: God receives glory when we seek him and make him known.

I.   **Seek His Mercy (57:1-2).**
II. **Trust His Salvation (57:3-7).**
III. **Wake Up and Make Him Known (57:8-11).**

How do I glorify God? Is there a more important question we could ask as Christians? We have a whole Bible that speaks to that question. Though this passage doesn't cover all Scripture says about a life that glorifies God, it does cover a lot of ground in a short space. It answers the question from a place of difficulty—from the valley rather than the mountaintop

In the superscription, "Do Not Destroy" seems to have been a well-known tune in ancient Israel, applied to various works of poetry, including Psalms 58 and 59. Given the name of the tune, I'm guessing this wasn't a happy-clappy song. The choir director only pulls this melody out and attaches it to psalms that have some dark overtones. Despite its darker aspects, this psalm has a discernable thread of trust in God, even a note of joy toward the end.

I was studying this passage when a text came from my wife asking me to go read my email. She had forwarded something from some dear friends of ours.

> Hematology has contacted me with a plan of action for [name of her daughter whom they adopted in the awareness of very serious physical issues]. We are holding her medicine until she is transfused next week, and they want her pediatrician to check her out this morning to make sure that this rash is not the serious condition which can be caused by the medicine [she] has to take. Prayers for wisdom for the pediatrician would be greatly appreciated . . . the condition that they are checking for is very rare, but almost always (from what I've been told) fatal. God's grace is always sufficient and He has shown us that repeatedly.

Take that in for a minute. How do you move from "almost always fatal" to "God's grace is always sufficient"? How do you live in the face of danger or disaster? How do you glorify God and have joy in God while your circumstances call for a tune titled "Do Not Destroy"?

We're also supposed to read this thinking of David hiding in a cave, being hunted by King Saul. The full story is told in 1 Samuel 22. We might be wondering where this hostility came from. Why is a king taking time from his busy schedule to hunt a young man down? Well, that hostility had been building over time (1 Sam 9–10). Saul had been chosen and anointed as Israel's first king. He *looked* like the perfect man for the job. Everyone kept talking about his height, his shoulders, how handsome he was.

A few chapters later we find out that he's disobedient to God; he directly disobeys the command given through the prophet Samuel. When confronted, Saul doesn't repent or humble himself. He minimizes his disobedience, saying something like, "I know I didn't obey everything to the *letter.* I know I was supposed to wait for you to come and offer the sacrifice. But in my defense, Samuel, you were late, the people were scattering, and the Philistine armies were mustering strength. I had to call an audible. Practical leadership had to be given. And yes, I know that *technically* I was supposed to destroy everything when we conquered Amalek. But think about it: I mean, why slaughter all those sheep when they could be offered as sacrifices to God? Those burnt offerings weren't for *me*; they were for God!"

Whatever reasons or excuses Saul offered, at the end of the day, there was just one problem: that's not what God told Saul to do. God didn't say, "This is roughly what I want you to do, but, you know, play it by ear. Improvise. Surprise me with something special." God didn't want Saul to think practically. He wanted Saul to obey.

This is where we encounter the famous words, "To obey is better than sacrifice." The prophet Samuel informs Saul, "Because you have rejected the word of the LORD, he has rejected you as king" (1 Sam 15:22-23). As a result, Saul becomes increasingly obsessed and paranoid about who will replace him as king.

So a little later when David, a shepherd boy, shows up to the battlefield with bread and cheese for his brothers and hears Goliath taunting the Israelite army, and when David asks why they're all sitting down while this giant talks smack to the God of Israel, and when David goes

out to fight Goliath in 1 Samuel 17, and when that same David comes
back with Goliath's sword in one hand and his head in the other, this
obviously gets Saul's attention. We have the beginnings of Saul's nasty
jealousy toward David. Then, when Saul makes rounds through the cities of Israel and the women come out to meet him singing songs, he
hears faintly, from a distance, the words of 1 Samuel 18:7, "Saul has slain
his thousands [he loves this song!], but David his tens of thousands" [he
hates this song!].

Jealousy has poisoned Saul's heart and mind. Through a series of
events, this hatred led to an all-out manhunt for David, who is at once
Israel's future king and the most famous fugitive in Old Testament history, which brings us to this song that was inspired when David was on
the run.

In the most significant ways, the world hasn't changed since Psalm
57. The outward stuff changes: the names of global leaders, the forms
of government, the territories and boundaries, the technology. But the
world remains fundamentally the same.

How do we live for the glory of God in a fallen world—a world that
hates God? How do we live for the glory of God in a fallen body, with
anxieties and pressures and a heart that easily drifts toward unbelief?

Seek His Mercy
PSALM 57:1-2

In verse 1 David prays, "Be gracious." The grace and mercy David seeks
in Psalm 57 is not exactly the same as the mercy he seeks in other
places. In Psalm 51, for example, after sinning with Bathsheba and
killing Uriah, David needs forgiving and cleansing mercy. He pleads
with God, "Completely wash away my guilt and cleanse me from my
sin" (51:2).

In Psalm 57 it's not that David has committed some grievous sin.
No, he's in trouble. He needs refuge (v. 1). His enemy threatens to
trample him underfoot (v. 2). When he lies down to rest, he feels like
he's "among devouring lions" (v. 4). His enemies have set nets and
traps to capture him (v. 6). So this is not so much "please forgive me"
as "please get me out of this!" We should get encouragement from the
fact that the psalms are filled with those kinds of prayers—prayers for
personal help.

I've often been refreshed by a quote from the great theologian and early president of Princeton Theological Seminary, Charles Hodge. He spoke this way about prayer as a child.

> In my childhood I came nearer to "pray without ceasing" than in any other period of my life. As far back as I can remember, I had the habit of thanking God for everything I received, and asking him for everything I wanted. If I lost a book, or any of my playthings, I prayed that I might find it. I prayed walking along the streets, in school and out of school. . . . I did not do this in obedience to any prescribed rule. It seemed natural. . . . I thought of God as an everywhere present being, full of kindness and love, who would not be offended if children talked to him. I knew he cared for sparrows. I was as cheerful and happy as the birds and acted as they did. (Hodge, quoted in Miller, *A Praying Life*, 71–72)

As Christians, sometimes we not only lack gentleness in helping fellow believers, but we neglect important biblical truths. We can accidentally give people the impression that God only gives two kinds of comfort: he comforts us with assurance when we confess our sin, and he comforts us in heaven as he wipes our tears away (Rev 21:4).

When our daughter, Ellie, was three years old and wasting away day after day, week after week in Children's Hospital, and they were loading her up with powerful antibiotics that were burning through vein after vein, until there were no more places they could stick her, if you came in and said, "Well, at least your sins are forgiven," I hope I would have been sanctified enough to say, "And that's the best news in the world," but I doubt it. I probably would say, "Are you serious? So is there no help with this? Is there no presence to comfort? Does God only come when we plead for forgiveness, or does he come when we're falling apart?" And there's great news in the Psalms. Believer, you get to say, after you've sinned grievously, "God, wash away my guilt. Restore the joy of your salvation to me." *And* you get to say, when life is too heavy, "God, I can't breathe. I can't sleep. I have no idea what to do. Please come!" If we ask the question, "Are there *many* mercies that come to us from the throne of grace?" Psalm 57 is a resounding yes!

How do you live for God's glory in the face of harsh realities in the world? Seek his mercy. But also trust his salvation.

Trust His Salvation
PSALM 57:3-7

David isn't pretending that his life is free of trouble. He's not denying reality. But neither is he *nurturing despair.* Notice his trust in God. He speaks of God as the one who "fulfills his purpose for me" (v. 2), and he considers God's power and grace to "reach down from heaven and save" (v. 3).

Is this a guarantee that everything that opposes us will lose? That Christians always come out on top? On top of our temptations? On top of those who oppose us? On top, when the Supreme Court is battling over something that directly relates to biblical truth? No. Psalm 57 isn't a one-way ticket into a life of triumph and unending bliss. However, we can have this confidence: God is good, and God is sovereign. God is big, and God is wise. He loves you. And from the moment you turn and trust in Jesus for salvation, you'll never live another day alone.

So, what does it mean for us to put this truth on? To "trust his salvation"? It means praying even though it seems like you're just talking to the walls. It means if God says this book is profitable for teaching, rebuke, correction, instruction, and training in righteousness, then we will read it. It means if God tells us that by the Spirit we put to death the deeds of the flesh, we should fight as if we believe that's true. And if my feelings are telling me that God has forsaken me, my feelings are lying.

Paul uses this phrase: "Let God be true, even though everyone is a liar" (Rom 3:4). And that's a useful statement in the fight of faith. The fight of faith is contending to believe that *whatever* contradicts God's Word is a liar. God is true; and every man, every humanistic philosophy, every cheap thrill, every nude image, every rival god, is a liar.

We have it on the authority of Scripture that this is the narrative sweep of our lives: God will send from heaven and save all who have trusted in Christ. If you have trusted in Christ, that's your life story. Christians are convinced of this: at the end of the day, every false refuge will cave in, and Christ will be seen as the one, true hope of the world.

Rebellion against him will not go overlooked or unaddressed. God will judge human sin. The reality of judgment against sin is one of the central claims of Christian faith. However, another central claim of Christian faith is this: God has provided a Savior. Jesus came and lived a perfect life. He died on the cross to pay for our sins against a holy God. He rose from the dead, and full forgiveness and new life are given to all who trust in what Jesus Christ has done! This is the message the Bible calls "the gospel." The psalmist speaks of a God of salvation who "reaches down from heaven and saves"—a God who "sends his faithful love and truth" (v. 3). The New Testament gives this Savior a name—Jesus. God reached down, through Christ, to save his people from sins. Jesus came "full of grace and truth" (John 1:14). God did in fact send his faithful love and truth in the person of his Son, Jesus Christ. Every passage in Scripture whispers this grand story and points to this great hero (Luke 24:27,44; John 5:39-40)!

Another feature that points to the psalmist's trust in God's salvation is a literary device called *epizeuxis* that involves repetition. You see the first one in verse 1. Why is this here? Because I need to remember daily to ask for every grace God would give. I need to pray for forgiveness. I need daily bread. I need protection from temptation.

The second *epizeuxis* is in verse 3. The ESV draws it out: "He will send . . . God will send." We need this truth on repeat mode. Why? Because I need to believe that God answers when I call, that no prayer for mercy goes unheeded. It needs to be said that God may give a different mercy than I asked for, but that would only be because there's a better mercy than the one I asked for.

The third repeated phrase occurs in verse 7. What a timely reminder to us about the vital place of confident perseverance. The Christian life is not one epic "seeking of mercy" and one epic "trusting his salvation." It's a daily seeking and a daily trusting.

Some of my favorite moments in family worship over the years have been our prayer times—to watch our children grow up and learn how to speak to God. It's an awesome thing! Several years ago we started something that would become a tradition. We took missionary photos off the refrigerator and passed them out. We took turns and prayed through the names of our friends who were serving Christ among the nations. That first night, our son, Hunter, mentioned the names of some friends and said, "God, I pray that you would help them to cling to Christ." I didn't hear a word after that because I was so deeply affected. As soon as the prayer was over, I raved about it in front of the whole family. I told him he was onto something huge. I told him I needed him to pray that regularly for me and that he should pray that for our family and for himself—that we would all "cling to Christ."

Where are we leaning, Christian friend? Is our confidence in ourselves, or are we boasting in him alone, confident that he who has begun a good work in us will complete it (Phil 1:6), just as he promised? This phrase has become a daily prayer I have for myself, for family, and for friends: God, help me cling to Christ today, for life, for righteousness, for joy, for purpose. In other words, help me trust your Word implicitly. Help me be able to say, "My heart is confident, God, my heart is confident."

According to the Bible, these things are the essence of what it means to live all of life for the glory of God: "The righteous will live by faith" (Rom 1:17).

This passage has one more thing for us. We are called to seek his mercy. We are called to trust his salvation. And we are called, friends—every Christ follower—we are called to wake up and make him known.

Wake Up and Make Him Known
PSALM 57:8-11

The central refrain and concern of this psalm is the proclamation of God's glory. You see the refrain in the middle and at the end (vv. 5,11). This shouldn't surprise us. Many of us are familiar with the first question of the Westminster Shorter Catechism—"What is the chief end of man?"—to which the answer is given, "Man's chief end is to glorify God and enjoy him forever."

We know from Scripture that to see God's glory in the face of Jesus Christ is to live: "This is eternal life: that they may know you, the only true God, and the one you have sent—Jesus Christ" (John 17:3). This is the only life that lasts forever. To miss knowing God through Jesus, whatever else we might have gained in this life, is to die empty. To die unfulfilled. It is to miss out on the purpose for which we were created. That's why Paul said, "For me, to live is Christ" (Phil 1:21). Paul counted everything else as garbage compared to knowing Christ. And Paul stated his ambition in Romans 15: he wanted to know Christ and make Christ known!

Remember those literary devices where words are repeated? The final *epizeuxis* is in verse 8: "Wake up! Wake up!" In verse 9 off he runs to praise the Lord among the nations, to the end that God's glory will be "over the whole earth" (v. 11). There's a note of joy.

If you follow NFL sports, you know the New Orleans Saints (the city where I was born) went through a rough patch for about, well, forty years. They stunk. Then something changed. The 2009–10 season was a winning season. The Saints went all the way to the Superbowl that year. The city halted while that game was played. As you came to the closing minutes, we were behind. The Colts, led by Peyton Manning, had possession. Manning was driving toward victory, and the Saints were one touchdown behind. Then, with three minutes and twenty-four seconds left on the clock, our own Tracy Porter intercepted the ball and ran back seventy-four yards for a touchdown.

Our family and a bunch of college students were in our house. As soon as the game was over, without any advanced planning, everyone in our living room ran out of our front door, yelling and screaming for joy. And when we got to the front yard, guess what we found? Our neighbors had done the same thing! Music was blaring. Mr. Dan, the safety engineer from across the street, was doing the robot in his front yard. This was a side of Dan I had never seen. Our college-student friends were dancing with our kids in the driveway. You could hear the blaring as people just sat on their horns throughout the city.

It was an unscripted, citywide response. It was an eruption of joy. But, on reflection, what was fascinating was that the joy had to be shared. Practically no one stayed inside. The joy of the city spilled out into the streets. And that's the picture in this psalm. The psalmist reaches for the harp and lute—instruments of joy and praise—and he sings God's praise among the nations (v. 9). He wants God's glory to cover the earth (v. 11).

As we strive to live for the glory of God, to fulfill our primary purpose, I hope you hear God inviting you to seek daily mercies from him, to trust him and cling to Jesus, and to spread the good news of what he has done to the ends of the earth!

Reflect and Discuss

1. What excuses are we prone to make when we disobey God? What is one area in which you have been justifying sin by minimizing your disobedience?

2. What does David's relationship and emotion toward God in this psalm reveal about God's personal care and relationship to his children—to you?

3. How have you asked God, unashamedly, to pour out mercy in your life recently, believing he cares for you?

4. Why are we so prone to turn away from God when things aren't going our way or when we are hurting beyond description? How can

we remain firm in the truth of God's character and his word when
life is falling apart around us?

5. If everything were taken away from you except what you cling to,
   what would be left? What does this reveal about our confidence in
   God's sovereign goodness and faithfulness in our lives?

6. In the midst of David's enduring struggle, what does his main purpose—to continue glorifying God—reveal about (1) our struggles
   and (2) our purpose?

7. How would you describe your purpose in life? How does that influence the decisions you make every day—from how you spend your
   money to how you spend your time?

The Judgment of Corrupt Leaders

PSALM 58

Main Idea: The gospel compels believers to oppose injustice from evil leaders in anticipation of Christ's future judgment and reign.

I. **The Rejection of Justice (58:1-5)**
   A. Reflect God's heart for the oppressed.
   B. Remember God's grace for ourselves.
II. **The Request for Justice (58:6-9)**
   A. Pray for God to restrain corrupt leaders (58:6).
   B. Pray for God to remove corrupt leaders (58:7-9).
III. **The Response to Justice (58:10-11)**
   A. The righteous will rejoice (58:10).
   B. The corrupt will be convinced (58:11).

In 1384 John Wycliffe wrote, "The Bible is for the Government of the People, by the People, and for the People" in the prologue to his translation of the Bible. But it was Abraham Lincoln who made the threefold phrase famous during his address at Gettysburg. The great president actually borrowed the phrase thirdhand. A preacher named Theodore Parker had used it in a sermon in Boston's Music Hall on July 4, 1858. Lincoln's law partner, William H. Herndon, had visited Boston and heard the sermon. He returned to Springfield, Illinois, with his notes from the sermon. Herndon recalled that Lincoln marked with pencil the portion of the Music Hall address, "Democracy is direct self-government, over all the people, by all the people, for all the people" (Langley, *Washington Post*).

A persecuted Bible translator, a respected preacher, and a revered president all anticipated government to be for the good of the people. What none of them wanted was for government leaders—or leaders of any kind—to turn the tables and use their authority and the people under their leadership for their own selfish agendas and gain. Certainly the escalation in recent years of public awareness of sexual and domestic abuse by politicians, preachers, and other people in positions of authority is indicative of their concern. Before it was their concern, however, it obviously was God's concern. Psalm 58 is attributed to David, although not associated with a specific event in his life. But we can be relatively confident that at least part of the reason he wrote it was to help the congregation lament the injustice of corrupt government leaders and to confidently anticipate God's ultimate judgment of evil at the end of the age (see Ps 14).

Paul declared that God's reign over evil rulers—both seen and unseen—is rooted in the deity of Jesus Christ and secured by his work on the cross:

> *He is the image of the invisible God, the firstborn over all creation.*
> *For everything was created by him, in heaven and on earth, the*
> *visible and the invisible, whether thrones or dominions or rulers or*
> *authorities—all things have been created through him and for him.*
> *He is before all things, and by him all things hold together. He is also*
> *the head of the body, the church; he is the beginning, the firstborn from*
> *the dead, so that he might come to have first place in everything. For*
> *God was pleased to have all his fullness dwell in him, and through*
> *him to reconcile everything to himself, whether things on earth or*
> *things in heaven, by making peace through his blood, shed on the*
> *cross.* (Col 1:15-20)

Old Testament prophets had seen this dominion coming through the eternal reign of God's Messiah (Isa 9:6; Dan 7:14). This divine domination has been God's plan all along.

God's Messiah—Jesus—emphatically claimed his position of authority after his resurrection from the dead when he declared, "All authority has been given to me in heaven and on earth" (Matt 28:18; cf. John 17:2; 1 Cor 15:20-28). Christ's reign over evil rulers was further realized in his ascension back to heaven, when God

> *exercised this power in Christ by raising him from the dead and seating*
> *him at his right hand in the heavens—far above every ruler and*
> *authority, power and dominion, and every title given, not only in this*
> *age but also in the one to come.* (Eph 1:20-21)

Ultimately, this universal authority will be manifested when "the kingdom of the world has become the kingdom of our Lord and of his Christ" (Rev 11:15; see vv. 15-18). The resurrected and exalted Christ is the ultimate expression of God's judgment against and reign over evil rulers.

The heartbeat of the psalmist here provides us with one model of praying like Jesus taught his followers to pray: "Your kingdom come. Your will be done on earth as it is in heaven" (Matt 6:10). That's what the psalmist is praying for, and that's what believers today must pray for.

The Rejection of Justice
PSALM 58:1-5

To flesh out the prayer for God's kingdom to come, believers need to speak out on behalf of the oppressed. This psalm begins with an aggressive verbal offensive against those who reject justice and use their authority to foster inequity. Various Bible versions translate "you mighty ones" (v. 1) differently, but the reference to the "wicked" in verse 3 supports the probability that the psalmist is addressing government leaders who abuse their positions to immoral ends. That's why the rhetorical questions in verse 1 about whether they "speak righteously" and "judge people fairly" are answered with an emphatic "No" in verse 2. The progression of "your hearts . . . your hands" (v. 2) indicates instead that these leaders exercise a calculated ruthlessness in dealing with their subjects. These rulers think through their evil intentions in advance, cunningly weigh out their options, and mete out their self-serving plans with the efficiency of shrewd businessmen. They blatantly and intentionally reject justice.

David's assessment of these evil leaders then shifts from rebuking them directly to reflecting on some of their specific qualities that lead them to reject justice. He highlights their depravity by calling them wicked "from the womb" and liars "from birth" (v. 3). Their corrupt conduct betrays the nature that has characterized them from conception. He then compares their effect on the victims of their deceit to "the venom of a snake" (v. 4). They poison those who have been entrusted to their care. And he concludes by accusing them of turning a deaf ear to any voice of reason or persuasion (vv. 4-5). The picture is of the deaf cobra who is swayed not by the voice of the enchanter but by the movement of his instrument.

Consider two applications of David's direct and indirect rebuke.

Reflect God's Heart for the Oppressed

The gospel of Christ compels its adherents to be aggressive advocates of the oppressed and careful critics of corruption. Both reflect God's heart. The direct address in verses 1-2 reveals that God is far from passive when it comes to injustice. David wasn't hesitant to speak against those who were unjust. He said it to their faces instead of talking behind their backs, gossiping about them, or accusing them only in the hearing of those who would be sympathetic with him. He models here the open and honest communication of charges with integrity. Such should be the practice of God's children when addressing grievances and inequities, even with those who oppose us.

Furthermore, we have a moral obligation to defend the oppressed in this world because God's Word is far from silent on his heart for them. He defends the oppressed (Job 36:6; Pss 9:9; 72:2,4; 103:6; 146:7; Isa 14:32; Jer 50:33-34), delivers them (Judg 10:11-12; 1 Sam 10:17-18; Pss 72:12,14; 76:8-9; 106:42-43; Isa 26:5-6), gives them hope (Ps 9:18; Isa 54:11; Zeph 3:19-20), hears their cry (Pss 9:12; 10:17-18; 22:24; 106:44-46), shows them compassion (Judg 2:18; Neh 9:27; Isa 49:13), and promises to punish those who punish them (Isa 10:1-3; Amos 2:6-7). So God's children are to emulate his heart. We are to encourage the oppressed (Job 6:14; Ps 34:2; Isa 1:17), help them (Isa 58:6-11; 1 Tim 5:9-10), and cry out to God on their behalf (Pss 74:18-21; 82:3-4).

As we advocate for the relief of those who are the victims of oppression, we must always do so through the lens of the gospel and with the character of Christ. Amid the political turmoil in recent years, many professing Christians have felt that social media is a license for bad manners and unchristian rhetoric, using various platforms to maliciously attack opposing candidates. Our denunciation of unethical leaders and shady governments must always be done with integrity. It needs to be firm, fair, and honest, and at the same time "gracious, seasoned with salt" (Col 4:6). Even our approach to and interaction with those who persecute others must always be the same as that with which we engage our own enemies: with love. Only then can we give testimony to the gospel and rightly reflect the heartbeat of God (Matt 5:43-48).

Remember God's Grace for Ourselves

The second application is one of honest introspection, of careful self-examination. As we can tell from Psalm 51, David obviously understood that the difference between himself and these wicked leaders was one of degree rather than nature. He confessed his own depravity: "Indeed, I was guilty when I was born; I was sinful when my mother conceived me"

(Ps 51:5). And it's the same for every person who's ever been born. The description of these evil leaders in Psalm 58:3-5 is eerily similar to Paul's assessment of us:

> *There is no one righteous, not even one. There is no one who understands; there is no one who seeks God. All have turned away; all alike have become worthless. There is no one who does what is good, not even one. Their throat is an open grave; they deceive with their tongues. Vipers' venom is under their lips. Their mouth is full of cursing and bitterness. Their feet are swift to shed blood; ruin and wretchedness are in their paths, and the path of peace they have not known. There is no fear of God before their eyes.* (Rom 3:10-18)

Before rushing past this portrait of corrupt government officials, we need to see it as a mirror. Remember, beloved, we should look at these sinful men and conclude, "There but for the grace of God go I." Don't ever forget the grace of God in your own life.

The Request for Justice
PSALM 58:6-9

If the rule of Christ Jesus is going to be experienced at all on earth as it is in heaven, it's going to take more than our activism on behalf of the oppressed. It's going to take the forces of heaven to intervene on their behalf. Consequently, living out those early lines of the Lord's Prayer will demand us to request God's help and cry out to him on behalf of those who are the victims of injustice at the hands of wicked political leaders. Once again we're likely to find ourselves wrestling to reconcile the psalmist's prayer with Jesus's command to love our enemies and pray for our persecutors (Matt 5:44-45) and Paul's exhortation for us to bless those who come against us (Rom 12:14). Yes, this is another one of those imprecatory prayers, one in which he appears to be calling down ill will on the enemies of the suffering (see comments on Ps 54:5).

So, as we move into this section of the passage, let's not forget to allow it to open a window into our own hearts. Take a moment to reflect on how you felt when you listened to the most recent news report of an ISIS bombing of a Christian church building in some other part of the world, or even the threat of the North Korean dictator to launch a nuclear missile. Similar to the self-reflections noted in the comments on Psalm 54:5, think about those Nazi Holocaust prisoners, South African apartheid victims, and killing fields survivors. Most of us will have to admit that our heart longs for justice when we hear these accounts. So we likely can identify with the psalmist as he pleads with God to take action to defend his suffering little ones. In righteous indignation David uses a series of metaphors and similes to articulate two requests believers can and should make of God regarding wicked rulers.

Pray for God to Restrain Corrupt Leaders (58:6)

The psalmist first asks God to render these evil leaders impotent, to restrain their influence on their victims. The imagery he's using at first seems extremely violent and harsh until we remember that the Holy Spirit isn't likening the corrupt leaders to domesticated kittens but to savage beasts. The psalmist isn't asking God to beat up someone who's bullying him on a Near Eastern playground but instead to break the deadly grip these wild carnivores have on their trapped prey. We must pray as if the stakes are high!

Pray for God to Remove Corrupt Leaders (58:7-9)

The psalmist ups the ante in the next three verses by going beyond asking God to go ahead and take them out! He wants them to evaporate, to become blunt and harmless, and to dissolve away and be completely removed as if they had never existed.

Should believers actually pray like this? The psalmist's prayer appears driven by outrage that these kinds of leaders exist at all. His desire for their end seems violent. Kidner says, "It prompts the question whether an impassioned curse of tyrants is better or worse than a shrug of the shoulders or a diplomatic silence" (Kidner, *Psalms 1–72*, 227). Jesus seemed to opt for the former, at least when it came to leaders who abused people and led them astray. In Matthew 23 he pronounced a series of curses on the scribes and Pharisees, all beginning the same way: "Woe to you, scribes and Pharisees, hypocrites!" (23:13,15,23,25,27,29). These lead-ins are all followed by some of Jesus's strongest and most damning words in the New Testament. While none of us are Jesus, and while our engagement of bad people must intend to overcome evil with good, our Lord did seem to affirm the practice of the psalmist in sometimes crying out for God to bring an end to malicious leaders.

The Response to Justice
PSALM 58:10-11

God will respond to the prayers of his children as they cry out to him with zeal and passion for justice and righteousness in the universe. He's been clear about this all along. The prophet Isaiah declared that God ultimately will levy his comprehensive judgment against the wicked rulers of earth (cf. Ps 2) as well as those in the unseen world (cf. Ps 82). He said, "On that day the LORD will punish the army of the heights in the heights and the kings of the ground on the ground" (Isa 24:21). The day will come when God will vindicate his children and give them something to celebrate. At the same time he will exercise final and complete judgment against all evil authorities seen and unseen. The psalmist describes how both groups, the righteous and the corrupt, will respond on that day.

The Righteous Will Rejoice (58:10)

The response of the righteous is the natural reaction of those who are passionate about justice being served. When they see the "retribution"— or punitive vindication—meted out by the righteous Judge of the universe, they "will rejoice" that justice is finally being realized. The picture of the righteous person as one who "will wash his feet in the blood of the wicked" magnifies the celebratory and triumphant atmosphere of this ultimate vindication. The expression is a traditional ancient Near Eastern way of describing the utter defeat of an enemy. So we're not looking at some kind of twisted and ghoulish foot-washing ceremony but at victors as they wade through the blood left over from the carnage of battle (Wilson, *Psalms*, 842).

This gruesome celebration at first seems morbid, and we are almost tempted to shy away from embracing it, yet it makes complete sense in light of the larger biblical picture of God's righteousness. He wants us to anticipate the day when he will make right all the wrong in this world. The psalmist's description of that justification pales in comparison to John's vision of the bloodbath that will take place upon Jesus's return at the end of the age:

> So the angel swung his sickle at the earth and gathered the grapes from the vineyard of the earth, and he threw them into the great winepress of God's wrath. Then the press was trampled outside the city, and blood

flowed out of the press up to the horses' bridles for about 180 miles.
(Rev 14:19-20)

Our Lord's righteous army will join him in this final exercise of justice
against the wicked:

> *The armies that were in heaven followed him on white horses, wearing*
> *pure white linen. A sharp sword came from his mouth, so that he*
> *might strike the nations with it. He will rule them with an iron rod.*
> *He will also trample the winepress of the fierce anger of God, the*
> *Almighty. And he has a name written on his robe and on his thigh:*
> *KING OF KINGS AND LORD OF LORDS.*
>
> *Then I saw an angel standing in the sun, and he called out in a*
> *loud voice, saying to all the birds flying high overhead, "Come, gather*
> *together for the great supper of God, so that you may eat the flesh of*
> *kings, the flesh of military commanders, the flesh of the mighty, the*
> *flesh of horses and of their riders, and the flesh of everyone, both free*
> *and slave, small and great."* (Rev 19:14-18)

God actually is appalled when his followers don't see themselves as
warriors of righteousness and fail to join him in his campaign for justice
(see Isa 63:1-6). This realization compels believers in Christ to long for
Jesus's return and his final vindication.

The Corrupt Will Be Convinced (58:11)

The response of corrupt leaders and their followers to the justice of God
will be different. They will not celebrate but instead regretfully and finally
acknowledge what the righteous have always known. They exercise their
self-serving and manipulative ploys during their reign with complete dis-
regard that there will ever be a day of reckoning, but in the end they
will be convinced of God's justice and forced to publicly recognize and
acknowledge that he never forgets his children. In fact, he ultimately will
"reward" them and condemn those who seek to manipulate them.

This reversal of perception and fortune is a picture of every person
who rejects Christ in this life. People live as if no judgment were coming,
no day when they would have to answer for their hard-heartedness and
self-service. They go through life looking out for number one and stepping on whomever they need to step on as they make their way to the top.

However, the Bible is clear that the day will come when their perception will be overturned and their understanding will be radically

different. Those whom they spent their lives abusing and manipulating will one day be rewarded, and they will finally be convinced that there is a righteous Judge on the earth. His name is Jesus, and all who hear his gospel should embrace it while they still have a chance.

Conclusion

To be sure, God's reign is no democracy, yet he does intend it to be for the good of the people he created (Rom 13:1-7). And he never intended for the governments he ordained to lord over people for the benefit of the leaders who run them. God ordained governments to benefit people, not to suppress and oppress them.

But evil governments and rulers seem to have free reign today. Yet the Bible is clear that God will have the last word. In that age "to come" to which Paul referred (Eph 1:21), every person who's ever lived and every principality and every power will know that Jesus is Lord over all. Why? Because

> *God highly exalted him and gave him the name that is above every name, so that at the name of Jesus every knee will bow—in heaven and on earth and under the earth—and every tongue will confess that Jesus Christ is Lord, to the glory of God the Father.* (Phil 2:9-11)

At the inauguration of the eternal kingdom, the host of heaven will declare, "The kingdom of the world has become the kingdom of our Lord and of his Christ, and he will reign forever and ever" (Rev 11:15), for "he has a name written on his robe and on his thigh: KING OF KINGS AND LORD OF LORDS" (Rev 19:16).

So we pray like Jesus told us to pray: "Our Father in heaven, your name be honored as holy. Your kingdom come. Your will be done on earth as it is in heaven" (Matt 6:9-10). And because we're reassured that prayer will be answered in Jesus's promise, "Yes, I am coming soon," we pray even more urgently with John: "Amen. Come, Lord Jesus!" (Rev 22:20).

Reflect and Discuss

1. Based on Psalm 58 and other supporting Scriptures, what is the biblical view of government? How should government leaders treat us, and how should we treat them?
2. What are some examples of injustices going on in today's world?

3. What keeps us from reflecting God's heart toward the oppressed?
4. What are some tangible ways we can speak out and take action on behalf of the oppressed?
5. David's rebuke toward the ungodly was public. How should we publicly rebuke the ungodly?
6. What role does self-examination play in publicly rebuking sin?
7. Based on David's prayer concerning ungodly rulers, how should we pray in regards to ungodly rulers?
8. How should we respond to the seemingly brutal and morbid images in the Bible of God's judgment? Why would God use such language?
9. Is it appropriate for us to pray that God would remove ungodly leaders, and, if he must, in a violent way?
10. While we can disagree on whether God may ordain war, what can we agree on concerning our role in fighting for the oppressed?

Praying to a Global God

PSALM 59

Main Idea: The gospel compels us to ask God to destroy his enemies and declare his glory to all nations.

I. **Recognizing God's Enemies**
   A. They try to discredit his people (59:3-4a).
   B. They try to destroy his people (59:6-7,14-15).
II. **Relying on God's Help**
   A. We pray for God to deliver (59:1-2).
   B. We pray for God to act (59:4b-5).
   C. We pray for God to destroy (59:11-13).
III. **Rejoicing in God's Strength**
   A. His sovereign deliverance (59:8-10)
   B. His steadfast delight (59:16-17)

I think I have a pretty good work ethic. I get that from my dad. He raised us kids to know that it was important to work hard at everything we did. As I was growing up, I watched him pour himself into his family, his work as a public school administrator, and even his care for our home. He especially seemed to be fond of keeping our yard looking nice. After one long Saturday of working outside all day, I asked him if he really enjoyed doing all that work on our yard. I'll never forget his reply: "I like the results." For him, the end result was worth the sacrifice of sweat and soreness.

David believed the long-term result was worth the immediate investment. The backdrop of this psalm is when Saul sent his men at night to reconnoiter David's house in an effort to kill him. Michal—David's wife and Saul's daughter—helped her husband make a narrow escape out a window (1 Sam 19:11-17). While the themes of urgency, vindication, and passionate prayer for God's deliverance aren't new to David's compositions, this psalm gives us a peek into a part of David's heart that we don't see in every psalm—his understanding of how the favor of God on his life in the present ultimately would affect all the people of the earth (Ps 59:5,8). This is especially impressive as this song was evidently composed prior to David's ascending to the throne of Israel! Yet he refers to "my people" (v. 11) as well as the global impact of the defeat of his enemies (v. 13).

Truly the gospel is at play in Psalm 59. David apparently had such intimacy with God that he had the spiritual foresight to understand that God's kingdom was intended to have a global reach and that he was ordained to play at least some role in bringing that about. Saul and his thugs are described here as enemies of God's overarching plan of global reign, a reign that would one day materialize in the kingship of God's Messiah, Jesus Christ. Here God's servant prays for God's enemies to be defeated in view of the ultimate advancement of his global kingdom.

Consider three major motifs in Psalm 59 that help us think about how we pray for the gospel to have unhindered access to all people and how our work in the present affects that result.

Recognizing God's Enemies

Let's start by looking at how David describes those who oppose him and hate God's agenda for his life. Believers must recognize the enemies of the gospel and their motives. David identifies the twofold agenda of these evil men.

They Try to Discredit His People (59:3-4a)

The Psalter never suggests that David overestimated his innocence or had an overinflated view of his ability to resist temptation (see Ps 51). At the same time, he wasn't shy about declaring his blameless condition when he knew he was in the right, and especially when he knew God's reputation was on the line. Such was the case most of the time when Saul and his men were in pursuit. Here David emphatically claims they're making up their allegations and trying to discredit him.

False accusations always are driven by impure motives and evil intents. On a different occasion the psalmist says, "For they do not speak in friendly ways, but contrive fraudulent schemes against those who live peacefully in the land" (35:20). People say things that aren't true about others in order to stir up trouble. This happens at every level of our society from school playgrounds to the White House. Sometimes people try to discredit others for revenge, sometimes to manipulate power, sometimes to gain an advantage.

But fabricated testimony is especially characteristic of those who oppose the gospel of Christ. The prophet Isaiah told us this kind of viciousness would be levied at God's Messiah: "He was oppressed and afflicted, yet he did not open his mouth. Like a lamb led to the slaughter and like a sheep silent before her shearers, he did not open his mouth" (Isa 53:7). And that's exactly what happened to Jesus: "The chief priests and the whole Sanhedrin were looking for false testimony against Jesus so that they could put him to death" (Matt 26:59; cf. Matt 9:34; 27:22-26; Mark 3:22; Luke 23:2; John 18:30). Although the Roman governor, Pilate, knew Jesus was innocent, he accommodated the Jews and allowed their false allegations to have the day (Matt 27:22-26). However—true to Isaiah's prophetic words—Jesus "did not open his mouth" (Isa 53:7; see Matt 26:63; 27:12-14; Mark 14:61; 15:5; Luke 23:9; John 19:9; 1 Pet 2:23).

Consequently, followers of Jesus Christ can expect the same (Matt 10:25). People who hate the gospel will try to discredit those who embrace it. But be encouraged, beloved. Jesus said,

> "You are blessed when they insult you and persecute you and falsely say every kind of evil against you because of me. Be glad and rejoice, because your reward is great in heaven. For that is how they persecuted the prophets who were before you." (Matt 5:11-12)

No matter what lies people make up about us, believers must resolve to trust in God's Word: "The arrogant have smeared me with lies, but I obey your precepts with all my heart. Their hearts are hard and insensitive, but I delight in your instruction" (Ps 119:69-70). When people try to discredit us, we depend even more on the truth of our Bibles.

They Try to Destroy His People (59:6-7,14-15)

With poetic prowess David characterizes his enemies by their desire to destroy him. He uses the same picture twice to describe them (vv. 6,14). These villains are branded as a pack of dogs that roam the city looking for helpless prey. David may have chosen this description because these attackers had tried to ambush him at night (1 Sam 19:11). Additionally, David was keenly aware that scavengers, murders, and adulterers like to operate after dark because they think it hides their shameful activity (v. 7; Job 24:13-17).

The psalmist recognizes their destructive and blasphemous speech, and he compares them to the Israelites murmuring in the wilderness, whining because they don't get what they want (v. 15). They are like a pack of wild animals bent on finding and consuming their prey, resolved to destroy their target, settling for nothing less.

Again, the gospel is in view here. Jesus's enemies didn't falsely accuse him just to mar his reputation or undermine his popularity. From the beginning of his life, they wanted to destroy him. In the cosmic view of his life in the book of Revelation, Satan is depicted as a dragon that "stood in front of the woman who was about to give birth, so that when she did give birth it might devour her child" (Rev 12:4). Jesus's life on earth began with an angel telling Joseph to "take the child and his mother, flee to Egypt, and stay there until I tell you. For Herod is about to search for the child to kill him" (Matt 2:13). At the end of his life, "the chief priests, the scribes, and the leaders of the people were looking for a way to kill him" (Luke 19:47). And everything in between was similar (Matt 12:14; 27:20; Mark 3:6; 11:18; 14:55).

The same is true for those who follow the Christ. Jesus told his followers that enemies of the gospel "will hand you over to be persecuted, and they will kill you. You will be hated by all nations because of my name" (Matt 24:9; cf. Matt 10:17-18; Mark 13:9; Luke 21:12-17). A sin-sick culture doesn't want merely to discredit the gospel; it wants to eliminate it along with all of its proponents. Consequently, they will try to destroy anyone who tries to promote it.

This oppression of gospel advancement has been the perpetual theme since the time of Christ. After his crucifixion, Jewish religious leaders fiercely opposed even the threat that his agenda would be furthered. They went to great lengths to pay the Roman soldiers to lie about his resurrection, instructing the soldiers to say, "His disciples came during the night and stole him while we were sleeping" (Matt 28:13). This reckless opposition to the gospel continued at the hands of Jewish leaders during the apostolic period. Rome also determined that Christianity was bad for their culture, so they decided to try to extinguish it.

During the Reformation, even the institutional church opposed the proclamation of the true gospel. Later, communism would take its turn at trying to destroy Christianity. In contemporary culture, groups like ISIS have unapologetically stated as their primary mission to eradicate Christianity and establish Islam as the only religion practiced on the earth. Yet, through it all, the gospel message shines and continues to advance in power! As Jesus promised, "The gates of Hades will not overpower it" (Matt 16:18).

Relying on God's Help

With the psalmist under such assault from the enemies of God's kingdom, he cries out to God for help and relies on his rescue. At three different points in the song, he pleads desperately for God to intervene in his plight. The things for which he prays provide good guidance for followers of Christ who are relying on God to come against the enemies of the gospel.

We Pray for God to Deliver (59:1-2)

The agenda of the psalmist's enemies is clearly articulated at the beginning of this song. They're described as "those who rise up against me" (v. 1), "those who practice sin," and "men of bloodshed" (v. 2). These men have chosen to make evil and violence their way of life. Their target here is David, who finds himself once again in a desperate situation and in need of help from outside of himself.

So his primary request is for God to "rescue" him from these opponents, an appeal he repeats in the first two verses. The poetry expands on his plea in both verses with the parallel entreaties "protect me" (v. 1) and "save me" (v. 2). The word *protect* is related to the word *stronghold* (vv. 9,16,17) found throughout the psalm, which carried the idea of being set high up, out of reach. David was asking God to do something he discovered his physical house couldn't do, so he cries, "My God" (v. 1). In the same way, our physical resources won't be able to stand against the enemies of the gospel. Only the name of our God is strong enough to defend us and to forge a pathway to victory (Prov 18:10-11). Believers must cry out to God "in his name" for deliverance from those who have adopted evil and violence as their modus operandi and have come against his character and mission (Ps 54:1,6).

We Pray for God to Act (59:4b-5)

The most general part of the psalmist's prayer is his cry for God to "awake" and "rise up." Obviously, David didn't believe God was sleeping. After all, God had promised David, "He will not allow your foot to slip; your Protector will not slumber. Indeed, the Protector of Israel does not slumber or sleep" (Ps 121:3-4). But neither did David always know why God wasn't responding immediately to his prayers. And he had such an earthy relationship with his Lord that he could talk to him as a child talks to his or her father. From a human standpoint, sometimes all we know is that God seems to be asleep and disconnected from our plight. So we use words that express what we feel, but we use them against the backdrop of knowing that our Father is sovereignly hearing and acting for our good and his glory.

This conviction becomes clear in the next verse as David applies his personal prayer to a broader context. He acknowledges that God is the "Lord God of Armies . . . God of Israel" (v. 5), a confident confession that wasn't unfamiliar to the young soon-to-be king (see 1 Sam 17:45-46). He was passionately resolved to protect, defend, and depend on the reputation of his God, so he wasn't hesitant about appealing to it in prayer. Basically, David is saying, "God, you are the God of armies, including your people, Israel. Now I'm asking that you act like it on my behalf!" The idea here is similar to praying in God's name (see comments on Ps 54:1,6). We would do well to appeal to God more often based on his character, person, and position. He delights when we do so, and he always acts consistently with who he is.

It's in this broader application of David's prayer that we see what he values the most. His greater concern is the advancement of the larger kingdom of God, not just his personal situation. He knows the wicked ways of his immediate enemies are simply a manifestation of a larger reality—the global evil that resists God's rule. So he asks God to protect his people and defeat all the enemy nations (vv. 5,8). He doesn't want God to let his immediate detractors off the hook, but he seems even more concerned that he would exercise his vengeance on all who deal faithlessly.

David's worldview provides a helpful pattern for our own praying. We should always be more concerned about God's global—and even universal—kingdom than we are about our own personal situation. The order in the Lord's Prayer is important. Jesus taught us to ask, "Your kingdom come. Your will be done on earth as it is in heaven" before we ask, "Give us today our daily bread" (Matt 6:10-11). That kind of praying will then temper and shape the praying we do for our personal circumstances.

We Pray for God to Destroy (59:11-13)

The psalmist continues asking God to act according to his global agenda and glory, but now he raises the stakes for his enemies. At first he doesn't want God to condemn them all the way to death (v. 11). The psalmist wants his people to be able to see these enemies of the kingdom stumbling around as an object lesson on the result of sinful rebellion against God (cf. Deut 8:11-20; Judg 2:22; 3:2; Pss 78; 106; Isa 10:5-6). And he wants his attackers to be "caught in their pride" and their "curses and lies" (v. 12). While slanderous rhetoric alone can destroy entire communities, it is especially deadly coupled with pride because it flies in the face of God himself (see Judg 9).

David ultimately wants his enemies to be destroyed, to completely disappear (v. 13). Why? David wants it to be clear to everybody that God—not those who oppose him—is the true ruler of Israel and of all the people on the planet. David's words in this prayer are similar to what he said to the giant, Goliath:

> *Today, the LORD will hand you over to me. Today, I'll strike you down, remove your head, and give the corpses of the Philistine camp to the birds of the sky and the wild creatures of the earth. Then all the world will know that Israel has a God, and this whole assembly will know that it is not by sword or by spear that the LORD saves, for the battle is the LORD's. He will hand you over to us.* (1 Sam 17:46-47)

The shepherd boy reminds us in both accounts that the mark of a true child of God is to see him acknowledged and glorified (cf. 1 Kgs 18:36). That was Jesus's motive for living, his model for praying, and the basis of his expectation for his Father's response. He said, "Now my soul is troubled. What should I say—Father, save me from this hour? But that is why I came to this hour. Father, glorify your name." And his Father responded, "I have glorified it, and I will glorify it again" (John 12:27-28). May we take our cue from him, praying for the destruction of enemies of the gospel to the end that God may be glorified throughout the whole earth!

Rejoicing in God's Strength

Once again the psalmist wades through the murky waters and miry clay of persecution and desperation, only to find himself resting on the solid ground of worship. We find his expressions of worship in two primary places in the song—verses 8-10 and 16-17. In these verses David intends to "keep watch" in faith and "sing" praises. His heart is overflowing—even in the midst of his suffering—with the glory of God and the anticipation of salvation.

At the heart of his worship in this text, David rejoices and rests in one primary attribute of God. Twice in these verses he addresses God as "my strength" (vv. 9,17), and he acknowledges him three times as his "stronghold" (vv. 9,16,17). Additionally, David says of God, "You ridicule all the nations" (v. 8), and he sings about God's "strength" (v. 16). Within this celebration of worship, we find two particular manifestations of God's strength.

His Sovereign Deliverance (59:8-10)

In stark contrast to the dogs that howl, prowl, and seek to destroy him in verses 6-7, the psalmist begins to acknowledge the sovereign God who delivers him. The contrast is marked by the phrase *But you* (v. 8), which begins a series of confident descriptions of God's rescuing hand on behalf of his servant. Although the vicious attackers think no one is watching because it's nighttime (see vv. 6-7), the omniscient God has a front-row seat. And, as in Psalm 2:4, the figurative language actually finds him entertained by their outrageous folly (v. 8)!

The psalmist, however, doesn't want God to be the only one entertained by the victory over his enemies. He's going to hold a vigil like the night watchman of a besieged city, sitting on the edge of his seat awaiting the arrival of reinforcements (v. 9). The stanza closes with the expectant realization that God will, in fact, let him see the overthrow of his adversaries (v. 10). The phrase *look down* here carries the idea of watching in triumph, like the winner of a race who revels in his victory over his competitors.

This commentary on the present enemies actually reflects God's attitude toward the rebellion of "all the nations" (v. 8) of the world who think they can get away with persecuting God's servants. When we're feeling the weight of persecution for the gospel, it's encouraging to keep in mind that God isn't caught off guard by it and actually considers it silly. While his assessment doesn't minimize the pain and suffering we feel, it does help us keep it in proper perspective (Ross, *Psalms*, vol. 2, 322). And that perspective gives us great confidence to see God as our "stronghold" (v. 9; cf. vv. 16-17) and our "refuge" (v. 16) when we're suffering. The reality of his sovereign perspective and defense helps us endure!

His Steadfast Delight (59:16-17)

In similar fashion to verse 8, the psalmist now contrasts the dogs that howl, prowl, and maliciously attack him (see vv. 14-15) with his God who steadfastly loves him. Once again the contrast is strong: *But I* (v. 16).

Although the wicked dogs had their say against God at night, his righteous servants will sing praises to him in the morning! David's poetic pen unfolds the primary reason that prompts the praise. He unpacks the idea of God's "strength" by paralleling it to his "faithful love" (vv. 16-17; cf. v. 10). God's strength on behalf of his children grows out of his steadfast love for them. That ought to be enough to cause all of us to break out in songs of worship!

As God's children, we don't trust him simply because he's our strength, fortress, and refuge. We don't even trust him just because we know he's sovereign and, therefore, we're on the winning team. In addition to those things, we trust him because he loves us. Not only is he our Creator and sustainer, and not only is he sovereign and omnipotent, but he's also loving. As Wilson points out,

> Without the last, God would be a powerful deity with whom
> we had to deal, but we would not likely *trust* him. It would
> be a little like living under a totalitarian dictatorship. The
> government would exercise the power of life and death over
> all aspects of our world, and we would have to deal with it and
> consider it in all our decisions and actions; but we would not
> have to trust it. (Wilson, *Psalms*, 856; emphasis in original)

God's love is described here and elsewhere by a Hebrew word that indicates "covenant loyalty." In contrast to the way humans love so often, his love for us isn't based on appearances, hormones, compatibility, or personal benefit. No, his love is rooted in his commitment to his relationship with us.

I've done a lot of weddings where the bride and groom wanted to write their own vows as opposed to using the traditional ones. And I'm happy to accommodate that request as long as I reserve the right to check their vows for biblical integrity. My wife's dad—who was the pastor who officiated over our wedding ceremony—didn't give us that option. And I'm kind of glad he didn't. I'm glad we stood at an altar many years ago and said, "For richer or poorer, for better or worse, in sickness and in health." Why? Because those words help depict marriage as the picture of the gospel it's intended to be (Eph 5:22-33; cf. Hos 1–3). Marriage reflects how God loves with a covenant love. It's not about emotions, feelings, or benefit to the one offering the love. It's about commitment.

That's the way God loves us in Jesus Christ. By coming to earth in pursuit of us, he demonstrated that he loves us with no reserve. And if he was willing to endure suffering on my behalf, field even my own rejection and rebellion, and become my sin on the cross, then surely I will trust him. Even when my world is falling apart, my world is spinning out of control, and the enemies of the gospel seem to have the upper hand against me, still I will rejoice and rest in him as my strength and deliverer.

Conclusion

We must see our suffering and pray for God's subsequent deliverance in view of his glory and gospel being intended for all nations of the earth. Consequently, our lives must be given to this end—to announce his glory and gospel to every person on the planet. Animosity and opposition toward the gospel and its adherents are going to get nothing but worse. Consequently, we must expect to suffer for our faith. As we do—and as we see other brothers and sisters in Christ doing the same—we should pray for God's help and intervention. But we should pray against the backdrop of a desire to see his glory recognized and received by all people, including those who persecute us.

As we wrestle with the tension of praying as David prayed, viewing our enemies like Jesus taught us to view them, we have to keep in mind a titanic truth. If we're going to pray for God to deliver us and destroy our persecutors, and to do it in a way that demonstrates his sovereign strength, we'd better make sure we're innocent! Ross insightfully says, "Whenever believers pray for things like this, they must first examine their lives to make sure they are living faithfully to God—they can trust him to vindicate them" (Ross, *Psalms*, vol. 2, 327). So let's pray this way, but let's do it as ones who are able to say with the psalmist, "Not because of any sin or rebellion of mine. For no fault of mine" (vv. 3-4).

A third application of this passage is that we can talk to God with the brutal honesty of a little child talking to his or her father *only* if we do it against the backdrop of his sovereignty and strength. The earthy relationship David had with God never sunk to irreverence or disrespect. His whining, complaining, and asking seemed to always wind up in worship. He cried out to God with imprecation against his enemies in view of God's character—his sovereignty, strength, justice, and righteousness. A big view of God will always temper our prayers of imprecation and keep them safely rooted in gospel motives.

Reflect and Discuss

1. When those outside the faith attempt to discredit us, how do we find strength, peace, and comfort?
2. The enemy has been trying to destroy God's people (and God's Messiah) since the beginning of time. How does it encourage you to look back on God's sovereignty and power through persecution?
3. Have you ever prayed for God to be awakened to your needs? What can we learn from David's prayer life?
4. Should a Christian pray for God to destroy his or her enemies?
5. What role does self-examination play in asking for God to destroy? How will we know if our prayer is right before God?
6. What is the balance between calling for God's judgment against our enemies and Jesus's command to love our enemies?
7. David says that God laughs at our enemies' plans. What does he mean by this, and how does this encourage us in the midst of facing our enemies?
8. What attributes of God does David lean on during times of trouble? Why, after knowing these things about God, do we still doubt?
9. Why is it difficult to see our suffering through the lens of God's glory?
10. What does David mean by referring to God as his "stronghold" and "refuge"? How would it change your life if you viewed God as David did?

Closing the Gap

PSALM 60

Main Idea: God restores his presence with his people when they repent of their sin and trust him alone.

I. Repent of Your Sin (60:1-3).
II. Run to Your Deliverer (60:4-5).
III. Rely on God's Promises (60:6-8).
IV. Remember Your Need (60:9-12).

On Wednesday, February 21, 2018, the gospel enterprise on earth recorded a loss while the kingdom in heaven celebrated a win. Dr. Billy Graham, the world-renowned and beloved evangelist, went home to be with the one he faithfully proclaimed for the better part of half a century. In the days following his death, a barrage of pictures and news articles about Graham's ministry flooded the news networks and social media. We revisited God's grace in his life and celebrated the countless victories of people who missed hell and made heaven because of the gospel he had preached across the globe. Billy Graham's death certainly was bittersweet for many of us—bitter because we're going to miss him terribly and sweet because we're thankful that God graced our lives with one of his choice servants.

Dr. Graham's passing, however, also reminded me of something else, something not so pleasant to recall. As I reviewed the pictorial account of his life—the packed stadiums, the flooded altar areas, the conversations with world leaders, the consultations at the White House—two thoughts kept coming to my mind. One, I couldn't help but think about how our secular culture, our evangelical culture, my own denominational culture, and so many of our local church cultures don't have the same feel as they did when Dr. Graham was preaching. There doesn't seem to be as much evangelistic fervor among believers, spiritual interest among unbelievers, and religious awareness in our society. Two, I found myself praying, "Lord, do it again." We seem to be at a different place spiritually than we were in those days. And we desperately need God to do something for us that not only can we not make happen, but we haven't seen him make happen in quite some time.

That's the desperate straits in which we find ourselves today. We've backslidden, and we can't fix it. There seems to be a gap in our fellowship with God, and we don't have the ability to close it. We need God to deliver us from our moral—and evangelistic—drought, and he's our only chance of deliverance. If he doesn't come through for us, we're toast!

King David knew what it meant for God's people to be separated from the sweet fellowship they once had with him. This psalm was birthed out of one such situation. The superscription describes an occasion for which we simply don't have all the information. The context seems to be when David was fighting the Aramaeans in the north while the Edomites were attacking in the south (2 Sam 8). The king deployed Joab to suppress the latter uprising. When David got news of Joab's victory, he may have penned this psalm to reflect both his worry over the southern conflict and his confidence in God's promises to conquer the opposing peoples (Ross, *Psalms*, vol. 2, 333). The song is a lament, possibly prompted by David's armies suffering a significant setback in the battles, the details of which the 2 Samuel 8 narrative doesn't divulge.

What is certain is that there seems to be a gap between God and his people. The Israelites were in a situation where their power and position weren't assurances they would survive. They didn't have any good options, but the psalmist knew their victories and their defeats both came from God (Ross, Vol. 2, 335). The only hope David and his people had was for God to make good on his word, and that hope gave him the confidence to cry out to him for help. So, how do we pray when there's a "fellowship gap" between us and God? Consider four applications regarding how we pray for God to close that gap on our behalf.

Repent of Your Sin
PSALM 60:1-3

Anyone who's ever participated in any kind of addiction intervention knows that one of the most important things for a person to do is admit there's a problem. The same is true if we expect God to intervene in our crisis situations. Sometimes we don't pray like the psalmist because we don't see our desperate situation, and sometimes we don't see our desperate situation because we're not willing to admit that something is awry. Sometimes things are cockeyed between us and God because of our sin, and we need to admit to God that we have a problem.

David knew something wasn't right between God and his people. The language in the first three verses implies Israel has experienced some significant military defeat at God's hand (cf. vv. 9-12; also Ps 44). The catastrophic setback is described first as having earthquake-like effects, shaking and ripping the people apart (v. 2). Second, the psalmist says God has made his people "suffer hardship" (v. 3), describing the weightiness of what they're enduring. Finally, he likens the consequences of the disaster to the effects of intoxication (v. 3). Ross says, "God made them drink it to the bitter dregs, so to speak. The image represents the staggering blow they received in their defeat, a blow that sent them reeling" (Ross, *Psalms*, vol. 2, 338).

Despite the graphic terms with which David describes the defeat on the battlefield, he knows the real problem is a spiritual one. His deepest concern in this text is for how the current circumstances reflect the nation's broken relationship with God. The psalmist comes right out of the gate stating what he understands to be the problem (v. 1). This weighty charge is couched in three descriptive verbs that suggest God's anger toward his people has caused him to both spurn and break them. While we're not told the reason for God's anger or the details of his discipline, the psalmist clearly underscores that it put a serious strain on their relationship.

After admitting to God that there is a rift between him and his people, David begins to cry out to God for help. He makes two specific requests for God to fix this cataclysmic problem: "Restore us!" (v. 1) and "Heal its fissures" (v. 2). The petition at the end of verse 1 could also be rendered, "Turn back to us." Although the psalmist offers no reason for God's anger, he obviously assumes it's the reason for his trouble. So he's asking God to turn back his anger. The request in verse 2 for God to "heal" the broken nation is a request for God to restore their relationship with him so they once again can rest in his defense.

The two appeals together are a plea for God to reestablish Israel's favored position by abandoning his anger and repairing the rupture in their relationship. The adversity had seriously strained their relationship with him. So the king asks God on behalf of his people not to spurn them but, instead, to come to their aid. While the pronoun *you* isn't emphatic in verses 1-3, its repeated and rapid-fire presence traces the nation's chaos right back to God. So David sees their predicament as being under his ultimate control. Consequently, he goes to the source with his appeal. God produced their dilemma, so only God can provide their deliverance.

These first few verses paint a beautiful picture of the gospel! Taking the initiative of admitting there's a problem between us and God paves the way for deliverance, just as it did for David. God is sovereign, and certainly it is only by his grace that we become aware of our predicament. However, like the psalmist, we can respond to that grace by confessing we have a problem we can't fix. Being willing to admit our need is part of the DNA of what the Bible calls *repentance*. God in his grace calls us to himself and demands that we confess there's a problem between him and us. He calls us to change our mind about our sin and about the person of Jesus Christ. Peter proclaimed, "Therefore repent and turn back, so that your sins may be wiped out" (Acts 3:19; cf. Matt 3:2,8-9; 4:17; Acts 2:38; 17:30; 20:21; 26:20). The only way we are saved is to change our mind about out sin and turn to the only one who can do anything about our situation, and that's Jesus Christ.

The same thing is true when we find ourselves in desperate situations in our Christian lives that result from our sin. If we want to tap into God's resources through prayer, we can't just start praying and expect him to act. The Bible indicates that when we pray with unconfessed sin in our lives, our prayers just bounce off the ceiling (see Ps 66:18; Isa 59:1-2; Matt 5:23-24; 1 Pet 3:7). We must always begin by admitting there's a problem between us and God and that we can't fix that problem. That admission forges a path for us to turn from our sin, come into his presence, and make our appeal for his strong help. Certainly, sometimes we find ourselves desperate for God's help when our predicament isn't the result of our sin. However, knowing the nature of our sinful flesh should always compel us to start with that as a possibility. And even if we are right with God, we still need to lay before him our awareness that we've got a problem we can't fix.

Run to Your Deliverer
PSALM 60:4-5

Sometimes efforts at affection can backfire on us. Our daughter is the youngest of our three kids, and she's our only girl. She's now grown, married, and has children of her own. But when she was just a little girl, I remember frequently saying to her, "You'll always be daddy's little girl!" I wanted her to know how much I loved her and that she and I would always have a special daddy-daughter relationship. When she became a teenager, however, my expression of affection came back to haunt me more than a few times. When she wanted something and was trying to convince me to approve, it wasn't beyond her to look at me with puppy eyes and say something like, "Oh, Daddy, please! Remember, you said I'd always be your little girl." She was playing the identity card in order to get what she wanted!

While God never desires that we make petty attempts to manipulate him, he delights in us using our identity card when we need him to act. While Bible translators differ on the exact meaning of verse 4, it's clear that the psalmist acknowledges that God has "given a signal flag" (v. 4) for his people. A signal flag was a type of standard or banner often used in war to be a rallying point for the troops. It was visible during battle and, therefore, served as an encouragement and motivation for the soldiers. But some interpreters see the rallying banner in verse 4 not as a help but as a way of exposing Israel to the barrage of arrows coming from the enemy archers (Wilson, Vol 1, 860-61). That makes verse 4 merely a continuation of the catalog of God's negative actions toward his people found in verses 1-3.

The apparent positive tone beginning in verse 5, however, seems to indicate that David's words should be understood as a positive offer of protection from the archers. The declaration provides a theological foundation for his prayer. God is giving his people a banner that represents their identity as belonging to him. It represents their calling and mission in life.

> They were called to be the people of God with a distinct
> inheritance and mission; and even in the midst of apparent
> chaos, they were to demonstrate the truth of their calling by
> crying out to God for deliverance and renewal. (Ross, *Psalms,*
> vol. 2, 338–39)

The Israelites were keenly aware of the identity of their signal flag. After their victory over the Amelekites in Exodus 17, Moses said Israel's banner was the Lord himself. He called him *Yahweh nissi*—"The Lord Is My Banner" (Exod 17:15; cf. Isa 11:10-12). God is the one who prevails on their behalf, and that's who the psalmist is petitioning. He appeals to God's delight in his chosen ones (v. 5). The Israelites are the apple of God's eye, and David knew he wouldn't abandon them. The "right hand" is a symbol of strength. David appeals to God for his people's deliverance from their enemies based on their treasured position as

God's children, and, consequently, he prays that God will deliver them with great force!

David's approach here is worthy of our imitation. What father will not come to the aid of his beloved children when they're in trouble, especially when they're crying out for help? What father will not exercise all of his strength, ability, might, and resources to rescue his children when they're hurting? Disciples of Jesus Christ are God's precious children (Rom 8:14-17), and he takes great delight in us. He promised that Christ would be our banner who would deliver us: "The Deliverer will come from Zion; he will turn godlessness away from Jacob. And this will be my covenant with them when I take away their sins" (Rom 11:26-27). So he wants us to approach him with our needs based on that identity. Somehow the prayers of God's little ones—made against the backdrop of our identity in Christ as his children—strangely work as the tender nerve that moves the muscle of omnipotence! God acts when his children rally around their identity as his children and cry out to him for deliverance.

Rely on God's Promises
PSALM 60:6-8

After establishing God as our banner, David appeals to the promises God made to his people long ago. He quotes something God had said "in his sanctuary" (v. 6)—in his separate and unique position as a warrior, as the leader, as the King, as the holy God (cf. Ps 69:35). This oracle was a confirmation of God's promises from the time Israel had inhabited the land. God is taking his people back to the conquest and distribution of the land, and he's assuring them of his faithfulness to love and preserve them.

This oracle begins on a note of triumph, portraying God as the victor who has won the day (v. 6). We really don't know if this prophetic word was given at the time of the current crisis or if God spoke it at some other time in Israel's history. Oftentimes God's people rehearsed oracles like this as reminders of his faithfulness. What matters is that it was timeless. Whenever God's people were threatened or attacked, or whenever their possession of the promised land was in jeopardy, oracles like this would remind them of his victory and his promise to "divide" the land and "apportion" it to his people (v. 6; see Ross, Vol 2, 340).

In the next three verses God employs the literary device known as a *synecdoche*. A synecdoche is when we use some parts of something to represent the whole of it. For example, in our treasured song "God Bless America" we find the words, "From the mountains, to the prairies, to the oceans, white with foam" representing the entire United States. Here in Psalm 60, God uses representative geographic locations in and around the promised land to represent the whole of it. While Shechem and Succoth (v. 6) specifically refer to territories on either side of the Jordan (Ross, Vol. 2, 341), they are meant to signify the allotment of land as an inheritance for the whole nation. In verse 7 God declares, "Gilead is mine, Manasseh is mine." Similarly, the former territory was east of the Jordan, and the latter straddled the river. Then he says, "Ephraim is my helmet; Judah is my scepter" (v. 7). The scepter represented kingship. Since Judah was the center of the kingdom, it often was seen as the head, and Ephraim to the north as its defense against invasion. So Ephraim was to the state what a helmet was to a soldier (Ross, Vol. 2, 341-42).

After painting this picture of Israel proper, God references surrounding states in verse 8. These countries gave Israel a lot of trouble during the conquest as well as throughout the early monarchy. They weren't ever fully part of Israel but were subjugated and controlled by her. Moab is pictured as a servant with a pot for washing. A warrior pitches his shoe to his slave Edom to be cleaned (Ross, Vol. 2, 343). And while the exact intention of the statement about Philistia is difficult to nail down, it obviously asserts God's victory over that land.

So in just a few sentences the early history and distinctive territories of Israel are rehearsed. The God of Israel owns the land (and surrounding territories) and can allocate it to whomever he pleases. And as he promised, he chose to divide it up among the Israelites. So this oracle is a reminder of his sovereignty over the land and his faithfulness to his promise. And under the inspiration of the Holy Spirit, David reminds his people that they can rely on God's word and rest in its certainty, even in the midst of their turbulent times.

What an encouragement for us when it comes to prayer! As God's children, we have his Word written down and preserved in the Bible so we won't miss it or forget it. This Bible is filled with God's promises to us about his sovereignty over all creation, his delight in us, his salvation for us, and his will for our lives. Those promises all find their fulfillment in Jesus Christ. Paul said,

*For every one of God's promises is "Yes" in him. Therefore, through him
we also say "Amen" to the glory of God. Now it is God who strengthens
us together with you in Christ, and who has anointed us. He has also
put his seal on us and given us the Spirit in our hearts as a down
payment.* (2 Cor 1:20-22)

God has made an irrevocable promise to us as his beloved children; he'll
never go back on it. And he wants us to cry out to him, recount to him
what he has said, and rely on him to make good on it. John wrote, "This
is the confidence we have before him: If we ask anything according to his
will, he hears us. And if we know that he hears whatever we ask, we know
that we have what we have asked of him" (1 John 5:14-15). The most
potent praying we do is when we pray according to God's will. And the
Bible is made up of sixty-six books of God's will! Consequently, we should
pray with an open Bible, appealing to God based on what he's revealed
and pledged to us. We should cry out to him on the basis of his character,
his attributes, his faithfulness, his commands, his promises, his mission,
and his glory. We can rely on God to come through on his word.

Remember Your Need
PSALM 60:9-12

One of the times have I felt most inadequate in ministry leadership is
when I left the faculty at New Orleans Seminary to be the pastor of
Riverside Church in Denver, Colorado. Riverside was a large church.
I had never pastored a large church before, and I had spent the last
eleven years of my ministry teaching in a seminary. When I was inter-
viewing with the search committee, that tension came up. One of the
team members told me they knew they were going to have to address
that issue with the congregation. So he asked me, "What makes you
think you can do this?" I knew what he was asking. My degrees weren't
enough. My experience didn't match up. Nothing on paper said this
would work. So as honestly as I knew how, I responded, "If God doesn't
show up, I'm in trouble."

The last stanza in this poem is about that reality. It's simply a
rehearsal of the psalmist's need for God. He asks who will help in verse
9. He admits utter failure at God's hand in verse 10. He recognizes the
vanity of man's strength in verse 11. And he declares God as the reason

for success in verse 12. Every verse is some acknowledgment of complete reliance on someone other than himself. David is repeating the truth that if God doesn't show up, he's in trouble. Remembering that need kept him in a healthy place—a place of utter desperation for and dependence on God.

The Hebrew parallelism in verse 9 identifies Edom as a "fortified city" that Israel couldn't penetrate. Apparently, the king had been planning an attack on Edom when God interrupted and caused the chaos among his own people (see vv. 1-3). In light of the setback, he's asking the rhetorical questions, "Who will bring me . . . ? Who will lead me?" (v. 9). And the emphatically implied answer is "Nobody—if God doesn't do it!" And the recognition of need for him continues in verse 10. The psalmist has a problem: only God can give them victory over Edom, but he's turned his back on them. Victory would be possible only if God showed up.

If David's armies were to expect victory, God would have to answer their prayer for help and healing. So he prays, and again the parallelism reveals why this is a lost cause and hopeless endeavor unless God provides some help (v. 11). David was keenly aware that "a king is not saved by a large army; a warrior will not be rescued by great strength. The horse is a false hope for safety; it provides no escape by its great power" (Ps 33:16-17). It would be ridiculous to trust in men and materiel (Ross, Vol. 2, 345). If he did, even the armies of the people of God would be toast!

Weighing the vanity of trusting in his own ability against the promise of God's sovereign power is a no-brainer. The psalmist is going with God on this one. Trusting in God's ability instead of his own assures him that God will provide victory in his military assault on Edom (v. 12). Because they were repentant of their own disobedience (vv. 1-3), and because they had God's word on the matter (vv. 4-8), David and his armies could be confident God's wrath was temporary and their victory was certain. And God won't merely act on their behalf; he will act "valiantly" (v. 12), or mightily. The Israelites will defeat their foe with vigor!

The psalmist finishes with a clear statement of his point: "He will trample our foes" (v. 12). The first word of this clause keeps our attention on the one who's the only guaranteed source of help. The construction is as if David is saying, "God himself will win this thing!" While the Israelite armies will physically engage in the battle, God is the warrior trampling the enemy under his foot. The metaphor is an anthropomorphism that speaks loudly of the utter defeat of the enemy (Ross, Vol. 2,

346). David's prayer was for victory as they mounted the attack, and he was confident God would come through because his people were relying on what he had promised.

I haven't given a lot of good answers during my days, but I think the one I gave that search team was one of them. Apparently it was acceptable because they called me to be their pastor. And for the almost eight years of my tenure at Riverside Church, I lived in that tension of dependence. It was glorious! Utter dependence on our God is a safe place. That's a healthy place for each of us. And the most potent praying any of us will ever do is when we pray from a position of total reliance on God, a position where we acknowledge, "If he doesn't show up, I'm in trouble!" When we pray from the position of remembering our need for God, he always seems to show up.

Conclusion

What a great picture of the gospel! Remember your need—you're a sinner and have fallen short of God's glory (Rom 3:23). Cry out to God in repentance and faith—he's made that possible through his Son, Jesus (Acts 2:38). Embrace and celebrate your position as a child of God— he's adopted you and made you a joint heir with Jesus (Rom 8:15-17). Live your life in complete confidence in God's promises—he's packaged them in Jesus and written them down in the Bible (John 1:1,14; 2 Cor 1:19-20; 2 Tim 3:16-17). And finally, remember every day that all you are, all you have, and all you do is completely dependent on Christ and Christ alone (2 Cor 12:9-10). That's what Jesus has made possible through his life, death, and resurrection.

Spurgeon said, "Faith is never happier than when it can fall back upon the promise of God" (Spurgeon, *Treasury of David*, vol. 3, 30). Ultimately, it is an act of faith to throw ourselves at the mercy of the promises God makes in his Word. God speaks; we respond yes. And at no time is that more refreshing than when we find ourselves at the end of our rope, having exhausted our own resources, and having brought bedlam into our lives through our sin. Psalm 60 gives us the hope that God can and will close that gap. It points us to the gospel and even tells us what to do. We must be willing to admit that we've messed up and God isn't pleased. We must cry out to him to turn back to us and fix our mess by his grace. We need to grab hold of our identity as his children and run to him as our banner. Through the mystery of prayer, we need to remind him of that truth and of the promises to which he's obligated himself in his Word. And then we need to rest in the confidence that he'll be faithful to come through for our good and his glory. That's a happy place for our faith.

Reflect and Discuss

1. What biblical pictures come to mind when you think of "sweet fellowship" with God?
2. How do we pray when there's a "fellowship gap" between us and God?
3. What is the correlation between seeing our need for God's intervention in our lives and a willingness to seek him to intervene?
4. How does our ongoing need in life and God's ever-present deliverance throughout our lives serve to paint a glorious picture of the gospel? Why should a recognition of our need also provide us hope in driving us to prayer?
5. Why is it important for us to know the multifaceted character of God as we approach him in prayer? How does knowing who he really is guide us in genuine conversation with him?
6. In what ways does our identity as children of God impact our assurance before God in prayer?
7. What is the connection between God's faithfulness in the past and our expectations of the present? In other words, how should God's activity in our lives in the past inform how we view our needs in the present and future?
8. How can a thorough understanding of remembrance in Scripture provide confidence for us to ask specific prayers with an expectancy of God's response?
9. Why is utter dependence on God actually a safe and healthy place to live?
10. In what area(s) of your life might you need to remember your need for God, repent of sin, run to him, and rely on his promises?

Praying When You're Ready to Quit

PSALM 61

Main Idea: When believers are fainthearted, God provides strength and safety in his eternal presence and reign.

I.   **Pray for His Eternal Protection (61:1-4).**
II. **Promise to Praise Him Eternally (61:5,8).**
III. **Pray for His Eternal Reign (61:6-7).**

Serious boxing fans are familiar with the rematch that took place November 25, 1980, in New Orleans between Sugar Ray Leonard of the United States and Roberto Durán of Panama. While Durán had won the first match between the two fighters, Leonard's speed and movement gave him the advantage in the rematch. He was able to land several solid punches in the first half of the fight, had his opponent on the defensive, and even started to taunt him a little bit. Then suddenly—toward the end of round 8—Durán turned his back to Leonard, waved his glove toward him, and reportedly said to the referee, "No más," or "No more." Durán was done. He quit the fight.

If I'm completely honest, I feel that way sometimes as a Christian. So many things make me tired and weary of the battle—the unraveling of our culture's moral compass; the undermining of the Christian faith by our judicial system, media, and Hollywood; the coldness of people to the gospel; and the constant battle of my own flesh against sin. These things and more cause me to want to throw up my hands and say, "No más." I just want the fight to be over. I'm tired, and I want to be done.

Apparently, David got tired sometimes. Many of his psalms are prayers on behalf of God's people when they're in desperate situations, but this psalm—similar in style to Psalms 62 and 63—is a personal heart cry at a time when he's overwhelmed, alienated, and tired. He's praying for himself. While God's sanctuary is firmly established as the locus of the kingdom, David appears to be away from home and in trouble (Ross, Vol. 2, 351). He's weary and longs once again to experience the safety of the sanctuary and the continuation of his service. He finds his strength in what he sees as his eternal relationship with his God. That's the common thread running throughout this passage: "forever" (vv. 4,7), "many generations" (v. 6), "continually," and "day by day" (v. 8).

King David's prayer foreshadows God's glorious and grand answer in the eternal reign of the King of kings, Jesus Christ. Sometimes even Jesus's servants feel overwhelmed and alienated, and they want the fight to be over. Like David, we can find strength in the lasting nature of our relationship with God in Christ, and we can ask for his protection as well as the ongoing extension of his reign according to his glorious promises. Consider three applications for our praying when we find ourselves ready to say, "No más."

Pray for His Eternal Protection
PSALM 61:1-4

The psalmist opens up in a familiar way by pleading for God's help. The word "cry" indicates a loud, *desperate* shout, an emphatic plea for God's help. His dilemma is *distant* because he's crying out "from the ends of the earth" (v. 2), an expression that refers to a remote area, possibly even a far country. This hyperbolic and figurative term expresses David's frantic feeling of estrangement. And his dilemma obviously is *distressing*. David is losing heart and the will to resist. He is discouraged and on the brink of saying, "No más."

He's not just wanting to be back home because he's homesick, however. Whatever the nature of his situation, it was threatening enough that he was looking for protection. He asks that God would "lead me to a rock" (v. 2) because in the past God had been his "refuge" and "strong tower" (v. 3; cf. Prov 18:10). He longs to be in God's "tent" and "shelter" (v. 4). All of these requests are filled with metaphors for the ancient tabernacle that represented the place God dwelt among his people. David had set it up in Jerusalem when he brought the ark there (2 Sam 6:17; cf. Exod 33:7-11; Num 11:16-17). So his request in this psalm is not for God to do something to his enemies but just to get him back home to that place and position of his safekeeping.

David understands that God's "rock" of protection is superior to anything he or anyone else can bring to the table (v. 2). This rock is a metaphor for God's sovereign protection, which towers in comparison to any human resources. God reigns from an exalted position over human affairs, and his protection will put David out of the reach of his adversaries (Ross, Vol. 2, 354).

David doesn't want such a secure arrangement to be temporary. While he knows he has no right to be in God's "tent" as a permanent citizen, he asks for the next best thing—to "dwell" permanently as a resident alien (v. 4; Wilson, Vol. 1, 870). He wants to hang there for the duration of eternity!

God's sovereign protection through his presence has been made available to his children through his Son, Jesus Christ. John declared that God "became flesh and dwelt [tabernacled] among us. We observed his glory, the glory as the one and only Son from the Father" (John 1:14). Paul identified this one who tabernacled among God's people as the rock that David was seeking. He said that when Israel was delivered from Egypt, they "all drank the same spiritual drink. For they drank from the spiritual rock that followed them, and that rock was Christ" (1 Cor 10:4). Speaking of his role as Messiah, Jesus told his disciples, "On this rock I will build my church, and the gates of Hades will not overpower it" (Matt 16:18). So when we're desperate for God's protection, we turn to Jesus and cry out to him for the help he promises and only he can give!

Jesus is the rock of God who provides not only the most powerful place of protection available but also the only permanent protection. He provides that eternal protection when people put their trust in him. Quoting from Isaiah, Paul declares, "The one who believes on him will not be put to shame" (Rom 9:33; cf. Isa 8:14; 28:16; 1 Pet 2:6-8). Whoever builds on the sure foundation of Jesus Christ will be delivered from the alienated situation in which prideful people will find themselves—ashamed when they stand in God's presence. Not so for those who trust in the rock that is Christ!

Promise to Praise Him Eternally
PSALM 61:5,8

When we find ourselves in desperate situations, it should always drive us back to the promises God has made to us as his children. In those promises we will find great comfort and assurance in his eternal security. At the same time, we will realize a renewed confidence when we give ourselves afresh to his worship. Verses 5 and 8 are related and are best understood when considered together. The thought of dwelling in the safety of God's presence boosts David's confidence and prompts him to promise to worship God ceaselessly when he gets out of his predicament.

The parallelism in verse 5 helps us understand what David is saying. The indication is that God has answered the prayer in verses 1-4. God strengthened and encouraged his faith with the reminder that he was a child of the covenant, an heir of all that God had promised. The "heritage" he promised not only included the promised land (Deut 2:19; 3:18), but all the other bounty and blessing that came in his covenant with his people. As one of "those who fear your name," David is confident the benefits include God's protection and safety.

Apparently David's prayer in verses 1-4 included some "vows" (vv. 5,8) he made in view of God's answering him. Those vows are specified for us in verse 8. In his alienated and desperate state, David promised to praise the Lord if he would deliver him! God heard his prayer and his promise, and he answered. He made it possible for David to make good on his commitment.

David doesn't want this arrangement to be short-term either. He resolved to praise his God "continually . . . day by day" (v. 8). The idea is uninterrupted continuity, not necessarily eternal perpetuation. David is vowing to sing God's praises as long as he's alive and able to sing. God's answer to protect him and prolong his life comes with a responsibility—to be a lifelong worshiper. More days to live means more days to praise.

Sometimes we feel alienated from God, like he's distant and disinterested in our situation. As we cry out for his help in those situations, we should always renew our vow to worship him when he comes to our aid and answers our prayer. God deserves our worship and takes great delight in it. And it's appropriate that we resolve to do it forever because that's exactly what we're going to be doing for all eternity. In his vision of eternity, John said that he "heard every creature in heaven, on earth, under the earth, on the sea, and everything in them say, 'Blessing and honor and glory and power be to the one seated on the throne, and to the Lamb, forever and ever!'" (Rev 5:13). That's why God responds to our commitment to do it. And that's why there's something particularly potent in prayers that are accompanied by the resolve to worship our God for all of our days. So promise to praise him as a permanent and perpetual part of your life.

Pray for His Eternal Reign
PSALM 61:6-7

If we're going to be worshiping God forever, then by implication he's going to be in a position to be worshiped forever. With the assurance that we are part of God's covenant people and the recipients of his abundant blessing, we should pray that his reign will last forever and ever. That's what the psalmist does. He makes the same request in three ways (vv. 6-7). He's praying for long life and for his legacy to continue through the lives of his descendants. So he asks God to "appoint faithful love and truth to guard him" (v. 7). He knows this is the only way his reign will be perpetuated (see Ps 15:2; 23:6).

While these petitions may seem like normal court lingo like "May the king live forever" (Dan 2:4), much more is at play here. The psalmist is praying for his dynasty to endure in keeping with the promise God had made to "establish his line forever, his throne as long as heaven lasts" (Ps 89:29). He had promised, "My faithful love will never leave him as it did when I removed it from Saul, whom I removed from before you. Your house and kingdom will endure before me forever, and your throne will be established forever" (2 Sam 7:15-16). Although David's immediate prayer here may have been for God to let him live and reign forever via an enduring royal dynasty, the language alludes to the eternal reign of David's greatest descendant, the Messiah who was to come (Ross, Vol. 2, 358).

David's prayer here essentially is for the perpetuation of God's reign through Jesus Christ. The prophet Isaiah foretold as much: "The dominion will be vast, and its prosperity will never end. He will reign on the throne of David and over his kingdom, to establish and sustain it with justice and righteousness from now on and forever" (Isa 9:7). Before Jesus was born, the angel told Mary,

> *"He will be great and will be called the Son of the Most High, and the Lord God will give him the throne of his father David. He will reign over the house of Jacob forever, and his kingdom will have no end."*
> (Luke 1:32-33)

The author of Hebrews understood Psalm 45:6 to be referring to Jesus: "But to the Son [he said], 'Your throne, O God, is forever and ever, and the scepter of your kingdom is a scepter of justice'" (Heb 1:8).

And when John reported his vision of Jesus's return, he said, "The seventh angel blew his trumpet, and there were loud voices in heaven saying, 'The kingdom of the world has become the kingdom of our Lord and of his Christ, and he will reign forever and ever'" (Rev 11:15).

The long life King David wants to extend from generation to generation ultimately is the life of King Jesus, the one whose reign will last for all eternity. We need to pray that way as well, especially when we're fainthearted and feel like God's presence is elusive. In those times it's important for us to pray for things that are certain, things about which we are sure. And nothing is surer than the eternal reign of our Lord and Savior, Jesus Christ. Again we find ourselves back at the Lord's Prayer: "Your kingdom come. Your will be done on earth as it is in heaven" (Matt 6:10). Because God always answers prayer according to his will (1 John 5:14-15), we should pray for the eternal reign of Jesus Christ to be manifested in our lives and world.

Part of Christ's perpetual reign in our immediate world involves his reign in the lives of every person who ever lives. When he declared, "All authority has been given to me in heaven and on earth" (Matt 28:18), he was claiming his rule over every tribe, nation, and tongue forever. And that claim provides the impetus for his commission for us to "go, therefore, and make disciples of all nations" (Matt 28:19). Jesus Christ was the rightful heir to the throne of Israel and, thereby, the rightful heir to the throne of every person's heart. And he's charged us with the responsibility of claiming what's his by sharing the gospel with every person on the planet. So when we pray for the perpetuation of his reign, we're praying in view of our evangelistic efforts. Let's pray for Christ's reign with the resolve to see it actualized in every life and in every nation.

Conclusion

In January 1983 my wife and I stood at a church altar in El Paso, Texas, and said "I do" to each other. We were agreeing to be each other's partner for the duration of our time on earth. We signed up for life! Our vows weren't just a one-time affair. The words we articulated spoke of duration, so that covenant has had to be renewed every day—day after day, year after year—just as it had to for the psalmist (v. 8). If we had limited our mutual commitment to the day we articulated our vows at that church altar, our relationship would have crashed and burned a long time ago.

God has called us into that kind of covenant relationship in Jesus Christ. He's in it for the duration. He bound himself openly to us when his Son hung publicly on the cross. God made good on his vow in Jesus Christ. And because he's a God of loyal love and enduring faithfulness, he calls us to be people who are characterized by the same kind of love and commitment. We, too, are bound by the vows we made openly to him, the public commitments we made to him in truth. Those vows should be renewed every day—day after day, year after year. If we really want to experience his functional protection—on his rock, up in his tower, in his tent, under his wings—we need to give ourselves persistently to prayerful pursuit of him, continual praise to him, and constant proclamation of his gospel.

Reflect and Discuss

1. Have you ever found yourself weary from the battle of the Christian life? Surely we will all face this at one time or another. What should we do?
2. Reflect on your recent prayer life. Would you characterize some of your prayers as "crying out" to God? What keeps us from doing so?
3. Have you ever asked God for something and then promised to praise him all of your days regardless of his answer? How can we pray more intentionally this way?
4. If we do assure God that we'll praise him all of our days, how can we be sure to not fall short of that promise?
5. What confidence, within God's promises and protection, do we have that David didn't have? How does the coming reign of Christ cement God's promises?
6. How does the coming eternal reign of Christ comfort us in times of trouble and suffering? How can we incorporate this eternally important truth into our prayer life?
7. When we pray things back to God that are sure and certain (like the coming eternal reign of Christ), what confidence does that give us?
8. How is praying for God's eternal reign tied in with God's mission? What is our role in both?
9. How does God's covenant faithfulness to us in Christ encourage us through periods of suffering?
10. How does God's covenant faithfulness to us in Christ push us to pray?

True and False Refuge

PSALM 62

Main Idea: Since God is the only true refuge, every source of refuge in this world will fail us.

I. False Refuge: Confidence in Men (62:1-9)
II. False Refuge: Increase of Wealth (62:10)
III. True Refuge: God Alone (62:11-12)

I love how God has chosen to reveal himself to us. He didn't just ordain that there would be lawgivers and prophets and apostles. He gave us poets. Under divine inspiration these poets offer us a vocabulary of faith, truths to believe and live by and sing to one another, so that we persevere in this life of faith until the end. In other words, these are not just songs. Psalms is a book filled with the kind of singing that prepares us for living in a real world with an unshakable hope in God.

This psalm feels more like testimony and exhortation than *vertical* worship or prayer. David addresses four audiences. He speaks to his enemies in a kind of defiant taunt (v. 3). He speaks to his own soul (v. 5). He speaks to the people of God as a whole (v. 8), and finally, the only time in this entire psalm, he directly addresses God (v. 12). All these exhortations come together to firm up the conviction that God is a refuge for us.

There are truths here that we're going to need for real life. How long do you have to live in this world before you're familiar with feeling threatened or in danger? Feeling like you're a tottering fence, a leaning wall? Feeling like there are people or circumstances in your life that are bent on bringing you down? The Psalms give us a vocabulary of faith in a fallen world. These truths are meant to be believed and internalized. More importantly, these truths are meant to offer us stability of soul.

As Christians, our problem is *not* that we don't trust God. We have to trust God, at least for our salvation, to even become a Christian. The problem is that we don't trust him *alone*. We always want to add in something else to trust. Here David gives you the big idea right out of the gate: "I am at rest in God alone; my salvation comes from him."

To help us not miss the point, the same Hebrew word occurs six times in the first nine verses, four of those times in reference to God. If you mark in your Bible, you might want to circle these: "God *alone*" (v. 1); "He *alone*" (v. 2); "They *only*" (v. 4); "God *alone*" (v. 5); "He *alone*" (v. 6), "people are *only*" (v. 9). Psalm 62 is aimed at one primary effect. It's not just that we would feel the truth that God is a refuge for us but that God *alone* is a refuge for us. In the course of pressing that point home, David exposes two areas of life in which we seek refuge outside of God.

False Refuge: Confidence in Men
PSALM 62:1-9

There's some back-and-forth going on throughout the passage as it relates to trusting in God versus relying on men. It goes something like this: Trust in God alone (vv. 1-2). You can't trust in man because men are sometimes malicious and deceptive (vv. 3-4). Rest in God alone—he is a rock (vv. 5-8). Don't trust in men because they're here today and gone tomorrow (v. 9). You see? It's David toggling back-and-forth: real refuge, false refuge.

The superscription indicates that David is the author of this psalm, so it's helpful to bear in mind things we know about David from the historical writings of the Old Testament. Knowing some of David's story will help us grasp some of the experiences he describes here.

David had what you might call an early break. He killed Goliath the giant. That tends to bring you out into the public eye. Everybody was talking about him. Popular songs were written about him, and Israelite girls sang them in the streets. In light of that, David would have known the temptation to find security in human approval because early on David became a magnet for powerful, beautiful, upwardly mobile people. Practically overnight, he was on a first-name basis with none other than Saul, the king of Israel himself.

Who wouldn't feel, "I've arrived"? "Finally, the ball is bouncing in my direction." However, if we keep reading David's story, we learn things change quickly for him. The thing that put him on the cover of magazines all over Israel is the very thing that aroused the jealousy of King Saul, turning David into a hunted man. By the time his story plays out, hostility from people he should be able to trust becomes a common theme (v. 4).

This psalm finds David calling this truth to mind—people are a faulty refuge for all kinds of reasons. One, because they can turn on you (vv. 3-4). Two, because they're not around forever (v. 9). "Those of low estate are but a breath; those of high estate are a delusion; in the balances they go up; they are together lighter than a breath" (v. 9 ESV). Low estate and high estate—it's a Hebrew expression that takes in everybody. All human beings are *but* a breath. Again, that's the same word translated "alone" or "only" in verses 1, 2, 5, and 6. Trust *only* in God because men are *only* a breath. The contrast is absolute. Human beings are a vapor, a breath. Here today, gone tomorrow. God is the only one we can trust "at all times" (v. 8).

You might be thinking, *Wait, hasn't God given us people to trust and look to?* Ephesians 6 speaks of children obeying parents. Hebrews 13 exhorts church members to submit to pastors as spiritual overseers. Proverbs 17 describes the way a true friend is reliable and present during adversity. Yes, that's how it's supposed to be. It's a good thing when friends are trustworthy, when parents are there for us. When they do this, they are *reflecting* God's image. He is faithful, dependable, and trustworthy. Here's the point: Those things that we are, on our best days and in our closest relationships, God is at all times. He can't be otherwise.

Are we Christians helping one another look to God in ways that we should? Are we helping our children understand that only one being in the universe will, at the end of the day, never fail them? Are we pointing out to friends (and remembering ourselves!) that God alone is able to be always listening, always working, always present?

We need to be present, but friends, we cannot pretend to be God. You don't have what it takes to keep me ultimately afloat. You can't keep my happiness gauge always reading full. The day you pull that off, you'll become an idol to me. I won't have to get something from God because, well, I always have you to meet every need of heart and soul. When we put all our stock in human friendship and then a friend disappoints us, our world collapses. When we pursue human approval at all costs and then discover that certain people don't like us, it shuts us down. Living in light of friends' approval means always trying to *be* something to stay in. Living in light of enemies' disapproval means always trying to *prove* something. We always have a chip on our shoulder.

Yes, David had enemies, and they were sometimes loud, sometimes dangerous, often deceptive. He addresses them in verse 3. He's aware of their motives. But he comes right back in verse 5 to where he started.

Resting in God alone is headquarters. This is truth. He lives right here. It was said about Jonathan Edwards that his happiness was wholly out of the reach of his enemies.

Even concerning friendships, we need to bring this truth on board. Our relationships with those closest to us are healthier when we give one another the freedom to not be God to us—the freedom to be a vapor, because God alone is my rock, my fortress.

False Refuge: Increase of Wealth
PSALM 62:10

David seems to speak of different ways of acquiring wealth, beginning with dishonorable ways of obtaining it: oppression and robbery. As king over Israel, he would certainly have had the ability to abuse his position to amass greater personal wealth. But he disavows dependence on wealth.

The word *increases* has to do with fruitfulness. This isn't a bad word. Here he's talking about the more natural and honorable way of obtaining wealth. We're called in Scripture to be diligent: to work hard, to be wise stewards, and so on. So what's he doing lumping all of this together—these warnings about wealth? David is saying something we hear Jesus and then Paul say a thousand years later: money is dangerous, however it comes. Wealth sticks to us. The power goes to our heads. The distractions money affords can divert us away from living to please God and serve others. So we have Psalm 62:10 and other verses like it because God knows how easy it is for wealth to turn from being a blessing to a refuge, from being a temporary good that we *steward* to being a ticket to the good life in a world that *worships* money.

It's not the increase of wealth that's wrong. The question is, What happens next, and what does that display? Do our hands close tightly over the money because we're convinced this is life? Money *spenders* say, "This is a handful of great experiences." Money *savers* say, "This is a handful of future security." Both are putting their hope in wealth.

Christian, there's another way to display our faith as wealth increases. We can enjoy God's blessing and give thanks that all of this comes ultimately from him. Then we can open our hands in ways that demonstrate this stuff isn't life! This isn't refuge. We can look at our resources through the eyes of faith, seeking first his kingdom, prioritizing the support of the church, the cause of the oppressed, and the spread of the gospel.

True Refuge: God Alone
PSALM 62:11-12

This song points to God for salvation (v. 1). Look at the metaphors for God: my rock, my salvation, my stronghold, my refuge (vv. 2,6,7-8). David has purposed to trust in God alone, and the foundation is in these final two verses.

First, God has spoken. This is the foundation of our faith and trust in God. God has gone on record to tell us who he is, how we may know him, and what he is like. David says, "God has spoken once; I have heard this twice." Just think about that. In parenting it's often the opposite. You say it twice (or ten times) before they hear it once. God says it once, and David hears it twice. This is his way of describing the soul-stabilizing effect of God's word in his life. God's word breaks in on David's life and circumstances in such a way that—only through grace—he can say, I don't get my security from the people who love me or the people who pretend to love me. I don't lose sleep over the people who want to destroy me. I don't get my security from my wealth.

Oh, to know this grace! Where God's Spirit works this truth down into our souls and we say, by grace, "God alone is my refuge. Let the world fall, I will never be shaken because he alone is my refuge, my rock, my salvation, my stronghold."

What does David hear God saying? That strength and faithful love belong to God because he repays people according to their works. David's faith is grounded in these glorious truths: God is sovereign. God is all powerful. And God loves David. God is committed to David's good. God is a God of both sovereign power and faithful love. Therefore, he can be a refuge for us. Church, if we only had a God of brute power, he could do anything, but we'd cower before him in fear. If we only had a God of love and kindness, we'd know his care but have reason to wonder whether he could keep us safe. But we hear the prophets speak of one who would eventually come and rescue his people. He would atone for their sins. He would take their guilt into the grave. He would welcome the weary and heavy-laden into rest and free them from powers too strong for them.

And then we see Jesus Christ show up on the scene of history. He really came to this earth! He made exclusive claims about himself: "I am the way, the truth, and the life. No one comes to the Father except through me" (John 14:6). He promised exclusive refuge for those who trust him. He went to the cross. He took our enemies to the grave and rose in triumph over sin, death, and Satan. Best news of all, he offers new life—absolute refuge (now and forever) to everyone who calls on him. This is the good news of the gospel. God uses this message to bring us from death to life. This is the hope of the world.

The apostles who saw him alive say, "There is no other name under heaven given to people by which we must be saved" (Acts 4:12). They preach Jesus Christ everywhere they go. We come to the final book of the New Testament and hear that the Lamb *alone* is worthy to receive all glory (Rev 5:8-14) because the Lamb *alone* has redeemed and rescued his people. In that way, having walked through the Scriptures, our eyes are open to read Psalm 62 in a new way, and we understand it is Jesus Christ who extends to us the refuge promised here. We can't do an end run around God to get security from money or other people. And we actually can't do an end run around Jesus to get to the God who alone is our refuge. No one comes to God the refuge but through him.

This is sobering news for those who depend on any other refuge besides Jesus. As verse 12 says, God will "repay each according to his works." You don't want that payment. That payment amounts to your soul receiving justice from a holy God. What sinners like us need is mercy from a holy God, and that mercy comes to us through the cross of Jesus Christ.

If we spend our lives propping up one false refuge after another while rejecting the God who made us, we'll give account for that. But there's good news. If we turn to the one refuge God provided, and we believe that he lived and died and rose again, and that he alone has power to rescue us, we will know God not as Judge but as rock and refuge.

Reflect and Discuss

1. How do we know if we are relying on something or someone more than we are depending on God?
2. Why are people a faulty refuge? While we know such truths in our head, how do we live in a way that reflects the belief that people are a faulty refuge?
3. How do we have healthy relationships with people without making those relationships an idol in our lives?

4. What can you do to repent and correct course if you realize you have made a relationship an idol?

5. How does giving others the freedom not to be God actually free us to have healthier relationships with those around us?

6. How do we keep our view of money in its proper place in our lives?

7. Read Psalm 62:11-12. How did the truths in these verses stabilize David's soul? Define these particular attributes of God. How have you seen God show these attributes in your own life?

8. What needs to happen for you to stay close to God's Word today? The rest of this week?

9. How does staying close to God's Word enable you to trust God alone as your refuge?

10. How is it true that the way our faith feels can and will change? How do we acknowledge and unpack how we feel yet not allow our feelings to dictate our lives?

Behold His Love

PSALM 63

Main Idea: When we realize God's love for us, we will delight in knowing and worshiping him, even in the midst of life's difficulties.

Four Effects of Realizing the Greatness of God's Love

I.   **Your Relationship with God Becomes a Consuming Addiction, Not a Convenient Addition.**
II. **Your Worship Is No Longer Mere Duty; It Is Immeasurable Delight.**
III. **You Want God More Than You Want Even His Greatest Gifts.**
IV. **Your Experiences in the Wilderness Become Experiences in Worship.**

---

s your heart in love with God? That may be the most important question I could ask you. Yet I'm concerned that, even for many professing Christians, words like *love, affection,* and *longing* don't describe our relationship with God. I'm concerned that many people in the church have faith in God, but for a variety of reasons they lack feeling for God. We may believe in God's love in our heads, but a passion for God is missing in our hearts.

We don't want to miss out on the satisfaction God has designed for us in our daily relationship with him. Even more, we don't want to miss out on *eternity.* James 1:12 and 2:5 talk about how heaven is prepared for those who love God, not for those who merely make a mental affirmation of belief in God. Even the demons believe in God (Jas 2:19)! And according to Jesus, doing things for God is also insufficient:

> *Not everyone who says to me, "Lord, Lord," will enter the kingdom of heaven, but only the one who does the will of my Father in heaven. On that day many will say to me, "Lord, Lord, didn't we prophesy in your name, drive out demons in your name, and do many miracles in your name?" Then I will announce to them, "I never knew you. Depart from me, you lawbreakers!"* (Matt 7:21-23)

Jesus says that "many" people will be shocked to stand before him one day, having assumed that their eternity was safe when it was not. That's why we need to honestly answer the question, Is my heart in love with God? This question is critical, both now and for eternity. So, how do you get that kind of love for God? The answer, according to the Bible, is that you realize the greatness of God's love for you.

Psalm 63 is one of the most beautiful expressions of love for God in all of Scripture. King David says of God, "Your faithful love is better than life" (v. 3). When we know this truth about God's love, we will long for God in this way.

This psalm was most likely written in response to King David's flight from his son Absalom (2 Sam 15–17). We know for sure that David was in a wilderness, both physically and spiritually. Physically, he was on the run with his life and his kingdom in danger. He talks about those who "intend to destroy my life" (v. 9), while claiming that he will "bless [God] as long as I live" (v. 4).

Spiritually, David was separated from the temple in Jerusalem, the place where God's glory dwelled palpably among his people. David missed being in the midst of God's worship. We have much to learn from David's longing, or we might even say obsession, for God. Based on this psalm, we will consider **four effects of realizing the greatness of God's love**.

Your Relationship with God Becomes a Consuming Addiction, Not a Convenient Addition

Psalm 63 is written by a man with a consuming addiction to God. The verb *seek* (v. 1) is related to the Hebrew noun for "dawn," which explains why the word *eagerly* has also been translated "early" (KJV). From the moment the day begins, David wants to be with God. He thirsts for God as if he's in the desert and hasn't had water; he's desperate. He knows that God is the source of his soul's replenishment.

In verse 5 the imagery switches from water to food. David craves God more than he craves food. And it's not just in the morning; it's all day and all night (v. 6). David sounds obsessed here, which is why I use the word *addicted* to describe the effect of knowing God's great love. An addict is driven by a desire for one thing, believing that if he can have it, he will be satisfied. David is addicted to God like that. It's similar to what he says in an earlier psalm: "I have asked one thing from the LORD; it is what I desire: to dwell in the house of the LORD all the days of my life, gazing on the beauty of the LORD and seeking him in his temple"

(27:4). Biblical faith is a consuming addiction to God. It's what Paul expresses in Philippians 1:21: "For me, to live is Christ and to die is gain." Paul couldn't wait to die because that meant he would be with Jesus. He wanted Jesus more than he wanted to live!

This kind of obsession may sound extreme, but in reality this is biblical Christianity. This is what Jesus taught: "If anyone comes to me and does not hate his own father and mother, wife and children, brothers and sisters—yes, and even his own life—he cannot be my disciple" (Luke 14:26). Scripture commands us to honor our father and mother (Exod 20:12) and to care for our children and families (1 Tim 5:8). Jesus is inviting us into a love relationship that makes our closest relationships in this world look like hate in comparison. "The one who loves a father or mother more than me is not worthy of me; the one who loves a son or daughter more than me is not worthy of me" (Matt 10:37).

Keep in mind that this is *initial* teaching from Jesus, not in-depth discipleship after many years. These are the basics of what it means to be a Christian. Christianity is obsession with Christ. It is a relationship with God that is like a consuming addiction. However, I fear this kind of relationship with God is foreign to many Christians today. Instead of God being a consuming addiction in our lives, we make God a convenient addition to our lives. We simply add God onto all sorts of other people and things we love in our lives—family, health, work, money, success, sex, sports, exercise, food, and a host of other things.

Sure, we'd say we believe in God, or we'd even say we worship God. But the question is, Do we want God more than we want anyone or anything else in this world? Do we want God more than we want our spouse or our kids? Do we want time with God more than we want an extra hour of sleep, or exercise, or so many other things we spend our days doing? Do we want God's glory in the world more than we want more comforts in the world? Do we want God's glory more than we want our money? When we want these things more than God, that may be a sign that we don't realize the greatness of his love for us. We are, after all, talking about the God of the universe, who is infinitely more beautiful and satisfying than anyone or anything in the world.

Your Worship Is No Longer Mere Duty; It Is Immeasurable Delight

In Psalm 63 David is not talking about the worship of God as something he *has* to do or *needs* to do, though, in a sense, worship is mandatory because God deserves our worship. No, worship is something he *longs* to do. It's not duty for him; it's delight! Look at the actions mentioned: David is singing (vv. 3,7) and lifting up his hands (v. 4).

This kind of joy and affection reminds me of attending a college football game. When you find your seats in the middle of a bunch of people you've never met before, you start to bond with them pretty quickly. When your team scores, you are standing up, screaming, and high-fiving all of these people. Thousands of you start going ballistic over a bunch of guys you don't know who are running around on a field with an object made of pigskin trying to cross a white line. I remember one night recently after I had taken my two boys to a game and I was tucking them into bed. One of them (without being solicited) said to me, "Dad, will you pray for me?"

I said, "Sure, buddy—how can I pray for you?"

"I need you to pray for my perspective. I feel like I'm more excited about our team winning the game today than I would be if I heard somebody had come to Christ. I was more excited about that than I am about going to church tomorrow. I just think I need a different perspective."

So I prayed that for him, for his brother, and for myself. Earlier that week, in our family Bible reading, we had read the parables of the lost sheep, the lost coin, and the prodigal son (Luke 15). The Bible says there was rejoicing in heaven over one person who turns and trusts in Christ. My son had reminded me of how easy it is for our affections to be so great for things in this world. These aren't bad things, but they need to be kept in perspective. How much more should we have strong affections for the worship of Almighty God?

We should also remember that this kind of love and affection for God is not driven by obligation. True love is driven by *passion*. It's not that we *must* worship God but rather that we *want* to. God is honored by heart-captivating, mind-exhilarating, breathtaking, awe-inspiring worship. This kind of worship not only glorifies him but also satisfies us. People who realize the greatness of God's love don't view worship as their duty. They view it as their delight.

You Want God More Than You Want Even His Greatest Gifts

Sadly, God's gifts can actually be one of the greatest barriers to true, God-glorifying worship. But this raises a question: If biblical Christianity involves a love for God that transcends love for anyone or anything in this world, then is it wrong to love your spouse or your kids deeply?

Or, for that matter, is it wrong to enjoy the good things God gives us in this world? The answer to that question, in light of all of Scripture, is clearly no.

It's altogether right to love your spouse and your kids deeply, and God exhorts us in his Word to enjoy all kinds of good gifts that come from his hand (Jas 1:17). However, it is possible to receive those gifts and love them more than we love the God who gave them to us. In fact, I would go a step further: it is dangerously easy for any of us to love family and health and hobbies and homes and all sorts of things, and even to thank God for these things, yet not actually love God. You can even love the forgiveness of sins and the promise of heaven but not love God.

Imagine you are stranded at sea, drowning in the water, and a ship arrives to rescue you. Just because you want that lifeboat to rescue you, and gladly receive its help in order to survive, does not mean you love the captain of the ship. So also the desire to escape hell does not mean you love God. If we're not careful, this is what our Christianity can become—a bunch of people who don't want to go to hell and who will gladly take a "lifeboat" to heaven. Yet our lives demonstrate little to no real love for the Captain of the ship.

Everything in Psalm 63 is focused on God, not his gifts. David says, "I eagerly seek *you*. I thirst for *you*; my body faints for *you*. . . . I gaze on *you* . . . to see *your* strength and *your* glory" (vv. 1-2; emphasis added). Then, in light of God's "faithful love" (v. 3), David says, "My lips will glorify *you*. . . . I will bless *you*. . . . *You* satisfy me. . . . I think of *you* . . . , I meditate on *you*" (vv. 3-6; emphasis added).

When David says that God's love is "better than life" (v. 3), he is taking what is arguably most valuable to him (and to us)—life itself—and he's putting it in perspective. Your life is more valuable to you than your money. If a robber were to confront you and threaten your life if you didn't give him your money, then you'd give him your money to preserve your life. Your life is also more valuable to you than comfort. We would endure all sorts of painful surgeries, procedures, and processes if a doctor told us this was the only way we could live. Yet when David is given the choice between the good gift of life and the God who loves him and gave him life, he chooses the Giver.

The heart that knows the greatness of God's love says the same thing with every other gift, even the most valuable gifts, in this life. The Bible is not saying that any of these things are bad in and of themselves; they are good gifts from God. Yet if we long for and love these good (even great) gifts more than we long for and love the giver of these gifts, then we are idolaters rather than worshipers of God. We have totally lost perspective.

Your Experiences in the Wilderness Become Experiences in Worship

By the end of this psalm, in the face of those who seek to destroy his life, David says that he rejoices in God (v. 7). How is it possible to rejoice in God when you're in the wilderness, when you're at the end of your rope, when you're not even sure tomorrow is going to come, or when you're not even sure you want tomorrow to come because you're so tired of the challenges and the trials you're facing?

Whether it is physical health, challenges in family or work, or fear of what tomorrow holds, each of us experiences some kind of "wilderness." That is, we all experience some good gift from God being taken away. In response, biblical faith trusts in the giver even when the gifts are taken away. When your health is fading, when your marriage is struggling, when your kids are wandering, when your work is wearing you down, or when your life is wearying, faith looks up and realizes that the giver, God, is still there. He loves you with a love that's better than life itself, and he will satisfy you in a way that no gift can ever satisfy you.

Consider why God's love is better than life itself. It's not simply because it stretches higher and deeper than anyone or anything in this world. His love is better because his love lasts longer than life. When the final day comes and your life draws to an end, the love of God for you will not end (Rom 8:38-39). It's the simple yet glorious truth of John 3:16—God showed his love for you by giving his only Son for you, so that through your belief in him (not just in your head but in your heart), you will never perish but have everlasting life, a life in which you will eternally enjoy God's love.

Reflect and Discuss

1. Respond to the following statement: "The Bible says we must *believe* in Jesus. Whether we *love* him is not that important."
2. How would you describe your relationship with God? Do words like *love* and *affection* come to mind? Discuss your answer.
3. What are some ways to grow in your love for God when you don't feel great affection for him?

4. What's the danger of professing faith with our mouths while having no love for God in our hearts? What are some passages in Scripture that speak to this danger?

5. What are some things in your life that tend to take priority over your relationship with God?

6. How might Psalm 63 speak to someone who prioritizes work or sports over gladly committing to the fellowship and mission of a local church?

7. How would you answer someone who asks, "Should I feel guilty for loving my new house?"

8. What gifts from God are you most tempted to turn into idols?

9. The reality of God's love does not mean we won't suffer. Nevertheless, how can God's love change our perspective on suffering?

10. What other passages of Scripture assure us of God's unfailing love?

Turning the Table on Terror

PSALM 64

Main Idea: God's children don't have to live in fear of the wicked when they trust in him for deliverance.

I. The Request for God's Protection (64:1-2)
II. The Résumé of God's Enemies (64:3-6)
III. The Response of God's Judgment (64:7-8)
IV. The Reaction to God's Justice (64:8-10)

It's always especially ironic when "what goes around comes around" and the tables are turned on injustice. Several years ago a commander at a secluded terrorist training camp north of Baghdad was conducting a demonstration for a group of militants. He unwisely chose to use a belt packed with live explosives for the training exercise. During the demonstration the explosives accidentally detonated, killing the commander and twenty-one other ISIS trainees. The weapons he intended for the destruction of some group of innocent people became the instrument of his own death. An employee working the counter at a nearby liquor store commented,

> This is God showing justice. This is God sending a message to the bad people and the criminals in the world, to tell them to stop the injustice and to bring peace. Evil will not win in the end. It's always life that wins over death. (Adnan and Arango, "Suicide Bomb Trainer")

This observer was correct in suggesting that ultimately God will turn the tables on evil and win the day. Since the attack on the World Trade Center in 2001, acts of terror have escalated dramatically across the globe. No longer can we get on an airplane, attend a sporting event or concert, or even go to a shopping mall without thinking about the possibility of something terrible happening. The term *terrorist* is appropriate. Evil men who manipulate others to do horrific things have the ability to strike *terror* in ordinary, innocent people. And often—by their own admission—they target followers of Jesus Christ. Most of us find

122

ourselves living in anticipation of the day when God will turn the tables on terrorism.

The temptation to live in terror isn't new. As Ross observes, "In every age there are malicious people who try to terrorize innocent people, either by their threats and taunts, or by actual physical violence" (Ross, *Psalms*, vol. 2, 395). David's day was no exception. Throughout most of his life, he faced the threat of terror at the hands of evil people who sometimes succeeded in causing violence and inflicting pain on innocent people. Yet, in spite of his seemingly frequent vacillation between fear and faith, he always landed on the confident ground that God would turn the wickedness of evil men back on them.

Psalm 64 gives us a clear example of how God's children can pray with confidence because we're convinced he ultimately will turn the tables on terrorists and all others who seek to incite fear in the lives of innocent people. His justice ultimately will win the day. Consider how the psalmist requests God's protection from his enemies, rehearses their résumé, asserts God's response of judgment, and identifies various reactions to his justice.

The Request for God's Protection
PSALM 64:1-2

The psalmist begins in a familiar place—with a cry for God's help. The imperative *hear* isn't just a request for God to listen but an urgent plea for him to respond with an answer. Specifically, he's asking God to respond to his lament over the circumstances (Ross, Vol. 2, 397). His situation has made him anxious and sorrowful, and he desperately needs relief. He's in a dire situation he can't resolve. He needs his God to do something he can't do.

David's specific request is for God's protection, a plea he expresses in two particular ways. The first request is that God might "protect" him from his "enemy." It would seem that the most complete way for God to do this would be to eliminate his enemy. However, in this context the word *protect* is a request that they wouldn't have any effect on him (Ross, Vol. 2, 398). The psalmist's second request is for God to "hide" him from the "wicked." What he wants is to be concealed from an apparent conspiracy, like a crowd of demonstrators or a frenzied mob (cf. Ps 2:1). The picture here is of a small group of evil men who are strategically lathering up a raging mob in order to assault and destroy the object of their hatred. This is a frighteningly familiar picture of what we know of today as terrorism. Quite often a small group of extremists can stir up large groups and manipulate them into hating and attacking innocent people.

Once again, we find David crawling up into God's lap like a little boy might do with his father. With uninhibited honesty and utter desperation in his voice, he asks God to act on his behalf. And just like a child in the strong care of his daddy, the danger of his situation already begins to disappear because he's making his appeal to a compassionate ear in a safe place. This is the way it should be when the righteous are being terrorized by their enemies. We find a safe place whenever we climb into the strong arms of our heavenly Father through prayer. Even when danger is still looming, we're comforted and strengthened just by talking to our omnipotent and loving Father.

The Résumé of God's Enemies
PSALM 64:3-6

Many of the psalms reflect the writer's affinity for reminding himself (and God!) about the extremely depraved character of his enemies. Apparently, he sees doing so as helpful—if not needful—in his prayers. Here he begins to review the résumé of those who are trying to kill him in this particular situation.

David identifies five primary characteristics that detail the frightening picture of the terrorists who are targeting him. They wage a war of words. They depend on the element of surprise. They attack innocent people. (The psalmist identifies himself as "blameless" and completely undeserving of their assault.) They act without fear and arrogantly. They are inherently evil. All their devising and perfecting is born in the deepest, darkest part of the heart that can't even be mined by human understanding.

Passages like this reaffirm my convictions about the Bible's supernatural, timeless nature. Could there be any more accurate picture of the nature of terrorism today? Terrorists fill the airways, Internet, social media, and printed propaganda with vicious rhetoric and threats. Just as verses 3-4 indicate, they launch malicious verbal attacks and slanderous accusations that incite naïve people to act. Often their words even inspire women and children to use themselves as weapons of destruction while the instigators remain safely in hiding.

Instead of valiantly attacking opposing soldiers, these terrorists act as cowards by blowing up and gunning down innocent people in public places, and they do it at the most unexpected times. These enemies of righteousness carry out their evil plots as if they have a license to exercise such diabolical plans and malicious violence, and they do it without any fear of retaliation from men or God. Truly they are aptly named—*terrorist*. Their strategy is to strike terror in the lives of their opponents. But their depraved character is nothing new; God has always had their number!

The Response of God's Judgment
PSALM 64:7-8

Though the heart is unsearchable with human capacities, and though the source of all the evil plots of terrorists is too deep for us to grasp, God is more than capable. He who "searches every heart and understands the intention of every thought" (1 Chr 28:9) weighs their motives and turns the tables on them. Just when they think they've carried out their plan successfully, they find themselves in the crosshairs of God's response of judgment. For he says, "I, the LORD, examine the mind, I test the heart to give to each according to his way, according to what his actions deserve" (Jer 17:10). Mark it down, beloved: God will condemn the wicked and preserve the righteous.

That's why we find the strong contrastive conjunction *but* at the beginning of verse 7. The psalmist now confidently states that—although the enemy attack comes out of nowhere and strikes terror—God will flip it on their heads! While the terrorists assume God isn't paying attention to their wicked ploys, suddenly he turns the tables. While the terrorists once shot verbal arrows and wielded verbal swords at the psalmist, God now "will shoot them with arrows; suddenly, they will be wounded." The attackers once waged a war of words to slander the psalmist, but now "they will be made to stumble; their own tongues work against them."

God isn't necessarily firing literal arrows; the language is figurative. He's pronouncing his word that will command the destruction of the psalmist's enemies, just as he did in an earlier messianic psalm: "Then he speaks to them in his anger and terrifies them in his wrath" (Ps 2:5). The attackers wield terrifying and malicious words, but God's decree is more powerful, causing these detractors to be "wounded" (64:7) and to "stumble" (v. 8). "The shooters will be shot; those who planned to destroy the innocent will be destroyed—by one powerful word from God" (Ross, *Psalms*, vol. 2, 402).

This kind of what-goes-around-comes-around economy isn't foreign to God when it comes to his just response to the wicked. He's sovereignly applied this principle to others in biblical history. The gallows Haman erected for Mordecai became his own place of execution. The furnace that was overheated and intended to consume Shadrach, Meshach, and Abednego ended up killing the king's servants who threw them in it. The jealous rulers who plotted to have Daniel killed in the lions' den ended up as the lions' dinner (Ross, Vol. 2, 395). Herod Agrippa, who executed the apostle James, later experienced an excruciating death from an illness. Turning the tables on those who attack the righteous is sometimes part of God's judgment.

The Reaction to God's Justice
PSALM 64:8-10

God's retribution on those who incite terror will bring different reactions from different groups of people. Believers should pray for both reactions.

The first reaction to God's justice is that of humanity in general (vv. 8-9). These are likely references to unbelievers in contrast to the righteous mentioned in verse 10, and their response is somewhat surprising. The terrorists who were planning to carry out their plans in secret will be the objects of public shame and disdain, even among those who are not part of the people of God. The tables of justice will be turned on them not only in their demise but also in the response of their fellow unbelievers.

God's judgment also will strike "fear" in the general populace, causing them to "tell about God's work." The verb *understand* means "to be prudent, to deal wisely." Unbelievers will talk about what they see among themselves and even give it an honest assessment! They will have to acknowledge that the judgment against these cruel terrorists is God's work and, consequently, they should revere him. While this certainly doesn't indicate that everyone will become a follower of God, some of them might. God's righteous retribution on the wicked could serve as an evangelistic catalyst in our day! At the very least, it will cause some people to take Christ and his followers much more seriously (Ross, *Psalms*, vol. 2, 403).

Believers should make pleading for God's justice a part of our rep-ertoire of prayer because sometimes the fear of God's judgment opens people's spiritual eyes. I trusted Christ when I was nine years old for one reason: I didn't want to go to hell. I wish I could say I understood things like God's love, goodness, and grace. I wish I had been moti-vated by the glories of spending eternity worshiping him in heaven. But I wasn't. I was motivated by the fear that God would judge my sin with eternal damnation. And he showed me the gospel, and I trusted Christ, and I was saved. The fear of God's judgment is a legitimate motivator, and we should pray that God will use it to draw some people to himself.

God's righteous judgment expands beyond the immediate subjects to include everybody on the planet. The consequences of his righteous retribution far exceed the local context of the psalmist. While we don't see this everywhere in the Psalms, it is in Psalms 56–68. "Because God upholds justice and protects those who are unjustly attacked, all human-ity will be drawn to proclaim and consider the works of God" (Wilson, *Psalms*, 900). The exercise of God's justice will be a means of making his glory known among all people!

The second reaction to God's justice is one the psalmist encourages among God's faithful (v. 10). The righteous can respond by celebrat-ing and resting in God's protection and care. So the psalmist's prayer in verse 1 to have his life preserved under God's safeguard is answered in abundance! While its realization may still be in the future, he finds confidence in knowing he will joyfully worship God in the safety of his presence. Kidner notes that this "is a sober joy, with the facts faced at their worst, but also at their overwhelming best" (Kidner, *Psalms 1–72*, 247). The sure hope of worshiping God for all of eternity serves as a sustaining force in the believer's life.

The increasingly expansive glory of God noted early in Psalms 56–68 also shows up here. A progression of praise to some degree begins in Psalm 61:8: "I will continually sing of your name." It continues in Psalm 63:11—"The king will rejoice in God; all who swear by him will boast"—and reaches new heights here in Psalm 64:9: "Everyone will fear . . . tell . . . understand . . . rejoices . . . takes refuge . . . offer praise." Then, in telescopic fashion, this sea of worship is broadened in Psalm 65:8 where "those who live far away are awed by your signs." Ultimately, it finds its crescendo in the two hymns of praise: Psalms 66:1-4 and 67:3-7. This sweeping flood of praise in this series then finds a suitable conclusion in

Psalm 68:32-35, where God receives the praise of the entire world after conquering the nations and entering his sanctuary.

Truly the reaction to God's justice should be worship. That response should certainly come from his righteous people. But ultimately, worship will be the universal response of all people to his greatness and his glory.

Conclusion

While Bildad the Shuhite's counsel to the suffering Job wasn't always on target, he did rightly recognize, "God does not reject a person of integrity, and he will not support evildoers" (Job 8:20). The general principle of this psalm is clear: when God's children are terrorized by evil men for righteousness's sake, he will show himself strong to them as deliverer and avenger. Consequently, when Christians face the wicked forces of this world for the sake of the gospel, he will be our refuge. When terrorists make those who trust in Christ the objects of their attacks, they act foolishly because God will avenge them. So once again, based on the reality of God's anticipated retribution, believers can pray confidently for God's strong help against the onslaught of terrorism. Terrorists will get what they deserve, and they may even get what they had planned to impose on others.

A word of caution is in order, however. The liquor store employee outside of Baghdad, mentioned earlier, actually found pleasure in the accidental death of the scheming terrorist. When he heard the news of the botched training exercise, he burst out laughing. "This is so funny," he said. "It shows how stupid they are, those dogs and sons of dogs" (Adnan and Arango, "Suicide Bomb Trainer"). Such a reaction should never characterize followers of Jesus Christ. Our God rhetorically asks, "'Do I take any pleasure in the death of the wicked?' This is the declaration of the Lord God. 'Instead, don't I take pleasure when he turns from his ways and lives?'" (Ezek 18:23; cf. Ezek 33:11). If the one we serve doesn't find pleasure in the death of terrorists, but instead desires that they repent and be saved, then we should have the same posture.

While we have a tendency not to have a whole lot of pity on a suicide bomber or any other terrorist who loses his life while trying to harm others, these scenarios in the psalms should always point us to the gospel. As Wilson observes, "When we rejoice in the destruction of the wicked, when we are glad that they 'get what they deserve,' we might want to be cautious. What if we were to receive what *we deserve*?" (Wilson, *Psalms*, 902; emphasis in original). Christ's disciples must always be careful not to be guilty of the same attitude as the unforgiving servant in one of Jesus's parables. His master said to him, "You wicked servant! I forgave you all that debt because you begged me. Shouldn't you also have had mercy on your fellow servant, as I had mercy on you?" (Matt 18:32-33). Because of Jesus's work on the cross, we didn't get *what we deserve*. That should always temper our prayers for God's retribution and clothe them with humility.

Reflect and Discuss

1. David, as he often does, is begging God to "hear" his voice. How does David's vulnerability and honesty encourage you in your prayer life?
2. David has a rugged and real prayer life because he understands his absolute dependence on God. How is your prayer life? Is its weakness due to your inability to understand your dependence on God?
3. Notice David's description of God's enemies in this psalm. Does God still have enemies today? Can similar descriptions be used?
4. David has confidence in God's righteous retribution against his enemies. Can we, as followers of Christ, have that same confidence?
5. Jesus says in Matthew 5 to "love your enemies." How can this be reconciled with what David is praying for? Can we rightly pray for God to condemn our enemies if we are also to love them?
6. Stepping back and looking at the broad picture, who are God's enemies? Who are our enemies? Is it important to define who the true enemy is?
7. What is the first reaction David anticipates in response to God's judgment? Does this happen today? What are some examples?
8. What is the second reaction David anticipates in response to God's judgment? What are some examples of this in your life?
9. We are expected to exult over God's judgment but not to gloat. What is the fine line between these two?
10. In regard to gloating in the presence of God's judgment, how can the gospel keep our exulting in God's judgment pure? In other words, how important is it to remember your own sin and guilt?

Why Should I Pray?

PSALM 65

Main Idea: In prayer we speak to the God who listens, provides, and satisfies.

I. God Listens and Rescues (65:1-8).
II. God Is Gracious and Provides (65:9-13).
III. God Is Worthy and Satisfies (65:1-13).

The nineteenth-century hymnwriter Louisa Stead gave voice to the deep desire of Christians over the centuries:

> Jesus, Jesus, how I trust Him!
> How I've proved Him o'er and o'er!
> Jesus, Jesus, precious Jesus!
> O for grace to trust Him more!
>   ("'Tis So Sweet to Trust in Jesus")

We want strong faith in Christ. We long for grace to trust him more. And we know God has provided three primary means of grace for this to happen: his Word, his ear, and his people. To put it another way: Scripture, prayer, and the local church. This psalm is itself a prayer packed with truths that fuel a life of prayer. Before we walk through the passage, let me offer a few observations about the struggle many of us have in cultivating a healthy life of prayer.

First, if you're a Christian, you have God's Spirit living in you. As a result, you want to cultivate fellowship with God. You want to run to him for help. Even though your desire to pray might feel like a dying ember in this particular season of your life, *if* you're a Christian, the basic desire to fellowship with God in prayer is there. It may just need cultivation.

Prayer isn't easy, and some struggles are common to many of us. If we're honest, sometimes we're bored or distracted to the point of not wanting to go on. This can lead to further inconsistency, which then leads to a sense of guilt and shame. We can wonder, *What's wrong with me?* as if we were the only ones who struggle this way.

Consider these words from a great Christian leader, Dr. Chuck Swindoll.

> I should tell you up front that this is not going to be your basic religious-sounding statement on prayer. Sorry, I just don't have it in me. No, I'm not sorry. To be painfully honest with you, most of the stuff I have ever read or heard said about prayer has either left me under a ton-and-a-half truckload of guilt or wearied me with pious-sounding clichés and meaningless God-talk. Because I didn't spend two or three grueling hours a day on my knees as dear Dr. So-and-So did . . . or because I wasn't able to weave dozens of Scripture verses through my prayer . . . or because I had not been successful in moving mountains, I picked up the distinct impression that I was out to lunch when it came to this part of the Christian life. ("Strengthening Your Grip")

It's no wonder Jesus told his disciples to "pray always and not give up" (Luke 18:1). Apparently, Jesus knew that his disciples, and generations of believers after them, would face just that temptation.

Psalm 65 has a fresh invitation for us. Here we have a potent reminder of who God is and the privilege we have to approach this God in prayer. This psalm offers us fresh motivation to praise God and to cultivate habits of the heart by which we look to him for all we need. It offers us three reasons to pray.

God Listens and Rescues
PSALM 65:1-8

Prayer is a true test of faith. Consider what the author of Hebrews said about faith: "Now without faith it is impossible to please God, since the one who draws near to him must believe that he exists and that he rewards those who seek him" (Heb 11:6). In prayer we come to God, believing he's there even though we can't perceive him by our senses. We come believing not only that he's there, but that we will come away with something—he rewards those who seek him. In other words, prayer holds up a sign that says, "I believe you are listening. I believe you are near and present to bless, sustain, forgive, and renew." In prayer, whether we feel this to be true or not, we always leave with more than we had when we came.

So here in Psalm 65 David is praising God. He says in verse 1, "Praise is rightfully yours." And the ESV captures the way the psalmist moves from God's worthiness to the mind-blowing fact that this God is attentive to our prayers: "Praise is due to you, O God, in Zion, and to you shall vows be performed. *O you who hear prayer*" (vv. 1-2 ESV; emphasis added).

God listens to us when we pray. Have you stopped to consider the gravity of this simple truth? Everything about that statement is staggering. Just turn it over, word by word. *God* listens to us when we pray. God *listens* to us when we pray. God listens *to us* when we pray. God listens to us *when we pray*. What a grace-driven motivation to pray and not give up!

David stacks the verbs up in these verses, saying God hears (v. 2), atones (v. 3), brings us near (v. 4), and answers (v. 5). Christian, what a picture of the God we have come to know through Jesus! This is the God who is there. He deserves praise, hears prayers, and intervenes in our lives to prove his faithfulness again and again. Psalm 65 motivates us to pray in much the same way the Bible as a whole motivates us to Christ-exalting living—by showing us how wonderful God is!

In 1986 I was in sixth grade, in Mrs. Rolfes's social studies class. The year before that, President Ronald Reagan laid out his "Strategic Defense Initiative." I remember hearing a lot about Mikhail Gorbachev and hearing the words *Star Wars* associated with President Reagan's plan. Something about a global shield to neutralize nuclear weapons. My imagination was running wild.

Mrs. Rolfes told us we could write a letter to President Reagan to share any ideas that might help. I took this assignment seriously. I went home, tore a page out of my notebook, and drew a picture of a tank, along with instructions, directly addressed to our nation's commander in chief. I had arrows and descriptions indicating which button lowered the beds for the tank drivers to sleep in, which button deployed the oil slick behind the tank, obviously to immobilize pursuing enemies, and which buttons triggered missiles, lasers, and flame throwers, respectively. I pictured President Reagan opening that letter, marching into the war room, slapping it on the table, and saying, "Build this!" I hoped he would name it "Gorbie's Worst Nightmare."

Here's the crazy part. I got a note back from the White House thanking me for writing. Who knew my tank drawing would make it all the way to the Oval Office! I was intolerable for days. In reality, I'm pretty sure my tank never made it into any war-room conversations. But that's not the point. I share the story because I'm still amazed that I sent a note from Elmwood Parkway to the most powerful office in the world, and it actually got there.

Friend, prayer is a far more awesome prospect. The God who is enthroned in heaven, sovereign over the nations, all-knowing, blindingly pure, and unspeakably holy is there when you pray. And he's listening.

We could go further back into the Old Testament and watch the story of Moses unfold. Young Moses was reared in the courts of Pharaoh. He grew up learning the names and the ways of the gods of Egypt. Then God revealed himself to Moses and called him to rescue the people of Israel. When Moses led the people of Israel out of Egypt, he began to introduce them to the one true, living God. Moses set God apart from the collection of Egyptian deities: "For what great nation is there that has a god near to it as the Lord our God is to us whenever we call to him?" (Deut 4:7).

The great prince of preachers, Charles Spurgeon, said this about prayer: "Prayer pulls the rope down below and the great bell rings above in the ears of God. He who communicates with heaven is the man who grasps the rope boldly and pulls continuously with all his might" (Spurgeon, *Quotable Spurgeon*, 178). We think and speak too modestly about prayer.

God Is Gracious and Provides
PSALM 65:9-13

When I was a kid, we sang a song that helped with some of the Hebrew names of God. I don't know if we pronounced them correctly, but we would sing about Jehovah Tsidkenu—the Lord our Righteousness; Jehovah Nissi—the Lord our Banner; Jehovah Rapha—the Lord our Healer; Jehovah Shalom—the Lord our Peace; and Jehovah Jireh—the Lord our Provider. Think about those names for a minute and realize, everything we need as weak and sinful people, living in a world filled with difficulties and hardships, God supplies. We need righteousness; he's got it for us. We need protection. We need peace. He is everything we need. Martin Luther famously said, "God is mine; everything is mine."

Starting in verse 9, God is seen as providing for and sustaining his creation. The rain we need for the fields, for crops to grow—where will it come from? God brings the growth. God clothes the hills with joy. Words that capture God's beneficence and generosity carry these verses along as God abundantly enriches, fills, softens, blesses, soaks the channels, overfills carts with plenty, carpets the hills with joy. What's the joy spoken of here? Verse 13 says it's flocks and grain. This isn't just God being good to creation for its own sake. Verse 9 says, "You prepare the earth in this way, providing *people* with grain" (emphasis added). In God's kind provi-dence, he cares about our everyday needs, our physical sustenance.

In the New Testament, when Jesus taught his disciples to pray, he invited them (and us) to ask for physical provisions: "Give us today our daily bread" (Matt 6:11).

Taken together we have, in God's Word, an open invitation to bring all our cares to God. Peter urged Christians to cast "all your cares on him, because he cares about you" (1 Pet 5:7). James wrote, "If any of you lacks wisdom, he should ask God" (Jas 1:5). He gives that too! And Paul says, "Don't worry about anything, but pray about everything" (Phil 4:6 CEV).

Charles Spurgeon said, "If you may have everything by asking in his name, and nothing without asking, I beg you to see how absolutely vital prayer is" (*Spurgeon's Sermons*, 28: 1882). What an incentive we have to pray!

God Is Worthy and Satisfies
PSALM 65:1-13

The greatest gift God gives us in prayer is himself. This psalm centers on God's worth and intervening grace. Right out of the starting blocks, David says, "Praise is rightfully yours." Then there is an unbroken series of "you" statements, featuring God as the one who hears (v. 2), atones (v. 3), chooses and brings near and satisfies (v. 4), answers and gives hope (v. 5), is robed with strength (v. 6), silences the roar of the seas (v. 7), brings joy (v. 8), and abundantly provides for his creation (vv. 9-13). This passage pulls God into focus. Martin Luther said, "Prayer is climbing up into the heart of God" ("Of Prayer"). To put it another way, prayer is a means by which God brings us in close.

Whether we always feel it at a conscious or emotional level, when we come before God in prayer, we leave with an imprint on the soul. Something of his delights, his compassion, his joy becomes ours, in a unique way, when we pray.

My father planted a church in New Orleans before I was born. He died when he was only forty-five years old (I was twelve), but while he lived, he had a contagious joy in Christ and love for people. I could tell stories all day, but no area of my dad's life was more compelling than his life of prayer. How often I caught him reading Scripture and praying! Especially after we went to sleep. I could see the lamp on down the hall and could hear him whispering his prayers, praising God, and mention-ing us and others by name, sometimes praying with great emotion.

After dad died, my mom told me, "Your dad used to say he didn't want his entrance into heaven to be like someone running into a brick wall. He wanted to live so close to God that death was like tearing through tissue paper." I have never known someone to be in such a continual state of prayer as my dad.

Prayer is oxygen for the Christian. That's why the moment you believe, God sends his Spirit to live inside you, and the Spirit's first order of business, according to Paul, is to create a cry in your heart that says, "*Abba*, Father!" (Rom 8:15). He comes and tells you and me, "You can call him Father now! And you can bring everything to him!"

Now, all of this hinges on the perfect work of Jesus Christ. Because Jesus came to earth, lived a perfect life, died in our place on the cross, and rose again, all who turn to Christ for hope and life are saved. We're washed clean of sin and guilt. We're brought into God's forever family. From then on, we live in the good of Jesus's perfect standing before God. The throne of judgment becomes to us a throne of grace. Jesus taught, "No one comes to the Father except through me" (John 14:6). That same Jesus is the one who makes real prayer possible.

Why pray? The God who rescues and who graciously provides for us, the God who is worthy and satisfies his people with abundant grace, is listening when we pray. What a privilege!

Reflect and Discuss

1. As a Christian, what can you do if you lack the desire to pray? How can you cultivate this desire?
2. Two common struggles with prayer include boredom and distractions, which easily lead to frustration, inconsistency, and guilt. How have you experienced these struggles in your own life as you pray? What have you done to address these struggles?
3. How do our motives affect our prayers? What is your aim when you pray?
4. What do your prayers indicate about where you are in your relationship with God?
5. Practically, what does it look like to pray at all times or to pray "without ceasing"? What keeps us from doing this as we go about our day? How can we abide with God throughout our day?
6. How should we respond when God does not answer our prayers the way we would like?

The Cosmic Cause of Christ

PSALM 66

Main Idea: God's supremacy and saving power in Christ should elicit our worship and our commitment to spread God's praise among all the peoples of the earth.

I. **Eleven Couplets**
   A.   Singing and shouting
   B.   Worshiping and witnessing
   C.   Invitation and admonition
   D.   General revelation and special revelation
   E.   Life from death
   F.   Trust amid trial
   G.   Past and present
   H.   Universal and personal
   I.   Speaking with our lips and surrendering our lives
   J.   Humble dependence and holy desire
   K.   Praise and prayer
II. **One Challenge**

The psalms don't always follow a logical progression like one of Paul's letters, where one truth leads to the next truth, which then leads to a conclusion. Instead, interlocking themes come together poetically in powerful ways. We find eleven of these interlocking themes in the form of couplets, or pairs, in Psalm 66. Together these couplets paint a picture of what I call *the cosmic cause of Christ*. Given, Christ isn't explicitly named in this psalm, but as with the whole Old Testament, we will see that Psalm 66 finds its fulfillment in the person and work of Jesus Christ (Luke 24:44).

Eleven Couplets

Singing and Shouting

In the first couplet in this psalm, in verses 1-4, we see the interplay between singing and shouting. The singing in Psalm 66 should inform the singing in Christian corporate worship. To an outsider who is not familiar with the church or with a worship gathering, corporate singing might sound somewhat strange. Why would a bunch of adults gather together for a sing-along? There's a reason our weekly gatherings include singing rather than only coming to hear a sermon. Sometimes we act as if the sermon is the main event and everything else is just lagniappe. However, singing is a vital, pivotal, biblical part of worship.

To be the church is to be a singing people. We're a community that can't help but sing praises to our God. This is one of the primary ways we worship; we *sing* the glory of his name. We also *shout*, though shouting is something many churches need to work on. The Hebrew word for "shout" in verse 1 is used in other places in Scripture as a war cry or a triumphant celebration of victory over one's enemies (1 Sam 10:24) (Kidner, *Psalms 1–72*, 233). For instance, Psalm 47:1-2 says, "Clap your hands, all you peoples; *shout* to God with a jubilant cry. For the LORD, the Most High, is awe-inspiring, a great King over the whole earth" (emphasis added). This is the kind of loud cry that "encourages the faithful while striking fear into the heart of the enemy" (Wilson, *Psalms*, 916), and this needs to be a part of our worship.

What does *shouting* look like in a corporate gathering? We might sing loudly as we give God praise, or it could be that during a song, or between verses of a song, we shout out praise to God. While singing "How Great Thou Art," we might shout, "Yes, God, you are great and greatly to be praised!"

This kind of shouting is appropriate not only in our singing but also in the preaching of God's Word. As God's glory is being revealed, we should have the freedom to shout! An "amen" here or there would probably help us get out of the spectator mentality where only the pastor is talking and the people are listening. So if the pastor says something that is true or that our heart resonates with, then we should not be afraid to shout out an "Amen!" or "Praise the Lord!" or "That's right!" And when somebody else does that, we should not look at that person and think, *Man, settle down.*

Worshiping and Witnessing

There is a constant back-and-forth between worship and witness in this psalm, as the following pattern demonstrates:

A. 1-4: Worship
B. 5-7: Witness
C. 8-15: Worship
D. 16-19: Witness
E. 20: Worship

After the singing and shouting in verses 1-4, we see witness in verse 5: "Come and see the wonders of God." And after the psalmist calls us to "bless our God" in verse 8, he later says, "Come and listen, all who fear God, and I will *tell* what he has done for me" (v. 16; emphasis added).

The psalmist sings worship *to* God and then gives witness *about* God. When he sees God's greatness, he can't help but call other people to see what he sees. This is the way it works in our lives as well. When we see something great, we say to people around us, "You've got to see this!" Like the psalmist, when we behold our God together in worship—the God who reigns over all nature and all nations, the God who saves us from sin and damnation, the God who reveals himself in his beauty and majesty and love and mercy—we should run to the world saying, "Come and see who God is! Come and see what God has done!" Passionate worship *always* leads to personal witness. Therefore, if we're not witnessing, there's a problem with our worship. We're not seeing God for who he is. We're not realizing the magnitude of what he's done for our souls.

Invitation and Admonition

The third couplet involves invitation and admonition. The psalmist is inviting the people of Israel and the peoples of the world to give glory and honor and praise to God. This is not just a personal expression of worship. The psalmist is inviting people to see the awesome deeds and the great power of God. He is reaching back into biblical history to recount reasons for blessing God, and he's inviting people to respond.

Alongside this invitation, you also have admonition. There's a note of warning in verse 7. That was a warning to people in the psalmist's day, and it's a warning to us today. Don't exalt yourself before God. He is watching you, and he knows everything you do. Don't rebel against him. Don't set yourself up as his enemy. If you do, you will eventually come cringing to him (v. 3).

General Revelation and Special Revelation

General revelation refers to the ways God reveals himself to all people everywhere. In Psalm 66 the nations surrounding Israel would have been able to see certain aspects of God's power and authority. Much like Romans 1:20 teaches us, all creation shouts the glory of God: "For his invisible attributes, that is, his eternal power and divine nature, have been clearly seen since the creation of the world, being understood through what he has made."

At the same time, Scripture teaches that general revelation, by itself, is not sufficient to bring us to a saving knowledge of God. It does leave us "without excuse" (Rom 1:20b). Because we are born with a sinful nature, we reject what we know of God through general revelation:

> *For though they knew God, they did not glorify him as God or show gratitude. Instead, their thinking became worthless, and their senseless hearts were darkened. Claiming to be wise, they became fools and exchanged the glory of the immortal God for images resembling mortal man, birds, four-footed animals, and reptiles.* (Rom 1:21-23)

If we only have access to general revelation, we inevitably dispense with what we know of the Creator in order to worship his creation. Responding to God in repentance and faith requires special revelation.

Special revelation refers to "God's words addressed to specific people, including the words of the Bible" (Grudem, *Systematic Theology*, 1254). Special revelation comes to us today through Scripture, for this is God's written revelation of who he is and what he has accomplished in Christ for our salvation. People must hear this message, the gospel, in order to believe and be saved. As Paul says, "So faith comes from what is heard, and what is heard comes through the message about Christ" (Rom 10:17).

Psalm 66 looks forward to the day when God's saving purposes will be known and embraced by all nations. That's why the psalmist invites the entire earth to see and understand what God has done on behalf of his people: "Come and see the wonders of God; his acts for humanity are awe-inspiring" (v. 5).

These concepts of general revelation and special revelation are important with respect to the church's mission. Many missionaries go to places and peoples in the world where there is an abundance of general revelation but an absence of special revelation. That is, these peoples can see the glory of God in creation around them, but they've never heard the good news about how this glorious God saves. Currently there are about six thousand people groups in the world, comprising over two billion people, who have never heard, not just about God saving his people at the Red Sea but more importantly about how God can (and will) save them from their sins and give them eternal life. Like the psalmist, they need someone to tell them, "Come and see the wonders of God" (v. 5).

This is the same thing we want to say to our non-Christian friends: God has not only created the world, but he has come to us in Jesus, who is God in the flesh (John 1:14). Christ has died on a cross in our place in order to pay the penalty of sin, and he has risen from the dead in victory over sin and death so that we can be saved from sin and restored to eternal life with God forever! That's worth singing and shouting about!

Life from Death

Psalm 66:8-9 is the primary testimony of the psalmist—that God is to be praised because he has delivered us from death and given us life. Everything we have is owing to God's power and grace, including our very lives. God's physical deliverance of the psalmist and of Israel from their enemies anticipated a greater deliverance to come. Here's how Paul describes this greater deliverance in Colossians 1:13-14: "He has rescued us from the domain of darkness and transferred us into the kingdom of the Son he loves. In him we have redemption, the forgiveness of sins." Through Jesus Christ, God's people have been rescued from the enemies of sin and death. We now experience redemption and eternal life.

Trust amid Trial

Verses 10-12 recount how God has tested and tried his people. The psalmist speaks of a refining process, recounting how God—whether in Egypt before he brought Israel to the Red Sea or in the wilderness before he brought them to the promised land—walked his people through trials. Notice the psalmist's high view of God's sovereignty: "*You* lured us into a trap; *you* placed burdens on our backs. *You* let men ride over our heads" (emphasis added).

The psalmist knows that God is ultimately in control of all things. Even amid difficulty, God has ultimate authority over that difficulty. Despite the fact that God let men "ride over our heads" as Israel "went through fire and water," the psalmist can still conclude, "but you brought us out to abundance" (v. 12). In the midst of trial and on the other side of trial, there's trust. And not just trust but "abundance."

This is not some trite faith the psalmist is speaking about, a faith that knows nothing of pain or difficulty. No, the psalmist knows what it's like to hurt, to feel heavy with the burdens of life. At the same time, the psalmist knows what it's like for God to bring him through trial to a place of abundance, and *that* is cause for worship. You can't help but think about God's words to his people through the prophet Isaiah:

> *Now this is what the LORD says—the one who created you, Jacob, and the one who formed you, Israel—"Do not fear, for I have redeemed you; I have called you by your name; you are mine. I will be with you when you pass through the waters, and when you pass through the rivers, they will not overwhelm you. You will not be scorched when you walk through the fire, and the flame will not burn you.* (Isa 43:1-2)

Past and Present

This psalm recounts God's past work among his people in order to inspire present worship in his people. In verse 13 the psalmist promises to sacrifice and pay his vows, and then in verses 14-15 he mentions vows he made in the past when he was in the midst of trouble and trial. The psalmist can look back to clear manifestations of God's power on behalf of his people—the way God brought his people through the Red Sea (Exod 14) and across the Jordan River (Josh 3)—which gives him confidence. God will be faithful to do the same in the present.

This is part of what we do as believers when we gather every week for worship. We read God's Word and see the stories of God's faithfulness to his people, and this inspires worship among God's people. With all kinds of people facing all kinds of different life situations, we find strength by hearing about how God has *always* brought his people through trial to triumph. So no matter what we're walking through in our lives, we worship.

Universal and Personal

This psalm progresses from the universal to the personal. It starts with all the earth shouting the praises of God (v. 1). Likewise, verse 8 is a call to all the "peoples" of the world. So we have a universal picture in Psalm 66, but then slowly, subtly, the psalmist begins talking about God's more personal revelation to his people, Israel, and you see a narrowing in verses 9-12. Notice the words *we*, *us*, and *our*.

Finally, after speaking about Israel with plural pronouns, the first-person pronouns *I* and *my* appear in verse 13 and then continue through the rest of the psalm. God has heard "*my* prayer," and he has not "turned his faithful love from *me*" (v. 20; emphasis added). That's not to say that the "us" isn't important, because it is. From the beginning, this psalm is calling on more and more people throughout the earth to praise God. But amid the universal worth of God, the psalmist doesn't lose sight of the personal nature of praise.

When you gather with the church to sing and shout to God, don't forget that you're singing and shouting to *your* God. This is the God you know, the God you love, the God who has worked a miracle in your soul. This is the God who hears your prayer, the God who has not withheld his steadfast love from you.

Speaking with Our Lips and Surrendering Our Lives

When the psalmist starts speaking in the first person in verse 13, he describes the offerings he's going to bring before God. He mentions "fattened sheep," the "fragrant smoke of rams," and the sacrifice of "bulls with goats" (v. 15). This is a picture of an extravagant offering before God.

Some commentators think this is an exaggeration made for effect; others think this expression means that this was definitely a king writing this psalm, given the amount of wealth needed in order to sacrifice this much. We don't know for certain, but what we do know is this: the psalmist knows that worship is not just about singing and shouting. Worship is also about sacrifice. It's about laying down before the Lord that which costs you. We must remember this every single week when we gather together for worship. If we sing and shout but fail to lay down our lives in surrender before God, then we have not worshiped.

We should give God total surrender of our lives in worship. Whatever he wants us to do, wherever he wants us to go, whatever he wants us to give, we yield to him. Our possessions, our plans, our dreams, our days are his to spend however he wants for the glory of his name.

Humble Dependence and Holy Desire

Do you feel the sense of humility and dependence in the psalmist in verses 16-17? He is humble before God. He fears God in a way that causes him to cry out in humble dependence. This man knows he needs God.

This humble dependence is coupled with holy desire. The psalmist cries out to God in prayer, knowing that if he cherishes sin in his heart, his prayer will have no place before God. Obviously, he is not perfect— no one but Jesus is sinless—but the psalmist realizes it would make no sense to worship and pray while cherishing or desiring sin. No, to worship and to pray is to desire God and a life of holiness that honors him. This is the kind of worship that pleases God. It's the desire reflected near the end of the book of Isaiah, when God says, "I will look favorably on this kind of person: one who is humble, submissive in spirit, and trembles at my word" (Isa 66:2).

May both humble dependence and holy desire mark our worship.

Praise and Prayer

Throughout this psalm you see praise and prayer, and it's encapsulated especially here at the end.

In one sense praise *is* prayer. Praise to God is communication with God. So as we sing and shout, we are, in a real sense, praying. We're calling out to God. But praise relates to prayer especially when we call out to God for needs in our lives (or others' lives). This is what the psalmist is doing at the end of Psalm 66. For when we call out to God for needs, we know God hears us (v. 19). What a thought! This is *God*, attending to *my* voice. He hears it, and he responds to it according to his steadfast love.

One Challenge

Earlier I mentioned how the eleven couplets I've identified in Psalm 66 come together to paint a picture of the "cosmic cause of Christ." The name of Jesus is nowhere to be found in this psalm, but that doesn't mean this psalm doesn't point us directly to him. Jesus is the epitome of God's special revelation.

The height of our worship does not revolve around the Red Sea or the Jordan River but the cross of Calvary. This is the place God dealt the decisive blow to sin and death. Through the sacrifice of his Son on the cross, he made it possible for you and me to be reconciled to him, both now and forever. *This* is cause for singing and shouting, for worshiping and witnessing.

All who know that Christ has come should testify in places and to peoples where Christ is not known. We must invite people to come to Christ, and we must admonish them not to turn away from his gracious gift of salvation. Christ alone can deliver us from death. He alone is the ground for trust amid the worst trials this life brings. What he did on the cross two thousand years ago for us is a picture of his promise to be faithful to us today. And, more personally, what he did for *you* is a picture of his promise to be faithful to *you* today.

So sing and shout with your lips to him, and surrender all of your life to him—in humble dependence, with holy desire, praising him as he taught us to pray: "Our Father in heaven, your name be honored as holy. Your kingdom come. Your will be done on earth as it is in heaven" (Matt 6:9-10). This is the cosmic cause of Christ. This is the purpose for which Christ came. He came to make worship like this possible in your life and in others' lives. Ultimately, Christ came to make Psalm 66 a reality, to make God's praise possible among all the peoples of the earth. In turn, making God's praise known should be the purpose of every Christian's life. So in view of the global glory of God and the cosmic cause of Christ, I challenge you: **Spend your life spreading God's praise among the peoples of the earth.** Say to the people you live around, the people you work with, and the peoples of the world, "Sing about the glory of his name; make his praise glorious" (v. 2). Say to your neighbors and say to the nations, "Come and see the wonders of God; his acts for humanity are awe-inspiring. . . . Come and listen, all who fear God, and I will tell what he has done for me" (vv. 5,16).

Reflect and Discuss

1. What should be distinctive about a church's corporate gathering? What role does singing play?
2. What is the relationship between worshiping and witnessing? What's wrong with having one without the other?
3. Many Christians think of worship solely as a personal expression of praise. In what sense should we be warned in our worship? (See v. 7.)
4. The psalmist calls on all nations to come and worship God. What is necessary for a person to know God in a saving way? How does Romans 10:14-17 inform your answer?
5. Why must the truth of the gospel be the central theme of our worship? What are some things that tend to crowd out the message of the gospel in our corporate gatherings?
6. How do trials reveal whether we are truly relying on God? How have you seen this truth demonstrated in your own life?

7. What is the difference between intimacy in our relationship with God and treating God casually?

8. Why do you think we so often doubt that God hears us when we pray? How can we have confidence when we pray, and what does this have to do with the gospel?

9. Psalm 66 doesn't mention Jesus Christ explicitly. How does this psalm relate to him?

10. Spreading God's praise to all peoples involves sharing the gospel. Articulate the message of the gospel as if you were sharing it with an unbeliever who was unfamiliar with the Bible. Try to keep your explanation under two minutes.

The Ultimate Disconnect[1]

PSALM 67

Main Idea: God blesses his people for the sake of his praise among all peoples.

I. **One Truth**
   A. The patriarchs
   B. The exodus
   C. Giving the law
   D. Taking the promised land
   E. King Solomon
   F. The Psalms
   G. Israel in exile
   H. The Prophets
   I. The Gospels and Acts
   J. The Letters of the New Testament
II. **One Danger**
III. **Three Realizations**
   A. Realize who God is.
   B. Realize why God blesses.
   C. Realize what this means.

Quite possibly more than any other chapter in the Bible, Psalm 67 has shaped my understanding of my life, my family, and God's purpose for the church in the world. I'll never forget where I was sitting the first time I heard this psalm taught and the way God used it to put my life on a totally different trajectory.

Psalm 67 contains one primary truth, and this truth forces us to address one common danger. We'll also consider what this psalm tells us about who God is, why he blesses, and what this means for us, his people.

---

[1] David Burnette contributed to some portions of this chapter.

One Truth

In a sense Psalm 67 is simple. It contains one primary, overarching truth, a truth absolutely critical to understanding Christianity and the purpose of your life in this world. **God blesses his people for the sake of his praise among all peoples**. Let's unpack this massively important statement.

There's a pause at the end of verse 1 in the middle of a sentence. It says *Selah*, which is basically a musical term that signifies some kind of pause, as if to say, "OK, don't move on too quickly in the song yet; just let it soak in." Verse 1 is a petition based on a high-priestly blessing in Numbers 6:24-26. People would go to the priest, and the priest would bless them, saying, "May the Lord bless you and protect you; may the Lord make his face shine on you and be gracious to you; may the Lord look with favor on you and give you peace."

The petition, "May God be gracious to you," is like asking God to show you, a sinner who has rebelled against him, unmerited love and undeserved compassion. It is asking God not only to not give you what you deserve (condemnation) but also to give you what you don't deserve (mercy). "May God bless you" is likewise a gracious petition for blessing. Even though in our sin we are all due the curse of God's condemnation, this is an appeal for the blessing of God's kindness and love. Asking for God to make "his face shine upon us" is like asking for the smile of the holy God of creation.

Is Psalm 67 talking about spiritual blessing or physical/material blessing? According to the text, the answer seems to be yes. Certainly the psalm has to do with spiritual blessing—the gift of God's grace, the light of God's face—but then in verse 6 the reference to the "earth" clues us in that the psalmist has in mind God's blessing on the land, most likely at harvest time. So in addition to spiritual blessings, there's a picture of physical and material blessings.

After verse 1 there's a pause, not a period. We don't simply ask for God's blessing and then move on to something else. No, the thought is incomplete. Yes, we pause, but then we keep going. And the most important words in the psalm are the first words of verse 2: "So that." Apparently God has a purpose behind his blessing.

God blesses his people for the sake of his praise among all peoples. He blesses so that his saving power might be made known among all the nations (v. 2). The psalmist then erupts in verses 3-5, calling on the peoples to praise God and the nations to "rejoice and shout for joy." The terms *peoples* and *nations* refer to tribes and clans and ethnic groups in the world. Scholars have identified more than eleven hundred different ethnic groups in the world today. These are groups of people who share a common language and cultural characteristics. In Hebrew the psalmist uses three different words for peoples and nations in this passage, underscoring that God aims to be praised by all (Goldingay, *Psalms 42–89*, 302–3). The psalmist wants people from the north to the south, from the east to the west, from the rich to the poor, from the young to the old, from the urban to the rural, in every tribe, in every language, and among every ethnic group on the earth to praise God. That's the reason God blesses his people.

God's desire for praise among all peoples is a theme that shows up throughout Scripture, as an all-too-brief tour will demonstrate.

The Patriarchs

In Genesis 12:1-3 God made the following promises to Abraham, the father of the people of Israel:

> Go out from your land, your relatives, and your father's house to the land that I will show you. I will make you into a great nation, I will bless you, I will make your name great, and you will be a blessing. I will bless those who bless you, I will curse anyone who treats you with contempt, and all the peoples on earth will be blessed through you.

Even though Abraham was an idolater, God chose to bless Abraham (and eventually Israel, the nation that came from Abraham) *so that* he might be a conduit of his blessing to all peoples. Genesis 12:1-3 is echoed in the purpose of God's blessing articulated in Psalm 67.

To Isaac, Abraham's son, God said, "I will make your offspring as numerous as the stars of the sky, I will give your offspring all these lands, and all the nations of the earth will be blessed by your offspring" (Gen 26:4). To Jacob, Abraham's grandson, God said, "Your offspring will be like the dust of the earth, and you will spread out toward the west, the east, the north, and the south. All the peoples on earth will be blessed through you and your offspring" (Gen 28:14).

God was doling out extravagant promises to the patriarchs, all for the sake of his global, self-exalting purpose.

The Exodus

When God delivered his people from Egypt, he declared, "I will harden Pharaoh's heart so that he will pursue them. Then I will receive glory by means of Pharaoh and all his army, and the Egyptians will know that I am the LORD" (Exod 14:4). God had brought his people to the edge of the Red Sea, which meant they had a massive body of water in front of them and the fast-approaching Egyptian army behind them. That's not good military strategy. You don't run into a dead end if an army's about to overtake you. So, why did God lead his people to the edge of the Red Sea? So that he would gain glory for himself among the Egyptians. He would split that sea in half and send his people through it on dry land. They were able to look in their rearview mirrors and see the water come crashing down on the Egyptians. The Egyptians found out that God is "the LORD." God blessed his people for his glory and for his praise among all the peoples.

Giving the Law

We can also see God's global purposes in his giving of the law.

> Look, I have taught you statutes and ordinances as the LORD my God has commanded me, so that you may follow them in the land you are entering to possess. Carefully follow them, for this will show your wisdom and understanding in the eyes of the peoples. When they hear about all these statutes, they will say, "This great nation is indeed a wise and understanding people." For what great nation is there that has a god near to it as the LORD our God is to us whenever we call to him? And what great nation has righteous statutes and ordinances like this entire law I set before you today? (Deut 4:5-8)

God gave Israel the law so that when they followed his commandments, they would show his goodness and wisdom to the surrounding nations. In other words, God gave Israel his law for the sake of his praise among the nations.

Taking the Promised Land

Once Israel finally made it to the promised land in Joshua 5–6, the first major city they came to was Jericho, a city with massive walls encircling it. Of the various military options available—going over the walls, going under the walls, breaking through the walls, sending in a decoy, or starving out the people inside the walls—God again chose a rather unusual strategy. He told Joshua to command the priests to blow trumpets and then have the people shout really loud. The walls would fall down, and Israel would take Jericho. That must have sounded like a strange plan to Joshua. Imagine telling an army that's been training for war for an entire generation that you're turning it over to the music guys! So why did God design this battle plan for the first major city in the promised land? Because he was orchestrating events so that only he would get the glory for the outcome.

King Solomon

Why, you might ask, was Israel's King Solomon given such wisdom? The queen of Sheba's reaction upon seeing him gives us the answer—that this pagan queen might praise God: "Blessed be the LORD your God! He delighted in you and put you on the throne of Israel, because of the LORD's eternal love for Israel. He has made you king to carry out justice and righteousness" (1 Kgs 10:9).

The Psalms

We see this pattern in the psalms as well. In Psalm 23 we hear that the Lord is our shepherd and that he provides, renews, and leads us. Why? He does it "for his name's sake" (23:3). In Psalm 25 the psalmist asks the Lord for forgiveness "for the sake of your name" (25:11). God carries out his saving work for his own glory.

Israel in Exile

We see something similar in Daniel 3 with the well-known story of Shadrach, Meshach, and Abednego. Why would God let three Hebrew boys who were standing up to worship him be thrown into a fiery furnace? We will miss the point unless we read the entire story. When Shadrach, Meshach, and Abednego spend some time in a fiery furnace and then come out on the other side without a drop of sweat on their brow, King Nebuchadnezzar, the pagan king of Babylon, praised God, saying, "For there is no other god who is able to deliver like this" (Dan 3:29). Likewise, when God delivered Daniel from the lions' den, King Darius, another pagan king, decreed that everyone in his kingdom "must tremble in fear before the God of Daniel" (Dan 6:26). He continued,

> For he is the living God, and he endures forever; his kingdom will never be destroyed, and his dominion has no end. He rescues and delivers; he performs signs and wonders in the heavens and on the earth, for he has rescued Daniel from the power of the lions. (Dan 6:26-27)

Once again, God's extravagant blessing was for his extravagant glory.

The Prophets

In Isaiah 43 God says some of the most beautiful words to his people in the whole Old Testament:

> Now this is what the LORD says—the one who created you, Jacob, and the one who formed you, Israel—"Do not fear, for I have redeemed you; I have called you by your name; you are mine. I will be with you when you pass through the waters, and when you pass through the rivers, they will not overwhelm you. You will not be scorched when you walk through the fire, and the flame will not burn you. For I am the LORD your God, the Holy One of Israel, and your Savior. I have given Egypt as a ransom for you, Cush and Seba in your place. Because you are precious in my sight and honored, and I love you, I will give people in exchange for you and nations instead of your life. Do not fear, for I am with you; I will bring your descendants from the east, and gather you from the west. I will say to the north, 'Give them up!' and to the south, 'Do not hold them back!' Bring my sons from far away, and my daughters from the ends of the earth." (Isa 43:1-6)

God speaks of blessing upon blessing for his people, but then in the next verse he says his people are "created for my glory" (Isa 43:7). In other words, he created his people for his glory, and he loves them for his glory.

When God gave his new covenant promise through the prophet Ezekiel, he told the prophet why he was going to act on behalf of his people:

> Therefore, say to the house of Israel, "This is what the Lord GOD says: It is not for your sake that I will act, house of Israel, but for my holy name, which you profaned among the nations where you went. I will honor the holiness of my great name, which has been profaned among the nations—the name you have profaned among them. The nations will know that I am the LORD—this is the declaration of the Lord GOD—when I demonstrate my holiness through you in their sight." (Ezek 36:22-23)

God was acting for the sake of his name among the nations.

The Gospels and Acts

God's global purposes don't change in the New Testament. When we get to the end of the Gospel accounts, Jesus says to his disciples, "Go, therefore, and make disciples of all nations" (Matt 28:19). Similarly,

Luke's Gospel teaches us that Jesus died and rose again so that repentance and forgiveness of sins "would be proclaimed in his name to all the nations" (Luke 24:47). Luke picks up that same story in Acts 1, as Jesus promises his disciples that they would "receive power when the Holy Spirit has come on you" (Acts 1:8). Why? Because "you will be my witnesses in Jerusalem, in all Judea and Samaria, and to the end of the earth" (Acts 1:8). This worldwide gospel witness is what we see happening in the rest of the New Testament.

The Letters of the New Testament

Paul tells the church in Galatia that God revealed Jesus to him "so that I could preach him among the Gentiles" (Gal 1:16). To the church at Rome, he says, "My aim is to preach the gospel where Christ has not been named" (Rom 15:20). There were peoples who were not praising God, and Paul was called to go to them. This is still the mission of the church today. Finally, in Revelation 7 we see how God's original promise to bless the nations through Abraham comes to fruition:

> *After this I looked, and there was a vast multitude from every nation, tribe, people, and language, which no one could number, standing before the throne and before the Lamb. They were clothed in white robes with palm branches in their hands. And they cried out in a loud voice: Salvation belongs to our God, who is seated on the throne, and to the Lamb!* (Rev 7:9-10)

This is the all-consuming, final, ultimate, glorious, global purpose of God. God blesses people for the sake of his praise among all peoples.

One Danger

Having identified God's desire to see all peoples praise him, there's a danger of which we all need to be aware: **We are prone to disconnect God's blessing in our lives from God's purpose for our lives.**

Our hearts resonate with the idea of grace, and for good reason. However, it is oftentimes a grace centered around us. So while grace is worthy of our attention, if disconnected from its purpose, the sad result is a self-centered Christianity that misses the purpose of God.

If you ask the average Christian in our culture, "What is the message of Christianity?," you will likely hear something along the lines of, "God loves me." But that's not Christianity. It's true, of course, but it's incomplete. In this me-centered version of Christianity, *we* become the focus. *We* make plans for our lives and careers based on what's best for *us*. *We* choose a house to live in, a car to drive, clothes to wear, even a way of living, based on what *we* want. However, the message of Christianity is "God loves me *so that* . . ." God is the end goal. So, does this mean God has an ulterior motive in blessing us? Yes!

To some people it sounds arrogant for God to claim that he is the center of the universe and to say that everything revolves around him. And it would be arrogant for any one of us to say that. But remember: you and I are not God! God lives to exalt himself. If that rubs you wrong, then ask yourself, "Who else should he exalt?"

This does not mean God doesn't love us deeply—he does! God possesses unusual, extreme, and intimate passion for his people. This is the beauty of the gospel! God glorifies himself by making his salvation known to us. He glorifies himself by saving you and me through the sacrifice of his Son on a cross. He glorifies himself by showering us with his grace, and that grace has a goal, namely, his glory.

What made Psalm 67 such a life-altering text in my life is that, for the first time, I realized that the blessing of God does not center on me. Instead, the blessing of God is intended to spread *through* me. God has given me the gospel for a reason, and that reason is so that all peoples might know the gospel. God has given me material blessings in this world for a purpose, and that purpose is *not* so that I can be more comfortable or have more luxuries or so that I can coast out my Christian life until I get to heaven. No, that's *not* biblical Christianity. God has given me wealth in this world for the spread of his worship in this world. All of his blessings ultimately center on him, not on me.

Out of more than eleven hundred people groups in the world, more than six thousand of these ethnic groups have never even heard of the saving power of God. That's over two billion people. It's not that they have heard the good news of God's grace in Christ and rejected it; it's that they have not even heard it. And the primary reason, it seems, that they haven't heard the gospel is because we who have the gospel have disconnected God's grace from God's purpose. We are sitting back with the gospel in the confines of comfortable churches where we're content to spend the majority of the time and money God has graciously given us on ourselves, never realizing that God gave it to us for a greater purpose.

Could it be that God might lead many, if not most, of us who live in a land of gospel saturation to go to the peoples of the earth for the praise of his name? That seems so far-fetched to us that we wouldn't even consider it, that is, until we realize that it's the purpose of our salvation. Psalm 67 helps us see that purpose, and in so doing it transforms our lives. Below we'll look at three realizations that spring from this psalm.

Three Realizations

Realize Who God Is

Psalm 67 helps us realize who God is by revealing to us various aspects of his character. That **he is the gracious Savior** means we have good news to tell the nations! We don't go to the peoples of the world with a message of condemnation; we go with a message of celebration. God loves you! He is gracious! He is merciful! He has sent his Son to save you from your sin! We say to peoples living in spiritual darkness, "The light of God shines on you! (See Matt 4:16.) Turn from yourselves, trust in him, and be saved forever!"

While God is gracious and loving, we must also see that **he is the righteous Judge** (v. 4). This is sobering news for all who don't trust in Christ, but it's news we must make known. Put yourself in the shoes of those who have never heard: if God is indeed the Judge of all people everywhere, and if we stand condemned before him, then wouldn't we want somebody to come and tell us how we can be pardoned? Wouldn't we want somebody to leave behind their comforts and take the risk of moving their family to where we are in order to learn our language so they could share this gospel with us? We would want everybody involved in this effort, not just a select few.

A third attribute of God is also found in verse 4: **he is the sovereign King**. God is the King over all the nations on earth. This is why the church should fast and pray fervently, give sacrificially, and go willingly: because Jesus is King of the nations! He doesn't deserve the praise of only some people groups; he deserves the praise of all people groups. "Let the peoples praise you, God; let *all* the peoples praise you!" (v. 3; emphasis added). The question is, Do we believe this? Do we believe this enough to give our lives to this?

Realize Why God Blesses

Psalm 67 helps us realize not only who God is but also why God blesses: for the sake of his praise among all peoples. More specifically, **he aims**

to be known among all peoples (v. 2). In order for the peoples to *praise* God, they obviously must *know* God. And when they know him for who he is, they will praise him for what he is worth.

Intellectual knowledge is not all that he is after. **He aims to be enjoyed by all peoples** (v. 4). God has used John Piper to open my eyes to the beauty of this psalm and this truth in particular. His book *Let the Nations Be Glad* is one of the most influential books I have ever read outside of the Bible. Piper says, "The goal of missions is the gladness of the peoples in the greatness of God" (*Let the Nations Be Glad*, 11). It's not only Psalm 67 that is expressing this truth. Consider a few more examples: "The humble will see it and rejoice. You who seek God, take heart!" (69:32). "Let all who seek you rejoice and be glad in you; let those who love your salvation continually say, 'God is great!'" (70:4). "The Lord reigns! Let the earth rejoice; let the many coasts and islands be glad" (97:1).

You may also be tempted to think God is using you, as if you are merely a pawn in his desire to bless others. You may wonder if he really loves you. In response, God *is* using you for his purpose, but his purpose for you is *good*. In fact, his purpose for you is evidence of his love for you. We tend to get this backward, thinking that if God loves us, then he must focus solely on us. However, what if God's love for us is most fully realized in sharing it with others? And what if our joy in God will increase, not when we hoard God's blessings for ourselves but when we spread God's blessings among others? I know few greater joys than leading people to joy in Jesus. Greater than all the comforts of this world is the satisfaction of seeing more and more men and women glad in God. *That* is a purpose worth living for!

God has designed our hearts to be glad in giving, not in hoarding. Yet, in our culture, we find ourselves swimming in an ocean of deceit. We're surrounded by the lie that says *getting* will make you happy. It's not true. God loves you, and in his love he tells you to *give* your life away so that you and others might be glad in him.

Also, **he aims to be feared by all peoples** (v. 7). Piper writes, "God is jealous to be known and praised and enjoyed and feared. He is displeased when people are ignorant of him or disrespectful to him or bored around him or unduly casual in his presence" ("Let the Nations Be Glad"). The God we make known in the gospel is not to be trifled with. He is holy, just, and all-powerful.

Realize What This Means

You may be wondering what Psalm 67 means for your life. It is not just for information. This psalm means **this prayer must be constant on our lips**. The desire for God to be known among all peoples should fuel prayer in our lives and our families and our churches.

Further, **this purpose must captivate our lives**. The time is short, and the need is urgent. We do not have time to sit back and soak in a message of grace that centers on us. God has given us much, including his gospel and many other temporal blessings, for the purpose of making his glory known among all peoples. Therefore, let us connect God's blessing in our lives with God's purpose for our lives. For when God's purpose captivates our lives, then the blessing of God will follow in our lives. God wants to be praised, known, enjoyed, and feared among the nations, and he will bless those who are aligned with what he wants. This is why Jesus gives us not only a Great Commission but also a promise to go with us and provide us everything we need to accomplish it (Matt 28:18-20).

Do we want to experience the fullness of everything God offers? Then let's give ourselves to the purpose God has ordained! Let's pray and give and go, and as we do, let's expect the blessing of God to follow the purpose of God. Again Piper notes,

> If God blesses his people for the sake of the nations; then God is most likely to bless us when we are planning and longing and praying to bless the nations. If God wants his goods to get to the nations, then he will fill the truck that's driving toward the nations. He will bless the church that's pouring itself out for unreached peoples of the world. And this blessing is not payment for a service rendered; it's power and joy for a mission to accomplish. When we move toward the unreached peoples, we are not earning God's blessings, we are leaping into the river of blessings that is already flowing to the nations. ("Let the Nations Be Glad")

The river of God's blessing is flowing to the nations, so let's jump in and enjoy!

God's global purpose for his praise among the peoples can't be a sideshow in the church; *it's what fuels the central mission of the church.* We have all been commissioned and blessed so that we would give our lives for the spread of God's praise among the peoples of the world. This is what it means to be the church.

Finally, while Psalm 67 is a prayer and a purpose, it's also a promise (vv. 6-7). God will bless us, and he will bring all the ends of the earth to fear him. **This promise must compel risk-taking, life-giving, death-defying confidence in our Lord.** In fact, this is happening already among our brothers and sisters around world. There is more to this life than having a nice job, a decent family, a comfortable life, and then tacking on church attendance. We have been created, saved, and blessed by God for the praise of God among the peoples of the world.

One day Christ, the sovereign King and righteous Judge and gracious Savior, will return, and God's face will shine on us in a much greater way. Revelation 22:4 says, "They will see his face." Let's live and die for that day.

Reflect and Discuss

1. In what ways has God blessed you physically and materially? In what ways has God blessed you spiritually? Make a list of each.
2. Respond to the following statement using Scripture: "God's desire to bless all nations began in the book of Acts."
3. When you receive more physical blessings—money, job promotion, house, car, etc.—what is your first impulse? Do you typically think about how to leverage those blessings for the gospel? If not, why not?
4. How does the overarching message of Psalm 67 clash with a culture that is heavily influenced by consumerism?
5. If God blesses others through us, does that mean he is only using us? How is it good news to be used to bless others?
6. How should the truth of God's sovereignty give us confidence in the church's mission?
7. Sharing the truth of God's justice and wrath with unbelievers can be uncomfortable. Why it is critical that we don't neglect these sobering truths?
8. How might Psalm 67 shape the way a church uses its resources?
9. Some people think Christians are simply trying to keep people from enjoying life. How does verse 4 speak to this misperception?
10. In light of the message of Psalm 67, what are some things that need to change about the ways you are currently leveraging your job, your money, your time, etc.?

God on the Move

PSALM 68

Main Idea: Based on God's attributes and works, he deserves our praise and the obedience of our lives.

I. **The Portrait of God**
   A. He is awesome (68:35).
   B. He is active (68:1,4-18).
   C. He subdues all who rebel against him (68:2,6,12,14,21-23).
   D. He satisfies all who trust in him (68:3).
   E. He is the one true God (68:4,8-9,33-34).
   F. He is the covenant-keeping Lord (68:4).
   G. He is Father of the fatherless (68:5).
   H. He is protector of the widow (68:5).
   I. He loves the lonely (68:6).
   J. He rescues the captive (68:6).
   K. He provides for the needy (68:7-10).
   L. He is sovereign over nature (68:8-9).
   M. He is sovereign over nations (68:12,29).
   N. He is powerful above us (68:14).
   O. He is present with us (68:15-16).
   P. He commands a heavenly army (68:17).
   Q. He conquers in earthly victory (68:18).
   R. He bears our burdens (68:19).
   S. He saves our souls (68:19-20).
   T. He is my God and King (68:24).
   U. He is our God and King (68:26-27).
   V. He draws peoples to himself (68:29-31).
   W. He deserves praise throughout the earth (68:32-35).
   X. He is the divine warrior (68:1-2,33).
   Y. He speaks a dependable word (68:11).

II. **The Implications for Us**
   A. Give glory to this God.
   B. Give your life to his mission.

Many commentators say this is one of the most difficult psalms to understand, particularly because of a few verses whose meaning seems somewhat obscure. My goal, however, is not to get down into the weeds but to step back from the landscape and see the beauty and wonder of what lies before us.

Maybe more than any other psalm, Psalm 68 contains all kinds of different names and titles for God. At least six different Hebrew names for God are used: *Yah, Yahweh, Adonai, Shaddai, El,* and *Elohim* (Boice, *Psalms 42–106,* 554). In addition, there are various titles for God interspersed throughout the psalm. All these names and titles come together to paint a majestic portrait of who God is and what God has done, and is doing, in history. Below we'll look at twenty-five different attributes and activities of God in Psalm 68. Based on this portrait God has revealed, I want to draw two simple (yet massive) implications for our lives and for the church.

The Portrait of God

He Is Awesome (68:35)

Before looking at verse 1, it's worth noting how the final verse of this psalm sums up everything: "God, you are awe-inspiring in your sanctuaries." This points to the earth-shaking power, mind-boggling majesty, and awe-inducing splendor of the God who saves. This psalm offers a full-orbed picture of God throughout history, marching across the heavens and the earth, riding on clouds, scattering enemies, causing the earth to quake and showers to fall. We step back in awe. We can't read this psalm casually. We can't consider this God without being overwhelmed by his greatness, which, as we'll see in the next attribute, is revealed in what he does.

He Is Active (68:1,4-18)

This psalm begins by saying, "God arises." This is a deliberate allusion to what happened when God's people were wandering in the wilderness. At Mount Sinai, God gave his people his law, including instructions for how he would dwell in their midst through the ark of the covenant, which would be a physical symbol of God's presence with and protection of his people. Numbers 10:33-34 says,

*They set out from the mountain of the Lord on a three-day journey with
the ark of the Lord's covenant traveling ahead of them for those three
days to seek a resting place for them. Meanwhile, the cloud of the Lord
was over them by day when they set out from the camp.*

God led his people during the day with a pillar of cloud that centered
on the ark of the covenant. "Whenever the ark set out, Moses would say:
Arise, Lord! Let your enemies be scattered, and those who hate you flee
from your presence. When it came to rest, he would say: Return Lord,
to the countless thousands of Israel" (Num 10:35-36).

Notice the similarities between Numbers 10:35 and Psalm 68:1. The
psalm begins with Israel's enemies scattering before the presence of
God as he is on the move, and the rest of the psalm shows God on the
move. He rides on the clouds (vv. 4-6), going out before his people,
and he marches through the desert (vv. 7-10), leading them to conquer the land of Canaan (vv. 11-14). Ultimately, God leads his people
from Mount Sinai in verse 1 to Mount Zion in verses 15-18, where his
presence settles among his people in Jerusalem. Some commentators
believe this psalm was sung when the ark of the covenant was brought
into Jerusalem (Boice, *Psalms 42–106*, 554). Regardless, the main point
is clear: God is active. He acts in history among and for his people, and
his actions affect all peoples.

He Subdues All Who Rebel against Him (68:2,6,12,14,21-23)

When God arises, his enemies scatter. Those who hate him flee like
"smoke" driven by the wind and wither like "wax" in front of a fire (v. 2).
While prisoners are led out to "prosperity," "the rebellious" experience
scarcity (v. 6). This theme of God's subduing his enemies continues in
the rest of the psalm (vv. 12,14,21-23).

While we don't know for sure what some of these images mean,
we cannot help but think about the fall of "Babylon" mentioned in
Revelation 18–19, a symbol of the world system arrayed against God.
Mark it down: God eventually, completely, and ultimately subdues all
who rebel against him.

He Satisfies All Who Trust in Him (68:3)

After talking of the destruction of the wicked, the psalmist assures the
righteous that they have nothing to fear before this God, for his favor is
on them. God satisfies to the uttermost all who trust in him.

He Is the One True God (68:4,8-9,33-34)

This psalm makes several references to God's work in the clouds. Many commentators believe this is a deliberate provocation of the followers of Baal. The Canaanites worshiped Baal, calling him the "the Rider on the clouds" and attributing the rain to his doing (Kidner, *Psalms 1–72*, 239n1). This is likely the background for the story of Elijah's showdown with the prophets of Baal in 1 Kings 17–18. David is making a similar point in this psalm: Baal doesn't bring the rain; God does. Baal can't bring fire from the sky; God does. Baal isn't god over the heavens; Israel's God is the only God over the heavens.

He Is the Covenant-Keeping Lord (68:4)

David uses the name *Yahweh* (translated "Lord"), the covenant name God revealed to his people as an expression of his commitment to love and to care for them. So this awesome, active God, this one true God who subdues rebels and satisfies the righteous, is committed to his people. We see evidence of this commitment in the characteristics of God mentioned below.

He Is Father of the Fatherless (68:5)

The majestic God over all creation cares for the orphan.

He Is Protector of the Widow (68:5)

This is who God is "in his holy dwelling." Wilson notes, "God's compassionate concern emanates from his divine residence" (*Psalms*, 937).

He Loves the Lonely (68:6)

God is a pursuing God who goes after those who are abandoned and alone.

He Rescues the Captive (68:6)

This God also goes after the imprisoned. He pursues the oppressed and the enslaved, bringing them from their imprisonment to his prosperity.

He Provides for the Needy (68:7-10)

In God's care for the fatherless, the widow, the lonely, and the captive, he provides for the needy. When you read verses 7-10, you can't help but picture God's provision for his people in the wilderness. When they were thirsty, he would give them water from rocks. When they were hungry, he would rain down bread from heaven. God is near to the needy. He delights in providing for the destitute. He finds pleasure in harnessing all of his power on behalf of the fatherless and the widow and the lonely and the captive and the needy. And, as James Boice notes, this makes God unique:

> The kings and other rulers of this world do not act like this. They surround themselves with the noblest and richest of their lands, those who can enhance their glory and strengthen their power. The highest glory of God is that he cares for the miserable and surrounds himself with them. (Boice, *Psalms 42–106*, 555)

Yet, as you see God surrounded by the weak, don't think for a second that he is weak.

He Is Sovereign over Nature (68:8-9)

God owns the rain. He determines when it falls and when it is withheld. We're reminded of God's questioning of Job:

> *Have you entered the place where the snow is stored? Or have you seen the storehouses of hail, which I hold in reserve for times of trouble, for the day of warfare and battle? . . .*
> *Who cuts a channel for the flooding rain or clears the way for lightning, to bring rain on an uninhabited land, on a desert with no human life, to satisfy the parched wasteland and cause the grass to sprout? Does the rain have a father? Who fathered the drops of dew? . . .*
> *Can you command the clouds so that a flood of water covers you? Can you send out lightning bolts, and they go? Do they report to you: "Here we are"?*
> *Who put wisdom in the heart or gave the mind understanding? Who has the wisdom to number the clouds? Or who can tilt the water jars of heaven when the dust hardens like cast metal and the clods of dirt stick together?* (Job 38:22-23,25-28,34-38)

The answer to each of the questions is clear: only God does these things. The author of creation has all authority over creation.

He Is Sovereign over Nations (68:12,29)

God is not only sovereign over nature but also over nations. It's not only the rain that responds to his bidding, but he causes nations to run from him (v. 12), and he causes them to revere him (v. 29). He holds the kings of the earth in the palm of his hand.

He Is Powerful above Us (68:14)

Psalm 68:14 and 91:1 are the only two times in the Psalms when the Hebrew word *Shaddai* is used to refer to God. It emphasizes his might and majesty.

He Is Present with Us (68:15-16)

In all his awe-evoking might, God is not just powerful above us; he is also present with us. God has chosen to dwell among his people. David does a bit of "trash talk" with the mountains, saying to Mount Bashan, which is a towering, many-peaked mountain, "You think you're great, but you look with envy on Mount Zion, where God has chosen to dwell." Zion is virtually a hill in comparison to a mountain like Bashan, but this hill in Jerusalem is the place where God chose to establish his people and where Solomon built his temple. Psalm 132:13-14 says, "For the LORD has chosen Zion; he has desired it for his home: 'This is my resting place forever; I will make my home here because I have desired it.'"

Mount Bashan may be marked by height, but Mount Zion is marked by holiness. Zion essentially becomes the focal point for the rest of the psalm. It's the place where the people of God and the enemies of God, and eventually the kingdoms of the earth, will come. It is symbolic, a picture of all the earth ultimately worshiping God, who has revealed himself to us.

He Commands a Heavenly Army (68:17)

God is coming to dwell among his people surrounded by "tens of thousands" of chariots. This psalm may have been sung when the people of God brought the ark of the covenant into Jerusalem. We can only imagine the thrill of that scene, as this journey that began at Mount Sinai centuries before culminated in the entrance of the ark into Jerusalem.

He Conquers in Earthly Victory (68:18)

God is likened to an earthly king returning victoriously from battle, now encompassed by all the spoils of that victory. God's people were brought out of slavery in Egypt and then, after wandering through the wilderness, they entered Canaan where they claimed the land God had promised to them. Entering the promised land required conquering pagan nations; and when Israel finally settled, they celebrated the God who had protected his people and conquered their enemies. God commands a heavenly army, and he conquers in earthly victory.

He Bears Our Burdens (68:19)

David has recounted centuries of history, but here he transitions to the present. God carries us even now, and he will continue to carry us in the future.

He Saves Our Souls (68:19-20)

David attributes "salvation" to God. God doesn't just daily bear our burdens; he ultimately saves our souls! Not only has he led us in the past, and not only will he carry us in the present, but he will deliver us in the future—ultimately from death. What confidence we can have in this God!

He Is My God and King (68:24)

When David says that God's procession is "seen," he is referring to the grand, majestic God whom he has described in the previous twenty-three verses. This is not just the God and the King over *all*; this is the procession of *my* God and *my* King into the sanctuary. There's a sense of pride here but not the sinful kind. This is boasting in God.

He Is Our God and King (68:26-27)

The psalmist's personal praise is not disconnected from the people of God, for he says, "Bless God in the assemblies." He then describes Israel's tribes, north and south. David clearly sees himself worshiping as part of the community of God's people.

He Draws Peoples to Himself (68:29-31)

You may wonder why David wants God to "show [his] strength" (v. 28). The answer is in verses 29-31. This picture of kings being drawn to worship God is prophesied throughout Scripture. The psalmist is describing the ingathering of all the nations to give praise and honor and glory to God—even the "beast in the reeds," which was likely a reference to Egypt, the nation that had for centuries oppressed the people of Israel (Kidner, *Psalms 1–72*, 244). The "bulls" and "calves" symbolize hostile peoples, both large and small, and the psalmist wants God to summon his power and draw them to himself (Kidner, *Psalms 1–72*, 244).

He Deserves Praise throughout the Earth (68:32-35)

God draws peoples to himself because he deserves their praise. The rest of the psalm is addressed to kingdoms all across the earth. David tells them all to "sing praise" and "ascribe power" to God because he is "awe-inspiring" and he "gives power and strength to his people."

Notice the connection with the previous psalm. God dwells among his people, protects his people, provides for his people, and shows his power among his people all for a purpose: so that all the peoples might come and give him praise (67:3,5). God doesn't just deserve praise from one nation but from all peoples. And he will get it. That's the whole point of Psalm 68.

He Is the Divine Warrior (68:1-2,33)

God is the divine warrior who is on the move in the world, blessing, leading, guiding, and empowering his people for the sake of his praise among all the peoples. He is caring for orphans and widows and the enslaved and the impoverished. He is conquering all of his enemies so that all the kingdoms of the earth might know that he is God.

He Speaks a Dependable Word (68:11)

This psalm is reveling in the reality that God will be praised among all the peoples. That was the point in verse 11, which harks back to Exodus 15, the response of God's people after he delivered them from Egypt, bringing them out of slavery and across the Red Sea. Miriam, the prophetess, took a tambourine in her hand, and all the women went out after her with tambourines and dancing, shouting, "Sing to the Lord, for he is highly exalted; he has thrown the horse and its rider into the sea" (Exod 15:21).

God gives the word. He conquers, he delivers, he leads, and he guides all things according to his purpose—and so his people sing. You might wonder how we know all these things about God. We know because Psalm 68 is not the end of this story of God on the move. Centuries later this awesome God actively came to us in the person of Jesus, the Christ. He subdued demons. He satisfied sinners. The one true God came to his people, announcing,

> *The Spirit of the Lord is on me, because he has anointed me to preach good news to the poor. He has sent me to proclaim release to the captives and recovery of sight to the blind, to set free the oppressed, to proclaim the year of the Lord's favor.* (Luke 4:18-19)

The one who is all-powerful above us came to be bodily present with us, and he came to conquer. He lived a perfect life, he died a sinner's death, and then he rose from the grave, conquering sin, Satan, and death itself, canceling the debt that stood against sinful men and women. Colossians 2:14 says God took our certificate of debt away by "nailing it to the cross." Through Christ, "he disarmed the rulers and authorities and disgraced them publicly; he triumphed over them in him" (Col 2:15).

Christ has conquered, and he has said, "Come to me, all of you who are weary and burdened, and I will give you rest" (Matt 11:28). He will bear our burdens today, and he will save us forever. The one who is sovereign over nature is sovereign over the nations, and one day "every knee will bow—in heaven and on earth and under the earth—and every tongue will confess that Jesus Christ is Lord, to the glory of God the Father" (Phil 2:10-11).

The Implications for Us

At least two mammoth implications follow from the twenty-five attributes and activities of God in Psalm 68. First, we should **give glory to this God** (vv. 4,34). Stand in awe of him. Do not be casual or complacent with this God. And do not rebel against this God. Instead, confess your sin to him. Receive mercy from his throne, find salvation from your sin, and experience satisfaction for your soul.

Second, as you give glory to this God, **give your life to his mission**. God is still on the move. He did not stop moving with an ark entering into Jerusalem or with the building of a temple in Mount Zion. When Jesus died, the curtain of that temple was torn in two. God's presence now dwells in every person on the planet who turns from his or her sin and trusts in his Son.

Christian, the Spirit of this God dwells in you. And his Spirit is on the move. He has not saved you from your sin and filled you with his power so that you can sit on the sidelines as a spectator in the church. He has saved you for the salvation of and spread of God's glory to the nations. Jesus possesses all authority in heaven and on earth, and he, our heavenly commander, has charged us: "Go, therefore, and make disciples of all nations" (Matt 28:19). Give your life to this mission, confident that God is on the move through you and all around you, bringing all the kingdoms, nations, and peoples of the earth to praise his name.

Reflect and Discuss

1. If you were to ask your non-Christian friends, "What is God like?" how do you think they would answer? What about your Christian friends?
2. Why is it so critical that we have a high, or right, view of God?
3. Why should Christians be comforted by the fact that God is a covenant-keeping God?
4. How would you describe God's relationship to those who are the most weak and vulnerable?
5. Psalm 68 teaches that God is sovereign over nations. How should that affect our response to the weekly news headlines?
6. The picture of God in this psalm is majestic and lofty. What attributes of God assure us that this same God also cares for his people?
7. How might Psalm 68 give hope to Christians who are persecuted?
8. How might the picture of God in Psalm 68 affect a church's corporate worship?
9. List some ways Psalm 68 gives you confidence as you seek to obey Christ's command to make disciples of all nations.
10. How does Psalm 68 speak to the idea that all religions are essentially the same?

Drowning for the Gospel

PSALM 69

Main Idea: God ultimately will vindicate his children because of their zeal for the gospel even though they presently face opposition.

I love movies based on true stories, in spite of the speculation and fiction that often characterizes Hollywood's depiction of historical events. One of the most gut-wrenching scenes I've ever watched is in the movie *Pearl Harbor*. After the *U.S.S. Arizona* is attacked by the Japanese, sailors are scrambling everywhere, some just trying to take cover and survive, others trying to help injured or trapped comrades. At one point a group of sailors are trying to free some others who are trapped in the hull of the ship, which is quickly filling with water. Some of the entombed men are frantically reaching their hands through a small hole in the ship's hull, desperately pleading for someone to save them. One of the sailors outside compassionately grabs the hand of one of his perishing shipmates. The scene ends when the hand of the trapped sailor stops moving. The water below overtakes him. His hopeless grasp for help ends in vain. The rescuing grip is too late. A soldier, zealous for his country, loses his life.

The psalmist understands what it means to be drowning and in desperate need of God's rescuing hand. His devotion to God and his house creates a life-threatening situation. In Psalm 69 he's drowning, and he's desperately reaching out for God to save him. Although this psalm was evidently penned by David, it likely was tweaked and applied to the circumstances of God's people long after it was written. They were either in exile or in some other dangerous situation, and they needed God's salvation. Once again, he gives them hope.

Believers may sometimes face the psalmist's predicament, as well as the predicament of the despairing sailor trapped in the *Arizona*'s hull. Our zeal for Christ, his church, and the other institutions of the Christian faith will sometimes put us in situations in which we feel like danger is overtaking us. Just this week I was reminded of this assault when I went to use the restroom in a restaurant, only to find a placard on the outside that stated that the facilities were "gender neutral." On the same day I read a story in the news about a teacher in Texas who was sent home to change her T-shirt because it had the words *Just Pray* on it. These two occurrences are merely a small sampling of the relatively new clashes being made against the Christian faith in America, which pales in comparison to the total war that's been assaulting global Christianity for decades and even centuries.

God's hand, however, will never fail to reach us in his time. In this song the psalmist's deadly dilemma points to the hope that believers have in Jesus Christ, the one who ultimately will enable them to reach their destination. Our God wants his people to zealously defend the faith, advance the gospel, and announce his glory in all the earth. However, doing so will often reap bitter opposition from people both inside and outside the community of faith. That's because zeal for the things of God always rubs people wrong who aren't on board. But this psalm—with its numerous pictures of God's Messiah—is a reminder that our Lord is worth our suffering and sacrifice.

The Crisis at Hand
PSALM 69:1-4

The psalmist describes his current crisis first by noting a lethal assault (vv. 1-2). His enemies have him in the deep end of the pool, and he doesn't know how to swim! His ship has sunk, and he's trying to stay afloat in the raging sea.

In the wake of this assault, the psalmist is making some attempts to get God's attention and marshal his help, but he's "weary" (v. 3). Neither his ceaseless cry for help nor his constant search for divine rescue has gotten any response, so the reality of his demise is setting in.

David drops his metaphorical description and identifies the tangible reality of his situation. His trouble is due to the innumerable host of false accusations being levied at him by enemies. The term *without cause* suggests their attack isn't due to a simple misunderstanding but instead is a purposeful distortion of the truth. His conclusion underscores the injustice at hand: "Though I did not steal, I must repay" (v. 4).

The Concern for Reputation
PSALM 69:5-6

I was a PK of sorts growing up. I wasn't a "preacher's kid," but a "principal's kid." During my entire high-school tenure, my dad was the superintendent of our small school system, so to some degree we lived in a glass house just like the families of preachers. What we kids did and how we acted not only reflected on our own reputations but on my dad's as well. My parents taught us the importance of guarding our reputation, their reputation, and especially Christ's reputation. They instilled in us the conviction that we should always be concerned about how our actions—whether right or wrong—might reflect on what other people thought about us and our Lord.

At the end of my senior year in high school, our coaches selected me to receive the Athlete of the Year award at our annual sports banquet. It was arguably the most prized athletic award at our school and one that was a huge honor to receive. However, when my dad found out about the selection, he went to the coaches and told them to give the award to someone else. I remember the night he came into my room and told me what he had done. He told me how much he loved me and how proud he was of me for being chosen by the coaches, but he said he didn't want anyone to ever think the only reason I received the award was because he was the superintendent. It wasn't wrong for me to get that award; it was a good thing. Doing so, however, would run the risk of reflecting poorly on both my reputation and my dad's.

The psalmist was concerned about reputation. In verse 5 his lament begins to expand in widening concentric circles of concern. His first concern is over his own guilt, or even just the public perception of his guilt. But he doesn't stop there. He broadens his alarm to how the charges against him will reflect poorly on the community of faith (v. 6) and even on God himself (vv. 7,9). We can examine these expanding concerns by looking at the psalmist's personal *responsibility* in causing the reproach and his *request* for God's help to prevent it.

We first see the *responsibility* the psalmist assumes for the marred reputation. In verse 5 the holy searchlight of the righteous Father ultimately finds its way to his drowning child. However, its effect is not what we might have expected. Instead of resulting in David's deliverance, it results in David's dissection! Instead of the outcome being his physical rescue, it turns out to be his personal responsibility! While we're not told the specifics of David's offense—or even whether the accusations against him are valid—the parallel acknowledgments of "my foolishness" and "my guilty acts" (v. 5) suggest multiple transgressions that offended God. The psalmist understands that none of his legitimate guilt ever escapes the probing gaze of his omniscient God.

It's funny how prayer works, especially when I feel like I'm drowning. I often come before God with an entire grocery list of things I need from him and—before I know it—he's showing me all kinds of stuff he wants from me. My praying frequently starts off with the expression of my physical needs, but the focus quickly turns to my spiritual needs. My prayer sometimes begins with objective wants, but it ends up with reflective needs. You can't rush into the light of God's presence and be there very long without his revealing glory turning back on you. That seems to be what happens to David as he describes his immediate crisis to God. He started off with a metaphorical account of his current state and his desperation for God to help (vv. 1-3), then moved to a more objective description of his state of affairs under the attack of his enemies (v. 4), but now ends up confessing his own sin (v. 5)! "Prayer is already doing its work" (Kidner, *Psalms 1–72*, 264).

O Christian, be encouraged and challenged with the beauty of God's economy in prayer! When we're drowning because of our faith, our faithfulness to "search" for his help in prayer most often will result in him searching us, a quest that always uncovers our own responsibility, or at the very least a healthy examination of our spiritual state. And while David's wrongdoing was not likely the direct cause of his current chaos, we can't dismiss the possibility (see v. 26). When we're praying out of desperate circumstances, we should first entertain the prospect that we've in some way contributed to their presence.

Next, the psalmist makes his *request* for God to stay the effects these accusations might have on the reputation of his people. The parallelism in Hebrew highlights this distress in verse 6. David appeals to God in desperation that "those who put their hope in you" and "those who seek you" wouldn't be "disgraced" or "humiliated." While such reproach would be horrific for any reason, his concern here is that it would happen "because of me." Whether the charges against him were valid or not, he knew they would reflect on God's people. For the Israelites, shame and disgrace as a result of an enemy's attack didn't prompt internal emotions alone but also visible actions of communal rejection and detraction (see Pss 70:2; 71:1,13). Whether the psalmist had to wear some sign of disgrace or experience some kind of public shunning by the community, the community's assumption of his guilt would have been manifested in some obvious and visible way (Wilson, *Psalms*, 952).

The Cause of Opposition
PSALM 69:7-12

In somewhat of a cause-and-effect fashion, the psalmist puts some specifics to the root and result of the reputation he's developed. He first identifies the ultimate cause for the tarnished reputation that's come his way. He says that it's because of "you" (v. 7) and "zeal for your house" (v. 9) that the criticism has come. Here he reveals what he really thinks about the scorn he's experiencing. It isn't actually the result of his personal failing but the repercussion of his commitment to God. Then he tells us the subsequent effect on his life. The descriptive terms *insults* (vv. 7,9) and *shame* (v. 7) both suggest public reproach that has been levied against him for God's sake. And that reproach, he says, has alienated him (v. 8). To be ostracized by family or friends in the ancient world was serious business.

The picture the psalmist is painting here is like that of an accused criminal leaving a courthouse. He's doing his best to hide his face from a reporter's camera while a group of angry citizens yells accusations and insults from the informal gallery behind a police barricade. To intensify the situation, his own embarrassed family is trying to blend anonymously into the crowd (cf. Num 12:14; Deut 25:9; Job 20:15; 30:10). This is not at all unlike what happened to our Lord on the night before he died. The religious gallery vehemently exclaimed, "'He deserves death!' Then they spat in his face and beat him; others slapped him and said, 'Prophesy to us, Messiah!'" (Matt 26:66-68). And just a short time later his close friend denied three times that he even knew him (Matt 26:69-75).

In verse 9 the psalmist says to God that his reproach is due to "zeal for your house." The descriptions in verses 10-11 indicate an open display of weeping, fasting, and wearing sackcloth, all of which represent the psalmist's public mourning over some kind of assault on the temple or at least the refusal of some people to humble themselves before God.

Apparently, those identified with this resistance saw David's mourning as an occasion to make him a "joke" (v. 11) or mockery, as well as the subject of insulting conversation among the city leaders and the sport of the drunkards (v. 12).

Again, the descriptions here point us to one who ultimately would suffer because of his zeal for God. While partial references to Christ are scattered throughout this psalm, the entirety of verse 9 finds its fulfilment in him. When Jesus drove out the money changers from the temple, "his disciples remembered that it is written: Zeal for your house will consume me" (John 2:17). And when Paul was appealing to the Roman believers to work to help the weak instead of pleasing themselves, he pointed out, "Christ did not please himself. On the contrary, as it is written, The insults of those who insult you have fallen on me" (Rom 15:3). What appears to be some weakness on the part of God in this psalm for not responding to the psalmist's desperate pleas now makes perfect sense. The theme of this song is redemptive, for it is a privilege for God's children to "be treated shamefully on behalf of the Name" (Acts 5:41). It is—despite its cost—a high compliment when we are drowning for the sake of Christ, his church, and all the institutions of the Christian faith.

The Cry for Help
PSALM 69:13-18

Awhile back I found out that a fellow believer was struggling with depression. Apparently he'd been battling with it off and on for some time. He told me that he hadn't disclosed it to anyone primarily because he was embarrassed that someone who had been a Christian as long as he had would have such weak faith. He finally got plugged into a godly Christian counselor to talk through his journey. In the first session the counselor made a good recommendation. He said, "When you get home today, I want you to sit down and just begin to list all of the ways God has been faithful to you through the years." My friend followed his directions. When he recounted the exercise to me, he shared how amazed he was at the comfort he experienced simply retracing the goodness of God in his life.

Believers in Christ learn to trust in God's faithfulness because he's so consistent with it! When we find ourselves drowning in some unwarranted attack or other personal crisis, we can find strength and encouragement by acknowledging and expressing that trust. That's what the psalmist does here. Notice the circumstances he's in, the cry he makes, and then especially the character of God that provides the foundation of his prayers.

The psalmist's **circumstances** are disastrous, so once again he returns to the imagery of drowning (vv. 14-15) and just generally being "in distress" (v. 17). The reference to the "Pit" in verse 15 is likely the picture of being buried alive in a well that somebody's about to close up by putting a stone on top. Death is imminent if God doesn't show up.

Because of his perilous plight, David **cries** out to God. The opening "But as for me" (v. 13) contrasts his appeal with the hateful attacks of his detractors in verse 12. While they decry him at the city gate and make fun of him at the local bars, he's going to pray. So he cries out for God to "answer me" (vv. 13,16,17), "rescue me" (v. 14), "don't let the flood-waters sweep over me" (v. 15), "turn to me" (v. 16), "don't hide your face from [me]" (v. 17), "come near to me," "redeem me," and "ransom me" (v. 18). Once again the little child crawls up in his heavenly Father's lap, grabs his cheeks and turns his face toward him and begs for his help. It's a safe place for the psalmist, and so it should be for us.

In verse 18, the word *redeem* describes the duty of a man's next of kin to stand up for him in trouble, to avenge his death (Num 35:19), or to buy back his land or liberty (Lev 25:25,48-49). The word *ransom* carries the basic idea of purchase (Ps 31:5). The two verbs are found together in Isaiah 35:9-10, where God's people are called "the redeemed" and "the ransomed" (Kidner, *Psalms 1–72*, 266).

The most significant implications of these actions aren't realized until the cross of Christ. Speaking about himself, Jesus says, "The Son of Man did not come to be served, but to serve, and to give his life as a ransom for many" (Matt 20:28; cf. 1 Tim 2:6). And Paul declares that Jesus "redeemed us from the curse of the law by becoming a curse for us" (Gal 3:13; cf. Titus 2:14). As we crawl up into God's lap to plead for help, we know that our access to that safe place is only possible through the work of Christ on the cross, and in him we look with faith and humility for God to deliver us from trouble.

The psalmist appeals to God's **character**. The grounds for assuming that it's "a time of favor" (v. 13) is that these are the times God has acted in faithfulness to his people in the past! David is confident that the time he needs help is the same time God hears and answers! So in humility and faith, he appeals to the forever love God has for his covenant people (v. 13; cf. v. 16). He reaches out and appeals to, literally, God's "truth salvation" (v. 13). These references underscore the trustworthiness of God to act on behalf of his children and deliver them.

David didn't learn these truths about God from a creed but from experiencing his faithfulness and deliverance through time. Just like my friend who was struggling with depression, every believer in Christ can recount a litany of times God has shown himself faithful and strong in our lives. Some of those times have been when we've asked, and some of them have even been times when we haven't! God's character should always be the object to which we appeal in prayer. His nature and attributes—manifested in Christ—reflect his glory and provide the sure basis on which he hears and responds to his children in time of need.

The Cup of Reproach
PSALM 69:19-21

The psalmist not only appeals to God's character, but he finds assurance in the fact that God is keenly aware of all of the details of his situation (v. 19). God knows about his enemies as well as their effect on him. The weight of the assault evidently has broken his spirit (v. 20). He can't go any further; he's ready to quit. He's about out of oxygen as the waters of hopelessness overtake him.

As if that isn't enough, there's no sympathy to be found anywhere (v. 20). His vain search for support just heaps coals on the fire of his loneliness and futility. Instead of finding sympathizers in his search, his empty stomach and dry mouth are only met with harmful and distasteful substitutes for satisfying sustenance (v. 21).

Much of David's description of his plight is clearly metaphorical, but his words look forward to an event and a person for whom this mockery, maligning, and maliciousness would be all too literal. Recounting Jesus's crucifixion, the Gospel writer says that at one point "they gave him wine mixed with gall to drink" (Matt 27:34). A short time later "one of them ran and got a sponge, filled it with sour wine, put it on a stick, and offered him a drink" (Matt 27:48). And while Matthew doesn't specify these events as prophetic fulfillment of the psalmist's words, John does: "When Jesus knew that everything was now finished that the Scripture might be fulfilled, he said, 'I'm thirsty'" (John 19:28).

This "poisonous" identification with Christ is only the culmination of the cross motif that runs through these verses, as well as the whole

psalm. The words *insults, shame,* and *disgrace* (v. 19; cf. vv. 6-12) reflect the
intense dishonor of public shame that was far worse in Old Testament
culture than in our own (cf. Num 12:14). Contrary to those who would
see this gesture as an act of compassion simply to numb Jesus's pain on
the cross, the New Testament writers see it as underscoring his intense
agony of abandonment and betrayal as he died—one that should compel us to faithfully endure the same:

> *Therefore, since we also have such a large cloud of witnesses
> surrounding us, let us lay aside every hindrance and the sin that so
> easily ensnares us. Let us run with endurance the race that lies before
> us, keeping our eyes on Jesus, the source and perfecter of our faith. For
> the joy that lay before him, he endured the cross, despising the shame,
> and sat down at the right hand of the throne of God.* (Heb 12:1-2)

The vinegar-soaked sponge was a definitive expression of mockery, a
"painful lack of concern—even sadistic toying with the urgent needs of
the suffering" (Wilson, *Psalms*, 955). Such was the cup of reproach our
Lord drank on our behalf. We should be willing to do the same.

The Curse of Enemies
PSALM 69:22-29

Up to this point in the psalm, we've seen so many allusions to Christ and his
passion (vv. 4,9,21) that we might expect the psalmist to now pray for God
to forgive his enemies, just as Jesus did on the cross. Instead—serving as a
reminder of the stark contrast of what Jesus did for us—David's anger
is kindled by his zeal for justice, about which the Old Testament largely
exists to remind us (Kidner, *Psalms 1–72*, 266–67). The next eight verses
are a catalog of curses he prays down on his enemies, all of which are
things God was going to do sooner or later. David's life was in danger,
and the reputation of God's community was hanging in the balance. So
he prays for judgment urgently and boldly, much as we should do on
this side of the cross when we're longing for Jesus to come.

These verses can be analyzed from three different angles. **What** he's
asking God to do is clear—he wants him to turn the tables on his enemies (v. 24). He's basically asking God to destroy his enemies and save
him. He wants him to flip the script!

Why the psalmist wants God to strike his enemies and deliver him
is stated in verse 26. This is a summary of his plight as narrated in the

whole psalm up to this point. Whether the psalmist was being disciplined for some sin, suffering for the purpose of sanctification, or just reaping the consequences of his faithfulness (vv. 4-12), he had found himself in a low state of affairs under the sovereign, heavy hand of his God (vv. 1-3,14-15). Instead of having pity on him, however, his enemies continued to turn up the heat, falsely accusing him (v. 4), taunting him (vv. 11-12), and even mocking him in his pain (vv. 18-21).

How David wants God to judge his enemies makes up the lion's share of these verses. In summary, he wants God to strike at the heart of both the physical and spiritual elements that sustain people in this world: food, health, shelter, and the grace that only God can give. First, in verse 22 he asks that, when they sit down to eat and celebrate the sign of God's presence, he would turn their table on them and let it be the means of their demise. "They had given him poison and sour wine for food and drink; it is fitting that their celebratory feasts become their undoing, as they are found out and destroyed suddenly" (Ross, *Psalms*, vol. 2, 498).

Second, in verse 23 the psalmist asks God to take away their health. The reference to dimmed eyes may mean he's asking God to physically blind them, or it may mean he wants them to lose their ability to reason and understand what's good and right. The reference to the hips speaks of their strength and vigor, which the psalmist wants God to weaken in terror. While David appears to be referring to physical elements in verses 22-23, Paul applies them to the spiritual condition of the Israelites who rejected God's great salvation in Christ Jesus (Rom 11:9-10). Those who reject the gospel are spiritually malnourished and blind.

Third, in verse 25 the psalmist asks God to remove their shelter. Just as their attacks on him had isolated him from his family and friends, he prays that God will do the same for them by causing them to have to abandon their abode. Peter, of course, applied this verse to Judas's default on his apostolic office (Acts 1:20). Spurgeon observes, "What occurs on a large scale to families and nations is often fulfilled in individuals" (Spurgeon, *Treasury of David*, vol. 3, 183). Rejection of the gospel results in rejection of the abode God intends for us.

Fourth, in verses 27-28 the psalmist prays against his enemies ever receiving God's grace. The first phrase literally means "add more iniquity to their iniquity" or let them continue to sin so both their guilt and subsequent punishment will increase. He wants God to abandon them to their own desires—or let them reap what they sow (Gal 6:7)—so they won't find favor from him and be forgiven of their sins. He thinks they should be "erased from the book of life" (v. 28). Although the New Testament will extend this "roll call" idea to indicate eternal life (Luke 10:20; Phil 4:3; Rev 3:5; 13:8; 17:8; 20:12,15; 21:27), here it refers to people living in this life. David's asking that they be removed from the roll sheet of the righteous who will inherit the earth (cf. Pss 25:13; 37:9,11,22,29,34; Isa 60:21; Matt 5:5). The bottom line: he wants his enemies to be excluded from the saving grace of God's salvation.

Before we leave these verses in which the psalmist—once again—is calling down fire from heaven, we need to be reminded of what this teaches us about prayer on this side of the cross. First, we put retribution in God's hands. There's no question David is spewing out his pain like an erupting volcano, but he's directing it to God. His suffering and anger are real emotions that we feel sometimes in the midst of our desperation, and we need to be open and honest with our heavenly Father about them. It's healthy—both physically and spiritually—for us to express our feelings to God. However, we should never act on them ourselves. All of the things for which the psalmist prays are God's actions against those who attack his people. In the same breath that we pray these kinds of things, we should also be asking God to forgive those who come against us and give us grace to love them (Rom 12:17-21).

Second, even if we're not drowning to the point of wanting to pray like this, let's always remember there are fellow believers in the world right now who—like David—are desperately feeling this way. They're experiencing this kind of anger and hate because the waters of despair are overtaking them. Their honest expression of these kinds of emotions, however, doesn't negate their relationship with God. Our brothers and sisters who are being abused, tortured, and unjustly accused need our empathetic, sympathetic, and fervent prayer, as well as our physical presence and aid if we can provide it. Jesus identifies with their suffering and pain, even if it results in death. "If God went so far to stand in solidarity with the suffering of the world, how can we do less?" (Wilson, *Psalms*, 960). Even if we're not suffering right now, let's never neglect to remember those who are.

The Concert of Praise
PSALM 69:30-36

The language in this last section suggests this song may have been tweaked for use in the communal worship of God's people during desperate times long after David's day, possibly even during the exile or beyond. Those "who are prisoners" (v. 33) and "the descendants of his servants . . . and those who love his name" (v. 36) anticipate the day when God will "build up the cities of Judah. They will live there and possess it" (v. 35). The reference to "Judah" alone implies the psalm's employment sometime during the divided kingdom, a time when many among God's people longed for restoration.

The fact that a number of psalms seem to have served this purpose should encourage us in their use in our own situations. Their application is timeless because God's people will always be in need, and he will always be there to help them. Furthermore, regardless of the particular situation that inspired this application, the predicament of the people of God reflects an eschatological hope that transcends its historical setting. The children of God's Servant, Jesus, and the ones who love his name ultimately will inherit his land!

As usual, God strengthens the faith of the psalmist in the midst of his drowning. As he's crying out to God, his heart is turned from despair to devotion, from worry to worship. Our Father will do this for us as we crawl up in his lap with our frantic faith and pray for him to deliver us. God himself will turn our distress to doxology if we will persevere in pursuing him. This praise issues forth in telescopic fashion from three concentric circles.

The first circle is the thanksgiving of the psalmist, the one who's been in dire straits. He resolves to praise and exalt God (v. 30). This personal, heartfelt praise is more pleasing to God than the most expensive religious sacrifices (v. 31). God delights in a joyous and grateful song that comes from a sincere heart more than he does religious ritual that's offered out of routine.

The second circle is the worship of the larger body of God's people. They're described as those who are "humble . . . who seek God" (v. 32) and "the needy . . . his own" (v. 33). When they see the psalmist's sincere worship, they will be inspired to join in and have their spirits strengthened (v. 32) because "the LORD listens . . . and does not despise" (v. 33) them. Beloved, God inhabits the praise of his people and answers their prayer, and that should be a great encouragement to us when we find ourselves drowning for the gospel's sake.

Verse 34 reflects the third circle of worship as the psalmist calls for "everything" to join in the praise to God. God is worthy of the worship of his whole creation! This universal praise—reinforced by the eschatological references to "Zion" and "Judah" in verse 35 (cf. Ps 37)—anticipates the time prophesied in Revelation 5; 20; and 21 when Jesus Christ will be revealed as the rightful owner of the title deed to the earth and the sole object of the worship of all creation. This is when "the prayers of the saints" (Rev 5:8) will find their ultimate answer in his redemptive work as all creation joins the church in praising him:

> *You are worthy to take the scroll and to open its seals, because you*
> *were slaughtered, and you purchased people for God by your blood*
> *from every tribe and language and people and nation. You made them*
> *a kingdom and priests to our God, and they will reign on the earth.*
> (Rev 5:9-10)

Then they will be joined by the thunderous voices of countless angels who will be declaring, "Worthy is the Lamb who was slaughtered to receive power and riches and wisdom and strength and honor and glory and blessing!" (Rev 5:12). And if that weren't enough, that universal choir will be joined by every creature in heaven, on earth, under the earth, and in the sea, singing, "Blessing and honor and glory and power be to the one seated on the throne, and to the Lamb, forever and ever!" (Rev 5:13).

The concert of praise ultimately will be the worship of our Redeemer, Jesus Christ, by everything and everybody in the whole universe. He alone is worthy to be enthroned on the praises of his creation!

Conclusion

The assaults on the teachings and institutions of the Christian faith are escalating at an unimaginable rate in our day. Our Lord has given us the stewardship of protecting and advancing the faith, even though it means we will be criticized, ostracized, and even criminalized for it. Surprisingly, sometimes the opposition will come from within our own camp, but even then, it's not an option to roll over and play dead. Because of Christ, we know God's truth will win the day, and his strong hand will be there to save us when we're drowning. We can always be confident that he will preserve his gospel and pronounce judgment against its enemies. He clearly promised that even the gates of hell won't be able to succeed in warding off the advancement of his church. So as his soldiers, we reach out to him to deliver us based on the hope he's promised.

Reflect and Discuss

1. David had no hesitation in crying out to God when he needed him. Have you ever been in such a desperate situation that you cried out like David, "Save me, O God!"?

2. What hinders our prayer life from becoming like David's?

3. While David is crying out for God to save him, what does God immediately reveal to him (v. 5)? Have you noticed this pattern in your life? Why does God do this?

4. God's enemies oppressing God's people is nothing new. What comfort does David find in the midst of oppression and persecution?

5. Is there a connection between zeal for God and increased persecution? What are some New Testament examples of this?

6. This would be categorized as a messianic psalm. What connections do the New Testament authors draw from this psalm to the life of Christ, and where are they found?

7. In David, but fulfilled in the life of Christ, what can we learn about standing strong in the face of opposition?

8. David is honest with God about what he wants him to do to his enemies. Did David let his temper get out of control? Are we, as followers of Christ, justified to pray like this about our enemies?

9. Even if we do not have physical enemies about whom we feel this way, how does this remind us of brothers and sisters across the world that do? How then can we pray for those who are physically persecuted?

10. What confidence do we have when, even though we cry out to God, he seemingly is *delaying* his deliverance? What if he *never* answers the prayer in the way we ask?

When God Drags His Feet

PSALM 70

Main Idea: Believers can pray with confidence for God to be glorified when he provides timely help and righteous vindication.

I.   Ask God to Help You Immediately (70:1,5).
II. Ask God to Humiliate His Enemies (70:2-3).
III. Ask God to Honor His Name (70:4).

The phrase *dragging your feet* is usually understood to be an idiom for moving slowly and reluctantly because you don't want to do something. From the perspective of eternity, God is always on time, and he never operates from a posture of not wanting to help his children. However, from our earthly perspective, it appears sometimes that he's dragging his feet a little bit, especially when we're feeling the weight of opposition to our Christian faith. The psalmist apparently knew that feeling. He prays here in Psalm 70 as if God were dragging his feet and in no hurry to answer him.

While Psalm 70 is attributed to David, the intent is for it to be performed "to bring remembrance." The only other time this term appears is in the heading of Psalm 38. Some see it as referring to the incense offering, in which case Psalms 38 and 70 were to be recited during the presentation of that ritual (Wilson, *Psalms Volume 1*, 967). The words are pretty much a repeat of Psalm 40:13-17; it may have been separated out as a stand-alone prayer for help to be offered during the ceremony mentioned above. Some commentators also see it as an introduction to the combined composition of Psalms 70 and 71 (see Wilson, Vol. 1, 966).

Whether seen as an introduction to the next psalm or as an independent piece, this prayer appears to be driven by the psalmist's perception that God is procrastinating. So he's crying out to him with three urgent requests. He wants God to help him immediately in the face of enemy attack, to humiliate his enemies, and to honor his own name. When we're in similar perilous and pressing situations and we need God to act *now*, believers can find help in making these three requests together.

Ask God to Help You Immediately
PSALM 70:1,5

This psalm is bookended by the psalmist's plea for immediate and urgent help. Three elements characterize his predicament. First, the psalmist's back is against the wall. The appeals "hurry" and "do not delay" are cries of desperation. Second, the psalmist has zero resources of his own from which to draw (v. 5). Third, the psalmist has his God. He cries for the Lord "to rescue me . . . to help me!" (v. 1), for he is "my help and my deliverer" (v. 5). The psalmist has great confidence in God's ability and faithfulness to deliver him because he's seen him do it so many times in the past.

These same characteristics illustrate the Christian journey on both sides of conversion. We're all in the desperate and urgent situation of not having any resources to deal with our sin problem. Outside of God's intervention we're doomed to eternal destruction away from his blissful presence. But in the cross event, God—in Christ—shows himself strong as our help and deliverer. When we cry out to him in repentance and faith, he saves us with a grand demonstration of divine faithfulness. This is exactly why we tend to think in terms of prayer when we are describing how a person comes to Christ. We often describe it as asking Jesus into our hearts or praying to accept Christ. There's nothing wrong with those depictions as long as we're using them to describe our desperate cry to God to save us.

For us as God's children, the same is true. Just as we have no fleshly ability to earn our justification, we're bankrupt of resources to live out the Christian life and experience sanctification. In our flesh we're vulnerable to the manipulation and control of Satan's influences. But we have God! We find ourselves at his mercy, the one whose mercies are new every day. Our spiritual and emotional dependence is on him through Christ's presence within us. And our natural and dependable recourse in the face of oppression is to cry out and trust in him for help. We pray for him to deliver us from the one who hounds us and who seeks to wreak havoc on our Christian lives. God is always faithful to respond.

In addition, he's always right on time in doing so. Paul said, "For while we were still helpless, at the right time, Christ died for the ungodly" (Rom 5:6). Of our desperate need for help in the Christian life, the author of Hebrews reminds us,

For we do not have a high priest who is unable to sympathize with our weaknesses, but one who has been tempted in every way as we are, yet without sin. Therefore, let us approach the throne of grace with boldness, so that we may receive mercy and find grace to help us in time of need. (Heb 4:15-16)

Whether we are coming to Christ or navigating tumultuous waters in our walks with him, God in Christ is always faithful to respond to our cries at just the right moment!

Ask God to Humiliate His Enemies
PSALM 70:2-3

At the heart of the psalmist's request is for his enemies to be ashamed, embarrassed, and perturbed over their efforts to oppose God and his people. Their defeat is not enough. The psalmist evidently looks toward a broader effect of God's judgment against them. He wants others to see his vindication and, subsequently, to fear God. When God responds to his prayer, the psalmist wants the righteous to rejoice and the disobedient to dread.

Still, David's petition certainly implies the utter defeat of those who are opposing him. His adversaries are described as those who mockingly say, "Aha, Aha!" Like an overconfident opponent in a professional wrestling match prior to the first bell, they taunt him and gloat with the arrogant expectation of his utter defeat. So David prays that they would be "turned back" by God's hand, that his utter embarrassment of them would make them "retreat" in shameful defeat. Essentially, David is asking for God to once again flip the script on his enemies and turn their haughty heckling into their own humiliation.

Few commentators and other interpreters make any direct application of David's prayer in these verses. On the surface it does seem strange for us to ask God to humiliate our enemies as opposed to just disciplining them. Even if we make direct application of the psalmist's imprecations for God to wipe out his adversaries, it's awkward to go to this extreme. After all, athletes are penalized for taunting their opponents. But once again the ultimate motive is the key. If all we want is for our enemies to see that we ultimately have the upper hand on them, then our motive is for our glory and honor, which is totally sinful and unacceptable. However, if our true desire is for the broader populace to see God's hand and honor his name, then it's perfectly good and right for us sometimes to pray for God to humiliate our enemies. The secret is that we pray for their humiliation out of the heartbeat of our own humility.

We once again should be reminded that to pray like this is to pray like Jesus taught us to pray: "Your kingdom come. Your will be done on earth as it is in heaven" (Matt 6:10). We know Jesus's arrival will be characterized by the humiliation of those who've opposed him and his gospel. When Babylon the great falls in the book of Revelation, a voice from heaven says,

> As much as she glorified herself and indulged her sensual and excessive ways, give her that much torment and grief. For she says in her heart, "I sit as a queen; I am not a widow, and I will never see grief." For this reason her plagues will come in just one day—death and grief and famine. She will be burned up with fire, because the Lord God who judges her is mighty. (Rev 18:7-8)

The arrogant boasting of the wicked one and his armies will be laid low for all to see. Their humiliation will be on display for everyone to behold and ponder (cf. Rev 18:9-20). When we pray for Jesus's kingdom to come, we're essentially praying for his enemies to be humiliated.

Ask God to Honor His Name
PSALM 70:4

Here's where we find solid ground on which to ask God to hurry up. The obvious counterpart to the humiliation of God's enemies is the honor of God's name. So it's perfectly natural for the psalmist to follow his request for the former with a request for the latter. He knows that the humiliating overthrow of God's enemies will not only give relief to him but also will give joy to all "those who love [God's] salvation" (v. 4). Ross observes, "The contrast is clear: shame for those who seek the life of the psalmist, joy for those who seek the Lord" (Ross, *Psalms*, vol. 2, 508).

Don't miss, however, the object of the joy for which David is asking on behalf of God's people. It's not their deliverance, their enemies' defeat, or even their joyful satisfaction itself. The end game for the psalmist is that God's people will proclaim his greatness!

Herein lies another balance for us as we wrestle with the ethic of praying for God's enemies to be humiliated. The glory of Christ and the glory of man cannot coexist. It's one or the other. Either he is exalted and mankind is principally humbled, or mankind is exalted and he is perceived to be humbled. We know that our great and glorious Lord ultimately will not allow anyone to steal his glory; he's the only one worthy of it. So, if he's exalted, it follows that those who try to steal his glory will be humiliated.

Furthermore, our assignment to make disciples among all people is the practical pathway of declaring Christ's glory among all nations (Ps 96:3; Matt 28:18-20; Rev 14:6-7). If we obediently follow his instructions, then the enemies of the gospel naturally will be humiliated. These words in Psalm 70 constitute another compelling argument for us to leverage all that we are and all that we have to proclaim Christ's glory and gospel to all people. When we do so, the name of Christ is honored and gospel haters—by default—are humiliated. When we don't, gospel haters are exalted, and the name of Christ—by default—is scorned. Our prayers for God's enemies to be humiliated and his name to be honored go hand in hand. In essence, they're two sides of the same coin.

Conclusion

Does God move too slowly for you sometimes? I often hear people say that when God answers prayer, he either says, "Yes," "No," or "Wait." In this psalm David won't take no for an answer (69:13), and he's not big on the idea of waiting. His prayer here seems to teach us that we can press God about the timing of his answer as well as about the subject of our prayer. "When the ax is about to fall, there is no time for 'Wait'" (Goldingay, *Psalms 42–89*, 361). When you're in a jam, throw your pride to the wind and don't be afraid to yell, "Help! Now!" But when you do, make sure your desperate cry is aired against the backdrop of a desire for God to be glorified among all people. That needs to be our ultimate motivation to secure his help sooner rather than later.

Reflect and Discuss

1. Have you ever found yourself questioning God's timing? What were the circumstances?
2. Looking back on those circumstances, do you see God's wise timing?
3. What are some specific things God has taught you while you were waiting on him?
4. How has God, in reality, already answered our eternal cries to him?

5. Even though we are firmly and eternally in Christ, why do we still have troubles in this life? Do we, like the psalmist, have enemies?
6. Notice David's desire for his enemies: that they be utterly ashamed. Does this contradict Jesus's teaching in the Sermon on the Mount to love your enemies?
7. Can the glory of man and the glory of God coexist? In what way is David actually praying according to God's will?
8. Is David's prayer one of vengeance or for God's glory? In other words, is David's desire for his enemies to be ashamed man centered or God centered?
9. In verse 5 David says that he is "oppressed and needy" and desperate for God's help. Even though our situation may be different from David's, are we still, in essence, oppressed and needy? How so?
10. Surely David knows God's will is immanent, yet he still cries to him. If God is sovereign, why petition him?

Finishing Well: A Prayer for Senior Adults

PSALM 71

Main Idea: Aging believers can trust God to continue to be faithful to help them now and forever.

I.   Rely on God's Help (71:1-4,9-13).
II. Reflect on God's Faithfulness (71:5-8).
III. Relay God's Greatness (71:14-18).
IV. Rest in God's Resurrection (71:19-21).
V.   Rejoice in God's Deliverance (71:22-24).

Joe Paterno, head coach of the Penn State Nittany Lions from 1966 to 2011, won more football games than any other coach in history. In addition to his 409 victories, he led his teams to eighteen post-season bowl wins, two national championships, and five undefeated, untied seasons. But just eleven days after his final victory, Paterno was fired as head coach amidst a child sex abuse scandal involving a beloved assistant coach. Paterno was accused of concealing information related to the case. Consequently, fourteen years of Penn State's wins were nullified, and Paterno plummeted in the ranks of college football's winningest coaches. The great coach died of lung cancer within three months of his dismissal with a dark shadow hanging over his celebrated career. While Paterno's wins were later reinstated, he likely will be remembered more for the way he ended than for his decorated run of almost half a century. Some will always say that the most victorious coach in college football history didn't finish well.

Psalm 71 is about finishing well in the life of faith. Although we can't identify the writer, he's obviously old (vv. 9,18). This prayer was written by someone in the later stage of life. And if just the normal hassles of growing old weren't bad enough, this aging brother is still being harassed for his faith in God (vv. 10-11). Unidentified people have plotted together to take him out and are just waiting for the most opportune time to implement their coordinated plan. At its core the attack is on the psalmist's faith and the God in whom he trusts. These people claim God has abandoned him and left no one to come to his rescue.

Senior adults in the faith not only have to deal with the difficulties of aging but also with the continuing taunts of evil people who oppose their gospel and want to discredit their Lord. If a believer continues to live out his or her faith in the later stage of life, suffering will still come with the territory, as well as the responsibility to defend the faith. But while Christian seniors aren't exempt from these challenges, they usually are better able to deal with them. Their long history of experiencing God's faithfulness enables them to look with confidence at the present and the future. Their trust in our Lord for many years helps them be confident in their faith in the often tumultuous season of senior adulthood. The firm faith many of them learned as children and retained through their lives positions them to finish well amid the trials of their later years.

This psalm speaks of an aging saint who wants to finish well. Here's how godly seniors can do the same, as well as how all believers can pray for them to do so.

Rely on God's Help
PSALM 71:1-4,9-13

Like the beginning of Psalm 31, the first three verses are grounded in the affirmation that God is "my rock and fortress." This confession is supported by the introductory resolve in verse 1 as well as the imperative appeal in verse 3. The psalmist is affirming his confidence in God as his sufficient help, relying on his help, and appealing to him to rescue him and bring him to safety.

This introductory verse is followed by a litany of requests for God to come to the psalmist's aid (vv. 2,4,9,12). Images like "power" and "grasp" represent the strength of wicked and cruel people who have seized control of the psalmist, posing a threat to his life and faith. The threat seems to have arisen because God hasn't responded. He appears to be far away. So the sinking senior citizen is extending an urgent plea for God to leap into action and deliver him from the clutches of his pursuers.

The aging saint has learned to appeal to God's nature when he needs his help. First, he appeals to God's faithfulness by pleading,

"Let me never be disgraced" (v. 1), a fate he actually wants God to mete out to his enemies (v. 13). The psalmist trusted God through the years and doesn't want egg on his face now by being let down, an outcome that surely would tarnish God's reputation. Next, the psalmist appeals to God's "justice" (v. 2) to deliver him from his enemies. After all, a just God wouldn't allow wicked people to destroy his people and make fun of their faith in him. Finally, he appeals to God's strength and ability by requesting, "Give the command to save me" (v. 3). Certainly, that's what anyone would expect from one who is both rock and fortress.

Senior adults who have walked with God for many years have learned that the Lord is their first recourse in times of trouble, not their last resort. Their first reaction is to cry out for help and ask him to come to their aid. Because they've seen him respond faithfully so many times, they can rely on him with great confidence to do the same again. Furthermore, their intimate walks with our Lord through the years have given them a knowledge of him that forms the basis of their appeals. They know how to implore him based on his nature, something to which God is especially inclined to respond. And practically, senior adults—especially those who have physical restrictions—are able to take advantage of their faith experience by devoting more and more time to prayer. In most cases, if an aging saint can't do anything else, he or she can pray.

Reflect on God's Faithfulness
PSALM 71:5-8

When trouble comes, aging saints normally don't have to muster up confidence in God on the spot. It's been developed over a lifetime. This evolutionary confidence forms the foundation of the psalmist's prayer (vv. 5-6). The verb *leaned* carries the idea of being braced or upheld by someone or something for security. The image here is of the Lord taking care of him to make his life safe and secure, even since before birth (Ross, Vol. 2, 519).

The benefit of this lifelong stockpile of confidence in God hasn't been limited to the psalmist. He reflects on the fact that his whole life has been "like a miraculous sign to many" (v. 7). Because God is the source of this sign, his guidance and care of the psalmist has served as a solemn signal that should inspire others to obedience and worship. Because God has been faithful to shepherd the psalmist through all of life's dangers to a place of present safety, others should marvel at his journey and put their trust in God as well.

Serious reflection on God's faithfulness through the years will always result in worship. Because God has taken care of the psalmist and been his strong refuge, he is filled with praise (vv. 6,8). The word *honor* reflects God's fame and summarizes all the wonderful things he's done for the psalmist. Rehearsing this résumé in his mind leads the aging child of God to rejoice in his refuge all the time (Ross, *Psalms*, vol. 2, 521).

Senior adults who have known the Lord for a long time have stockpiled an arsenal of memories that will serve them well during the difficult days of growing old. There's something supernatural about reflecting on God's faithfulness that brings otherworldly help when tough times come. The grand assurance that the great "I AM" gave to Moses (Exod 3:13-15) belongs to every aging saint of God as well—he will continue to be what he has always been. He will do that through the person of Jesus Christ (John 8:56-58). Christian seniors can lean into their relationships with their Savior and trust him to see them through. They can be assured that he will be for them what he has always been.

Relay God's Greatness
PSALM 71:14-18

Strong confidence in God and his faithfulness is bidirectional. It not only prompts us to look back at the goodness he's demonstrated to us in the past, but it spurs us on to relate his greatness to others. As they become worshipers, the heritage of godliness is perpetuated into the future. The psalmist expresses a resolve to continue in faithful reliance on God and to pass that legacy on to others. Notice three outcomes.

First, relaying God's greatness means you never stop growing. Finishing well in the Christian life implies continuing to trust God and serve him all the way to the end. The psalmist determines to hope in God "continually" and to praise him "more and more." There's no sense here of a satisfaction that he's served his time and now it's somebody else's turn to step up. God is worthy of the praise of his people, and so the psalmist is intent on increasing his contribution as God faithfully comes to his aid. He vows to testify of God's saving acts of righteousness "all day long"—or continually—because God's awesome deeds are innumerable, and he's discovering more of them every day. This guy refuses to "get over" the greatness of God! Senior adults who finish well in the Christian life never let the glories of the gospel stop gripping them, and they never stop mining its depths.

Second, relaying God's greatness means you never stop testifying (v. 16). Because he's talking about praising God, he's likely referring here to his resolution to keep coming to the sanctuary to report on God's mighty acts. As long as he's physically able, he plans to gather with God's people and testify to his greatness. Further, only God's righteousness will be the subject of his testimony because he knows God's righteousness is his only hope of deliverance. Senior adults who finish well aren't consumed with the nostalgia of their own lives but instead with the résumé of God's righteousness. They are stingy protectors of his honor, and they never stop declaring it among his people.

Third, relaying God's greatness means you never stop discipling. The psalmist is committed to passing his godly heritage on to others who will continue the legacy (v. 17). He acknowledges that he was taught about God's greatness as a child and has faithfully run his leg of the race by proclaiming it during his lifetime. Now, as an aging man, he prays for God's grace to be faithful to pass the baton of trust in God on to those who will carry it forward (v. 18). One can't help but think here of Paul's allusion to carrying the gospel baton in a relay race and passing it on to others (2 Tim 1:3–2:2). Senior adults who finish well are those who continue to disciple younger people and pass the gospel heritage on to them.

Rest in God's Resurrection
PSALM 71:19-21

The psalmist seems to sigh with relief as he once again finds comfort in God's nature. God is a resurrecting God, one who lifts up his people even from their deathbed. Specifically, the psalmist finds rest by reflecting on the incomparable nature of God's righteousness that is beyond human comprehension. He intensifies his acknowledgment of this unparalleled quality, however, with a rhetorical question in the line that follows: "God, who is like you?" (v. 19). The psalmist finds great solace in remembering that God has done something that no other god can or would do: rescue the living from among the dead.

There may very well be an allusion to the exodus, especially in the phrase "Who is like you?" (cf. Exod 15:11), as well as with the picture of deliverance "from the depths of the earth" (cf. Exod 15:5). While it's not indicated in most English translations, some manuscripts have the aging saint shifting from the singular to the plural in verse 20 ("us" instead of "me"). This could be due to him seeing his dilemma as shared with others in the community of faith. He's not just expressing confidence in God for himself but on behalf of the whole nation (Ross, Vol. 2, 524-25). He's certain that same unrivaled God who brought the Israelites out of Egypt and through the Red Sea will once again show himself to be the strong deliverer of his people from their current predicament. He will raise them up in similar fashion.

The psalmist continues to rest in the assurance of God's righteous salvation in verse 20. The "depths" from which God's people will surely be raised likely refers to the subterranean abysses where masses of water were believed to be stored and where Sheol was located. The psalmist is comparing God's deliverance of his people with being rescued from the underworld. If God doesn't intervene, they will be lost forever! But he is confident God will come through (Ross, *Psalms*, vol. 2, 525).

Surely there's a foreshadow here of our resurrection in Christ. We are lost in our sins and are objects of the wrath of God. If he doesn't work on our behalf through the cross, then we are lost forever. Paul says,

> *But God proves his own love for us in that while we were still sinners, Christ died for us. How much more then, since we have now been declared righteous by his blood, will we be saved through him from wrath. For if, while we were enemies, we were reconciled to God through the death of his Son, then how much more, having been reconciled, will we be saved by his life.* (Rom 5:8-10)

So now we can say, "Indeed, we felt that we had received the sentence of death, so that we would not trust in ourselves but in God who raises the dead" (2 Cor 1:9). Although God makes us feel the weight of the troubles and calamities that come with being under the sentence of death (Ps 71:20), he delivers us by raising us from the dead in Christ Jesus! This new life alone makes it possible for us to run well and finish well.

The expression of the psalmist's rest in God's righteous salvation reaches its pinnacle in verse 21. He's confident God will not only rescue him from his current difficulty, but he will enable him to share in the honor of being a part of a revived and restored people. God will once again console him as he's done so many times before. The psalmist is certain God will give him the blissful rest that comes from being under his watchful eye, protecting hand, and resurrecting power.

In 1 Corinthians 15 Paul offers similar assurance to those whose hope is in Christ:

> *What I am saying, brothers and sisters, is this: Flesh and blood cannot inherit the kingdom of God, nor can corruption inherit incorruption. Listen, I am telling you a mystery: We will not all fall asleep, but we will all be changed, in a moment, in the twinkling of an eye, at the last trumpet. For the trumpet will sound, and the dead will be raised incorruptible, and we will be changed. For this corruptible body must be clothed with incorruptibility, and this mortal body must be clothed with immortality. When this corruptible body is clothed with incorruptibility, and this mortal body is clothed with immortality, then the saying that is written will take place:*
> *Death has been swallowed up in victory.*
> *Where, death, is your victory?*
> *Where, death, is your sting?*
> *The sting of death is sin, and the power of sin is the law. But thanks be to God, who gives us the victory through our Lord Jesus Christ!* (1 Cor 15:50-57)

In what Jesus Christ did when he died on the cross and rose from the dead, this psalm reaches its ultimate reality in the believer's life. In the gospel and its assurance of victory over death, God will increase our honor and comfort us again!

Rejoice in God's Deliverance
PSALM 71:22-24

The hope and confidence we have in God's deliverance provides great reason for worship. A final aspect of finishing well involves rejoicing in the salvation we know is to come. The last three verses of this psalm find the writer doing just that as he anticipates God providing strong deliverance. Kidner says, "So, with his name cleared and his faith con-firmed, this veteran can set his mind at rest, and his fingers, lips and heart to the praise of God and the telling of his story" (Kidner, *Psalms 1–72*, 272). This summary provides a pretty good outline for examining these verses.

First, the psalmist gives himself fully to the praise of God. He praises God by playing instruments, singing, and shouting. Even in his old age, the psalmist will continue to praise his God with every means possible because those who sought his life will be destroyed.

Second, the psalmist will tell God's story all of his days. He will speak constantly of God's faithfulness, redemption, and righteousness. To his dying breath, he will never stop telling others about how true God has been and how he has redeemed him from his darkest hour.

Third, the psalmist rests in the fact that his name has been cleared and his faith confirmed (v. 24). In Hebrew "disgraced" and "confounded" use the past tense to indicate the certainty of the fulfillment (Ross, Vol. 2, 526). The ones who once said, "God has abandoned him; . . . there is no one to rescue him" (v. 11) will have to eat their words because God has come to the aid of his servant. And having already addressed God as the "Holy One of Israel" (v. 22; cf. 78:41; 89:18), he acknowledges that his deliverer is distinct from the gods of the ancient world in his nature and works and that he's consecrated Israel to himself. The covenant God is the one who's cleared the psalmist's name and confirmed his faith.

What a description of the hope that aging saints have in the gospel of Christ! As their lives wind down, they can be confident that the Lord of the church will vindicate them in glory and that all of the enemies of truth will know of his victory (Rev 15:3; 18:20). They can worship him with all their hearts through instruments and songs and shouts. And they can use their voices—however frail and weak—to testify until their last breath how God in Christ has been faithful to all his promises to them, has redeemed them from sin and death through the cross, and has demonstrated his righteous salvation to them over and over again.

Conclusion

As I've worked through this passage, many in our denominational camp are still hurting from the news of another one of our leaders who has resigned in the wake of an inappropriate relationship. While this is just one of a way-too-long list of preachers and pastors who've lost their ministries amid similar scandals, this one has been particularly painful. This brother is one that so many of us saw as a model preacher, pastor, and kingdom leader. I've not been able to avoid the thought that if this can happen to him, it can happen to any of us!

Sexual and financial indiscretions aren't the only tragedies that can keep senior adults from finishing well. Aging Christians can be plagued by depression, anxiety, self-pity, pride, bitterness, laziness, and many other things that infiltrate their later years and cause them to be immobilized in the Christian life and the advancement of the gospel. Satan has so many ways he wants to attack older believers in order to undermine the many faithful and fruitful years they've served our Lord. But by God's grace older saints have so much to offer God and his people. Ross gets it right when he says,

> Blessed indeed is the congregation that has men and women who have walked with the Lord all through their lives. While it is important to bring young people, young families, into the Church to build for the future, that future will be shaped to a large degree by mature believers. And so it is encouraging to find a psalm that was written by a believer approaching old age who had trusted in the LORD all his life and continued to trust. His psalm draws on past experiences to build confidence for his prayer in the current crisis; and he draws on that confidence for his praise when the prayer is answered. (Ross, *Psalms*, vol. 2, 526–27)

As opposed to seeing Christian senior adults as liabilities and just anxiously waiting for them to die off, we need to learn from and lean on their faith. Our faith is strengthened by the testimony of these saints who've walked with God for many years and experienced his faithfulness time and time again. Security in our spiritual lives, stability in our congregations, and our faithfulness to the practice of desperate prayer all largely will hinge on the mature faith of these aging saints.

Reflect and Discuss

1. The psalmist is confident in God's sovereignty and ultimately his protection and deliverance. Does this, though, keep the psalmist from petitioning God? What can we learn from the psalmist's prayer?

2. An aging saint doesn't need convincing that God answers prayer. Wherever you are in your life, how does this example encourage you?

3. What does the psalmist appeal to in his prayer? In other words, on what basis does he invite God to act? Why does he do this?

4. Notice the psalmist's desire to relay God's greatness. Verse 14 implies that he desires to grow continually. What about you? How would you rate your desire to grow more and more in the Lord?

5. If you find yourself in a season that you aren't growing (or have no desire to grow), what is the problem, at its core? What steps can you take to cultivate spiritual growth in your life?

6. In verses 15-16 the psalmist desires to continually proclaim the Lord's goodness. Can your life be characterized by proclamation of God's goodness?

7. If your life is characterized by proclamation, in what ways do you do that? How can you encourage others to join you?

8. If you cannot say that your life is characterized by proclamation, in what ways can you grow in this area?

9. The psalmist desires to disciple others in the knowledge of God. Are you handing the baton of the gospel to the next generation? How can you make this a part of your life?

10. The psalmist, though he knows not yet fully the resurrection of Christ and our resurrection in him, is confident in God, who gives life from the dead. We, however, are in Christ. How should this encourage us?

Praying in View of the Coming Kingdom

PSALM 72

Main Idea: Jesus Christ ultimately will reign over an earthly kingdom marked by his righteousness, blessing, and eternal worship.

I. **Anticipate His Coming Kingdom (72:1-11).**
   A. Righteous judgment (72:1-7)
   B. Global dominion (72:8-11)
II. **Appeal to His Compassionate Heart (72:12-14).**
III. **Ask for His Concentric Blessing (72:15-17).**
IV. **Adore His Consecrated God (72:18-19).**

---

ouston, we have a problem." Those are the famous words spoken by actor Tom Hanks in the 1995 movie *Apollo 13* about the near-tragedy of the NASA spacecraft in 1970. The original words and their Hollywood edit reflected the discovery that one of the module's oxygen tanks had exploded, leaving the crew with a declining amount of breathable air. So a team of scientists and engineers were tasked with figuring out a way to generate oxygen. One of my favorite scenes in the movie is when the mission control guy comes into the room with the team of experts, dumps out a bunch of items on the table, and says, "Listen. This is what they have up there, and this is what you guys have right now. Let's build a filter, boys." In other words, "You have to solve the problem down here with only the resources they have up there."

Most Christians recognize that our world is in a mess. Because of the effects of sin, our planet is spinning out of control and destined for ultimate destruction. Yet God has assigned his children to dwell on this celestial ball and live out his redemptive mission until Jesus comes back for us. And sometimes—if we're honest—it doesn't appear that we have what we need to fulfill the task. That's why Jesus told us to pray, "Your kingdom come. Your will be done on earth as it is in heaven" (Matt 6:10). To say it another way, "Materialize on earth now what's going to characterize your kingdom later." Jesus wants us to pray that God will let us experience now some semblance of what we're going to experience when his kingdom finally comes.

The psalmist prays this way in Psalm 72. In its historical context this is one of the royal psalms focused on the life and well-being of Israel's king. It's one of only two psalms attributed to Solomon. While we can't be sure whether the superscription means this song was *to* him, *about* him, or *by* him, it's clearly associated with the vision of his enduring kingship, one that never ends! The psalmist is praying that God will establish and extend the king's righteous rule so that all nations will submit to his reign and experience God's blessings through him (Wilson, *Psalms*, 984).

The royal flavor of this song, however, extends far beyond Israel's monarchy. The idealistic language eclipses the reign of all of Israel's earthly kings and anticipates the glorious reign of the coming Messiah, Jesus Christ. As Ross says, he "will be the ideal king, what the world has been looking for; and his kingdom will be one of righteousness, peace and prosperity, the likes of which have never been seen on earth" (Ross, *Psalms*, vol. 2, 533). In anticipation of his long life and eternal reign, we can take our cue from Jesus and pray now for a deposit of what's coming in full later on. We can ask God to make a reality right now what we know is going to be a reality in the future kingdom to come. Here are four ways we can pray for the manifestation down here on earth of what we know they have up there in heaven—Christ's impending righteous rule.

Anticipate His Coming Kingdom
PSALM 72:1-11

Jesus teaches his disciples always to pray against the backdrop of his coming kingdom. He says, "Therefore, you should pray like this: Our Father in heaven, your name be honored as holy. Your kingdom come. Your will be done on earth as it is in heaven" (Matt 6:9-10). In Psalm 72 the psalmist unpacks two specific qualities he believes should mark the temporal king's reign. His requests help us know what we should expect to be manifested on earth through the reign of Christ Jesus.

Righteous Judgment (72:1-7)

The primary characteristics of the desired reign reflected in verses 1-7 are God's righteousness (vv. 1-3,7) and justice (vv. 1-2,4). Together they form his righteous judgment among the people. The request for God to "give" (v. 1) these qualities to the king is the only imperative verb form in the psalm and, therefore, seems to summarize the heartbeat of the entire poem. The psalmist is praying for God to give the king the necessary resources to rule justly and righteously over his people. He knows this coveted characteristic can only be found in God. Like Solomon's prayer for wisdom in 1 Kings 3:9-28,

> the petition is not simply that the king make good decisions, but that he do it according to God's decisions and God's righteousness. But the prayer would go beyond that to appeal for God's decisions and God's righteousness to govern the heart and mind of the king. If the king is God's representative, he must think like God. (Ross, *Psalms*, vol. 2, 536)

The only chance the king—or "the king's son" (v. 1)—has of exercising righteous judgment is if God gives it to him.

If God graciously grants this request for the king to have his character and subsequent ability to reign in righteous judgment, four results will occur. The first result is that the king will rule accordingly. If God grants the capacity, the king will act fittingly because such righteous judgment is the first virtue of government in Scripture. The Mosaic law forbids partiality in judgment, regardless of whether it favors the poor or the rich (Exod 23:3,6). While not everyone in the nation was poor, the poor needed impartial treatment more than anyone else. So if the king didn't judge them with righteousness and justice, he wasn't truly a righteous king.

We find a second result of the king's reigning with God's character and ability in verse 3. The Israelites believed the stability of their theocratic nation was manifested in nature. In other words, if the people were obedient, then their land would be blessed (Ross, *Psalms*, vol. 2, 537). If the king shepherded the people in righteousness and justice, they would benefit from a fruitful harvest.

The third result of having God's character and ability is that the king will vindicate the oppressed. If a righteous king is going to defend the poor and deliver the needy under his care, he also will have to defeat those who oppress them.

The fourth result is that the king's reign will be prolonged. The qualifying phrases (vv. 5-7) all reflect the desire for the king's administration of righteous judgment to be perpetuated as long as physical creation exists. The language of the psalmist here seems to extend past the reign of whichever king was currently on the throne. The author likely is thinking about the king's dynasty, in which his righteous reign will be perpetuated through his descendants.

This sustained rule will be marked not only by the people's physical prosperity but also by their spiritual prosperity: fear of God (v. 5; cf. 2:11) and peace with God (v. 7). The Israelites knew that a righteous king always influenced his subjects for good, while a wicked king influenced them for evil. The king who is the subject of this prayer will be a blessing to the spiritual lives of the people, just like rain on dry ground (v. 6). The similes here suggest that the king's reign will benefit the people with both spiritual nourishment and refreshment (Ross, Vol. 2, 538). If the king judges righteously, then his people will fear God and experience the spiritual prosperity of righteousness and peace.

Is it any wonder that our Lord spent so much of his time with the poor, needy, neglected, and outcast? Jesus's kingship was marked by a mission to relieve their suffering. In the synagogue in Nazareth, he read from Isaiah's prophecy:

> The Spirit of the Lord is on me, because he has anointed me to preach good news to the poor. He has sent me to proclaim release to the captives and recovery of sight to the blind, to set free the oppressed, to proclaim the year of the Lord's favor. (Luke 4:18-19; cf. Isa 61:1-2)

Then he closed the scroll and said, "Today as you listen, this Scripture has been fulfilled" (Luke 4:21). That's just another way of saying, "Isaiah was talking about me!" Jesus knew that God anointed him as King to bring the good news of release, relief, and recovery to those who are suffering. The psalmist's words foreshadowed the coming of one who reigns with this kind of righteousness and justice.

If this kind of righteous rule and justice is the agenda of our Lord, it certainly compels his disciples to pray and work to the same end during our time on earth. Jesus said the criteria of his final judgment would be based—at least in part—on whether we ministered to him by ministering to "the least of these brothers and sisters of mine" (Matt 25:40). Consequently, we'd better be about the business—both in prayer and in deed—of meeting the needs of the hungry, thirsty, strangers, naked, sick, and imprisoned. Christians should be on the front lines of prayer and action that aims to eliminate all forms of abuse, racial prejudice, and other social injustice. Additionally, we must give ourselves to sacrificial prayer on behalf of our brothers and sisters in Christ who are being persecuted for their faith all across the globe.

While the human author speaks of the current king's dynasty and the people's subsequent spiritual benefit, and even implies our own ministry of righteous justice and compassion, the divine author in Psalm 72 surely has more in mind. The descriptions in verses 5-7 clearly anticipate the earthly rule of the eternal King who one day will reign on the earth. In the book of Revelation, John witnesses the host of heaven worshiping the only one who is able to secure the title deed to the earth:

> And they sang a new song: You are worthy to take the scroll and to open its seals, because you were slaughtered, and you purchased people for God by your blood from every tribe and language and people and nation. You made them a kingdom and priests to our God, and they will reign on the earth. (Rev 5:9-10)

The aged apostle also says the redeemed subjects of this earthly kingdom "will be priests of God and of Christ, and they will reign with him for a thousand years" (Rev 20:6; cf. 20:4). While many questions are yet to be answered about what all this looks like, Scripture indicates that Christ one day will reign supremely over an earthly kingdom for an extended period of time, and righteousness and justice will be the order of the day (Matt 25:31-46). Everyone will fear the Lord, and peace will abound. Disciples of Christ must always pray for his exercise of justice in view of this ultimate outcome.

Global Dominion (72:8-11)

After praying that the king will reign in the righteousness and justice of God, the psalmist asks that his power and authority extend throughout the whole earth. This planetary power begins with geographic governance and concludes with human homage. This progression highlights the important theme in Psalms 56–72 of the growing anticipation that God will rule the earth and that all kings and nations will acknowledge his reign and worship him.

If there's going to be global dominion, then all the kings of the earth must submit to God's chosen king (cf. Ps 2:10-12). So the psalmist specifies the adherence he thinks the king deserves. He first prays for the allegiance of the "desert tribes," likely the nomadic tribes on each side of the Arabian Gulf who typically were difficult to control. The "kings of Tarshish and the coasts and islands" refer to those in the western part of the Mediterranean Sea. "Sheba and Seba" were kingdoms in the southern Arabian Peninsula and possibly even Ethiopia. All of these will "kneel before him . . . lick the dust . . . bring tribute . . . offer gifts," expressions indicative of their complete defeat, humiliation, subservience, and allegiance (Ross, Vol. 2, 539).

One can't read the psalmist's prayer here and not see allusions to the Davidic covenant in 2 Samuel 7 as well as the descriptions of the extent of the Solomonic empire in 1 Kings 4:21-24, especially the tribute that came from all the kingdoms. However, the answer to this prayer was never fully realized in any of Israel's historical kings. And—while in exile—the people continued to long for one who would restore Israel and fulfill God's purposes; "this language of hope in *human* kingship is transferred to a future 'son of David'— the Messiah—who will usher in the kingdom of God" (Wilson, *Psalms*, 988). The prophet Daniel said,

> *I continued watching in the night visions, and suddenly one like a son of man was coming with the clouds of heaven. He approached the Ancient of Days and was escorted before him. He was given dominion, and glory, and a kingdom; so that those of every people, nation, and language should serve him. His dominion is an everlasting dominion that will not pass away, and his kingdom is one that will not be destroyed.* (Dan 7:13-14)

Such must be the focus of our prayer. The psalmist's prayer certainly looks beyond any political kingdom to a worldwide kingdom, one that is only realized through the fulfillment of messianic prophecies in the reign of King Jesus over all the earth (Matt 28:18; John 17:2; Eph 1:20-22; Phil 2:9-11; Col 1:16; Rev 11:15). To that end believers in Christ must pray today.

Appeal to His Compassionate Heart
PSALM 72:12-14

Before getting caught up in this description of the king's reign, the psalmist models a second way to pray for his kingdom. He appeals to his compassionate heart. These verses reveal the primary reason the writer believes the nations of the world should submit to this righteous king: this king makes it his practice to show compassion for the oppressed, both in emotion and engagement. Expanding the thought of verse 4, the psalmist articulates the king's responsibility to defend the defenseless and to help those who can't help themselves.

The objects of the king's kindness are the poor, afflicted, and "helpless." All of these people are victims of "oppression and violence." The word *oppression* means "to tread underfoot" and describes the exploitation of powerless people by those who have power. The word *violence* reflects the insensitive indifference toward the lives of these helpless and hopeless people being abused. "Their lives" refers to their souls, the core of their identity as created by God (Wilson, Vol. 1, 989). The stakes are high here. Even if these helpless people don't lose their lives physically under this oppression, they're still in danger of losing their self-worth as human beings as well as their will to live.

The primary feature of these verses is the response of this king. He is described here as a champion of justice on behalf of the oppressed. His compassionate response is shocking and puts him in a class by himself. The psalmist says that when the poor cry out, this ruler of righteousness springs into action. He acts out his compassion as he rescues them and saves their lives. Because this righteous ruler highly prizes them and considers their lives to be "precious," he "redeems" them. He acts as their kinsman-redeemer, rescuing them, paying off their debts, vindicating them, and preserving their property and name.

In that day royalty just weren't known for acting this way toward their subjects! "It is hard to imagine any ruler paying so much attention to those with the greatest needs" (Ross, *Psalms*, vol. 2, 542). This king is different, however, because he has "pity" on those he shepherds. This word is particularly descriptive and actually reflects the idea behind all the other responses described in these verses. While it means to be troubled about something or to look compassionately on someone, it goes a step further. To pity someone includes the idea of sparing them. Two-thirds of the times this word is used, the eye is its subject, whether the eye of God or of a human. To have pity involves action—doing something about the person's plight when you see it. Ross says, "It is difficult to withhold compassion and pity when one is looking at the sufferer" (Ross, *Psalms*, vol. 2, 541). So this king has a sentiment of concern on steroids—he acts on his attitude and puts feet to his feelings! His "defense is not the result of some cold, legalistic administration of law but flows from a true sense of compassion that mirrors the compassion of God" (Wilson, *Psalms*, 989).

Four particular applications come to mind. First, thank God for his mercy and grace toward believers in Christ. Let's not fail to see ourselves in this passage. We were the oppressed, needy, and poor because of our sin. We were weak and had no helper. But Paul said, "For while we were still helpless, at the right time, Christ died for the ungodly" (Rom 5:6; cf. Eph 2:1-10; Titus 3:5), and "Christ redeemed us from the curse of the law by becoming a curse for us" (Gal 3:13). When we were helpless to do anything about our sin problem, our Redeemer protected and provided for his own. Our King assumed the responsibility to restore the oppressed. Because he considered our blood precious, he shed his own on our behalf that we might flourish in his righteous kingdom. May we never cease to praise and thank him for his mercy and compassion!

Second, pray regularly for our fellow Christians who are the victims of oppression and violence because of their faith. In the last year it's estimated that as many as 215 million believers experienced high or extreme levels of persecution in the fifty countries where it's most difficult to live as a follower of Christ (https://billygraham.org/story/franklin-graham-persecution-on-an-unprecedented-scale/). Our brothers and sisters in Christ are facing beatings, abductions, rape, torture, forced marriages, and death. If Psalm 72:12-14 accurately reflects the nature and demeanor of our King, then he stands ready to act accordingly in response to the prayers of his people. Let's cry out to our heavenly helper on behalf of those in our family who have no helper. Pray for their boldness to speak for Christ (Eph 6:19-20), their rest in the sufficiency of God's grace (2 Cor 12:9), their reliance on God's power (2 Cor 1:7-9), their deliverance by God's strong hand (Matt 26:39; Acts 12:1-17; 2 Cor 12:8), and their positive influence on their persecutors (Luke 6:27-31). As the Puritans said, let's sue God for his help for them based on his compassionate nature and his just and righteous reign.

Third, appeal to Christ's character on behalf of those in our society who are the victims of domestic and sexual abuse, prejudice and discrimination, and all other forms of social injustice. Thankfully, in the United States we currently are experiencing a heightened sensitivity to unfair practices toward segments of our population who've been the objects of all kinds of unfair practices. Believers in Christ should be leading this charge because it's our Lord's heartbeat. In his own hometown synagogue Jesus claimed Isaiah 61:1-2 as his marching orders:

> *The scroll of the prophet Isaiah was given to him, and unrolling the scroll, he found the place where it was written:*
>   *The Spirit of the Lord is on me, because he has anointed me to preach good news to the poor. He has sent me to proclaim release to the captives and recovery of sight to the blind, to set free the oppressed, to proclaim the year of the Lord's favor.*

> *He then rolled up the scroll, gave it back to the attendant, and sat down. And the eyes of everyone in the synagogue were fixed on him. He began by saying to them, "Today as you listen, this Scripture has been fulfilled."* (Luke 4:17-21; cf. Matt 25:31-46)

As Christians, we know that the ultimate answer to all injustice is the gospel. And we have a King who has a sensitive ear to the cries of the suffering, as well as to the cries of his children who advocate on their behalf. Let's pray for our righteous and just Judge to deliver the oppressed.

Stemming from this responsibility of praying for victims is the obligation to pray for and work toward the election and administration of government leaders who will work for social justice. The prophet Micah is clear when he says, "Mankind, [God] has told each of you what is good and what it is the Lord requires of you: to act justly, to love faithfulness, and to walk humbly with your God" (Mic 6:8). Because Psalm 72 looks forward to the messianic kingdom, it passes judgment on the failure of Israel's monarchy to meet the expectations of God for justice, equity, righteousness, mercy, and compassion. Such is true for every government before and after that time. Because God is the one who made us, he holds us all—believers and unbelievers alike—to his standard and leaves us without excuse (see Rom 1:32–2:1).

This accountability includes our politicians and other government leaders. They are responsible for executing God's expectations for social justice whether they acknowledge him or not. Wilson is right:

> While we may need to modify our strident, religiously oriented rhetoric in order to gain a hearing from secular politicians and leaders, we need not sacrifice God's standards of justice, equity, compassion, and truth to the modern "god" of pragmatism. God calls us, Psalm 72 calls us, not only to pray for the well-being of our leaders but for their wisdom to see that all justice is ultimately God's justice and that righteousness is not measured by what works but by the character of God, who empowers leaders and who will ultimately set all things right. (Wilson, *Psalms*, 995)

While Christians don't believe righteousness can be legislated, we do have the responsibility of fostering—through prayer and involvement—the election and action of government leaders who reflect God's character and standards.

Ask for His Concentric Blessing
PSALM 72:15-17

A third way to pray for the coming kingdom is to ask God to use his king as an impetus for blessing the whole world. The psalmist next summarizes his desire for the enduring, prosperous, and comprehensive reign of this king. In keeping with all of Psalm 72, the universal accolades desired here certainly reflect the wisdom, affluence, and sway that characterized Solomon's reign, all of which were illustrated by the visit of the admiring queen of Sheba (Wilson, *Psalms*, 990; see 1 Kgs 9–10). The psalmist specifically asks that God's blessing on the king be effectual in ever-widening concentric circles of influence. Like the ripples created by a stone thrown into a calm pond, he prays for these blessings to start with the king himself and then extend to the nation and ultimately to the entire world.

The widespread blessing of the king begins with God's favor. The psalmist prays that the king will have long life. Who wouldn't want a righteous king who loved his people and led them well to live a long time? So the psalmist asks that the king be given tribute to fund an extended reign. While the riches of Sheba are specifically mentioned based on Solomon's experience, all kinds of homage are desired. The psalmist also requests that people constantly intercede for the king and bless him. The people should cry out to God on behalf of this king and express praise and thanksgiving for his leadership.

The psalmist anticipates that God's favor on the king's life will be extended to the people he shepherds. He prays that God's blessing would cause both the land and the people to flourish under his reign. Regarding the land, he wants the fertile fruit of the land to be visible to all and to be of a quality equal to the best known to mankind. Regarding the people, the psalmist asks that they multiply and flourish in the same way as the fruit of the land.

The psalmist foresees the favor of God on the king ultimately affecting everybody on the planet. As the population and produce of the kingdom swell, the king's reputation certainly will expand in like manner. As his reputation expands, the psalmist desires that the beneficiaries of the blessing will naturally become the ones who bless. Ross explains: "The blessing that people derive from this king would be so great that they consider it the highest blessing they can have, and so they praise and honor him for the bliss that he imparts" (Ross, *Psalms*, vol. 2, 544).

As we think about praying for the widespread blessing of the king, we need to consider it from three standpoints. From a **civil** standpoint, we as citizens are the beneficiaries of the concentric circles of God's common and uncommon grace on our nation's leaders. Paul says,

> *Let everyone submit to the governing authorities, since there is no authority except from God, and the authorities that exist are instituted by God. So then, the one who resists the authority is opposing God's command, and those who oppose it will bring judgment on themselves. For rulers are not a terror to good conduct, but to bad. Do you want to be unafraid of the authority? Do what is good, and you will have its approval. For it is God's servant for your good. But if you do wrong, be afraid, because it does not carry the sword for no reason. For it is God's servant, an avenger that brings wrath on the one who does wrong.* (Rom 13:1-4)

That's why he also charges that "petitions, prayers, intercessions, and thanksgivings be made for everyone, for kings and all those who are in authority, so that we may lead a tranquil and quiet life in all godliness and dignity" (1 Tim 2:1-3). As believers in Christ, we must assault the throne of God on behalf of our political leaders because we know God's favor on them reverberates outward into our lives.

From a **missional** standpoint, disciples of Christ must pray for the advancement of the gospel to the farthest corners of the earth. The prayer that people be blessed in the king and that all nations bless him is arguably an allusion to God's promise to Abraham that all nations will be blessed through his seed (Gen 12:3). That promise is to be fulfilled through the Davidic covenant. So as we make disciples of all nations (Matt 28:18-20), the blessing people receive from the gospel of King Jesus will not only be the greatest blessing they ever receive, but it will compel them to worship him for the blissful happiness they experience. He is worthy of that worship, so let's pray to that end.

Finally, from an **eschatological** standpoint, Christ's disciples should pray for his eternal kingdom to come. Notice the qualifiers "forever" and "as long as the sun." Again, the psalmist obviously is tipping his hat—whether knowingly or unknowingly—to a kingdom that extends far beyond that of the current king. This kingdom is an *eternal* kingdom. In the heavenly reign of our Lord, the kingdom will have no end because King Jesus will reign forever and ever (Rom 11:36; Eph 3:21; 1 Pet 4:11; 5:11; Jude 25; Rev 1:6; 5:13). So let's always be praying that his name endures and his fame continues as long as the sun, forever and ever! Come quickly, Lord Jesus!

Adore His Consecrated God
PSALM 72:18-19

Psalm 72 is a prayer for the king to reign with righteousness and justice, which is a worthy expectation because of his godly nature. So the psalmist is compelled to turn his attention to the God who has established him (v. 19). Many scholars believe verses 18-19 were added to Psalm 72 as the closing doxology of this whole section of the Psalter (see Goldingay, Vol. 2, 395). Psalm 72 is the final psalm in Book II (see v. 20) and concludes in a similar way as Books I, III, and IV. The combined praise of Psalms 146–150 form the conclusion of Book V and of the whole Psalter. But while the high praise of verses 18-19 certainly serve to conclude Psalms 42–72, they also add vivid color to the worldwide vision that has just unfolded in 72:1-17 (Kidner, *Psalms 1–72*, 277). These words of worship provide a fitting response to the message of this particular royal psalm and prompt the reader to a fourth prayer response for the coming kingdom. Christ followers should continue to adore the one true God who has raised up this king and who is to be consecrated above all.

The psalmist praises God by acknowledging, attributing, asking, and agreeing. He first acknowledges that God "alone does wonders." God does wonderful works in nature and in history, and in heaven and on earth, but the zenith of his work—according to this psalm—is raising up a king like no other king, one who rules with righteousness and justice. The God of the universe is to be adored for establishing a king and a kingdom characterized by his own nature of compassion and uprightness.

On the heels of this acknowledgment, the psalmist attributes to God the glory he deserves. He previously prayed for the king's name to endure forever (v. 17). The foundation of such a request is the fact that the good reputation of the king will last because the glorious reputation of the God who set him on his throne will last.

Then the psalmist extols God by proclaiming, "The whole earth is filled with his glory." He wants the praise for the majesty of God's being to be known to all of mankind. This affirmation is a fitting end to the theme that's been developed in Psalms 56–72, where there's been an increasing emphasis on the universal rule of God. The nations acknowledge his authority and submit to it, and they join together in an expanding chorus of praise to his name. Phrases like *the whole earth* and *the ends of the earth* repeatedly announce the boundless nature of the worldwide dominion of God (Wilson, *Psalms*, 991). What an appropriate conclusion to this psalm and this whole book in the Psalter, and what an appropriate prayer for the people of God in every generation. Let the whole earth be filled with his glory!

Finally, the psalmist ends with a statement of reinforced, universal agreement: "Amen and amen." It's the only suitable way to respond to this glorious God who does wondrous works, whose glorious name deserves eternal worship, and whose glory must one day fill the whole earth. These closing words of this prayer foreshadow the believer's longing for the ultimate arrival of the King of kings and for the grace we need to wait faithfully for him. John writes, "He who testifies about these things says, 'Yes, I am coming soon.' Amen! Come, Lord Jesus! The grace of the Lord Jesus be with everyone. Amen" (Rev 22:20-21). When that time comes, the worthiness of this righteous and just God will rule the day!

Again, however, the psalmist's attention in these final verses isn't on the king but on the God who establishes him. Mysteriously, Paul suggests believers must live in a similar tension when it comes to our ultimate anticipation of the coming kingdom. While we long for the eternal reign of our Lord Jesus Christ, we are compelled to set our long-term sight on the glory of the God who ordained the rule of King Jesus. Unfolding the events at the end of the age and the coming of Christ, Paul writes,

> For he must reign until he puts all his enemies under his feet. The last enemy to be abolished is death. For God has put everything under his feet. Now when it says "everything" is put under him, it is obvious that he who puts everything under him is the exception. When everything is subject to Christ, then the Son himself will also be subject to the one who subjected everything to him, so that God may be all in all. (1 Cor 15:25-28)

I've never claimed to be able to explain the mystery of the triune God, and I certainly can't do it here. But by faith, as we pray for the eternal reign of Jesus Christ, let's do it in an atmosphere of adoration for the God who inaugurated his reign, the one who ultimately will be "all in all."

Conclusion

Psalm 72 closes with the only instructional postscript in the entire Psalter: "The prayers of David son of Jesse are concluded" (v. 20). While David is the dominant author in Books I and II, some of the psalms are anonymous (e.g., Pss 10; 33; 44; 66; 67) or attributed to other people (Asaph in Ps 50; Solomon in Ps 72; Sons of Korah in Pss 42; 44–49). A common denominator, however, is reflected in the term *prayers*, which indicates petition or entreaty on behalf of a sufferer. The pervasive presence of laments in this section of the Psalter makes this an appropriate description of its primary emphasis (Wilson, *Psalms*, 992).

However, while these *recorded* laments are ended, the longing is not. The immediate expectation of the psalmist and his fellow Israelites was that an earthly king would usher in a prosperous, golden age like Solomon's that would be characterized by the content of Psalm 72. But that didn't happen (see 1 Kgs 10–12). The nation of Israel never had a king that ruled like this. In fact, the entire world has never seen that kind of a truly righteous king or a righteous government. We so desperately need one! So the children of Israel continued to lament, and we continue to lament, longing for

> a king and his country; for a leader and his enterprise; for *the* King and the consummation of his kingdom, into which "the kings of the earth shall bring their glory", and "by (whose) light shall the nations walk" (Rev 21:24). (Kidner, *Psalms 1–72*, 257; emphasis in original)

This psalm gives us hope, however. It moves toward an eschatological restoration of God's original creation through the work of the coming Messiah. The prophets told of his reign on earth, and the New Testament confirms their words in its testimony of the second coming of Jesus Christ. Right now, he sits enthroned at the right hand of God. But all things haven't yet submitted to his rule (1 Cor 15:20-28). His righteousness doesn't currently fill the earth. The entire creation is groaning, waiting for the day of his redemption (Rom 8:18-25). But make no mistake—he is coming. When he does, he will reign over a kingdom on earth. Righteousness and justice will win the day and flourish. The land will overflow with fruitfulness. And every tribe, nation, tongue, and government on earth will submit to him and be blessed through him (Ross, *Psalms*, vol. 2, 546). Come quickly, Lord Jesus! Long live the King, and may he give us a taste right now of what's coming in the future!

Reflect and Discuss

1. Jesus told us to pray, "Your kingdom come. Your will be done on earth as it is in heaven." What are some of the current realities in heaven that we should be praying and expecting to experience here and now on earth?
2. What are some relational dynamics in heaven that we should be living here on earth?
3. According to Revelation 21:1-7, what are some things about heaven that we can begin prayerfully implementing here in our relationships with others?
4. What are three to five recent ways God has shown mercy and compassion toward you?
5. Who in your circle of influence is in need of experiencing God's mercy and compassion afresh?
6. How might you be merciful and compassionate to them on God's behalf?
7. Which specific local and national leaders could you begin praying that God's favor and blessing would rest on?
8. How might you begin regularly and strategically interceding for them?
9. How do we live in the tension of the now/not yet of the kingdom? What can we legitimately expect to manifest here and now versus that for which we will have to wait?
10. We say, "Your kingdom come. Your will be done," and we hope that some aspect of God's rule will be manifest in the here and now. What role does our relationship with God in prayer play in our discerning what we should expect to see?

Good to Be Near God

PSALM 73

Main Idea: While focusing on the wicked leads to envy, regret, and doubt, focusing on God and on his Word gives us a proper perspective on sin, judgment, and the faithfulness of God to his people.

I. **Two Perspectives**
   A. When he sees the wicked (73:1-16)
      1. He envies how they live.
      2. He regrets how he lives.
      3. He wrestles with how God works.
   B. When he sees God (73:17-28)
      1. He remembers their future.
      2. He realizes his foolishness.
      3. He rejoices in God's faithfulness.
II. **Two Exhortations**
   A. Trust in God's goodness.
   B. Tell others about God's greatness.

While I was in college in Athens, Georgia, I vividly remember the preacher in a Methodist church walking verse by verse through Psalm 73. I was at a pretty pivotal, and you might say vulnerable, point in my relationship with God. By God's grace, I had come to know Christ at an early age, and I had grown up in the church, grounded in my faith. When I went to college, I began to see a number of friends who I thought were pretty grounded in their faith begin to turn aside from God. They began to compromise their faith in Christ, choosing instead the ways of the world. Here's the catch: *they seemed to enjoy it.*

Quite honestly, my friends seemed to be having a lot of fun. I, on the other hand, seemed to be missing out on a lot of things. In this way, I felt a lot like the psalmist. I looked at the world around me, even at the way of those who had turned aside from God, and everyone else seemed to be prospering and enjoying life in a way that I wasn't. I could identify with verse 13. It seemed that the pursuit of holiness on this campus was all in vain. Where does it get you? And look at all that it keeps you from—socially, sexually, and in a myriad of other ways.

I could also identify with verse 2. In some ways my feet did stumble, and my steps did slip. I now look back on that time with the perspective of verses 21-22: "I was stupid." What was I thinking?

Many Christians are prone to struggle in the same way the psalmist struggled. There is, for example, a huge tension when it comes to an issue like sexual immorality. Scripture tells us to flee all sexual activity outside of marriage (1 Cor 6:12-20), and we know God is looking out for our good. However, the ways of this world can certainly *look* a lot better than God's ways. God's Word can start to sound too extreme. The same is true when it comes to the pursuit of pleasure and the achievement of status. We see non-Christians and nominal Christians prospering, and it seems as if things are going better for them than for us. We feel like we're missing out, and our feet begin to slip.

Maybe your feet have slipped, or maybe your steps are on the verge of stumbling. It could be that God, in his grace and in his love for you, has brought you to this psalm. Faith is a struggle, and this psalm deals with real life.

The author of this psalm is Asaph, a Levite who is basically serving as a worship leader among God's people. Deep down in his heart, he knows God is good (v. 1). This psalm is not the doubting of someone who is opposed to God or someone trying to prove God isn't good. No, this is the doubting of someone who believes God is good. At the same time, the psalmist is honest about his struggles. We will consider this psalm, then, from two perspectives.

Two Perspectives

In the first half of this psalm Asaph speaks from the perspective of one who is observing the wicked. In the second half he speaks from the perspective of one who has seen God. Seeing God rightly changes the way we see everything else.

When He Sees the Wicked (73:1-16)

When the psalmist sees the wicked flourishing, three things happen.

He envies how they live. The psalms are arranged into five books, and Psalm 73 is the first psalm in Book III. However, if you go back to Psalm 1 (the first psalm in Book I), there seems to be a tension between it and Psalm 73. In short, Psalm 1 says that the righteous will prosper and the wicked will perish. But then in Psalm 73 the psalmist essentially asks whether this is true. When he looks around, it certainly doesn't *seem* to be true. He envies the wicked. They enjoy sexual pleasure and success (as defined by the world) and the luxuries this world offers. He hears God's radical call to obedience, but when he looks around at the wicked, there seems to be another way, a better way, in this world.

In Psalm 73 the psalmist describes those around him who are disobeying God:

- They die peacefully (v. 4).
- They're blessed physically (vv. 4-5).
- They flourish with pride (vv. 6,9,11).
- They avoid pain (v. 12).
- They enjoy prosperity (v. 12).

He regrets how he lives. When the psalmist focuses on the flourishing of the wicked, he looks at his own life, and he concludes that *he has pursued purity in vain* (v. 13). That's quite a statement, but it's one we can identify with. We wonder whether it's really worth it to live in radical obedience to the commands of Christ, to submit to Scripture's standards of sexual purity, to simplify life in this world in order to sacrifice and give more away. Is there really a reward in righteousness?

In addition, Asaph concludes that *he has suffered constantly in silence* (vv. 14-15). It's as if he knows nothing of the man described in Psalm 1: "He is like a tree planted beside flowing streams that bears its fruit in its season and whose leaf does not wither. Whatever he does prospers" (v. 3). No, he feels the exact opposite, and he acknowledges that he has kept his suffering to himself. He did not want to lead the people of God to question God. This struggle is yet another way in which this psalm is so helpful, because it shows a healthy way to wrestle with doubt.

He wrestles with how God works. The psalmist wrestles with his faith honestly, but he keeps it between himself and God rather than letting it become a hindrance to others in their faith. He shows us how to ask questions and how to struggle in our faith while not pulling other people away from God. Again we can identify with the psalmist. There is much to wrestle with in a world where sex traffickers are flourishing, godless leaders are ruling, and sinners are succeeding. Why does God allow all this? Is he not powerful enough to stop this? If he is just, then why doesn't he put an end to this wickedness?

Thankfully, in the second half of this psalm there's another perspective. The transition begins in verse 16. When you try to understand the wickedness of the world in light of the goodness of God, it can wear you out. It certainly did for the psalmist. Then he "entered God's sanctuary."

When He Sees God (73:17-28)

When the psalmist goes into the presence of God, even amid all his questions, his entire perspective changes. We'll consider three ways he is affected.

He remembers their future. In verse 17 it's as if he was looking at a fat cow enjoying a meal on its way to the slaughter. Despite his earlier evaluation the psalmist realizes he doesn't want to head in the same direction as the wicked. He remembers their future.

A dream can seem so long and real, but then we wake up and realize it was only a matter of seconds and it was never real. That's the way of the wicked (v. 20). They are phantoms, these seemingly delightful men and women who in a matter of seconds find themselves despised by God.

The language in these verses is severe. The wicked will "fall into ruin" (v. 18) and "become a desolation!" (v. 19). They will be "swept away by terrors" (v. 19). Oh, how our perspective changes when we lift our eyes to God! We're reminded of Paul's words in 1 Corinthians 6:9-10:

> Don't you know that the unrighteous will not inherit God's kingdom?
> Do not be deceived: No sexually immoral people, idolaters, adulterers,
> or males who have sex with males, no thieves, greedy people,
> drunkards, verbally abusive people, or swindlers will inherit God's
> kingdom.

Similar warnings come in the book of Revelation: "Come out of her [the sinful world system], my people, so that you will not share in her sins or receive any of her plagues" (Rev 18:4). "But the cowards, faithless, detestable, murderers, sexually immoral, sorcerers, idolaters, and all liars—their share will be in the lake that burns with fire and sulfur, which is the second death" (Rev 21:8).

What is it about seeing God that causes the psalmist to remember the future of the wicked? The psalmist sees the justice of God. He sees that the wicked will ultimately be judged for their sins. And the same is true for the wicked around us today. God is not asleep when it comes to sex trafficking or sexual immorality or any other sin in this world. *He* will rouse himself, and *he* will assert his justice. God is active: "*You* put them in slippery places; *you* make them fall into ruin. . . . *You* will despise their image" (vv. 18,20; emphasis added).

He realizes his foolishness. In verses 21-22 the psalmist acknowledges his error. It's as if the psalmist steps back with an entirely new perspective and thinks, *Who do I think I am to be qualified to question the judgment of God or the goodness of God?* Seeing God rightly helps us see how foolish it is to view the world without considering his judgment against sin and his gracious purposes for his people.

He rejoices in God's faithfulness. Beginning in verse 23, the rest of this psalm is a poetic masterpiece that celebrates the majesty and mercy of God. This psalm ends with a description of how the fullness of pleasure in God far outweighs the fleeting, phantom prosperity of the wicked described in the first part of this psalm. With God there is real joy, real pleasure, and real delight. Indeed, Psalm 1 is ultimately true: The one who fears the Lord is blessed.

Asaph describes the faithfulness of God in four ways. First, *God grasps him* (v. 23). I love those moments when one of my kids reaches up and grabs my hand, and we walk together holding hands. Now picture the God of the universe holding you by the hand!

Second, *God guides him* (v. 24a). In this life we don't always know what to do or what is best for us. Whether we're talking about small decisions or big decisions, we look for counsel from people around us. That is good and wise, but it's even better to look for counsel from God—and find it! As he promised, God counsels us by his Holy Spirit who dwells in us, the one described as the "Counselor" (John 14:16).

Third, *God will glorify him* (v. 24b). Having just remembered the future of the wicked, the psalmist now remembers the future of the righteous (those who put their hope and their trust in God). He anticipates what Jesus will later say in the Sermon on the Mount: "Blessed are the pure in heart, for they will see God" (Matt 5:8).

Ultimately, the psalmist concludes that *God is good to him* (vv. 25-26). What a turnaround! Here's a psalmist who had almost stumbled when he perceived the wicked, but now, with a new perspective, he concludes, "Those far from you will certainly perish; you destroy all who are unfaithful to you. But as for me, God's presence is my good. I have made the Lord GOD my refuge, so I can tell about all you do" (vv. 27-28).

Two Exhortations

Based on verse 28, at least two exhortations are appropriate.

Trust in God's goodness. In a world where we are surrounded by wickedness, worldliness, and temptation, trust in the goodness of God. His presence is good, so trust that it is good to be with God. And his Word is good, so trust that it is good to listen to God. Don't be an "unthinking animal" toward God (v. 22) by buying into the deception of the world around you. Purity is not in vain, for the pure shall see God (Matt 5:8).

While nearness to God is good, this idea of purity does present a problem given that no one is perfect. For each of us, our feet have slipped and our steps have stumbled. We have all turned aside from God and his Word to the ways of this world, and as a result, we all deserve the destiny of the wicked described in verse 19: "desolation." Who among us could stand before the holy justice of God? We are all sinners, and we all need a Savior. The good news is that God has provided a Savior in the person of his Son, Jesus Christ. Paul says that God sent Christ to die on the cross "so that he [God] would be righteous and declare righteous the one who has faith in Jesus" (Rom 3:26). In Christ we stand justified before a holy God.

Tell others about God's greatness. Finally, the psalmist does not keep God's greatness to himself (v. 28). The impulse to "tell" only makes sense. Once you have a right perspective of God, you can't sit back in silence.

People all around us are living for fleeting pleasures. They believe the way of the world is good; but we know it's not, and we know where the way of the world is headed. So, how much do we have to hate someone *not* to tell them where it's headed? Let us, then, tell friends, coworkers, neighbors, and the nations that God is good. Tell them that he seeks us and satisfies us, and that while the pleasures of this world will pass in a moment, the goodness of God will last forever.

Reflect and Discuss

1. In what areas of your life are you most tempted to envy others?
2. Respond to the following statement: If you live in sin, then you'll always be miserable.
3. Does living a godly life ever seem pointless to you? What does this reveal about your faith in God's promises?

4. The psalmist says that he stayed silent in his suffering. Does this mean we should never discuss our doubts with trusted Christian friends? Explain your answer.

5. What questions have you wrestled (or are you wrestling) with in relation to your faith? Make a plan to talk about these questions with a church leader or another mature believer.

6. Describe in your own words what brought about the psalmist's change of perspective in verse 17.

7. Many Christians avoid the topic of God's judgment. Why is that a bad idea according to Psalm 73? How does God's judgment help us make sense of the seeming prosperity of the wicked?

8. Some people claim God will give us material blessings if we have enough faith. How does Psalm 73 speak to this error?

9. How can regular exposure to God's Word—both in preaching and in personal reading—prevent us from envying unbelievers and their so-called success?

10. The psalmist was initially envious, regretful, and doubtful. How would you describe him at the end of the psalm after he sees life from God's perspective?

Desperation Amid the Ruins

PSALM 74

Main Idea: God hears our desperate cries and acts for the sake of his name.

I. The Approach (74:1-2)
II. The News (74:3-11)
III. The Truth (74:12-17)
IV. The Ask (74:18-23)

The backdrop of this psalm seems to be Jerusalem after the Babylonian invasion in 586 BC. It looked like a perpetual ruin (v. 3). The Babylonians destroyed the sanctuary—smashing, burning, and looting Solomon's temple (vv. 3-8). God's chosen people were carried off into exile in Babylon, a dark place indeed (v. 20)—doves among savages (v. 19).

The fuller story of the Old Testament reveals God pleading with his people to turn back to him in faithfulness. He sent prophets to warn them, but the prophets were disregarded. So the warnings became reality and judgment fell. King Nebuchadnezzar marched up to Jerusalem. The city was conquered. The treasures of the temple were stolen or desecrated. The people were deported except for the poorest (2 Kgs 24:14). Then comes an interpretation of the events from God's own perspective: "Because of the LORD's anger, it came to the point in Jerusalem and Judah that he finally banished them from his presence" (2 Kgs 24:20).

What do you do when it seems everything is caving in around you? Does God hear his desperate children even if they've been wayward? In this psalm we learn a vital truth: God hears his people's desperate cries and acts for the sake of his name. The passage opens up in four sections.

The Approach
PSALM 74:1-2

Of our three children, one is more resistant to what we often call "small talk." He would call me from his college dorm. I would answer the phone, and he would greet me with a "Hi, Dad," then immediately jump into the reason for the call. No, "How are you and Mom doing?"

Here the psalmist dispenses with formalities. Why? Because the heat is on, and it won't let up. He is giving voice to the desperation of God's chosen people. The conversation begins with pain. In verse 1 the pain is expressed in the form of a question about God's rejection and anger.

It is, as the late pastor James Montgomery Boice described it, "a fierce complaint, bordering just possibly on impropriety as an address to God. But we should not miss the fact that it is at least addressed to God" (*Psalms 42–106*, 619). We cannot command God to give us answers and reasons for why he is permitting difficult circumstances in our lives, but as this and many other psalms demonstrate, the question is not prohibited. God does not cut off the voices of his desperate people.

In one sense we might push back on the psalmist. Doesn't the psalmist know that Babylon and what happened on that dark day in Jerusalem were God's judgment against the tenacious waywardness of the people? But read the question again. He asks why God has rejected them "forever." We see the same emphasis down in verse 10, with "how long" and "forever." And in verse 3 the psalmist invites God to look at the "perpetual ruins." The emphasis seems to be on the duration of God's judgment on his people. When will God's anger against their sin be satisfied?

The psalmist, in verse 2, trades questions for pleading. His request employs a key word: *remember.* He is calling on the Lord as a God who has made promises. They were promises to people who were unimpressive when God first found them. The people of Israel were not chosen by God because they were morally upright. Abraham the patriarch hailed from a family of idol worshipers, and God, if you will, interrupted their idolatrous worship and introduced himself and began making promises. God would be their God. They would be his people. God would make Abraham a nation. He would bless all the nations through him. Right from the start, the psalmist is hitching his hopes to the promises God had made to this people. Yes, they've been wayward, but they are his sheep (v. 1), his congregation that he purchased long ago and redeemed for his own possession (v. 2).

Have you ever sensed a distance from God—like he's a million miles away? Like the weight you are under will never lift? This psalm not only

helps you express your experience, but, more importantly, it helps you
seek the Lord from that place.

The News
PSALM 74:3-11

The psalmist, as it were, takes God by the hand and leads the Lord (and
the reader) on a tour through the ruined city where God's name had
dwelt. In a sense the sights and sounds are all wrong. Instead of fortified
walls around the city of God protecting the people of God, we see bro-
ken-down walls. Instead of the sounds of the worship of God's people,
the only thing we hear from the temple courts are the roaring taunts
of God's enemies. We expect the smell of incense and sacrifice when
approaching the temple, but instead the sanctuary itself is burning
(v. 7). Everything is out of sorts. The sound of prayers has been replaced
by a cacophony of vandalism, destruction, and mockery. Axes wreak-
ing havoc. Sacred things reduced to smoldering embers. This tour ends
with the tour guide, the psalmist, saying in verses 10-11, God, surely, you
won't let this be the last word. You won't tolerate insults hurled at your
name from the burning ruins of your house!

The Psalms make abundantly clear that argument is a form of prayer.
The psalmist is formulating a powerful argument. If the devastation of
Jerusalem was an act of God's judgment against his people's idolatry—
the way they kicked him to the curb and treated him as an insignificant
thing—was he listening to the voices of these mockers? Was God going
to let this slide?

This is where the tone of the prayer begins to change. He moves
to the truth about who God is and who God has been for the people
of Israel.

The Truth
PSALM 74:12-17

As impressive and foreboding as "the news" was in the last section, the
psalmist calls to mind his God—"my King" (v. 12)—a God who performs
saving acts. He speaks of God's power in the salvation of Israel, opening
up the sea (v. 13a) so they passed through on dry land. The psalmist's
faith is expressed here. His eyes are up. God has power over forces of
evil too strong for us (vv. 13b-14). God opens springs and streams (v. 15)

and rules over the day and the night (v. 16), the changing of seasons and the establishment of all earthly boundaries (v. 17).

Our God is the sovereign King. He rules over creation. Not only does he have untold, infinite power, but he also presses his power into the service of his people's salvation. In the Old Testament God saved his people through a mighty act of rescue—the great exodus. His people passed through the waters of death and emerged on the other side. However, that great redemptive act pointed forward to the mightiest of God's mighty deeds. God sent a deliverer, his Son, Jesus Christ. Jesus performed God's "saving acts on the earth" (v. 12) through his perfect life of obedience, his sin-bearing death on the cross, and his glorious resurrection from the dead. As a result, Jesus leads God's chosen people out of slavery to sin, and he promises to be our God forever—never to leave us or forsake us. This is the message of the gospel. This is the believer's hope.

Christian friend, take this truth to heart. God has shown us his saving acts. Jesus is our King, and he has power over all earthly powers. He has power to deliver us from powers too strong for us. He has power to sustain us in this present darkness.

This Old Testament saint doesn't know the fullness of the messianic hope we now see on this side of the cross, but he's onto something back there. He knows God as a covenant God who keeps his promises. He knows God as a saving, redeeming Lord who shepherds his people. He knows God as the King who rules and reigns and cannot be defeated. He knows that God contends for the glory of his own name and will not sit by and watch Israel's enemies gloat over his peoples' enfeebled condition. The psalmist is preaching truth to his soul.

Do you do the same? Have we learned the art of preaching the gospel to ourselves? Or do we only sit and listen to our fears mount their case? This psalm is instructive for us. He is bringing the grave "news" of his circumstances into contact with the truth of God's character and promises. This sets the psalmist up to make specific requests.

The Ask
PSALM 74:18-23

The superscription attributes this psalm to Asaph. If the background of this psalm is the Babylonian invasion in the sixth century BC, this could not be the Asaph who was a contemporary of King David. It could be either a later Asaph or, as many scholars believe, the name *Asaph* was "affixed to many psalms produced by this body of musicians" (Boice, *Psalms 42–106*, 617).

This writer deeply understands the character and nature of God. His prayers here at the close have a covenantal cadence about them. He uses this word *remember* again (v. 18) as he begins a series of earnest petitions.

Remember, Lord: this enemy has mocked you (v. 18). At this point, the psalmist is not focused on the way Israel's enemies oppress *Israel* (v. 8). His focus is the glory of God. When Babylon mocks Israel, Babylon is mocking Israel's God.

You may remember that when the risen Jesus confronts Saul of Tarsus on the road to Damascus, he says, "Saul, why are you persecuting me?" (Acts 9:4). Jesus so identified with his disciples that to persecute them was to persecute him. Asaph says that these foolish people insult God's name (v. 18).

The psalmist then represents Israel as easy prey for the great military might of Babylon (vv. 19,21). Asaph knows God hates oppressors—those who crush the powerless and gloat over them. "The one who mocks the poor insults his Maker, and one who rejoices over calamity will not go unpunished" (Prov 17:5). "The LORD executes acts of righteousness and justice for all the oppressed" (Ps 103:6).

Asaph asks God to remember the covenant promises he has made to his people (v. 20): You have never abandoned your promise. You didn't choose us because we were impressive. You weren't magnetically drawn to our moral beauty. We've tested you throughout our history and yet you've borne with us. You've given us your law. You've sent prophets. You've pleaded with us. You've wooed us, provided for us. You've disciplined us. But you've never abandoned your purpose.

On this basis the psalmist says, "Rise up, God, champion your cause!" (v. 22). Don't let the history books proclaim the great power of Babylon! Don't let the headline say, "Israel: Protected by God, Until Broken by Babylon!"

Conclusion

Here are six implications for the Christian life.

First, **God is not put off by our desperation**. We can come to him and bring our pain and our questions to him. Far better to bring them to him than to let our questions drive us away.

Second, **our hope in prayer is not anchored in our worthiness or merit but in God's saving grace**. This means all Christian praying is gospel-driven praying. We come confidently to a throne of grace (Heb 4:16) because of the work of our mediator, Jesus Christ. In Christ we have full access to God. We are invited to draw near and find the grace and help we so deeply need.

Third, **prayer involves theology and even argument**. We come to God as the one who is all powerful. We pray in a way that manifests our desire for God's glory to be revealed in the world and through his people.

Fourth, **we size up our circumstances against our all-powerful, loving, and faithful God**. The tour through fallen Jerusalem was a terrifying display of Babylon's strength; but God is King over the sea, Leviathan, day, night, seasons, and boundaries. This God is our God. He is a refuge for us. The best posture for us is to lift our eyes upward and outward.

Fifth, even when our desperate condition is owing to our own sin and failure, **God delights to run to the rescue of a humble people**. God's patience is great. The arm of God's mercy is long. There is no depth of sin we can find ourselves in where God cannot reach and restore us.

Sixth, **the church of Jesus Christ is meant to reflect the character of God**. Since God champions the cause of the poor and the afflicted, we, his people, are called to the same. God protects the vulnerable. God takes their side against their oppressors. The kingdom of God is not for the strong and mighty but for the poor in spirit. Therefore, the church is called to display God's heart to the vulnerable, the outcast, the poor, and the oppressed.

So we see yet again that God's Word exalts his character. He hears our desperate cries. He acts, he saves, for the sake of his name. We find all the grace and help. He gets all the glory.

Reflect and Discuss

1. Have you ever felt so overwhelmed by hardship that you didn't want to run to him—didn't want to pray or read his Word? What does this psalm teach us to do in such situations?
2. If we're confident that God is gracious toward us in Christ, how will that shape our prayer life?
3. What does it mean to look "up and out" in the midst of trials?
4. What would Psalm 74 sound like if Asaph didn't look up and out? How does this help you think about the way you pray?

5. How do our beliefs about God (theology) inform the way we pray? Think of examples of how wrong ideas about God might negatively impact our faith or hamper our effectiveness in prayer.
6. What are some good ways to cultivate right thinking about God so that we are able to preach truth to ourselves in times of hardship?
7. How is it good news that God saves "for the sake of his name"?
8. The psalmist presents prayers like arguments, giving reasons God should act in a certain way. Have you considered that before? How would you help someone else grasp this truth?
9. As Christians, how can we display God's heart for the poor and the afflicted?

God the Judge in a "Judge Not" Culture

PSALM 75

Main Idea: God's righteous judgment is bad news for the proud and good news for the believing.

I. The Source of Judgment: The Lord (75:2-3)
II. The Target of Judgment: The Proud (75:4-7)
III. The Goal of Judgment: Salvation (75:8-10)

The sixteenth-century Protestant Reformer Martin Luther summarized his theology this way: "One must always 'Let God be God.'" This is a classic example of "easier said than done." No one has trouble letting God be God as long as God is doing what we would do if we were God. However, the God we're talking about is a God who does things that are out of step with—even contradictory to—our cultural preferences.

This God defines right and wrong. And he doesn't do this after polling our culture, or any other culture for that matter. He gives us a list of dos and don'ts, many of which are as binding today as they were in ancient times. He tells us that if we live life our own way and reject him as the loving Creator and Lord, we will be condemned. When we read the Bible to learn about this God, we discover the unflattering news that God doesn't need us. He doesn't have a human-shaped hole in his heart that only you can fill. He doesn't run a democratic republic; he runs a kingdom. He is a generous King, a gracious and loving King. But he is a King, and he shares his throne with no one. This is the only God there is. There are no other God candidates.

To a culture where our favorite verse is "Judge not, that you be not judged" (Matt 7:1 NKJV)—to a culture that stands ready to quote this verse to God *himself* should he start to get any ideas—to this culture, God comes in Psalm 75 and unapologetically asserts his right to judge, his competency to judge, and his title as Judge.

As Christians we want to think biblically about God's judgment. Psalm 75 is going to lead us. Along the way, we want to carefully avoid three wrong responses to the biblical teaching concerning the judgment of God: ridiculing judgment, boasting in judgment (gloating), and minimizing judgment.

Something else I hope we see before we're done is that judgment is at the heart of the good news of Christian faith. There is no gospel without judgment. In a fallen world there is no salvation without judgment.

This is why a passage that is dominated by the idea of God's judgment could begin with thanksgiving (v. 1). Let's not miss this. The attitude one has toward the judgment of God reveals one's view of the character of God. In that way this psalm begins by urging us to consider the source. The one doing the judging is the Lord God himself.

The Source of Judgment: The Lord
PSALM 75:2-3

Consider verses 2 and 6-7. Psalm 75 is not a reluctant admission on God's part, "OK, I might as well admit it," his holy head lurching downward, "I am the sovereign Judge." No, this psalm, unlike our culture, views the judgment of God in a positive light. Look at how God speaks of judgment in verse 3. When God judges the earth, he is stabilizing it.

Humanism tries to offer us the hope that we can establish peace and righteousness and justice in the world apart from God. In our time and culture, that hope is often built on a theory of evolution coupled with the importance of education. There's only one problem: It's not happening. It's not working. Our advancements in education have only made the tools of war more sophisticated.

When we think of divine judgment, sometimes we think of God *shaking* the world with judgment. There are passages that speak that way (e.g., Heb 12:25-29). But it's fascinating to me that this passage comes from the other direction. It's telling us when unrighteousness and evil and injustice are left unchecked the world is tottering, and when God acts in judgment, he is *steadying* the world.

One of the reasons we find people not taking judgment seriously is they simply do not believe in the biblical God. Psalm 94:3-9 describes the foolish, arrogant, judgment-dismissing attitudes of the wicked as assuming that God is blind or indifferent. But Psalm 75 views judgment in a positive light because it views God in a positive light. Again, our view of judgment takes its cue from our view of God.

What does this mean practically? It means that if I trust God's character, then I'm convinced that he will judge rightly. So, for example, before I even read that difficult chapter of the Bible where God comes in judgment, I'm convinced that what God does is right. And after I have read that passage where God comes in judgment, I'm convinced that what God did was right. Why? Because we consider the source. We ask the simple question: Who is doing the judging here? When we discover it's God, we call to mind what we know about the biblical God.

First, he is slow to anger and abounding in faithful love (Exod 34:6). God isn't trigger happy. Second, he is righteous in all his ways (Ps 145:17). He doesn't have temper tantrums. He doesn't wake up on the wrong side of the bed. No, his judgment is a measured expression of his righteous character. Third, God is all wise (Ps 147:5; Rom 16:27). Scripture says the Lord founded the earth by wisdom (Prov 3:19). He also runs it by wisdom (Job 12:13-35). He judges with perfect wisdom. He is never in the dark. He never lacks all the information. We humans, even at our best, often lack context or comprehensive awareness of motives and contributing factors. God knows all. God rules and governs in righteousness, wisdom, and truth.

Paul brings God's wisdom and his judgments together. "Oh, the depth of the riches both of the wisdom and of the knowledge of God! How unsearchable his judgments and untraceable his ways! For who has known the mind of the Lord? Or who has been his counselor?" (Rom 11:33-34). Paul brings up an important and associated theme—namely, mystery. He uses the words *unsearchable* and *untraceable.* Isaiah 55:9 tells us that God's ways and thoughts are infinitely higher than ours. We may not fully understand the why or the how of God's judgment, but the upshot is faith in God means we come to these passages with a humble trust and confidence that God is good.

This brings us to the first wrong response to biblical teaching on God's judgment.

Wrong Response 1: Ridicule Judgment

Bill Maher sums up the story of Noah and the great flood this way: "It's about a psychotic mass murderer who gets away with it and his name is God" (Howell, "God a 'Psychotic Mass Murderer'"). There's an underlying assumption behind statements like this: that our sense of fairness and justice is *the* standard of fairness and justice. We give the impression that justice and righteousness is a moral code that exists outside of God—if you will, above God. God is answerable to that moral code. God is only righteous insofar as he conforms to that external standard, which (often) happens to perfectly match my sense of justice and righteousness.

One of the reasons our culture is so allergic to biblical teaching about God's judgment is because it reminds us of something we, in our pride, hate hearing: God is above us. I am not God's accountability partner. He's not asking me or you if it's going to be all right to flood the earth (Gen 6) or if it seems heavy-handed to annihilate the Amalekites (1 Sam 15).

We're allergic to hierarchy—unless we're at the top. This is not just a modern thing or an American thing. Isaiah 29:16 says it's a fallen humanity thing:

> You have turned things around, as if the potter were the same as the clay. How can what is made say about its maker, "He didn't make me"? How can what is formed say about the one who formed it, "He doesn't understand what he's doing"?

The *ridicule response to judgment* is wrongheaded because it assumes we have a better sense of right and wrong than God does. Those who ridicule God's judgment are not just self-righteous enough to look down their noses at other sinners, they are self-righteous enough to look down their noses at God himself.

The God of the Bible is who he is. He can't be taken in a piecemeal way. He is Creator, Lawgiver, Judge, Savior, Comforter, and returning King. It's a package proposal. We take him as he is for our everlasting joy or reject him to our everlasting destruction. As Christians, we don't say that to an unbelieving world with smirks on our faces but with pleading and through tears. In a way the doctrine of God's judgment draws a line in the sand between those who submit to God as he is and those who take what they like and leave the rest aside—those who make a god in their own image.

One author put it this way:

> But far from owning that they hate God, the vast majority of men will not only vehemently deny it, but affirm that they respect and love Him. Yet if their supposed love is analyzed, it is found to cover only their own interests. While a man concludes that God is favorable and lenient with him, he entertains no hard thoughts against Him. So long as he considers God to be prospering him, he carries no grudge

against Him. He hates God not as One who confers benefits, but as a Sovereign, Lawgiver, Judge. He will not yield to His government or take His law as the rule of his life. . . . The only God against whom the natural man is not at enmity is one of his own imagination. (Pink, *Doctrine of Human Depravity*, 114)

Here in Psalm 75 it is manifestly obvious: God is not ashamed of his title as the Judge of the earth. It's the first thing out of his mouth when he speaks in verse 2: "When I choose a time, I will judge fairly." Scripture reveals that God is ultimately the source of judgment. Given what we know from Scripture about his character, we should not want any other in charge of determining what is right and just.

The Target of Judgment: The Proud
PSALM 75:4-7

From beginning to end—from the moment proud Satan and his angels were cast down, to Adam and Eve eating the fruit so they would be like God, to Pharaoh arrogantly refusing to let God's people go, to the throwing down of the great Babylon in Revelation 18:7-10—God's judgment always hits its target, and it targets human pride.

There are these moments as you read through the Bible when your hair stands up a little, and you think, *He probably shouldn't have said that.* Take Daniel 5, for example. Quick background: God's people are in exile. Jerusalem has been torched. The Babylonian ruler, Belshazzar, is throwing a big party. The theme of the party is "Nobody is bigger, badder, and richer than Babylon." Since Belshazzar is the ruler of Babylon, this is basically a "look how awesome I am" party.

Then Belshazzar does something really dumb. He orders his subjects, "Fetch the gold and silver vessels, the ones we stole from the Jerusalem temple before we burned it to the ground. Go get those! A round of drinks for all my lords, my wives, and my concubines. Drink to the glory of my kingdom, from the holy vessels of the temple of Yahweh. Drink to our gods!" And the text says,

> At that moment the fingers of a man's hand appeared and began writing on the plaster of the king's palace wall next to the lampstand. As the king watched the hand that was writing, his face turned pale, and his thoughts so terrified him that he soiled himself and his knees knocked together. (Dan 5:5-6)

Then God addressed Belshazzar through Daniel, reminding him that the sovereign God placed his predecessor, Nebuchadnezzar, on the throne, "But when his heart was exalted and his spirit became arrogant, he was deposed from his royal throne and his glory was taken from him." Belshazzar didn't learn from history: "But you his successor, Belshazzar, have not humbled your heart, even though you knew all this. Instead, you have exalted yourself against the Lord of the heavens" (Dan 5:20,22-23). This party and the Babylonian kingdom were brought to an abrupt end that very night. The Medeo-Persians came, they killed Belshazzar, and Darius took over.

There it is: God's judgment always hits its target, and it always targets human pride. This is not only true when it comes to pagan pride but religious pride as well. Both James and Peter remind believers, "God resists the proud, but gives grace to the humble" (Jas 4:6; 1 Pet 5:5).

Wrong Response 2: Boast in Judgment

Some of us read passages that speak of God's judgment of evil and assume an attitude of moral superiority. Remember the Pharisee's prayer in Luke 18? He prayed, "God, I thank you that I am not like that guy over there." This is a classic case of what has come to be known as the humble brag because this prayer basically says, "I'm better than you, but it's only by grace."

But look at Jesus in the Gospels. Find the places where he is shouting, rebuking, and condemning. Who's he talking to? Professing members of the community of faith. These weren't atheists or idol worshipers, the Belshazzars of the world. They were churchgoers. They taught and memorized large portions of the Bible. Jesus reserves his strongest rebuke for them: "Blind guides! . . . whitewashed tombs. . . . Brood of vipers!" (Matt 23:24,27,33).

When we watch Jesus's manner with the self-righteous, we are seeing "God opposes the proud" in living color. "I have not come to call the righteous, but sinners to repentance" (Luke 5:32). This was not a compliment. He wasn't saying, "You guys are so righteous. You don't need me. Let me go help these other people." He was passing them by on account of their pride. It was an act of judgment.

The great Puritan pastor Thomas Watson said, "The greatest of all disorders is to think we are whole and need no help" (Wilson, *Works*, 81). In the book of Proverbs we come to a list that should bring us to the edge of our seats because it starts this way: "The LORD hates six things; in fact, seven are detestable to him: arrogant eyes . . ." (Prov 6:16-19). Verse 5 of our passage warns against speaking arrogantly.

The *boasting* response is arrogant because it assumes that when God judges evil and injustice in the world, I'll be safe because I'm so righteous. However, when the Bible speaks to the problem of evil in this world—injustice, anger, malice, vengeance, lust, greed, selfishness—we are *inside* the problem of evil, not outside. "All have sinned and fall short of the glory of God. . . . The wages of sin is death" (Rom 3:23; 6:23).

Someone said, "Pride is the AIDS of the soul." No one dies of AIDS. AIDS breaks down your body's ability to fight off illnesses of many kinds, and one of those illnesses kills you. Pride is like that. Pride lowers our defenses against all kinds of destructive sins. It makes us think we're above temptation. "Even if everyone falls away, I will not." Remember Peter saying that to Jesus? Famous last words. This is sobering. Pride left unchecked will take us places we never thought we'd go. Pride destroys friendships and marriages. Pride leads to divisiveness in the church. Pride is killing our witness before a watching world. Pride leads us to disciple our children to be nothing more than little Pharisees, with all the outward trappings of religious observance, yet having no sense that grace is amazing—where they never feel any sense of wonder at the mercy of God toward us in Christ.

What a tragic miss it is when we look at biblical judgment and all it produces and say, "Thank God I'm not messed up the way those people are!" Where is my heart? Why am I smirking? This boasting is not good.

In Romans 10 Paul tells us why his Jewish brothers and sisters by and large rejected God's salvation and God's Messiah:

> Brothers and sisters, my heart's desire and prayer to God concerning
> them is for their salvation. I can testify about them that they
> have zeal for God, but not according to knowledge. Since they are
> ignorant of the righteousness of God and attempted to establish their
> own righteousness, they have not submitted to God's righteousness.
> (Rom 10:1-3)

In this case the rejection wasn't because they wanted to eat, drink, and be merry with the dying pagan world around them. They rejected salvation because they were so righteous. They looked in the moral mirror and liked what they saw. "We don't need a handout. We're not God's charity case!" they said.

No wonder, when Jesus begins the Beatitudes, he starts his list of virtues with, "Blessed are the poor in spirit, for the kingdom of heaven is theirs" (Matt 5:3). In Scripture, blessing comes to those who are poor in spirit, the meek inherit the earth, and battles are not won by trusting in horses, chariots, weapons, or human strength. Oh, to be a church full of people who are poor in spirit! Oh, to be a man, a husband, a father, a pastor who is poor in spirit! Pastor Jonathan Edwards was intensely committed to live a godly life on a daily basis, and yet he would say years after his conversion, "I have had a vastly greater sense of my own wickedness, and the badness of my heart, than ever I had before my conversion" (*Works*, vol. 1, 57).

Is that your experience? In Scripture, the closer holy people got to the holy God, the less holy they felt themselves to be. Charles Spurgeon famously wrote, "It is easier to save us from our sins than from our righteousness."

The kingdom of God has a predictable pattern. God exalts the lowly and brings down the proud. We rightly say pagan pride is a stench in the nostrils of God, but we often neglect to realize that religious pride is just as offensive.

Friends, don't miss who is in the crosshairs of judgment in Psalm 75: the proud. So there can be no more important response to this truth than to humble ourselves before God. We must cast ourselves on his mercy because if we don't think we need mercy, we need it more than ever.

The Goal of Judgment: Salvation
PSALM 75:8-10

God's judgment is a terrifying thing because God is infinitely holy and we have sinned against him. The sobering thing is that when all is said and done, God's judgment is not poured out sparingly. There is a cup filled to the brim with God's just judgment against human sin, and that cup will be drained all the way down to the dregs. That cup will be turned over on the last day, and there will be no drips. God's just wrath will have been fully poured out. Yet no one will be able to charge God with overreacting to evil.

David cries out in Psalm 51, "Against you—you alone—I have sinned and done this evil in your sight. So you are right when you pass sentence; you are blameless when you judge" (51:4). Those words are a fitting response to every act of judgment we read about in the Bible. For example, what happened in the great flood? "Against you—you only—did they sin and do evil in your sight. So you are right and blameless in this flood." The Amalekites are destroyed. "You are right and blameless." The earth opens up to consume the sons of Korah. Fiery serpents are sent into the camp of Israel. "You are right and blameless when you judge." This applies all the way up to the final day of judgment, when God's just wrath is poured out on all rebellion. These words could even be written over the door of hell itself. "Against you have these sinned and done what is evil in your sight. You are right and blameless in this eternal judgment."

This is what our sins deserve. Scripture points this out time and time again: "Lord, if you kept an account of iniquities, Lord, who could stand?" (Ps 130:3). It's a rhetorical question whose answer is obvious: no one. Again: "And you—you are to be feared. When you are angry, who can stand before you?" (76:7). The answer: no sinner. And we have all sinned against God. There is no one righteous, not even one.

So, how is it that we can say the goal of judgment is salvation? How is it possible for us, far from ridiculing judgment or boasting in judgment, to humbly give God thanks in the midst of a song about God's judgment? The answer has everything to do with this cup in verse 8 and a prayer from Jesus in the garden of Gethsemane. Do you remember what Jesus asked? "My Father, if it is possible, let this cup pass from me. Yet not as I will, but as you will" (Matt 26:39). The Father's silence in the face of Jesus's plea for the cup to pass makes it abundantly clear that it was not his will for the cup of wrath to pass from Jesus.

What was the Father's will in sending the Son? The cup of God's justice against our sin sat there for thousands of years. God could not simply pour it out on the ground. That would be to deny his commitment to justice. It would be a denial of his own character, which is impossible (2 Tim 2:13). So the cup must be drunk.

The glory of the good news is this: in the fullness of time, Jesus Christ came to give his life as a ransom for sinners. The prophet Isaiah predicted the Father would lay on Messiah the iniquity of us all (Isa 53:6). So as we look forward from Psalm 75, the next time we see the foaming cup of judgment is when, on a hill outside Jerusalem, on the darkest day in human history, God puts it into the trembling hands of his only Son and says, "Drink it." Jesus took the cup and drained it for all who believe!

Christian, that is your salvation! No wonder there's salvation in no one else. No wonder it's such an insult to speak of "other ways" of salvation when Jesus alone became our substitute. Jesus alone became sin for us (2 Cor 5:21). He alone bore our sins in his body on the tree (1 Pet 2:24). The judgment of God on Jesus is our only hope of rescue.

So here is the final response we must avoid.

Wrong Response 3: Minimize Judgment

The *minimize* response is also arrogant because, if God in his Word makes judgment a prominent theme, then when I push this aside, however humble I might look or sound when I'm doing it, I have assumed the position of God's editor, his PR agent. Friends, read the Bible and think about this. If God's primary goal was to be accepted by our culture, he would've given us a much different book because our culture doesn't like a lot of what's here.

Beyond that, when we downplay the judgment of God, we are stealing glory from the cross. When we look at the cross, we see the greatest expressions of God's justice and mercy in all of history. God's justice was glorified in that moment because the cup of wrath was drained to the dregs. God's mercy was glorified in that moment because the cup of wrath was drained by the Son, not you and me.

That's why Paul says, "You want to boast? Go for it! Boast in the cross!" (Gal 6:14; author's paraphrase). On the cross we see that God is both "just and the justifier" (Rom 3:26 ESV) of the one who believes. He is seen, there, as Judge of all the earth and Redeemer of his people.

But we must respond to this news! Jesus is not automatically the substitute for every person on the planet. If that were true, we would be universalists; everyone would be saved because Jesus died. But it's not true, which is why response to Jesus is utterly vital. At the end of the day, all God's judgment will be poured out in fullness. Here's how it will play out. Either Jesus Christ drinks the cup of God's judgment in your place because God is merciful, or you will have to drink it yourself because God is just.

The one who turns from sin and trusts in Jesus will never drink a single drop of wrath. Why? Because Jesus drank the cup for all who trust him, and God is just—which means he can't charge all your sin to Jesus and still leave part of the bill for you.

This is why I love the verse of "It Is Well" that says, "My sin—oh, the bliss of this glorious thought! / My sin—not in part but the whole / Is nailed to the cross and I bear it no more, / Praise the Lord, praise the Lord, O my soul!" (Spafford, "It Is Well," 447). For all those who trust Jesus and embrace him as Lord, the just penalty for your sins against a holy God has already been satisfied. There is literally no wrath left.

That's why Romans 8:1 says, "Therefore, there is now no condemnation for those in Christ Jesus." Your condemnation wasn't *swept* under the rug somewhere. It was *absorbed* by Christ who stood in your place. When we look at the cross, we see God's judgment accomplishing God's salvation for all who believe.

If it was appropriate for the psalmist to begin a psalm of judgment with a word of thanksgiving, how much more so for us? We can say with even more heartfelt conviction, "We give thanks to you, God; we give thanks to you, for your name is near. People tell about your wondrous works" (v. 1). His most wondrous work of all is that God the Father found a way in his wisdom to be, at the same time, the Judge of the earth and the Savior of his people.

Reflect and Discuss

1. In what ways do we as humans struggle with God being God? Why are we so allergic to the idea of God being the Judge?
2. What is your attitude toward God as the Judge? Why?
3. How does pride lower our defenses against other sins? In what ways does pride manifest itself in your life?
4. How can we humble ourselves before God? What does this practically look like?
5. How is salvation the goal of judgment (see Ps 75:8; Matt 26:39,42)? How does downplaying the judgment of God steal glory from the cross of Christ?
6. How should this psalm inform how you pray, how you praise God, and what you pray for?

Behold His Wrath

PSALM 76

Main Idea: While we deserve the wrath of God due to our sin, God provides salvation from this just punishment through the sacrifice of his Son, Jesus Christ.

I. **God Is Infinitely Worthy of Our Worship.**
    A. God is glorious above all.
    B. God is sovereign over all.
    C. God is feared by all.
    D. God is the just Judge of all.
II. **We Are Infinitely Deserving of God's Wrath.**
    A. We have denied the glory of God.
    B. We have denounced the sovereignty of God.
    C. We have failed to fear God.
    D. We have dared to judge God.
III. **We Need God to Save Us from God.**
    A. At the cross God expressed his wrath toward sin.
    B. At the cross God endured his wrath against sin.
    C. At the cross God has enabled salvation for sinners.

As we read the Psalms, we should begin with the assumption that our greatest need is to know God, to have a high view of him in all of his glory. Unfortunately, however, we are constantly tempted in our lives, in our families, in the church, and in our culture to have a low view of God. More specifically, we are tempted to ignore or minimize characteristics of God that are not comfortable to us. That's certainly true when it comes to the wrath of God, a characteristic highlighted in Psalm 76.

We live in a day, even in the church, when we rarely talk about God's wrath. Even when we do, it's almost as if we're apologetic about it, as if we're ashamed of who God is. Here's how Francis Chan put it:

> Like the nervous kid who tries to keep his friends from seeing his drunken father, I have tried to *hide* God at times. Who do I think I am̶̶̶̶̶̶. truth is, God is perfect and right in all that He does. ̶̶̶̶̶̶̶̶ol for thinking otherwise. He does not

need nor want me to "cover" for Him. There's nothing to be covered. Everything about Him and all He does is perfect. (*Erasing Hell*, 133)

Similarly, Ajith Fernando writes,

Evangelicals are often apologetic about the biblical view of [God's judgment]. They say that they wish that what the Bible says about the punishment of sinners is not true, that they find it hard to accept this doctrine emotionally, but that because the Bible teaches it they are forced to believe it. This type of thinking is understandable, given our human frailty and inability to fully understand God's ways. We do not see the seriousness of sin as strongly as God sees it. But many today seem [almost] to be proud that their hearts rebel against the judgment of God. The message they convey to an outsider is that they think God is wrong and unfair, but that's what he is going to do, so they reluctantly include it in their statement of faith. (*Crucial Questions*, 133–34)

It is not our job to apologize for God or to hide anything about him. Instead, we need to hear what God has revealed about his glory in his Word, and we need to realize what this means for our lives. We should pray that God would use the message of his wrath to do what he has done at various times in church history, namely, bring revival. The book of Hosea talks a lot about God's judgment against sin and sinners, and in Hosea 10:12 the Lord says, "Break up your unplowed ground. It is time to seek the LORD until he comes and sends righteousness on you like the rain." Don't you long to see that in your church and even in your own life? By the grace of God, Psalm 76 just might be a text that God uses to do this. It shines a light on the seriousness of sin, and it should cause us to cry out for God's mercy.

The first half of Psalm 76 depicts a historical event when God poured out his wrath on a specific nation that had opposed him and his people, Israel. The second half then takes that historical event and raises it to another level in order to show that, ultimately, God's wrath will be poured out on all people who oppose him. We don't know for certain the specific historical event that's referenced in the first half of this psalm, but the Greek translation of the Old Testament (the Septuagint) includes a note from the translators that it is referring the Assyrians' attack on Jerusalem (2 Kgs 18–19) (Boice, *Psalms*, 6, 634).

The Assyrian army was on the assault against God's people. They were taking over city after city in Judah, and they ultimately surrounded Jerusalem with 185,000 troops. The people of Israel were scared. Hezekiah, the Israelite king, was urging Israel to trust God. The Assyrian commander, on the other hand, was threatening them, saying,

> But don't listen to Hezekiah when he misleads you, saying, "The LORD will rescue us." Has any of the gods of the nations ever rescued his land from the power of the king of Assyria? Where are the gods of Hamath and Arpad? Where are the gods of Sepharvaim, Hena, and Ivvah? Have they rescued Samaria from my power? Who among all the gods of the lands has rescued his land from my power? So will the LORD rescue Jerusalem from my power? (2 Kgs 18:32-35)

The Assyrian commander taunted God, which was a huge mistake. God's response comes in the next chapter:

> Who is it you mocked and blasphemed? Against whom have you raised your voice and lifted your eyes in pride? Against the Holy One of Israel! You have mocked the Lord through your messengers. . . .
> Have you not heard? I designed it long ago; I planned it in days gone by. I have now brought it to pass, and you have crushed fortified cities into piles of rubble. Their inhabitants have become powerless, dismayed, and ashamed. They are plants of the field, tender grass, grass on the rooftops, blasted by the east wind.
> But I know your sitting down, your going out and your coming in, and your raging against me. Because your raging against me and your arrogance have reached my ears, I will put my hook in your nose and my bit in your mouth; I will make you go back the way you came. (2 Kgs 19:22-23,25-28)

Then God keeps his word:

> "Therefore, this is what the LORD says about the king of Assyria: He will not enter this city, shoot an arrow here, come before it with a shield, or build up a siege ramp against it. He will go back the way he came, and he will not enter this city. This is the LORD's declaration. I will defend this city and rescue it for my sake and for the sake of my servant Davi[...]
> That ni[...]ent[...]enci[...]l of the LORD went out and struck down one hundred eig[...] 42-1[...] in the camp of the Assyrians. When the people got u[...]r—there were all the dead bodies! So

King Sennacherib of Assyria broke camp and left. He returned home and lived in Nineveh.

One day, while he was worshiping in the temple of his god Nisroch, his sons Adrammelech and Sharezer struck him down with the sword and escaped to the land of Ararat. Then his son Esar-haddon became king in his place. (2 Kgs 19:32-37)

The takeaway from this episode is clear: You don't mess with God. His wrath is real. He struck down 185,000 troops in an instant, and then he had the Assyrian king struck down by his sons in the house of his (false) god.

This background is illuminating as we consider Psalm 76. This psalm as a whole leaves us with at least three conclusions, two exhortations, and one response.

God Is Infinitely Worthy of Our Worship

The language in verses 1-2 evokes something awesome, which makes sense in light of God's judgment against Assyria in 2 Kings 19. The words translated "tent" and "dwelling place" are used in other parts of the Old Testament to refer to a lion's den (Boice, *Psalms 42–106*, 633). In Jerusalem, God is like a lion in his lair, and he is "ready to pounce" on anyone who attacks his glory and his people (ibid.). Consider several reasons, according to this psalm, that God is worthy of our worship:

God Is Glorious above All

No nation, including the mighty Assyria, can stand against him. He breaks their arrows, their shields, their swords, and their weapons of war (v. 3). He is "resplendent and majestic" (v. 4). At God's rebuke, "both chariot and horse lay still" (v. 6). In verse 10 the psalmist explains how even man's wrath against God ultimately brings God glory, for God has the final word. Survey the silent battlefield filled with slain Assyrian soldiers, and stand in awe of the God whom they defied. God is infinitely worthy of worship because God is glorious above all.

God Is Sovereign over All

For God to be sovereign means that he has all power and all authority over all things. That was the focus of 2 Kings 18–19. God demonstrated that both Assyria and Israel were in his hands. We must see the wʳ ʳ today in light of this reality. Whether it's the United Stateʳ ᴵ

Russia, or North Korea, God is sovereign over all of them. *He* governs the world with power and authority.

God Is Feared by All

The concept of fear appears four times in verses 7-12. No one can stand before this God in all of his holiness, glory, sovereignty, and wrath. Every mouth is silenced before him.

God Is the Just Judge of All

When was it that the earth "feared and grew quiet" (v. 8)? When "God rose up to judge and to save all the lowly of the earth" (v. 9). This is one of those points where Psalm 76 takes things to another level, for this is not just about Assyria. One day every person on the planet will stand before God as Judge. He will be just. God's wrath is a demonstration of God's just judgment. The wrath of God doesn't just come out of nowhere. It's not an emotional outburst, like we might think of fury in people. No, divine wrath is the inevitable expression of divine justice. If we take the time to consider, this is a good thing.

In our hearts we all long for justice. When we see a gunman shoot and kill people, or a terrorist drive through crowded streets murdering men, women, and children, we long for justice to be served. When we read about Nazi Germany systematically exterminating millions of Jewish men and women, we long for justice to be served. When we think about America's history involving slavery and other forms of injustice, we should long for justice to reign. And when we see the effects of sin in our own lives—adulterous spouses, abandoned children—something in us cries out, "Surely this is not all there is!" We long for goodness and justice to have the last word. And the Bible makes clear that God, the just Judge of the universe, will have the last word.

We Are Infinitely Deserving of God's Wrath

God's justice is a good thing, but it is also a terrifying reality when you realize who we are and how we have responded to him. Each of us is confronted with the reality of sin in our life. Many people are OK with God's justice and wrath when expressed toward people who have done particularly heinous things. However, when it comes to our own sin, many of us believe justice and wrath are wrong. We are fine with God's judging Assyria, but we fail to realize that *we are Assyria*. Each of us has God to his face. Consider what the Bible teaches about our Judge.

We Have Denied the Glory of God

Romans 3:23 says, "For all have sinned and fall short of the glory of God." We have all turned aside to other gods, whether it be money, possessions, sex, success, or whatever. We have turned aside to worldly pursuits and worldly pleasures. We have centered our lives around ourselves.

We Have Denounced the Sovereignty of God

We have looked into the face of the God, who is sovereign over all, and just like Assyria we have denounced his rule and reign over our lives. This is the God who speaks to creation and everything obeys his bidding, except when it comes to us. You and I have the nerve to look God in the face and say, "No." We think we know what is best for our life.

We Have Failed to Fear God

We have not feared the God who is to be feared. We have feared so many other things instead. Fear is such a prevailing problem in so many of our lives. We fear failure, ridicule, embarrassment, the unknown, sickness, death, etc. Could it be that the reason we fear so many things is because we don't fear God?

One indication that we don't fear God is that we don't fear sinning against God. We treat sin lightly, as if it's no big deal; and we're stunned, even offended, by how seriously God treats sin in Scripture. For example, in Genesis 19 Lot's wife was turned into a pillar of salt for looking back toward Sodom. In Numbers 15 a man was stoned for picking up sticks on the Sabbath. In 2 Samuel 6 Uzzah was struck dead for touching the ark of the covenant. Some people claim that the God of the Old Testament was more severe, but the God of the New Testament is different. That's not true. In Acts 5:1-10, to take one example, Ananias and Sapphira both lied about their offerings, and God struck them down dead. Think about what that would do to your church's attendance next Sunday.

If we are honest, we sometimes read these stories and think God is being overly severe. That's because we have a man-centered perspective of sin. But the key is not how severe the sin is; the key is the one who is sinned against. Think about it: if you sin against a rock, you're not very guilty. If you sin against a man, you're guilty. However, if you sin against an infinitely holy God, you are infinitely guilty. Sinning just once is infinitely serious in God's sight. According to Romans 5:12-21, one sin led to the curse of God, the curse that affects the entire world today. In Genesis 3 Adam and Eve ate a piece of fruit, and from that one sin has come all the evil and injustice in the history of the world—world wars, holocaust, cancer, disease, tsunamis, earthquakes, hurricanes, tornadoes, terrorism, pain, suffering, and death. Yet you and I have committed thousands upon thousands of sins! We are clueless when it comes to the seriousness of our sin against a holy God.

We Have Dared to Judge God

We, as sinners, actually have the audacity to point the finger in God's face and question his judgment. We ask how a good God can condemn sinners, as if we're the ones who are right and God is in the wrong. We actually say things like, "I could never worship a God who _____." It's as if we cannot tolerate a God whose holiness is higher than ours, a God whose wisdom is greater than ours, or a God whose righteousness is greater than we can even begin to comprehend.

We Need God to Save Us from God

Every human being will one day stand before God as Judge, which means we will stand before him guilty of sin. We will be deserving of his just judgment and eternal wrath, and we can do nothing to change that. All kinds of people today all over the world try all kinds of ways to appease God— religion, church attendance, good deeds—but none of these things can eliminate the stain of sin and guilt on our hearts before a holy God.

Some people wonder why a God who is loving can't simply forgive us of our sins. But, as John Stott recognized, this gets the problem completely backwards. Stott called forgiveness "the profoundest of problems" for God because God's forgiveness of sinners is a threat to his holy character (*Cross of Christ*, 110). If God simply forgives sin and acquits sinners, then he is not a just Judge. Just think—if a judge today knowingly acquitted guilty criminals, we would want that judge off the bench in a heartbeat. So if God is just and we are guilty, then the question is not *why it's difficult* for God to forgive sinners; no, the question is *how it's possible* for God to forgive sinners. We need God to do for us what we cannot do for ourselves.

The good news of the gospel is that God has done everything necessary to provide for us the forgiveness of sins and the hope of eternal life. He has done this by satisfying his own justice through the life, death, and resurrection of Jesus, his Son. Sadly, minimizing God's wrath also minimizes God's love. **At the cross, God expressed his wrath toward sin.**

At the same time, **at the cross, God endured his wrath against sin**. Jesus was enduring the wrath of God that we deserve.

What happened at the cross was so much more than the physical picture of what we see there. Yes, the cross was physical, and Christ's death as our human substitute is critical to our salvation. But we are not ultimately saved from our sins because of what a bunch of Roman soldiers did physically to Jesus. We are saved from our sins because of what God did and what Jesus chose to do.

In the garden of Gethsemane, Jesus was not sweating because he was afraid of what some Roman soldiers were about to do to him. Countless people have died martyrs' deaths in the name of Christ since that day, and many of them went to their deaths singing. For example, one Christian in India was being skinned alive, and he said to his tormenter, "Take off my outer garment. Today I put on a new garment of righteousness." Christopher Love was about to be led to the gallows and he wrote a note to his wife that said, "Today they will sever me from my physical head, but they cannot sever me from my spiritual head, Christ" (Platt, *Radical*, 35). Love went to the gallows singing with his wife applauding him. However, these martyrs were not braver than Jesus. Jesus was sweating blood in the garden, not because he was a coward about to face Roman soldiers but because he was a Savior choosing to endure divine wrath.

In the garden Jesus prayed, "My Father, if it is possible, let this cup pass from me" (Matt 26:39). The cup Jesus referred to was a cup filled with the fury of God's judgment due sin (Ps 75:8); it was a cup filled with the winepress of God's wrath due sinners (Isa 51:17; Jer 25:15-16; Rev 14:10,19-20). Jesus was sweating blood because he was about to endure all that we deserve in our sin.

We stand before a holy God deserving holy wrath in our sin, but Jesus went to the cross in our place. He swallowed down the full cup of God's wrath, and then he turned that cup over and cried out, "It is finished!" (John 19:30). Therefore, **at the cross, God has enabled salvation for sinners**. God's wrath is ultimately a demonstration of God's love! Becky Pippert said, "God's wrath is not a cranky explosion, but his settled opposition to the cancer of sin which is eating out the insides of the human race he loves with his whole being."[2] This fits with the aim of

---

[2] Will Metzger uses this quote from Becky Pippert's book *Faith Has Its Reasons* as he cites Tim Keller, "Brimstone for the Broadminded," *Christianity Today*, July 13, 1998, 65. Will Metzger, *Tell the Truth: The Whole Gospel to the Whole Person by Whole People* (Downers Grove: IVP, 2002), 49.

God's judgment as it is expressed in Psalm 76:9: "When God rose up to judge and to save all the lowly of the earth."

God wants to save all who humble themselves before him. Therefore, turn today from your sin and yourself, and trust in Jesus as your Savior and Lord. Heed the words of A. W. Tozer:

> The vague and tenuous hope that God is too kind to punish the ungodly has become a deadly opiate for the consciences of millions. It hushes their fears and allows them to practice all pleasant forms of iniquity while death draws every day nearer and the command to repent goes unheeded. (*Knowledge of the Holy*, 80)

Even if you've already trusted in Christ, let the reality of God's wrath lead you to stop toying with sin in your life. Humble your heart in holy awe before God.

Reflect and Discuss

1. When was the last time you heard a sermon about hell and the judgment of God? Why do you think this is such a neglected topic today?
2. What are some signs that a church or an individual has a low view of God?
3. Respond to the following statement: "A loving God would never send anyone to hell."
4. Is God's eternal wrath too severe a punishment for the sins we commit? Why?
5. What is the relationship between God's holiness and his wrath?
6. How would you respond to someone who said, "Jesus is much more kind and forgiving than the God of the Old Testament"?
7. If God is perfectly just, then how can he forgive sinners?
8. How does the Bible's teaching about God's judgment make the message of the gospel more precious?
9. If God's wrath turns some people away from Christianity, then why should we mention it in our evangelism?
10. How does a right view of God's judgment affect our missions strategies?

Truths for Your Trials

PSALM 77

Main Idea: Healthy believers process their pain in the presence of God.

I. **We Get to Be Weak (77:1-10).**
II. **He Gets to Be Strong (77:11-20).**

Here's a challenge I've been noticing more recently as I've shared the gospel or had spiritual conversations with unbelievers. They know the message. They may even self-identify as Christian. However, when you hear them talk about God or Jesus, it's not obvious that Jesus is actually real or alive. You wouldn't get the impression that Jesus Christ is ruling and reigning—that he must be known and treasured; that he is available, listening, acting; that he has the power to make all things new.

How real is your Christianity? Do you actually interact with God? When you talk about him (do we talk about him?), does it sound like we're talking about an awesome friend and King? Or does Christianity sound more like a spiritual exercise program that, at least for you, seems to yield some good results?

Dallas Willard, professor of philosophy for forty-six years at the University of Southern California, was a compelling Christian. He had a tremendously painful childhood. He lost his mom in a tragic accident when he was two. His dad remarried quickly in order to find someone to mother Dallas. She hated Dallas, so he ended up being raised by his brother and sister-in-law. As a teenager Willard had a hungry mind and read every book in the high school library by the time he graduated. His favorite book was Plato's *Republic*, and he carried it with him as he worked on a farm in his home state of Missouri. Then God found young Dallas and completely changed his life.

As a professor, Dallas was a magnet for students curious to hear more after class about his views. Another professor at USC tells of a conversation with a philosophy student that went this way:

> "Do you think Jesus can walk up to you?" he asked me. So I asked the student, "What do you mean by that?" And he said that he came from Dallas' office and "He told me about Jesus,

247

and he said, 'Now when you pray, Jesus will walk right up to you and he will listen to you.'"

I met that student twenty years later at a philosophy conference and he was still talking to Jesus. . . . Now who talks like that, "Jesus can walk up to you"? It is a person that truly believes that invisible things like the Trinity and the kingdom are actually real. (J. P. Moreland, quoted in Moon, *Becoming Dallas Willard*, 108)

So, again, how real is your Christianity? Do you believe in a God who hears your cries? In a way, this psalm speaks to the nature of our real relationship with God. The first reality is this:

We Get to Be Weak
PSALM 77:1-10

This is a psalm of lament. It's a believer running to God for help, for strength. In verse 2 we see his hand stretched out all night.

I grew up watching cartoons like *Tom and Jerry*. It's basically a cat and a mouse constantly fighting each other. You'd see one of them hit the other one's finger with a hammer, and what would happen? It would throb and pulsate and change colors.

The first time I smashed my thumb with a hammer, I realized it was all true. I also discovered at bedtime that it didn't hurt as badly if I held my thumb up in the air. So there I was lying in bed, arm straight, elbow locked, thumb up. You're thinking, *That's so cute.* I was in my thirties! The moonlight was coming through the window on my side of the room, and my wife rolled over and saw this strange silhouette—my arm straight and thumb pointing at the ceiling. And yes, she mocked me just a little. Here's the thing: I didn't care how weird it looked; I just wanted relief!

For the ancient Hebrew, physical postures were often a window into what was happening on the inside. They would tear their outer garments to show what they were experiencing on the inside. Here in verse 2 his lifted hands are an outward sign of a heart that was reaching toward God for help.

If you're allergic to being thought of as needy, poor, and helpless, you're not going to like the Bible—the Psalms especially. If you happen to be a person whose life has mostly gone as planned, the Psalms might honestly just seem whiny. It might seem like King David huddled up with all his angsty, music-major friends—a bunch of Eeyores with guitars—hit the record button, and poof, the Psalms.

However, if you've tasted hardship, I hope, as we read these words, there is a welcome realism here reminding you you're not alone. The Christian life isn't about pretending everything is going great. This is one of the things that is so refreshing about the Psalms, particularly psalms of lament. If you don't wake up every day feeling like a world changer, the Psalms are your new best friend.

This psalm is assuring you in line after line that God hears his people when we call to him. What's this psalmist saying? I think author Eugene Peterson captures it: "I found myself in trouble and went looking for my Lord; my life was an open wound that wouldn't heal. When friends said, 'Everything will turn out all right,' I didn't believe a word they said" (Ps 77:2 *The Message*). He refused to be comforted. It's like his soul is so blistered, so raw. He doesn't want a hug; he wants an answer.

As a friend, you encourage him, "Think about God's goodness; meditate on his faithfulness." He says, "That's exactly what I've been doing! But," verse 3, "when I think of God, I groan. When I meditate, my spirit becomes weak." In other words, "None of the exercises of faith seem to be working." Think, for example, of what it's like trying to turn a nut that's rusted. You can have the best wrench in the world, but if the nut is rusted, it's nearly impossible to turn it. That's how the psalmist feels.

He thinks about God's grace in days past (vv. 5-6), and that seems to make it worse. He starts asking hard questions (vv. 7-9). It's hard to figure out how to translate verse 10. "I am grieved" could also be translated "my plea/appeal," and the word *changed* could also be translated "years." So it's difficult to sort that out with certainty, but the idea is clear. To the psalmist, it *feels* like God's strength was more readily available in the past than right now.

What a statement! Just stop and think about so many places in Scripture where, if God managed his Word like we manage our Facebook page, he'd edit a bunch of stuff out. Peter denying Christ. Paul and Barnabas having a heated argument about John Mark. The entire book of Judges. You come to Genesis 9: Noah is fresh off the ark. It's a new start for him and the world, until verse 18. If I were the editor of the Bible, I'd say, "Let's take the camera off Noah. Let's get some B roll, capture some nature shots, until Noah is presentable. And by 'presentable' I mean dressed . . . and sober." But no. All of that material made it into the Bible.

And here in Psalm 77 God doesn't edit out the psalmist's feelings. Were I the editor, I might've said, "I don't like what he's suggesting in verses 7 through 9. I don't want people to be encouraged to say anything remotely like this in prayer, so let's leave that out." However, please don't mistake why these verses are here. They are not here to get us to think, *Apparently, it's possible for God's faithful love to cease. I mean, here we church folk have been singing 'his mercies are new every morning' all these years. But, hey, in light of verse 8, maybe they aren't.* These verses aren't the expressions of a hardened skeptic. The true skeptic says, "Why bother? I stopped talking to the walls years ago."

No, the beauty here is God allows the psalmist to express what he feels. Psalm 77 is a believer trying to breathe. Christian friend, the fight of faith involves discerning the difference between our feelings and the truth. These verses don't want to encourage you to fall in love with doubts you may be having about God. No, what we're supposed to hear in this is God saying, "You don't have to presort everything. Bring all of that mess to me. I want you to cast all your cares, all your anxieties on me (1 Pet 5:7). You don't have to be the hero. You don't have to keep your chin up. You don't have to smile. You don't have to be strong. Put away your glossy-brochure (non-real) Christianity, and come fall into my arms."

He Gets to Be Strong
PSALM 77:11-20

When our kids were little, we spent every night for several years reading a brief passage in the Bible, a few minutes praying, and a few minutes teaching through the Westminster Shorter Catechism, a series of brief questions with memorable answers drawn from Scripture.

A few years later I was in a car with a minister, and he was going on and on saying he thought the Heidelberg Catechism was better than the Westminster. I couldn't let the Westminster go down without a fight, so we playfully bantered back and forth. I wasn't really prepared for this exchange since, in fact, I had never read the Heidelberg Catechism. So I went to my hotel room that night (we were at a conference), and I read the first question of the Heidelberg.

1. Q. What is your only comfort in life and death?

A. That I am not my own, but belong with body and
soul, both in life and in death, to my faithful Saviour
Jesus Christ. He has fully paid for all my sins with
his precious blood, and has set me free from all the
power of the devil. He also preserves me in such
a way that without the will of my heavenly Father
not a hair can fall from my head; indeed, all things
must work together for my salvation. Therefore, by
his Holy Spirit he also assures me of eternal life and
makes me heartily willing and ready from now on to
live for him.

I read that and thought, *OK, it's a tie.* There are much worse ways
to begin instructing new believers about the faith. I'm not my own. I'm
his. He's got me. He can save me and preserve me. I can be weak, and
he can be strong.

One of the great truths we see in the Psalms is that the Christian life
is conversation with God. Here the psalmist starts by unburdening his
soul before God. Then, by God's grace, his soul finds another gear, and
he starts remembering, reflecting, and meditating. Verses 11 and 12 are
the hinge of the passage. Before that, we hear, "I cry aloud . . . refused to
be comforted. . . . I think of God; I groan. . . . I am troubled and cannot
speak." Then he says, "I will remember . . . yes, I will remember."

There's a key difference between "I *might* remember," "I'll *try to*
remember," and "I *will* remember." This is not the psalmist finding his
bootstraps. This is Spirit-empowered faith that keeps talking to God.
He's talking about God's strength and grace and saving power in real
history. Verse 16 is a reference to the exodus, where God brought his
people to the shores of the Red Sea, and the waters retreated. And the
*I*s of honest complaint are replaced with the *you*s and *yours* of Godward
trust: "*Your* way is holy. . . . *You* are the God who works wonders; *you*
revealed *your* strength. . . . *You* redeemed *your* people" (vv. 13-15).

What's he doing? He's believing! He's fighting the fight of faith,
but not in his own strength. There's no boasting, no chest thumping in
verses 11-20. His eyes are up and out.

In a sense we might have expected verse 4 to be the end of Psalm 77.
We hear him say, "I am troubled and cannot speak"—but he keeps
speaking. Day and night he's calling on the God who hears his cries.

This is real faith in a real God who is really listening. We need to know that, in light of the rest of what Scripture says, none of this happens apart from Jesus. We can't run around Jesus Christ to get an audience with a holy God. This is why the holy God sent his only Son. And Jesus said, "I am the way, the truth, and the life. No one comes to the Father except through me" (John 14:6). All the good that God has for you and me is wrapped up in Jesus. That's why Jesus came: so that our sin would no longer separate us from God. Jesus went to the cross and paid for our sins. He rose from the dead so that whoever believes has eternal life, sins forgiven, and a Father who is available right now.

I love stories in the gospels where Jesus intervenes. When he does, we are seeing him making spiritual truths visible. In Mark 9 there's a boy who is possessed by evil spirits. The boy's dad says this evil is trying to destroy his son. "If you can do anything," he pleads, "have compassion on us and help us." And the Gospel writer records, "Jesus said to him, 'If you can'? Everything is possible for the one who believes." Then the dad says, "I do believe; help my unbelief!" (Mark 9:21-24).

How real is your Christianity? Does it express itself in the way you run toward God in trials? As if he is as real as everything you're up against? Where we come to seek the Lord's strength and Jesus "walks right up" to us and listens?

Christian friend, we have a God who listens when we pray. We have a God who intervenes and sustains and rescues. Let's not live this life of faith relying on our own strength. Let's not present to unbelievers a Christianity that's for all the happy people who are winning in life. Let's cast our cares on him. Let's cling to hope in Christ. Let's offer that hope to the world. Let's remember the gospel. Let's look up and out to the God who hears our cries.

Reflect and Discuss

1. How do you get to a point in your relationship with the Lord where it sounds as though you are talking about a real friend when you mention him?

2. How can we discern the difference between feelings and truth?

3. As Christians, how should we respond when our feelings do not match God's truth?

4. Why does God want us to bring our mess to him, not presort it? What keeps us from coming to him with our mess?

5. How would you answer the question, How real is your Christianity? Why?
6. If you were to unburden your soul before God right now, what things would you address with him (e.g., past and present hurts, wounds, memories, questions, sorrows)?
7. Is your Christianity as real as your pain? Why or why not? If it's not, why? What would hinder you from turning to God and trusting him fully in your pain?
8. How will you allow this psalm to shift your view of God in the midst of a trial or how you respond to a trial when it occurs?

The Gospel for Generations Past and Future

PSALM 78[3]

Main Idea: The church should tell the next generation what the Bible teaches about God and his salvation in order to warn them against sin and encourage them to entrust their entire lives to Jesus Christ.

I. **What We Do**
   A. We teach the Scriptures (78:4-8).
      1. We teach the next generation who God is.
      2. We teach the next generation what God has done.
      3. We teach the next generation what God has said.
   B. We tell the stories (78:10,13-16,23-31,38-39,44-51,53,55,59-64,67-72).
   C. We warn against sinfulness (78:10-11,17-18,32,36-37, 40-42,56-58).
   D. We exalt the Savior.
      1. God responds to his people's failures with his forgiveness.
      2. God responds to his people's faithlessness with his faithfulness.

II. **What We Hope**
   A. They will know God in their minds.
   B. They will trust God in their hearts.
   C. They will obey God in their lives.

III. **Some Practical Steps Forward**

In this lengthy psalm Asaph sets the stage by talking to his own generation and to future generations based on God's work among the generations past. At least four generations are implied in the first four verses.

Psalm 78 is a reminder that we want to lead our children to know and to trust in God. I pray specifically for my boys to be the men God has created them to be and for my little girl to be the woman God has created her to be. I also pray for their future spouses. But my prayers don't stop there. I pray for the gospel to be passed on, with passion,

---

[3] David Burnette contributed to some portions of this chapter.

254

through my children to their children, and then to their grandchildren and beyond. This kind of praying changes parenting. We find ourselves asking the question, What can I do to pass on the gospel of God's grace and God's greatness to future generations?

Nevertheless, this question is not just for parents. This question is for all of God's people. God has given his church responsibility for passing the gospel on to the next generation, and we all have a part to play in this. We have been commissioned to make disciples, not just of all nations but among every generation.

What We Do

Based on this desire to pass on the gospel of God's grace and greatness to future generations, this psalm encourages four activities.

We Teach the Scriptures (78:4-8)

God has given us his Word, and we want to pass on this Word to the next generation. God gives instructions through Moses in Deuteronomy 6:6-7: "These words that I am giving you today are to be in your heart. Repeat them to your children. Talk about them when you sit in your house and when you walk along the road, when you lie down and when you get up." In short, the Word of God should be taught all the time. So what specifically do we teach?

First, **we teach the next generation who God is**. We tell our children that everything begins and ends with God, that he is the supreme Creator, sustainer, and ruler of all, and he alone is supreme. We don't just teach them convenient rules to obey and religious rituals to follow and life skills to know: we teach them God.

Second, **we teach the next generation what God has done**. The last part of verse 4 mentions the "wondrous works he has performed." The rest of this psalm recounts all that God has done in the history of his people. The psalmist wants God's people to tell future generations about the plagues, about God's provision of manna and quail from the sky, and the rest of God's faithful and powerful provisions for his people from generation to generation.

Third, **we teach the next generation what God has said**. The psalmist mentions God's "law" (v. 5) and his "commands" (v. 7). Make this book the center of your instruction in your home. Let it trump all other books. If God has spoken, then what else is more important for you to tell your children? More important than teaching them to play a sport or learn a subject in school, we need to teach them the Word of God. It's the only thing that will last. As Jesus told his disciples, "Heaven and earth will pass away, but my words will never pass away" (Matt 24:35). From generation to generation, God's Word will never fade. It is a rock on which our children and their children and their children can stand for eternity.

We Tell the Stories (78:10,13-16,23-31,38-39,44-51,53,55, 59-64,67-72)

This is the longest historical psalm in the Bible, and it summarizes some of the most important and foundational stories in the life of God's people. Time and space do not permit an exhaustive treatment of each of these stories, but consider some of the stories we have to tell:

- God's giving of the law (v. 10; Exod 19–40)
- God's parting of the Red Sea (vv. 13,53; Exod 14–15)
- God's guidance through the wilderness (v. 14; Exod 13:21; Num 10:34)
- God's provision of water and food (vv. 15-16,23-29; Exod 17:6; Num 20:8-11)
- God's judgment against sin (vv. 30-31; Num 11:33-34)
- God's mercy toward his people (vv. 38-39; Exod 34:6)
- God's signs and wonders against Egypt (vv. 44-51; Exod 7–11)
- God's victory over Israel's enemies and provision of land (v. 55; Joshua)
- God's rejection of his sinful people (vv. 59-64; 1 Sam 4)
- God's choosing of David as king (vv. 67-72; 1 Sam 16:1-13; 2 Sam 7)

By passing along these stories, we are telling our children that we all find ourselves living in the midst of a story that began a long time ago. In other words, we're not the first ones on the scene, and neither are our children. We want our children to know that the world doesn't revolve around us or them. The world and all of history revolves around God, and he is weaving together a grand story made up of all our individual stories.

We Warn against Sinfulness (78:10-11,17-18,32,36-37,40-42,56-58)

In the process of telling the stories of Israel's history, Psalm 78 gives us some sobering warnings. In spite of God's mighty acts, his protection and provision, his compassion and mercy, Israel continued to rebel and doubt God's promises. Notice this recurring pattern: God acts on behalf of his people, his people turn from him, and then God restores them through repentance. We should learn from Israel's failures.

In the first part of 1 Corinthians 10, Paul talks about God's bringing his people out of Egypt and then their wandering in the wilderness. He says, "Now these things took place as examples for us, so that we will not desire evil things as they did" (1 Cor 10:6). These Old Testament stories serve as a warning. Paul says, "Don't become idolaters as some of them were" (1 Cor 10:7). The Israelites turned from God and tested him, and they paid the penalty for their sin. Many of them were destroyed. Then Paul reiterates, "These things happened to them as examples, and they were written for our instruction. . . . So, whoever thinks he stands must be careful not to fall" (1 Cor 10:11-12).

Scripture is telling us to read these stories and realize that the same thing could happen to us. We are supposed to warn one another and our children. There are dreadful consequences to come when you turn from God. It leads to destruction, and God's judgment is real! So don't turn from God or test him. Trust God.

We Exalt the Savior

We tell the next generation about God's mercy toward his people. We tell them of how God's grace triumphs over man's sin. The story of Israel's history is the story of how **God responds to his people's failures with his forgiveness**. In fact, God's forgiveness is the only reason this story keeps going!

Israel's story is also about how **God responds to his people's faithlessness with his faithfulness**. This is good news, and it gets even better. This recounting of God's grace, mercy, forgiveness, and faithfulness ultimately points not backward but forward to Christ. Israel's history was pointing to the day when Christ, the promised Son of God, God in the flesh (John 1:14), would come to pay the price for all our failures and endure the penalty for all our faithlessness. This is a story worth telling. This is a God worth speaking about to the next generation. This is a gospel worth spreading to the generation after them . . . and the one after them.

We don't want this story to stop with us; we want this story to spread through us. So this is what we do: we teach the Scriptures, we tell the stories, we warn against sinfulness, and we exalt the Savior. And, as we'll see below, we do all this with the hope that it will have certain effects in the lives of future generations.

What We Hope

We proclaim God and his mighty acts to the coming generation for specific purposes. Notice, for instance, the words *so that* and *then* in verses 6-8. This is not teaching and telling and warning and exalting simply for the sake of information but for the sake of transformation. We hope for at least three things.

They Will Know God in Their Minds

We want the children in our homes and in our churches to know God deeply. We want teenagers to have an intimate knowledge of who God is. Amid all the awards and scholarships that they might get at the end of a school year (achievements for which we give thanks to God), the achievement that matters most is this:

> This is what the LORD says: The wise person should not boast in his wisdom; the strong should not boast in his strength; the wealthy should not boast in his wealth. But the one who boasts should boast in this: that he understands and knows me—that I am the LORD, showing faithful love, justice, and righteousness on the earth, for I delight in these things.
> This is the LORD's declaration. (Jer 9:23-24)

They Will Trust God in Their Hearts

In verse 7 the psalmist wants the knowledge of God in their heads to lead to the hope in God in their hearts. We're not just after head knowledge; we're after heart trust. We tell stories so that children will believe that God is trustworthy and will put their trust in him. We want them to trust God to satisfy them, which involves turning aside from the pleasures of this world because they have found greater treasure in God. We hope that their hearts will belong to God.

They Will Obey God in Their Lives

The psalmist wants future generations to keep God's commandments faithfully (vv. 7-8). The end goal for the next generation is not just to *survive* spiritually but rather to *thrive* spiritually. We want them to run into the world with the gospel, ready to use whatever gifts, experiences, education, resources, and anything else God entrusts to them. We want them to spend it all for his glory among all peoples.

Some Practical Steps Forward

One practical way to put this psalm into practice is through regular times of family worship. This would apply to families with children as well as families without children. It could also apply to singles who may have the opportunity to regularly spend time with other believers. Just as you set aside a time and a place to be alone before God, set aside a time and a place to gather regularly in your home to worship God with others. Such time involves reading, studying, and memorizing God's Word together, as well as praying and singing together.

If you have children, be sure to include them and to explain difficult concepts. Keep it simple and enjoyable. Remember, this doesn't have to be an exhaustive exegetical study followed by a season of prayer and a set of worship songs. You are aiming to shepherd their hearts in the truth and the love of God. Regardless of your family situation, the goal of family worship is to bring glory to God, produce joy in the home, and effect change in the world. Indeed, we want to "tell a future generation the praiseworthy acts of the Lord, his might, and the wondrous works he has performed" (v. 4).

Reflect and Discuss

1. What are some barriers to passing along the faith to the next generation?
2. Why must the Scriptures be primary in terms of what we teach to the next generation?
3. What's the danger in teaching our kids to behave morally without emphasizing the Bible's teaching about God and the gospel?
4. How does the telling of the stories of the Bible (including the overarching story of redemption) help fight against our natural, self-centered tendencies?
5. Respond to a parent who says, "It's the church's job to teach my child the gospel."
6. Based on Psalm 78, what does Israel's example teach us not to do? Make a list.

7. How can we teach about God's mercy and forgiveness and, at the same time, warn about the seriousness of sin?

8. What is our end goal for the next generation in passing along the faith? What role does the Holy Spirit play in this?

9. What are some specific ways churches and families can be intentional about passing along the faith to the next generation?

10. Have you ever been a part of regular family worship? What might family worship look like for your family or group of friends? Write down a simple plan.

Behold His Jealousy

PSALM 79

Main Idea: God is jealous for his own glory and for the good of his people, which means we should live zealously toward those same ends.

I. **What Does It Mean for God to Be Jealous?**
   A. God is zealous for his glory.
      1. God desires and deserves all glory.
      2. God is completely secure.
      3. God is supremely satisfying.
   B. God is zealous for the good of his people.
      1. In love, God cares for his people with compassion.
      2. In love, God saves his people from their sin.
      3. In love, God sustains his people in their suffering.
      4. In love, God leads his people to eternal life.
II. **Why Does It Matter That God Is Jealous?**
   A. We should live with zeal for his glory.
   B. We should live with zeal for our good.

We are constantly tempted to have a low view of God. We ignore or minimize characteristics about him that make us uncomfortable. Psalm 79 highlights the jealousy of God—one of those characteristics. When most of us think of jealousy, we think of the sin of selfish envy, even anger, that breeds resentment within us and destroys relationships around us. So, how is it possible for jealousy to be good?

Jealousy can be a good thing when we think about the love of a husband for his wife. For example, Heather Platt is my bride, and I am jealous for her. By that I mean that I am jealous for her good, jealous to see that she is cared for well. I'm jealous to provide for her. I am jealous to protect her from anything that would harm her. I'm jealous to promote the purity of my love for her and her love for me. In a similar way the jealousy of God is good for *you* and good for God. Now, don't carry the marriage analogy too far because as much as I love my wife, I am an imperfect husband. There are, then, some significant differences between God's jealousy and my jealousy.

Psalm 79 was written in light of the destruction of Jerusalem. Previously, God had protected Jerusalem from Assyria. But years later, because God's people persisted in sin, Babylon came and attacked the city, destroying it completely. This psalm is written from the perspective of the few Israelites who were still alive and left behind, now surrounded by ruins. Massive devastation makes this a hard, emotionally raw psalm to read.

Notice the psalmist's question in verse 5: "How long, LORD? Will you be angry forever? Will your *jealousy* keep burning like fire?" (emphasis added). What does it mean for God to be jealous, and why does this matter for our lives? We'll attempt to answer those two questions as simply as possible. And when I say "simply," I mean "straightforwardly," not "modestly." These are not modest truths; these are massive truths.

What Does It Mean for God to Be Jealous?

God Is Zealous for His Glory

I use the word *zealous* here because both the Old Testament and the New Testament words for "jealousy" are sometimes translated using the word *zeal*. Jealousy is zeal for something. So, what is God zealous for?

God is zealous for his own glory. It's all over this psalm and all over Scripture. Even here in the beginning of Psalm 79, amid the disaster that has come on the people of Jerusalem, God is the focus. The word *your*, referring to God, is used four times in verses 1-2. The psalmist is talking about this destruction from a divine perspective. In verses 9-10 the psalmist cries out for help, and he appeals to God with emphasis on God's glory, name, and vengeance in the eyes of the surrounding nations.

The psalmist knows that God is zealous for his glory. The first time we clearly see this attribute in God is when God gives Israel the Ten Commandments:

> *I am the LORD your God, who brought you out of the land of Egypt, out of the place of slavery.*
>
> *Do not have other gods besides me. Do not make an idol for yourself, whether in the shape of anything in the heavens above or on the earth below or in the waters under the earth. Do not bow in worship to them, and do not serve them; for I, the LORD your God, am a jealous God, punishing the children for the fathers' iniquity, to the third and fourth generations of those who hate me, but showing faithful love to*

a thousand generations of those who love me and keep my commands.
(Exod 20:2-6)

These foundational truths for God's covenant people remind us that **God desires and deserves all glory.** There is only one true God, and because he alone is God, he is jealous for all worship *as* God. Many people recoil at that idea because they think it is inherently wrong for anyone to be jealous for their own worship. In fact, we're repulsed by anyone who would dare to think that they deserve worship. They don't deserve glory, and they are totally deceived if they think they do.

But not God. No, he's not deceived. God knows he deserves all glory and that there is no other god. He is the God who is worthy of all worship in all the world, which means it's not wrong for him to desire worship. It's altogether *right* for him to desire his own glory, his own exaltation. The moment that God were to exalt anyone or anything else, he would no longer be *the God* who is worthy of all worship.

All the references to God's jealousy in Scripture are grounded in God's zeal for his glory. Exodus 34 provides another example of this truth, as God gives his people instructions about what to do and how to live when they enter the promised land, a land where all kinds of false gods were being worshiped: "You shall tear down their altars and break their pillars and cut down their Asherim (for you shall worship no other god, for the LORD, whose name is Jealous, is a jealous God)" (Exod 34:13-14 ESV).

It makes sense that God's name is Jealous, because there's no one greater than God. While it is wrong for us to want worship, since we don't deserve it, it's right for God to want worship because he *does* deserve it. Realizing this is the secret to true worship.

Our jealousy is different from God's jealousy in other ways too. When we are jealous, it is oftentimes due to our insecurity or envy. We see something someone else has, and we become jealous because we want it. For example, when I was in high school, the girl who is now my wife was dating another guy for months, and I was jealous of him. In fact, jealousy was eating me alive because I was insecure.

This kind of insecurity plays out in so many different ways throughout our lives. Most of us could think of something—even a good thing— we want that someone else has because there's insecurity in us. But not in God. **God is completely secure.** There is no envy in him because he desires nothing that is bad, and everything that is good belongs to him. He is supremely good and supremely glorious. He's not jealous of anything we have, because every good thing we have comes from him in the first place.

There's another way God's jealousy is different from ours. Once I finally started dating the girl who is now my wife, I would become jealous if other guys were flirting with her. Why? Because I would worry that she would like one of them more than me, that she would find more joy and fulfillment and satisfaction in being with them (particularly if the guy was more attractive and enjoyable to be around than me). But again, this is where God is so different from us.

God is supremely satisfying. He knows there's no one better than him. He is not worried that if you worship another god you're going to find more joy or fulfillment or satisfaction. No, God knows there is no one who can even come close to comparing to the joy and fulfillment and satisfaction that is found in him. God is zealous for his glory because God alone is glorious.

God Is Zealous for the Good of His People

Throughout Scripture God glorifies himself by showering his goodness on his people. From the start God creates man and woman in his image so that they will enjoy him as they glorify him with the life he gives to them (Gen 1–2). And they do for a time.

Adam and Eve soon turn aside from the security and satisfaction they have in God, and they instead worship other gods, namely, themselves. They turn aside from the God who is zealous for their good. At that point sin enters the world, and it affects every person in all of history. Now every person is born in sin, and they turn aside from the one true God and follow false gods (see Rom 1:18–3:20). This sinful nature is evident in the lives of each of us.

But God in his mercy set in motion a plan to make it possible for sinners to be reconciled to him, to be restored to satisfaction in him (Eph 2:4-7). In the Old Testament he called a particular people to himself. According to Genesis 12, Abraham and his descendants became known as the people of Israel, and, through Moses, God entered into a covenant with them (Exod 19–40). This covenant was akin to a marriage relationship in which God said, "I am going to pour out my love on you in a special way, and you're going to demonstrate my love to all the peoples of the earth."

Israel said yes and entered into that covenant relationship with God, committing their lives to him. But before the seal of that marriage-like covenant had time to set up, Israel was already turning aside to fashion a false god (Exod 32). In this way physical idolatry became a picture of spiritual adultery.

Like a husband who loves a wayward wife, over and over again God would pour out his love on his people, forgiving them of their sins, drawing them back to him, only to have them turn away repeatedly to idols. Oh, the hurt and horrors involved in adultery against the Almighty!

This is exactly what happened in Psalm 79. The people of God in Jerusalem had all the security and satisfaction they could ever want in God, and yet they turned aside and crafted idols with their own hands, bowing down to worship them. Those gods were not able to provide for them, care for them, lead them, or guide them. This idolatry led to all kinds of gross immorality, eventually bringing destruction on them.

Israel's spiritual adultery was like an addiction. An alcoholic knows that drinking will lead to disastrous consequences, yet he or she drinks anyway. So also we are prone to turn away from God, away from his glory and his goodness, despite what it will do to us. We choose to trust in ourselves and the things of this world when they will ultimately and inevitably lead to our downfall. Therefore, when you picture the jealousy of God, picture God as a husband who loves his wife deeply. Picture this husband as one who possesses all his wife could ever need or want, yet she turns aside from him and runs after other men instead (Ezek 16; Hosea). This husband is perfect, good, and faithful, but his wife continually sleeps around on him with all kinds of other men. This is the sense in which God is a jealous husband.

Again, God is not insecure. He is completely secure and supremely satisfying. And he loves his bride so much that he is jealous for her good. He will not give up on her, which means he is zealous to bring her back to himself. The psalmist knows this when he cries out, "How long, LORD? Will you be angry forever? Will your jealousy keep burning like fire?" (Ps 79:5). He knows the people of God were experiencing the consequences of idolatry, of spiritual adultery. The worship of other gods had led to their destruction and to death. They got what they asked for, what they deserved. So the psalmist turns back to God in sin and cries out for his mercy.

As the psalmist cries out, he shows us that he knows **in love God cares for his people with compassion**. From the beginning of this psalm, the psalmist pleads with God about the shame and destruction God's

people had experienced. In verse 8 he begs for "compassion . . . quickly."
In other words, "Hurry, O God, to help us."

The psalmist knows that Israel is in despair because they've sinned
against a holy God, and they need him to cover over their sins. So he
cries out, "God of our salvation, help us—for the glory of your name.
Rescue us and atone for our sins, for your name's sake" (v. 9). The
psalmist knows that **in love God saves his people from their sin**. He is
the God of our "salvation." God's people were caught in the clutches of
sin, and they needed to be saved.

The Hebrew word for "atone" means "cover over" (BDB, 497), for
we need God to cover our sins. In the Old Testament, sacrifices were
offered to atone for sins. On the Day of Atonement, for example, the
high priest would offer a sacrifice in the place of those who had sinned.
This sacrifice showed that the penalty for sin, which is death, had been
paid. The priests would offer this sacrifice over and over again, year
after year. But these Old Testament sacrifices were only intended to set
the stage for the New Testament, when Jesus would come and sacrifice
himself, once and for all, on the cross, to make salvation possible for
sinners before a holy God (Heb 10:1-14). This is the greatest news in
the world to every sinner anywhere: God has made a way for your sins
against him to be covered over.

God's love not only results in the forgiveness of sins. We see in
verse 11 that **in love God sustains his people in their suffering**. Notice
God's jealous love. He will not leave his people alone in their suffering.
According to his great power, he will preserve them. The same holds
true for God's people today: God is a faithful husband who will never
abandon his bride.

Finally, **in love God leads his people to eternal life**. Look at how
the psalm ends: "Then we, your people, the sheep of your pasture, will
thank you forever; we will declare your praise to generation after generation" (v. 13).

God is a jealous God, a zealous husband who loves his bride and will
lead his people in such a way that they will never, ever, ever run out of
reasons to give him thanksgiving and praise.

God is zealous for his glory, and, at the same time, God is zealous for
the good of his people.

Why Does It Matter That God Is Jealous?

We Should Live with Zeal for His Glory

God alone deserves all glory. Therefore, God desires all glory. So we *must* turn aside daily from all false gods and idols in this world—whether it's handcrafted, wooden figures or far more subtle (yet just as sinful) gods of money, sex, success, sports, entertainment, family, health, food, position, power, pleasure, comfort, acclaim, etc. We put our trust in things, even good things, instead of in our God. We pursue avenues that steal our affections from the God who is worthy of supreme affection and absolute devotion.

Scripture gives many examples of those who lived with zeal for God's glory. Elijah the prophet describes himself as "very zealous for the LORD God of Armies" (1 Kgs 19:14). God said of Phinehas, son of Eleazar, that "he was zealous among [the Israelites] with my zeal" (Num 25:11). May this be the mark of our lives—that we were as zealous for the honor of God as God is.

This kind of zeal should also mark our corporate worship. We should refuse to walk away from a worship gathering and think, *How did I feel about the service today?* as if the service was about us. No, what should drive us in worship is the question, How does God feel about the service today? The service is about him.

This kind of zeal should mark our families, our singleness, our marriages, our parenting, our work, our schooling, and everything we do. We ought to be driven, not for the pursuits of this world but for the glory of our God. For those who aren't sure if they're willing to let go of certain things and pursuits, I want to remind you of the second implication.

We Should Live with Zeal for Our Good

You might be thinking, *I thought I was supposed to live for God's glory, not my good.* However, this is where we need to realize that our greatest good is found in living for God's glory. Do you honestly think the way you're spending your money to indulge in more comforts and pleasures in this world is satisfying? You have no idea about the indescribable joy you're missing out on that comes with sacrificial giving. You're not living with zeal for your good but for your bad.

Do you think sexual immorality satisfies? You have no idea that in that moment of fading pleasure, you're missing out on unfading treasure. C. S. Lewis said,

> We are halfhearted creatures, fooling about with drink and sex and ambition when infinite joy has been offered us, like ignorant children who go on making mud pies in the slum because we cannot imagine what is meant by the offer of a holiday at the sea.

Then Lewis says these piercing words: "We are far too easily pleased" (*The Weight of Glory*, 26).

In other words, we think we give in to the temptations and things of this world because our desires are so strong, but that's not true. Our desires are weak. It takes so little to satisfy us. We settle for the slums instead of holding out for the Riviera.

God is supremely satisfying, so live with zeal for your good as you live with zeal for God. He loves you with a jealous love—an altogether right and good kind of jealous love. He is jealous for your affections, and he's worthy of them because he's the only one whose love can satisfy you. So I implore you to run from sin and reorient everything you do around zeal for God's glory. In the process you will be living with zeal for your good.

Reflect and Discuss

1. What do you normally associate jealousy with in your own life?
2. How is God's jealousy different from human jealousy?
3. Why is it good that God is jealous for his own glory?
4. Explain a specific way God's jealousy is good for his people.
5. How should God's zeal for his own glory shape the church's corporate worship?
6. How should God's jealousy shape the way we treat sin?
7. How does Psalm 79 speak to a culture that views all religious views as equally valid?
8. What are some idols that you have to guard against in your own life?
9. What are some signs that a church is taking a man-centered approach (rather than a God-centered approach) to evangelism and corporate worship?
10. Explain the following statement: Seeking God's glory is actually the best way to seek our own good.

The God Who Restores

PSALM 80

Main Idea: Our deepest needs are met when we see God in his glory.

I. The Shepherd: Who God Is (80:1-3)
II. The Struggle: Where We Are (80:4-7)
III. The Solution: What We Need (80:8-19)

Evidence suggests that the historical backdrop of this psalm is the Assyrian invasion in 722 BC that led to the fall of the northern kingdom of Israel. First, the tribes mentioned in the first two verses occupied territory in the northern kingdom. Second, the Greek translation of the Old Testament included a superscription: "Concerning the Assyrian."

About two hundred years before the Assyrian invasion, the united kingdom of Israel was divided: Israel in the north and Judah in the south. The northern kingdom dove headfirst into all kinds of wickedness. God sent prophets like Amos and Hosea to call them back, but Israel blew them off. That's what led to their fall. While Assyria had her own evil motivations, ultimately the Assyrian exile was God's judgment against the sin of Israel.

You can almost imagine the psalmist perched at the northern edge · of Judah, looking out at smoke rising in the distance over the lands of Ephraim, Benjamin, and Manasseh.

That's the historical situation. However, this isn't in the Bible just for us to become acquainted with history; it has profound relevance for God's people today. Psalm 80 answers the question, How do you pray when you realize you (or people close to you) are far away from God?

We love that God restores his people. That's really good news. But the restoration we *need* isn't always the kind we *want*. Psalm 80 is not a restoration that conjures up images of green pastures and still waters. Psalm 80 is a restoration that hurts. It hurts because sometimes we get hooked on things that are killing us.

What do we do when we realize we've drifted from God? This psalm directs our attention to three places.

The Shepherd: Who God Is
PSALM 80:1-3

In verses 1-2 the psalmist thinks about God's title as Shepherd and the promises God had made about his people.

Joseph, Ephraim, Benjamin, and Manasseh are Rachel's tribes. Rachel was married to Jacob. At first she can't get pregnant, then the Lord opens her womb and she has Joseph, the one famous for his fancy coat. God is gracious, and Rachel gets pregnant again, and Joseph gets a baby brother (Gen 35), but he loses his mom in the process. With her last breath, Rachel names her youngest son "Ben-oni" (later called Benjamin). Joseph had two sons who were considered so special to their grandpa that they were adopted and treated as his own sons (Gen 48:4-5).

In Jacob's dying hour he pronounces a blessing on these tribes. Fast-forward eleven hundred years, and Rachel's tribes are being carried off in judgment. To the naked eye, it looks like the Shepherd of Israel has no more interest in leading Joseph like a flock. It looks as if God's promise has failed. But notice two primary pictures of God: as gardener (vv. 8-17) and as Shepherd (vv. 1-2).

When the people of Israel speak of God as Shepherd, they're speaking of God's attentiveness, care, and provision for his people. These two statements—the Lord is God (Exod 3:14-15) and the Lord is Shepherd (Ps 23:1)—were massive pillars of faith in the Old Testament. How many Israelites across the centuries sang, "The LORD is my shepherd; I have what I need" (Ps 23:1)? Believers still quote this often in times of grief and loss. God as Shepherd wasn't just a theological formulation but a soul-steadying reminder of God's intention toward his people. This psalm is pointing up and out from the very start, directing our eyes to the central claim of the Old Testament but also of the New Testament.

Jesus comes on the scene, and what does he say in John 10?

> *I am the good shepherd. The good shepherd lays down his life for the sheep. The hired hand, since he is not the shepherd and doesn't own the sheep, leaves them and runs away when he sees a wolf coming. The wolf then snatches and scatters them. This happens because he is a hired hand and doesn't care about the sheep.*
>
> *I am the good shepherd. I know my own, and my own know me.* (John 10:11-14)

Then he does just that: he lays down his life for the sheep by dying on the cross in our place.

The central prayer of this psalm is repeated in verses 3, 7, and 19: "Restore us, God; make your face shine on us, so that we may be saved." In the fullness of time, the way God did this is Jesus. Jesus restores us (reconciles us) to God. John 1 speaks of the entrance of Jesus into human history in terms of God's glory shining on us: "The Word became flesh and dwelt among us. We observed his glory, the glory as the one and only Son from the Father, full of grace and truth" (John 1:14).

God's glory shines most brightly on the cross. There God's love and justice are on full display, as Christ becomes our substitute and bears the punishment we deserve, and he rises to give new life to all who trust in him. All the restoration work God is doing in the world is that kind. God is making people right with him through Jesus. If you have run to Jesus Christ in faith—what a privilege this is!—you can pray in the knowledge that God is sovereign and he is your Shepherd.

Psalm 80 displays such beautiful faith and trust. This psalmist is confident in God. This psalmist looks at the billowing smoke to the north, which testifies to Assyria's military power, and he prays something audacious: shine and we are saved (vv. 3,7,19).

The psalm moves from who God is to where we are.

The Struggle: Where We Are
PSALM 80:4-7

Here again he starts with God and describes him as the "Lord God of Armies" (v. 4). It's sometimes translated Lord of Hosts, and it refers to God's absolute rule over all forces in the world and in heavenly places.

We see this truth in many places in Scripture. Psalm 135:5-6 says, "For I know that the Lord is great; our Lord is greater than all gods. The Lord does whatever he pleases in heaven and on earth, in the seas and all the depths." And Daniel 4:35 affirms, "All the inhabitants of the earth are counted as nothing, and he does what he wants with the army of heaven and the inhabitants of the earth. There is no one who can block his hand or say to him, 'What have you done?'"

The books I was reading as a young adult twenty years ago didn't prefer to think of God in Psalm 135/Daniel 4 kinds of ways. I read books that told me God didn't know Adam and Eve were going to sin in the garden. He rolled the dice. He took a chance. It didn't go the way he expected. Dr. Bruce Ware of Southern Seminary wrote a great little book that helped me out of that: *Their God Is Too Small.* Ware takes the reader into the Scriptures to see that the God of the Bible is not worried or confused or wringing his hands. He is large and in charge. So we can trust him, even with things we don't understand. Christian friend, your view of God will shape the size of your prayers.

This psalmist knows something of the power of God, the one "enthroned between the cherubim" (v. 1). The physical place on earth where God's blazing holiness was most concentrated was between the cherubim, their golden wings extended over the mercy seat. This is a picture of God's glorious holiness. And the psalmist asks a question in verse 4. We might expect it to say, "How long will you be angry with your people's *transgressions?*" Instead it says, "How long will you be angry with your people's prayers?"

In the Old Testament hypocrisy reached such heights that the people of God would say "the temple of the LORD" three times in a row (Jer 7:4) as if it were a spell that warded off evil, as if nominal adherence to religious forms guaranteed that God would bless them. So they offered sacrifices. They attended this or that Old Testament church event. Welcome to the Christian fortress where we live, where everyone "knows" God, where everybody has walked an aisle and prayed a prayer. Friends, often where nominalism thrives, the aspect of God's character that gets left aside is holiness.

Here is the truth about God's justice and his judgment: He is a God who does not tolerate evil, who doesn't wink at our rebellion, who doesn't let us define right and wrong, who won't be your copilot, who doesn't invite us to haggle over the terms of repentance. This is the biblical God. There are no other God options. We take him on his terms or we perish.

You can be born and live your whole life and die telling yourself you knew God when in fact there was no evidence of his lordship in your life. In Matthew 7 Jesus tells us in no uncertain terms that hell will be full of people who think doing spiritual, churchy activities can be a substitute for following Jesus as Lord. Oh, how we need to reckon with this truth as the church of Jesus Christ! There's nothing more dangerous than playing religious games. The ultimate reason Israel is eating bread soaked in tears (v. 5) isn't because Assyria had a bigger army. It's because Israel didn't take God seriously.

In verse 5 Israel finally breaks. But even there God's chosen people are not weeping because of their sin against God, having tested his patience for a thousand years. No, they weep because it stinks to be in exile. How true that can be for us as well. We're often more concerned about our hardships than our sins. Israel's sorrow was merely worldly grief (2 Cor 7:10), not grief leading to repentance. It was the sorrow of a person who *thought* he could outrun the reaper; then the consequences of his actions caught him.

Oh, for a comeback of true repentance before our God, where we confess our sin individually, where we corporately lament the many failures of the visible church of Jesus Christ: *Instead* of displaying contentment in Christ, we have the same insatiable appetite for worldly wealth that our neighbors are defined by. *Instead* of taking risks of faith and obedience, we cling to the safety of what's familiar. *Instead* of holding fast to the word of life in a crooked and perverse generation, we are the crooked and the perverse. Church, we have one job:

> But you are a chosen race, a royal priesthood, a holy nation, a people for his possession, so that you may proclaim the praises of the one who called you out of darkness into his marvelous light. Once you were not a people, but now you are God's people; you had not received mercy, but now you have received mercy.
>
> Dear friends, I urge you as strangers and exiles to abstain from sinful desires that wage war against the soul. Conduct yourselves honorably among the Gentiles, so that when they slander you as evildoers, they will observe your good works and will glorify God on the day he visits. (1 Pet 2:9-12)

We are to be light bearers. Sadly, we can be the kind of church that dabbles in the things of God. And we can become so insensitive that we quench the Spirit and he leaves, and amid all the entertainment, we don't even notice he's gone.

What words do we say to God when this is where we are? Here's what we say: "Restore us, God of Armies; make your face shine on us, so that we may be saved" (v. 7).

Church, please hear me. Apostasy isn't hard. It's really easy. Ask Ephraim. Ask Manesseh. Ask Judah. Ask Demas. Ask Laodicea. Because of this, every Sunday is a gospel renewal ceremony for us. Every Sunday is a reminder that, while we are thankful for many things, we serve no God but Jesus Christ. We proclaim no message but Christ and him crucified. We commit to no purpose but that of praising, reflecting, and spreading the knowledge of Christ's glory to the ends of the earth.

The Solution: What We Need
PSALM 80:8-19

We need God to do something about our wayward hearts. Hope comes as we remember God's story. The psalmist says to God, "I know what you're up to." This psalmist travels back hundreds of years to God's mighty act of redemption, and he tells the story under the metaphor of God planting a garden. He's walking us across eight hundred years of history. Verse 8 is the middle of the fifteenth century BC, the exodus. God digs up a vine from Egypt. Verse 9 fast-forwards forty years when the walls of Jericho fall. God clears a place in the promised land. Verses 10-11 fast-forward another four hundred years to the height of the united kingdom in Israel. David is on his throne and Israel's vine is flourishing, running from the Mediterranean Sea to the Euphrates River, flourishing in God's place under his rule and blessing. Verse 12 stops the music with an allusion to the Assyrian invasion in 722 BC.

He knows the story, and he knows that God told his people even before they went into exile that exile wouldn't be the end of the story. There would be a return. God would send Messiah. God's hand would be with the man at his right hand, the Son of Man whom he would make strong (v. 17). That Son of Man would be the true vine. He would embody Israel. He would take her place in a story gone sideways. He would obey where they disobeyed. He would fulfill the prophecy in Isaiah 40:11: "He protects his flock like a shepherd; he gathers the lambs in his arms and carries them in the fold of his garment. He gently leads those that are nursing."

Isaiah 40 was like an Old Testament sneak peek at Romans 8, a reminder to God's sin-addicted people that he wasn't finished with them. He would gather his people, and nothing would separate them from the love of their covenant Lord. To gather sin addicts to himself and begin his mission of restoration, Jesus went to the cross. "As for me, if I am lifted up from the earth I will draw all people to myself" (John 12:32).

Here in Psalm 80:17, God taps the man at his right hand, the son of man; God makes him strong and he completes his task. The effect in verse 18 is that people call on his name.

This psalmist knows both how sinful a nation they are and how strong a Redeemer God is. He's saying, "God, listen; Shepherd of Israel, lead us like a flock!" Or to borrow from Psalm 68, "Lead captivity captive!" (see Ps 68:18 KJV). We can say the same thing as we plead for the deep restoration we need from God. We say to him we are weak. Our resume is pitiful. Temptation is powerful. The pleasures of sin are so enticing. The comforts of this world make us so spiritually sleepy. Then this chorus comes barreling in: Restore us, Lord, God of Armies. Shine and we're home! You shine and we are delivered!

Church, always remember: We're not changed by looking in but by looking up. Where he shines, his people are saved. Here's the good news; if you have trusted in Jesus, you will find this to be true: God will never give up on the work he began in you. The restoration we *need* isn't always the restoration we *want*.

If you've trusted Jesus, you can't sin and enjoy it the way you used to. And, because God is determined to get you home, he will pull out all the stops. Sometimes God's presence feels more like burning than blessing. He may bring heat to your life if it means you will be more fully his. When we cling to things that are killing us, God won't always whisper gentle warnings. He might not knock on the door; he might blast it off its hinges and tear you out of the grip of your idols.

Look at this awesome God of restoration in Psalm 80. Look at the verbs he has with him. He leads. He sits enthroned. He rallies his power. He comes to save us. He restores, shines, digs up, drives out, plants, clears. He makes vines spread and flourish. He cuts and burns away whatever is hindering us. Maybe we didn't realize it fully, but those are things we asked God to do when we asked him to save us.

Our final assurance is not something we produce in ourselves. Our final assurance is that God's face shines on us in the gospel: "The things of earth will grow strangely dim in the light of his glory and grace," and he preserves our faith to the end (Lemmel, "Turn Your Eyes upon Jesus").

Reflect and Discuss

1. When you face a difficult situation, how do you view God? As your Shepherd? Why or why not? How would you respond if you did view him as Shepherd?
2. How does your view of God, particularly of his sovereignty, influence the way you pray and the things you ask him to do? How *should* our view of God affect the way we pray?
3. When we face hardships, what's the difference between worldly sorrow and godly sorrow?
4. What does it look like when we play religious games today?

5. When are we more concerned with our hardships than our sins? What does that indicate about our hearts? How should we respond when we realize that this is where we are?
6. The psalmist's prayer in verse 7 for favor and salvation is answered for us in the person and work of Jesus. How do you pray when you're struggling? What kind of restoration do you hope for?
7. What can we as Christians do to prevent ourselves from drifting from God? What implications does this have for you this week?
8. What are some specific ways we can remember God's story (Deut 6:4-9)?
9. How do we gain a deeper knowledge of God through his Word? How does this deeper knowledge deepen our hope?

This Do in Remembrance of Me

PSALM 81

Main Idea: Unconditional obedience is the only acceptable response of God's people to the glorious gospel of Jesus Christ.

I. **Rejoice Regularly (81:1-5a).**
II. **Remember Intentionally (81:5b-7).**
III. **Respond Appropriately (81:8-12).**
IV. **Receive Expectantly (81:13-16).**

George Santayana, an early twentieth-century Harvard professor known for his pithy aphorisms, said, "Those who cannot remember the past are condemned to repeat it." That phrase is not only catchy but haunting. If our past—driven by human nature—has been ugly at times, then a healthy reflection on it ought to at least inform how we live in the present. In like manner, if our past bears clear reflection of God's incomparable grace, then we are compelled to greater allegiance to him in the present.

God's people tend to become a bit complacent about the historical roots of their faith. Based on a reminder about the reason God had instituted the Festival of Shelters (or Booths or Tabernacles), Psalm 81 speaks to that tendency. The memories of God's people had lapsed when it came to what he had done in delivering them from bondage in Egypt. Not only had they become lax in praising him, but they had ceased to obey him in response to what he had done. Consequently, they were missing out on his blessings. As a whole, Psalm 81 reflects the hope that God—based on his track record—will turn his people's affliction into rich blessing in the present and future if they will respond in obedience to his great salvation.

On this side of the cross, it remains true that unconditional obedience is the only acceptable response of Jesus's disciples to our deliverance from sin through the glorious gospel. We, too, tend to forget. Consequently, while we don't celebrate the Festival of Shelters to remind us of God's salvation, our Lord did give us the Table of Communion to help us remember his salvation and the obedience to which it constrains us (Matt 25:26-29; Luke 22:14-20; 1 Cor 11:23-34). This psalm seems to foreshadow the Lord's Supper and compels us to respond to God's salvation in four ways.

Rejoice Regularly
PSALM 81:1-5A

The opening verses of this psalm comprise commands for the people to celebrate God's great deliverance through singing and instruments (vv. 1-2; cf. Deut 32:43). The verbs in these verses represent a summons for the people of Israel to offer their loudest expressions of joy, which is the only suitable response to God's mighty works from people who've been blessed by what he's done (Perowne, II:94). The atmosphere described here would characterize the arrival of a king or the celebration of a victory (cf. 1 Sam 10:24; Zeph 3:14). The people were to pull out all the stops in the expression of their jubilation.

The people's delight isn't to be merely a testimony *about* God but expressions "to God," to the one who is "our strength" (v. 1; cf. 29:1) because he delivers and protects his people by his power. The parallel phrase "the God of Jacob" reflects on the innumerable ways he showed himself strong to his people since the time of the great patriarch (cf. 20:2).

One of the psalmist's primary points here is that the celebration of worship that characterized the Festival of Shelters was a prescribed gathering, not a suggested gathering. We see this first in the command to "blow the horn" (v. 3)—or *shofar*—which was the ram's horn used to convene an assembly, initiate a military attack (Josh 6; Judg 7), inaugurate certain festivals, or otherwise move a group to action. Blowing the shofar marked both the new moon and the month of appointed festivals (v. 3; cf. Lev 23:23-25; Num 29:1-6). It was blown on the first day of the seventh month. Ten days later was the Day of Atonement. Five days after that the trumpet would be blown again to mark the Festival of Shelters.

The regulatory nature of this celebratory gathering also is indicated in that the psalmist calls it a "statute," "rule" (ESV), and "decree" (vv. 4-5). The use of the name *Joseph* signifies historic Israel in general; and while the remainder of the verse is a bit obscure, it likely refers to God's judgments against Egypt when he delivered his people. The summons to exult in God's great salvation wasn't an option or a suggestion.

It was a binding decision of God that the people didn't have the freedom to dismiss. It was an appointed time to recall the history of their faith (Ross, *Psalms*, vol. 2, 707–8).

On this side of the cross, some believers tragically push back against the suggestion that we are to rejoice on command. Grace, they say, implies that we celebrate "when our hearts are in it" or "when the Spirit leads" or "as we feel led." This is a curious suggestion, however, since the gospel provides us with a compelling reason to be consumed with constant joy in God (Eph 5:18-20; Col 3:15-16). The prescribed festivals and observances in the Old Testament merely serve as a shadow of the constant joy we have because of God's grace in Christ Jesus (Col 2:16-17; cf. Rom 14:5-9). We are warned, however, against the Lone Ranger Christianity that's exhibited in "neglecting to gather together, as some are in the habit of doing" (Heb 10:25). "No time is amiss for praising God . . . but some are times appointed, not for God to meet us (he is always ready), but for us to meet one another, that we may join together in praising God" (Henry, *Matthew Henry's Commentary*, 861).

The New Testament, however, isn't limited to general instructions for believers to gather together and to express joy and thanksgiving. After our Lord transformed the Passover celebration—a memorial of God's redemptive work in delivering Israel from Egypt (Exod 12:26-27)—into a commemoration of Christ's blood atonement, he commanded his followers to celebrate it regularly (Luke 22:19-20; 1 Cor 11:23-26). He knew we would be prone to forget the magnitude of his great salvation, so he graciously commanded us to engage in welcomed, anticipated accountability. Contrasting God's greater salvation in Christ Jesus with his deliverance of Israel from Egypt, Matthew Henry is right:

> Now if they, on their solemn feast-days, were thus to call to
> mind their redemption out of Egypt, much more ought we,
> on the Christian sabbath, to call to mind a more glorious
> redemption wrought out for us by Jesus Christ from worse
> than Egyptian bondage, and the many gracious answers he
> has given to us, notwithstanding our manifold provocations.
> (Henry, *Matthew Henry's Commentary*, 862)

Believers should never shy away from prescribed times to remember and rejoice in God's great salvation. The gospel compels us to rejoice regularly in what God has done in Jesus Christ!

Remember Intentionally
PSALM 81:5B-7

The people's praise suddenly is interrupted when God's spokesman offers an oracle on his behalf. The prophetic voice claims to hear "an unfamiliar language," which likely is just a claim of God's inspiration. The first part of the oracle recounts God's gracious dealings with Israel. While they were weighed down with a "burden," weary from carrying "the basket" of heavy labor, and "in distress," God came to their aid with strong help (cf. Exod 1:11; 2:23; Pss 50:15; 116:8). He "relieved . . . freed . . . [and] rescued" them, setting them free from their burdensome toil. And then in dramatic displays of the use of nature, he led them through the sea and on to Sinai and spoke from a "thundercloud" (v. 7; Exod 14:19; 19:16-20; 20:18-21; Deut 4:12; Ps 18:11-13).

He further reminds them how he disciplined them because of their disobedience. God led them to a place where there was no water in order to strengthen their trust in him, but they rejected the opportunity on two occasions and resisted him (Exod 17:1-7; Num 20:1-13; cf. Deut 33:8; Ps 95:8). If Sinai was where God educated his people by encounter, Meribah was where he educated them by silence and apparent neglect (Kidner, *Psalms 73–150*, 325).

This oracle warns God's people in every generation, including those who call themselves Christians. The Psalmist speaks in clear and tangible terms. He doesn't use abstract concepts like oppression and redemption, but concrete words like *shoulder, burden, hands,* and *basket* (Kidner, Vol. 16, 325). God wants us to be gripped by the reality and emotion of what he's done for us. Jesus surely had the same purpose in mind when he gave us the Table of Communion. Paul said, "For as often as you eat this bread and drink the cup, you proclaim the Lord's death until he comes" (1 Cor 11:26). Jesus wanted us to be intentional about remembering what he did for us on the cross that we might be saved.

Respond Appropriately
PSALM 81:8-12

God wants us to *act* on what we remember. The only appropriate response is unqualified obedience. The Festival of Shelters included a public reading of the law every seventh year (Deut 31:10-13), which provided a potent reminder for the people to obey God fully. So God

reaches back into the wilderness wandering and captures some snap-
shots of what he's said and done that capsulize his law and compel the
people to respond appropriately with obedience.

The first snapshot is of the heartbeat of the law and is reminiscent of that great commandment in Deuteronomy 6:4 known as the
Shema. The psalmist here records the voice of God as saying, "Listen, my
people, and I will admonish you" (v. 8; cf. 50:7). The following parallel expression reflects God's desire for his people in deeply emotional
terms: "Israel, if you would only listen to me!" (v. 8; cf. Deut 4:1; 5:1;
6:4). He gave the law to the people in view of their obeying him. The
implication here, however, is that they failed to comply, a tragedy that's
clearly articulated in verses 11-12.

The second snapshot is of the exclusivity of the law and alludes to
the first of the Ten Commandments (v. 9). The declaration reminds the
people of their responsibility of absolute allegiance to Yahweh as the
only true God. Israel was prohibited not only from worshiping pagan
deities but even from having them in their possession (Exod 20:3;
Deut 5:7).

The third snapshot is of the obligation to the law and serves as a
reminder of its prologue (v. 10; Exod 20:2; Deut 5:6). God's strong deliverance provides the convincing reason for the people to obey his commandments. The promise expresses the assurance that God gladly will
give his word to those who will receive it by faith and subsequently give
testimony to it. The people are not only indebted to God because of
his deliverance, but they have access to its blessing and benefit through
obedience.

The spiritual nostalgia ends on a sad note. Although God's intent
in giving the law was for the people to obey, they would have none of
it. And although he affectionately called them "my people," nothing
in their actions indicated they belonged to him. So he abandoned
them (v. 12); he sent them away from the safekeeping of his grace. His
patience with their stubbornness ran out, and he freed them up to live
according to their own devices.

This response by God arguably is the greatest and most fearful manifestation of his punishment (Perowne, *Psalms*, vol. 2, 99). Furthermore,
it's indicative of the plight of all mankind as we high-handedly spit in
the face of our Creator by choosing sin over accountability to him. Early
in his letter to the Roman believers, Paul repeatedly lamented the consequences of this rebellion:

> *Therefore God delivered them over in the desires of their hearts to sexual*
> *impurity, so that their bodies were degraded among themselves. . . .*
> *For this reason God delivered them over to disgraceful passions.*
> *Their women exchanged natural sexual relations for unnatural*
> *ones. . . .*
> *And because they did not think it worthwhile to acknowledge God,*
> *God delivered them over to a corrupt mind so that they do what is not*
> *right.* (Rom 1:24,26,28)

This is what's so amazing about the gospel of grace! "But God proves his own love for us in that while we were still sinners, Christ died for us" (Rom 5:8). Although we arrogantly refused to listen to his voice and submit to him, he loved us anyway and sent Jesus to die for us. And he invites us to open our mouths wide so he can fill us with his saving Word (Ps 81:10). Paul—referencing Deuteronomy 30:14—beckons us to this righteousness by faith: "If you confess with your mouth, 'Jesus is Lord,' and believe in your heart that God raised him from the dead, you will be saved" (Rom 10:9; see Rom 10:5-13). Like the Israelites, none of us can keep the law (Rom 3:9-18,23), but we can respond appropriately to God's grace by embracing Christ Jesus.

Once again we can see in this psalm a foreshadowing of the Lord's Supper. Whenever we remember Christ's sacrifice for us, we are reminded that the only appropriate response to the gospel is our obedience. Again Paul connects the dots for us:

> *So then, whoever eats the bread or drinks the cup of the Lord in an*
> *unworthy manner will be guilty of sin against the body and blood of*
> *the Lord. Let a person examine himself; in this way let him eat the*
> *bread and drink from the cup. For whoever eats and drinks without*
> *recognizing the body, eats and drinks judgment on himself. This is*
> *why many are sick and ill among you, and many have fallen asleep. If*
> *we were properly judging ourselves, we would not be judged, but when*
> *we are judged by the Lord, we are disciplined, so that we may not be*
> *condemned with the world.* (1 Cor 11:27-32)

Disobedience never meshes with the gospel of Christ. As he did with the Israelites, our Father takes seriously when we as believers harbor sin in our lives and yet still try to engage in gospel activities. Such mockery of God's grace always reaps his loving discipline.

Receive Expectantly
PSALM 81:13-16

God doesn't want the current generation to repeat the same mistakes as the Israelites who came out of Egypt. Instead, he wants them to experience all of his blessings and goodness. So with the affection and tenderness of a loving father, he laments that they would not "listen to me and . . . follow my ways" (v. 13). These words bear a striking resemblance to those of Jesus when he moaned over Jerusalem with a burdened and compassionate heart, even in the context of judgment (Matt 23:37-39). The difference is that here in Psalm 81 there is still hope, there is still time to repent. God is yearning for his people to obey him.

Why is God so desirous of his people's allegiance and affection? Partly because his blessing is contingent on their obedience. He doesn't want them to miss out on any of the showers of his grace. God is willing and able to force his people's adversaries to bow at his feet (vv. 14-15). The last line of verse 15 means that the enemies' fate is sealed. While they may think their current submission to God is temporary, they're actually doomed to that fate for eternity. God's blessing of protection and victory for his people—should they choose to accept it—will also be forever.

God's blessings, however, won't be limited to the overthrow of Israel's enemies. If the people will obey, he will feed and fulfill them (v. 16). The promise here is again reminiscent of the Song of Moses where God was praised for feeding his people with "honey from the rock" and "the choicest grains of wheat" (Deut 32:13-14). The assurance is that he will bless the land in such a way to provide abundant and constant provision for his people.

The oracle concludes, then, with a strong reminder of God's strength, sustenance, and supply. If his people will obey, they can expect him to defend them against all their enemies and provide for their every need. They will be the recipients of a never-ending stream of his goodness and grace. If they refuse, however, they'll be on their own.

Conclusion

As a young boy, the imperative exhortation "This do in remembrance of me" was indelibly etched in my mind. How could it not be? Every time I went to church, it burned in my sight for an entire hour from its perch on the side of the Communion Table that sat in front of the pulpit. From an early age, I learned that obedience to that command was exactly what Jesus wanted me to do every time I took the Lord's Supper. He wanted me to celebrate afresh his great salvation in Christ Jesus and renew my commitment to obey him. Yet he knew I would be prone to forget the glory of how he freed me from slavery to sin through his death on the cross.

I'm embarrassed that my memory fades sometimes when it comes to the weight of the grandeur of the gospel. Ross is right:

> It is amazing that believers have to be reminded to praise God for this, or to understand its ramifications for that matter. The central focus of the Christian celebration is holy communion, which is a reminder that we have been brought into covenant with the Lord. That covenant includes obligations, and so at the time of the festival God's oracle reminds us that we are to obey. As with ancient Israel, so today many professing believers choose to ignore God's claims on their lives and live their own lives as they please. When they do that, they live without God's protection and provision—they often find themselves in various troubles. It does not have to be that way. (Ross, *Psalms*, Vol. 2, 713)

No Christian has ever experienced the full benefit of complete obedience to Jesus. Most of us just use grace as an excuse and quit trying. If we ever did fully obey him, however, he would rescue us from all our troubles and grant us the total overflow of his blessings. Whenever we come to the Lord's Table, we should resolve to make that our pursuit.

Reflect and Discuss

1. In what ways does God's grace toward us in the past compel us to allegiance to him in the present?
2. Why is it a good thing that we are commanded to rejoice in God rather than merely suggested to do so?
3. How is it a sign of God's graciousness to us that he commands us to regularly celebrate what he has done for us through the memorial of Communion?
4. How does regular and corporate commemoration of our redemption in Christ serve to prompt our rejoicing in God?
5. What is the connection between remembrance and rejoicing?

6. What purpose does recalling the Lord's discipline in our life serve toward impacting our remembrance of what he has done and our rejoicing in who he is?

7. "Those who cannot remember the past are condemned to repeat it." Is there a place for the regular remembrance of our disobedience in the past and God's graciousness in the midst of it? If so, how does that actually lead us to worship and not to self-condemnation?

8. How does the practice of partaking of the Lord's Supper provide an opportunity for us to judge ourselves while also keeping us from the judgment of God? See 1 Corinthians 11:27-32.

9. In what ways does regular remembrance of Israel's past sins serve to provoke our obedience in the present?

10. Why is God so adamant on our obedience to him? Said differently, what does God desire to do for us in our obedience based on Psalm 81:14-16?

A Plea for Justice

PSALM 82

Main Idea: God is sovereign, just, and merciful, and his people should pray and work for his will to be done and his saving mercy to be made known.

I. **Who God Is**
   A. He is the sovereign King over all.
   B. He is the good Judge of all.
   C. He is the merciful Savior for all.
II. **What We Do**
   A. We plead for God's justice to reign.
   B. We anticipate God's kingdom to come.
   C. We spread God's salvation to the needy.

Psalm 82 speaks directly into our context today. The psalmist talks about the weak and the fatherless, the afflicted and the destitute, the poor and the needy, and we live in a world where the following statistics are reported:

- 1 billion people live today in desperate poverty, lacking food, clean water, and simple medicine.
- 153 million orphans need to be protected, provided for, and loved.
- 42 million babies are murdered in their mother's womb every single year.
- 27 million people live in slavery right now, many of whom are bought, sold, and exploited for sex in a trafficking ring that has become one of the fastest-growing industries on earth.

In short, we live in a world of massive injustice. So, how are we to *understand* this world given that we are worshipers of the just God over this world? And how are we to *live* in this world as worshipers of this just God?

This is a question I have found myself wrestling with after a trip to the Himalayas. I saw poverty, heard stories of persecution (of people being stoned for faith in Christ), and came face-to-face with little girls who had been sold into sex slavery, all the while knowing that most of these people had never heard the name of Jesus. I've read similar stories of various places around the world. So what do you do? Do you just turn away from it and go on with your comfortable life as if these realities don't exist? Surely not!

Surely there's more to understanding this world than turning a blind eye and a deaf ear to injustice around us. And surely there's something to be done in this world about the injustice we see. Based on Psalm 82, we get a picture of who God is and, in light of that, what we should do in a world filled with massive injustice.

Who God Is

Psalm 82 reveals at least three characteristics, or attributes, or we might even say titles, describing who God is.

He Is the Sovereign King over All

One of the things that makes this psalm difficult to preach and to understand is confusion over who the "gods" are in verse 1. There are two main possibilities. The first option is that these "gods" are demons and evil spirits, what the New Testament calls "the rulers, . . . the authorities, . . . the cosmic powers of this darkness, . . . evil, spiritual forces in the heavens" (Eph 6:12). These are fallen angels and false gods who work to spread evil in the world. The other option is that these "gods" are human judges and rulers in the world who are promoting injustice. This argument is based on instances in the Old Testament when the judges whom God had set up to rule in Israel were (in the original language) referred to as gods.[4] This second option is bolstered by Jesus's words in John 10:35-36.

Ultimately, the answer doesn't change the primary meaning of the passage. There is one God (capital "G" God) who reigns over all gods. He reigns over all men and women, over all rulers and leaders, and over all the principalities and powers, the devil and his demons who influence men and women. Verse 7 says that these "gods" will "die like

---

[4] For example, the word translated as "judges" in Exodus 21:6 is *elohim*, which can also be translated as "God" (see Gen 1:1) or "gods" (see 95:3). The ESV translates the term as "God" in Exodus 21:6.

humans and fall like any other ruler." God will outlast them all because he is the sovereign King over all. God alone is on the throne of the world.

He Is the Good Judge of All

From the beginning of this psalm, God is presiding as Judge in the "divine assembly" (v. 1), and his goodness is clearly contrasted with the wickedness of the gods who surround him. He holds judgment over them. So this is not a trial where God is sitting at a court bench, listening to facts, trying to discover who's right and who's wrong. No, God alone is right, and all these gods are wrong.

These other "gods" are unjust. They show the wicked "partiality" (v. 2), and with their position they oppress the "needy and the fatherless" (v. 3). They are not maintaining the rights of the "oppressed and the destitute" (v. 3). Instead, they are handing the weak over to the wicked. The result is given at the end of verse 5: "All the foundations of the earth are shaken."

When the justice of God is not reflected in the judges, rulers, leaders—or the presidents and the politicians of the world in our day—the result is a shaking of the earth's foundations and a spreading of evil. This is what happens when evil judges on the earth turn away from the good Judge over all. May God help us be warned about this in our own churches and in our own culture and across our world today. The fabric and the foundations of our lives and our families and our culture crumble when we turn away from the one true Judge. The effects are devastating on the poor, the weak, the needy, the afflicted, the fatherless, and the destitute. Injustice spreads when we rebel against the good Judge of all.

He Is the Merciful Savior for All

As a reflection of God's goodness, we see a picture of God's mercy. He loves the weak and the fatherless. He cares for the afflicted and the destitute. He rescues the weak and the needy. This psalm is arguably the most spectacular of all because of its definition of God who ties "his divinity to the fate of the poor and dispossessed" (Hossfeld, Lothar, and Zenger, *Psalms 2*, 337, cited in Goldingay, *Psalms 42–89*, 570).

There is debate over whether the "they" in verse 5 is referring to the weak and the needy or to the gods (judges). If the reference is to the gods/judges, then this verse is talking about how they don't have knowledge or understanding, and they walk in moral darkness. If this is a reference to the "poor and needy" in the previous verse, it describes the plight of all humanity living in an unjust world. When judges and rulers and leaders do not judge and rule and lead according to the good judgment, rule, and leadership of God, the result is a lost world, walking about in darkness with no foundation to stand on. In other words, this is a picture of humanity in need, not only of a sovereign King and good Judge but also of a merciful Savior to deliver and rescue from evil and injustice.

The scenario that has been set up in verses 1-7 leads directly to the last verse of this psalm. This final prayer calls us to think about what we must *do* in response.

What We Do

What do we do in a world of injustice? What do we do when we open our eyes to the world around us and open our ears to the Word before us? There are at least three ways to respond.

We Plead for God's Justice to Reign

We say with the psalmist, "Rise up, God, judge the earth" (v. 8). We ask God to come and show his good judgment. We ask him to act. We pray and we plead for him to do something—to stop injustice, to show his justice. This is what we do based on what we know. We know God is the King, Judge, and Savior to all. And we know he's the Father to the fatherless, the defender of the weak, and the provider for the poor, so we plead for God to rise up and judge this earth accordingly.

We Anticipate God's Kingdom to Come

The psalmist says the nations do belong to God (v. 8). Therefore, we anticipate God's kingdom to come. Isn't this precisely what Jesus taught us to pray in the Lord's prayer? "Our Father in heaven, your name be honored as holy. Your kingdom come. Your will be done on earth as it is in heaven" (Matt 6:9-10).

We ask God to judge, and then we anticipate God to come and claim his inheritance. We look forward to his establishment of a new heaven and a new earth where evil and injustice will be no more, where goodness and justice will reign forever (Isa 65:17-25; 2 Pet 3:13; Rev 21:1-4). We plead for God's justice to reign, and we keep pleading with anticipation in our hearts because we want God's kingdom to come.

We Spread God's Salvation to the Needy

As important as the first two responses are—pleading and anticipating—we don't stop there. We also spread God's salvation to the needy. We do what this psalm says to do.

This psalm was likely addressed to judges in Israel, so there was specific application to them, which in some ways (not every way) applies to those who rule, judge, or lead today. But what God commands here, he also commands his people to do throughout Scripture. We are told over and over to give justice to the "needy and the fatherless," to maintain the "rights of the oppressed and the destitute," and to "rescue the poor and needy; save them from the power of the wicked" (vv. 3-4).[5]

God has not called you and me to sit back in a world of injustice, content to wring our hands in pious concern while praying our prayers in relative comfort. No, he has called us to give our lives spreading the salvation of our good God to those who are in need. We are to lay down our lives, showing his mercy to people in our communities and to people around the world.

This is not just what God *calls* us to do; this is what Christ *compels* us to do!

See yourself in the psalm. In our sin we are weak and needy, afflicted and destitute. We are wicked and destined to die. But God in his mercy has sent his Son to die for us in our place. He has pursued us, and he has brought us from death to life. He has become poor so that we might become rich (2 Cor 8:9). He has come to preach good news to the poor, to proclaim liberty to the captive, to set at liberty those who are oppressed (Luke 4:18). Thus, it just makes sense for all those associated with this Christ to spread the salvation we have received to others who are in need.

Micah 6:8 provides us with a concise summary of what the Lord requires of each of us: "Mankind, he has told each of you what is good and what it is the Lord requires of you: to act justly, to love faithfulness, and to walk humbly with your God" (Mic 6:8).

---

[5] For only a small sample of the many passages that instruct God's people to care for these needy and vulnerable groups, see Exod 22:22; Deut 15:11; 24:17; 26:12; Prov 31:9; Isa 58:6-7.

Reflect and Discuss

1. What are some recent news headlines that have highlighted injustice in your own community? What about in the world?

2. When you see reports of some of the terrible injustices in the world, what is your typical reaction? Do you tend to get angry? Do you ignore them or simply turn away?

3. What does our view of the character of God have to do with the way we view the injustice we see in the world?

4. Why is it such good news that God is sovereign even over injustice?

5. How does a biblical view of God's justice affect the way you respond when you are wronged or when others are wronged?

6. Describe the difference between God's view of the weak and needy and the world's view of these vulnerable individuals.

7. What are some specific areas of injustice that you can pray about regularly? Make a list.

8. What is the relationship between the gospel and addressing injustice?

9. How can a church ensure that the proclamation of the gospel is not de-emphasized in its efforts to care for the weak and needy?

10. List some specific ways you and your church can engage injustice around you from a gospel-centered perspective.

Praying within the Tension

PSALM 83

Main Idea: Believers should pray for God to glorify himself by both defeating and saving those who oppose his people.

I. Pray for God to Show His Concern (83:1-8).
II. Pray for God to Show His Consistency (83:9-15).
III. Pray for God to Show His Compassion (83:16-18).

When Charles Spurgeon was asked how he reconciled divine sovereignty and human responsibility, he replied, "I never have to reconcile friends. Divine sovereignty and human responsibility have never had a falling out with each other. I do not need to reconcile what God has joined together" (*The New Park Street Pulpit*, vol. V, 120). Spurgeon was honest in his acknowledgment that "where these two truths meet I do not know, nor do I want to know. They do not puzzle me, since I have given up my mind to believing them both" (Spurgeon, *The Metropolitan Tabernacle Pulpit*, vol. XV, 458). Spurgeon refused to go where Scripture doesn't go, but he firmly believed what Scripture says where it does go.

We as believers have to get comfortable doing the same thing with imprecatory psalms (see also Pss 35; 58; 69; 109; 137). They contain another mysterious tension between praying for God to wipe out enemies of the gospel and asking him to save them. Nowhere is that more evident than in Psalm 83. While we can't be sure about the exact occasion of this psalm, it likely served as somewhat of a war oracle whenever Israel was being threatened. The psalmist prays for God to deliver his people from enemy nations that are trying to destroy them. However, his prayer contains both a request for these adversaries to be destroyed and put to shame and an appeal for them to turn and seek the Lord.

This desperate appeal for God's help gives birth to three practical applications for contemporary Christians. First, because God will ever be faithful to his promises, we must ask for his protection and deliverance whenever nations attempt to eradicate the nation of Israel. Second, we must cry out to God on behalf of our fellow believers around the world who are being persecuted for their faith. Third, we must pray for enemies of the gospel worldwide to repent and trust Jesus Christ for salvation. To those ends, the following are three prayers we should pray within the tension for God to glorify himself by both defeating and saving people who oppose the gospel.

Pray for God to Show His Concern
PSALM 83:1-8

As we see so many times in the Psalms, the writer starts this poem like a desperate child who climbs up into his father's lap and unloads his honest and sincere heart on him. He knows he's talking to his good Father, whom he knows to be far from disinterested in or unfeeling about the suffering of his people. This is God he's talking to. The first verse begins and ends with "God" in Hebrew, which makes clear that the psalmist's hope is in the one who cares deeply for his children and comes to their aid when they suffer. So he prays for this compassionate God—not to *have* concern but to *show* the concern he certainly already has in his people's current crisis.

The psalmist begins his appeal by putting his two hands on God's cheeks, turning his face toward his own, and pleading for him to give careful attention to the persecution of his people and demonstrate his concern for them (v. 1). In a way that a child might address a seemingly distracted parent, he pleads with God not to be indifferent to his people's plight by remaining quiet and showing no response.

What is this current crisis? Multiple groups of wicked people are plotting together to destroy God's children. So the psalmist grabs hold of God's heartstrings. The last phrase of verse 3 describes God's people as those whom he cherishes and protects. He wants him to spring into action and do something about the need of his treasure!

These enemies of God, however, are zealous for their cause and passionate about their mission. They lather themselves into an emotional frenzy and rise up in confident hostility against his people (v. 2). And their united front and joint conspiracy are clear (vv. 3,5). Still today a hatred of God's people seems to rally so many groups that wouldn't otherwise play well together. It's an amazing thing that people who disagree on so many political and religious issues find common ground in their opposition to the things of the kingdom of God.

To validate the psalmist's alarm, he provides a roll call of some of Israel's frequent opposers a few verses later (vv. 6-8). Some of the ten nations on this list reflect close blood relationships with Israel. Consequently, their hatred of God's people was evident and off the charts. Others we don't know as much about, but we can be sure about two characteristics they have in common. One, they all attacked Israel numerous times throughout their history. Two, they all had the same goal of extinguishing Israel from the planet.

The specific aim of these enemies is clarified in verse 4. They want a complete annihilation. Their goal is that no one would even remember Israel's name. Hosts of people and nations in the Middle East and beyond have shared this agenda throughout history and continue to do so today. If they had their way, Israel would have been exterminated long ago.

This hatred of Israel, however, is deeper than political rivalry and national rift. It's actually an attack on two deeper realities—God and his gospel. The persecution of Israel and the hatred of her God ultimately is an attack on him. He is the object of the rage and jealousy of those who come against his children. The psalmist says these are "your enemies . . . those who hate you" (v. 2). He says this conspiracy is levied against "your people . . . your treasured ones" (v. 3). Ultimately their plot is aimed at "you" (v. 5). Ross says,

> The hatred cannot be explained simply as rivalry for the land, or even for world dominion. There is something more evil at work behind this constant tension, and the psalm hints at it with the clarification that these nations are God's enemies. If they could destroy Israel, they would in effect destroy the work of the LORD in bringing people to faith in him, and they would also destroy his prophetic word, especially concerning Israel, in which believers place their confidence. (*Psalms*, vol. 2, 735)

Whenever the people of God are attacked and assaulted for their faith, the real motive is the destruction of God (Ps 2:1-3). The bottom line is that people don't like him and his reign over their lives, so they go after the only tangible representation of him they can find—those who worship him.

The animosity levied against Israel is not just a diverted hatred of God; it's also a hatred for the salvation he's provided. It's a spiritual matter rooted in the opposition to God's work of redemption through the gospel, and it should come as no surprise to believers. It's as old as the conflict revealed in God's prophecy to the serpent in the garden of Eden: "I will put hostility between you and the woman, and between your offspring and her offspring. He will strike your head, and you will strike his heel" (Gen 3:15). The agenda in Psalm 83 to exterminate Israel is merely one attempt among many that Satan has made and is making to foil the advancement of the gospel of Jesus Christ, the offspring of Israel who crushed his head on the cross.

Two clear applications emerge from this first prayer in the text. First, **believers everywhere should pray for God to defend the nation of Israel and defeat her enemies**. I guess I'm one of those guys without a country when it comes to many aspects of eschatology. I believe Christ's church is the true "Israel of God" (Gal 6:16) and that believers are truly "Abraham's sons" (Gal 3:7; cf. Gal 3:8-9,29; Rom 2:28-29; 9:1-33). However, I'm old-fashioned enough to believe that—based on his covenant promises—God still has a place for ethnic Israel in the eschaton. I don't claim to understand all that it entails, but I believe a remnant of the nation will play some role in the eternal kingdom (Matt 19:28; Luke 22:28-30; Acts 26:6-7; Rom 11:1-36; Rev 7:1-8; 21:12-14). This conviction compels me and all believers to pray for God to defend his name by defending the nation of Israel, overcoming their opponents, and bringing peace to their land (Ps 122:1-9).

Similarly, **believers should pray for the persecuted among the true Israel, the church of Jesus Christ**. The oppression of God's people this psalm describes is not something with which most Christians in the Western world can identify. Many of our brothers and sisters elsewhere, however, are all too familiar with it. They wake up every morning and go to bed at night with a keen awareness that it could be their last day alive, or at least outside of a prison cell, simply because they profess faith in Christ. Someone needs to be an advocate for them like the psalmist was for persecuted Israel. Believers everywhere must step up to that role and cry out to the Father on behalf of our spiritual siblings who are suffering for their faith.

Pray for God to Show His Consistency
PSALM 83:9-15

A second prayer in this passage is for God to act in the current situation the same way he's acted in the past—to be faithful and true in the present to the way he's demonstrated who he is and what he does in the past. He calls to mind how God has glorified himself through some of the great victories he's brought about in Israel's history.

In the fashion of young children recounting the great Bible stories they learned in Sunday school, the psalmist first appeals to two of Israel's great campaigns recorded in Judges 4–8. Regarding the current enemies, he wants God to "deal with them as [he] did with Midian" (v. 9) by the hand of Gideon, who overcame his adversary with just three hundred men, armed only with trumpets, jars, and torches (Judg 7:19-25). The psalmist asks God to make their rulers like Midian's four rulers (v. 11). He destroyed them because they wanted to destroy Israel.

The songwriter also refers to the story of Deborah and Barak. He asks God to do to the current oppressors what he did to "Sisera and Jabin at the Kishon River" (v. 9), when he sent heavy rains that enabled Israel to defeat the Canaanites in their iron chariots and to deny them an honorable burial by spreading them like "manure" (v. 10; Ross, Vol. 2, 737). And the psalmist goes on in verses 13-15 to ask God to bring natural disasters like he did in Judges 4–5. He wants God to be consistent with his judgment in the past, cursing them with the same devastation they intended for Israel (v. 4).

Regarding his present battle, the psalmist's resounding cry in these verses is, "Lord, do it again!" He's asking God to exercise the same divine force as in those great Bible stories. And that's how we should pray today when we're asking God to defend and deliver his children. We don't need to ask him to make us like the great judges of the Old Testament so we can deliver ourselves. We need to appeal to these great Bible stories in which he showed himself strong on behalf of his people. We need to revisit those tales of his strength from the past and cry out, "Lord, do today what you did back then."

Beloved, the lesson for our children in the great stories of the Old Testament is not, "Be like these heroes." Do we really want our children to be like Gideon, who doubted God's wisdom and then set up idols that people worshiped even after his great victory (Judg 8:22-28)? Do we want them to dream about being strong like Samson, who was the Old Testament poster child for arrogance, sexual immorality, and spiritual infidelity (Judg 13–16)? Do we truly want our kids even to aspire to be like Deborah and Barak, whose victory was short-lived and who still needed a better judge to rise up after them (Judg 6:1-10)? These Bible characters were not heroes! They were men and women who needed God to do for them what they couldn't do for themselves and whose lives testified that Israel still needed a righteous Judge and Deliverer to give them true victory.

Believers can and should appeal to the same Bible stories we learned in Sunday school when praying for national Israel. We should ask God to be consistent with the way he's sovereignly rescued his people and defeated their enemies at critical junctures throughout biblical history. In addition, we should pray for our persecuted brothers and sisters in Christ around the world by not only appealing to those same Bible stories but by invoking the promises of Christ to go to battle on behalf of his own. He assures us that "the gates of Hades will not overpower" his church (Matt 16:18) and that his sheep "will never perish. No one will snatch them out of my hand" (John 10:28). On behalf of our suffering fellow believers, we're obligated and privileged to ask our Lord to be consistent with what he's pledged regarding his care for his disciples and the overthrow of their enemies.

Pray for God to Show His Compassion
PSALM 83:16-18

The first two prayers in this psalm come down on the side of God's eradicating his enemies and thereby ending their oppression of his people. But at the end of this psalm we see the tension similar to what Spurgeon addressed, and that frees us up to live and pray within it. Here we catch a glimpse of God's showing compassion toward them for a larger purpose—that everyone on the planet would know and revere his glorious name.

The psalmist knows that the global acclaim of who God is and what he does will somehow come about through the mysterious tension between destroying his enemies altogether and turning their hearts toward him. This tension is nowhere more vivid than in verses 16-17. Seeing how the psalmist prays in these verses helps guide our understanding of how we should pray the previous two prayers in this song. He asks for God to both *shame* his enemies and *save* them.

Three requests mark the author's prayer for God to shame his enemies and condemn them completely, just as he's asked God to do in verses 1-15. First, he asks that God make their facial expressions show their fear of him (cf. Dan 5:6). Second, the psalmist prays for them to be completely disgraced so that they are no longer formidable military foes but rather terrified enemies running for their lives. Third, he prays that all their plans are foiled and they are utterly destroyed. Needless to say, the psalmist's prayer list comprises a series of vivid requests for God to show his strength in complete judgment.

These appeals for God's terrible sword, however, are tempered in almost oxymoronic fashion by the psalmist's prayer "that [these enemies] will seek your name, Lord" (v. 16). In the same breath in which he asks for their destruction, he asks for their salvation! Although he wants these enemies defeated, he compassionately appeals that—once they see the demonstration of God's power—they will realize the foolishness of their ways and cry out to God for his mercy. Somehow the psalmist acknowledges a place for the richness of God's salvation in the midst of his awful judgment.

The psalmist's ultimate desire is that even God's enemies would know that he is the one true God who is sovereign over the whole planet (v. 18). God doesn't just reign over Israel—or America for that matter. He controls the destiny of the entire universe (Ross, Vol. 2, 741). So he's not interested in merely defending his name as the God over one nation. In the Old Testament God's "name" is always a reflection of his nature. He wants his name—who he is and what he does—to be acclaimed by all nations.

Such is part of the mystery that characterizes the imprecatory psalms. At times—under the inspiration of the Holy Spirit—the psalmist appears to be calling fire down from heaven out of one side of his mouth while pleading for God's mercy out of the other. That must be our posture as we read these psalms and learn to pray from them. As we pray for God's kingdom to come and for his will to be done on earth as it is in heaven, we pray in this tension. Out of one side of our mouths we pray that Jesus Christ might reign in righteousness and condemn those who oppose the gospel. Out of the other side of our mouths we pray that those same opponents of the gospel will repent of their sin and place their faith in Christ.

All the while we know that both of those things can't happen in the same person's life. Someone who opposes the gospel can't be damned forever and yet at the same time repent and be saved. However, we must remember that salvation and eternal destiny is the business of God, not of his children. Our business as his children is to pray for justice and to pray for grace. We don't have to understand how the two can be friends but simply to be faithful to pray for both. We pray for both to the end that God's acclaim will be widely known among all people.

Conclusion

The tension between awful judgment or merciful salvation actually shouldn't baffle us as believers in Christ. Those two realities that appear to be in juxtaposition to each other actually are at the heart of the mystery of the gospel. They're reconciled in the two-dollar theological word *propitiation*. In Greek one of the words translated by it came to denote the mercy seat, or covering, of the ark, which foreshadowed reconciliation by the blood of Christ. God "presented [Jesus] as an atoning sacrifice [propitiation] in his blood, received through faith, to demonstrate his righteousness, because in his restraint God passed over the sins previously committed" (Rom 3:25; cf. Exod 25:17-22; 30:6; Heb 9:5). A related Greek word also translated by "atoning sacrifice" similarly refers to Christ becoming our substitute and assuming our obligations, thus expiating and covering our guilt by the vicarious punishment he endured (1 John 2:2; 4:10).

On the cross Jesus incurred the wrath of a holy God in our stead. He died the death that we should have died. In so doing, he provided mercy and forgiveness for those who would believe. Both judgment and salvation happened at the same time. As Christ followers, that's the end to which we must pray for enemies of the gospel. Maintaining this tension between asking for judgment and for salvation, we pray through the lens of the gospel for every nation on the planet and every citizen of those nations to believe in Christ and bow to the "Most High over the whole earth" (v. 18).

Reflect and Discuss

1. What are we to do with the seeming tensions in the Word of God?
2. How are we to handle the tension of praying for God to wipe out enemies and asking God to save them? Is there a balance here?
3. How do we live with a consistent perspective and attitude toward the enemies of God?
4. Should we focus our prayers more on the annihilation of God's enemies or for God to defend and uphold those who are his? Why?
5. How do we get our hearts and minds wrapped around Christian persecution throughout the world in such a way that it moves and motivates us to intercede for the persecuted church on a regular basis?

6. How does God's activity in the past, through biblical examples, instruct us in how to pray concerning the enemies of God's people?
7. What are some specific prayers that we can pray on behalf of our persecuted brothers and sisters around the world based on Matthew 16:18 and John 10:28? How should these New Testament promises inform our present intercession?
8. What's the connection between God's shaming his enemies and saving them?
9. How does God's judgment against sinners make way for his salvation of sinners?
10. In what ways does the cross of Christ display both the judgment and the mercy of God?

Blessed before God

PSALM 84

Main Idea: God has always provided refuge and hope for his people as they worship him, and this is true today as God dwells in and blesses those who trust in Jesus Christ.

I. **Three Blessings for God's People Then**
   A. It was a blessing to work in the temple.
      1. He longed to be in God's presence.
      2. He loved to sing God's praise.
   B. It was a blessing to journey to the temple.
      1. Hope in God brings strength amid weakness.
      2. Hope in God brings joy amid weeping.
   C. It was a blessing to live with trust in God.
II. **Three Blessings for Christians Today**
   A. It is a blessing to be the temple.
   B. It is a blessing to journey to heaven.
   C. It is a blessing to live with trust in Christ.
      1. Then the psalmist prayed for God's favor on an earthly king.
      2. Now the Christian enjoys God's favor through our eternal King.

In his book *When I Don't Desire God: How to Fight for Joy,* John Piper asks, "How can we help Christians who seem unable to break out of darkness into the light of joy?" Piper is speaking about depression, and for those who find it odd to hear of Christians who struggle with depression, Piper adds,

> Yes, I call them Christians, and thus assume that such
> things happen to genuine believers. It happens because of
> sin, or because of Satanic assault, or because of distressing
> circumstances, or because of hereditary or other physical
> causes. (*When I Don't Desire God*, 210)

After acknowledging the reality of different degrees of depression and different reasons behind depression, Piper goes on to conclude,

"For most people who are passing through the dark night of the soul, the turnaround will come because God brings unwavering lovers of Christ into their lives who do not give up on them" (ibid., 229). That is what pastors, and all followers of Christ, should want to do: walk alongside fellow Christians in unwavering love for Christ and for one another. We should be determined not to give up on others, even when they may want to give up on themselves.

We may be tempted to look down on those who suffer from depression, as if the problem is some grave sin or spiritual weakness. However, as Charles Spurgeon reminds us, this may not be the case:

> I know that wise brethren say, "You should not give way
> to feelings of depression." If those who blame quite so
> furiously could once know what depression is, they would
> think it cruel to scatter blame where comfort is needed.
> There are experiences of the children of God which are
> full of spiritual darkness; and I am almost persuaded that
> those of God's servants who have been most highly favoured
> have, nevertheless, suffered more times of darkness than
> others. . . . No sin is necessarily connected with sorrow
> of heart, for Jesus Christ our Lord once said, "My soul is
> exceeding sorrowful, even unto death." There was no sin in
> Him, and consequently none in His deep depression. . . .
> [T]he way of sorrow is not [always] the way of sin, but
> a hallowed road sanctified by the prayers of myriads of
> pilgrims now with God—pilgrims who, passing through the
> valley of Baca [lit: of weeping], made it a well, the rain also
> filled the pools: of such it is written: "They go from strength
> to strength, every one of them in Zion appeareth before
> God." (Spurgeon, "The Valley of the Shadow," 230–31,
> 234–35)

At the end of that quote, Spurgeon is citing from Psalm 84:6-7.

Three times the psalmist refers to how "happy," or as some translations have it, "blessed," certain people are (vv. 4,5,12). These three acknowledgements of blessing will form the outline for how we walk through this text (Boice, *Psalms*, vol. 2, 691–93).Then, drawing on the entirety of Scripture and the finished work of Christ in the gospel, we will find three blessings for followers of Christ today.

Three Blessings for God's People Then

It Was a Blessing to Work in the Temple

The superscription says, "A psalm of the sons of Korah." To find out who they are, we need to look at 1 Chronicles 9.

God appointed different people from different tribes and families for all the work that went on in or around the tabernacle and the temple. When Israel returned from exile, God once again named those who would serve in the temple in 1 Chronicles 9. After mentioning the priests (vv. 10-13) and Levites (vv. 14-16), 1 Chronicles 9:19 mentions the sons of Korah:

> *Shallum son of Kore, son of Ebiasaph, son of Korah and his relatives from his father's family, the Korahites, were assigned to guard the thresholds of the tent. Their ancestors had been assigned to the LORD's camp as guardians of the entrance.*

The sons of Korah were gatekeepers who stood at the threshold of the tabernacle. They worked as doorkeepers of the place that symbolized God's presence among his people.

Other psalms, such as 42–43, express a longing for the presence of God when the psalmist is away from the temple (42:4; 43:3-4). It makes sense that the sons of Korah love what they do. They're not bored. Psalm 84:10 expresses their enthusiasm.

The psalmist, representing the sons of Korah, is singing about how **he longed to be in God's presence**. He loved the dwelling place of God so much that he longs, yes faints, to be there! And this from a guy who's always there. He's talking about the temple in the language of love poetry. The appetite for God here is insatiable. He wants more and more of God.

It's not the place itself the psalmist longs for but the person whose presence dwells in that place. We have to be careful when we think about the tabernacle or the temple, this place that symbolized the presence of God. God was not present *only* there. Solomon, when he was dedicating the temple, said, "Even heaven, the highest heaven, cannot contain you, much less this temple I have built" (1 Kgs 8:27). But then he goes on to pray the following:

> *Listen to your servant's prayer and his petition, LORD my God, so that you may hear the cry and the prayer that your servant prays before*

> *you today, so that your eyes may watch over this temple night and*
> *day, toward the place where you said, "My name will be there," and*
> *so that you may hear the prayer that your servant prays toward this*
> *place. Hear the petition of your servant and your people Israel, which*
> *they pray toward this place. May you hear in your dwelling place in*
> *heaven. May you hear and forgive.* (1 Kgs 8:28-30)

The Bible talks about how God dwells in heaven, yet it also talks about God dwelling on earth in a temple (earlier in a tabernacle). At the same time, the Bible talks about God being omnipresent, that is, dwelling everywhere on earth and in heaven. So instead of thinking of the tabernacle or temple as the *only* place God dwells, we should instead think of it as the place God chose to dwell in a particular, powerful way among his people in the Old Testament. If that's the case, this psalmist wanted to be there. He longed for communion with God in the courts of the temple. One day there was better than a thousand anywhere else. He loves that place because he longs for God's presence.

The psalmist even looks up into the structure of the temple, and he sees sparrows and swallows that have set up a nest there (Ps 84:3). What great imagery—the presence of God as the place *where the humble find a home.* The sparrow is used throughout Scripture to describe a humble, lowly, common, seemingly worthless bird. Jesus pointed out how two of them are sold for a penny (Matt 10:29). Yet this simple bird finds majestic meaning by having a house in the presence of God. It's really a great description, in a sense, of the people of God—humble, lowly, common people who find majestic meaning in the presence of God. Donald Grey Barnhouse compared the church to sparrows, saying,

> I look down some little street and see a humble chapel where
> a group of simple people worship the Lord in the beauty of
> holiness, despised and rejected of men, even as was their Lord,
> and I know that this is the rich reality of spiritual truth. Here
> are the sparrows who find their nest at the cross of Jesus Christ.
> Here is worthlessness that finds its worth because the Savior
> died. (*God's Remedy*, 239, as cited in Boice, *Psalms*, vol. 2, 690)

The presence of God is also *where the restless find a refuge.* Psalm 84 mentions the swallow (v. 3), a fast-moving bird that flies back and forth in different directions, wearing out anyone who tries to watch its movements (Boice, *Psalms*, vol. 2, 691). And yet here, in the presence of God, this same bird builds a nest and settles down to rest with her young. What a great illustration of what Augustine once said: "Our hearts are restless till they find rest in Thee" (*Confessions*, 3, as cited in Boice, *Psalms*, vol. 2, 691).

Not only did the psalmist long to be in God's presence, but also **he loved to sing God's praise**. More than a simple song, verse 2 refers to a loud cry (Kidner, *Psalms 73–150*, 303). This longing for God in the psalmist's heart and flesh overflows into crying out, not just in songs but in shouts to God. Biblically it is right to both sing and shout to God.

We are commanded repeatedly in the Psalms (e.g., Pss 66:2; 68:4), and all over Scripture (Eph 5:19; Col 3:16), to sing to God. In addition to singing, we also shout: "Let the whole earth shout joyfully to God!" (Ps 66:1). The word for "cry out" that's used in Psalm 84:2 (*ranan*) is used in other places in the Bible as a cry of celebration (see Deut 32:43; 1 Chron 16:33; Pss 20:6; 32:11). And that's what's going on in verse 2 in the presence of God; this psalmist overflows in praise (see v. 4). This blessing comes not for those who merely talk or think about God's praise but rather for those who celebrate God. The blessing is for those who sing with joy and shout aloud over God and his Word in worship. This kind of response is entirely appropriate for the church's corporate gathering on Sunday.

Our singing and shouting is a response to who God is. There are at least twelve different names and attributes and activities of God specifically mentioned in Psalm 84.

God is the covenant-keeping Lord. "LORD" in small capital letters is a translation of *Yahweh*, the name by which God revealed himself to Moses and to Israel when he called them out to be his people and entered into covenant with them (Exod 3:19; 6:3). He is the God who reaches down his hand of mercy and enters into covenant with unworthy sinners. He makes a commitment to them, and he keeps his covenant.

God is the commander of heavenly armies. He's the LORD of hosts. Literally, he is "Yahweh of heavenly armies," which points to the security that is found in God's presence, a reality the psalmist will later rejoice in.

God is the living God. The God I long for, the psalmist says, is not dead. He is the God whose presence is active among his people.

God is my King. As with the next statement below, the psalmist begins thinking of God in personal terms. God is not only the King of the world or even of Israel—he is *my* King.

God is my God. Put yourself in the psalmist's shoes for a minute: he looks up and sees the glory and grandeur of God commanding armies in heaven, living and active all across the earth, and he says, "He's mine." This is pride, but in a good sense. It's like the pride of a groom who sees his wife walk down the aisle. He says, "That's my wife! She chose me! She's with me!" So also the people of God ought to look up to God in all of his greatness and grandeur and glory and majesty over heaven and earth and think, *That's my God. That's my King! He chose me! He's with me!*

God is the only God. Verse 8 uses another Hebrew word for God— *Elohim*—to describe God as the one true God. Then in verse 8 the word *Elohim* is combined with *Yahweh* so that we have "Lord God of Armies."

God is the faithful God. He is the God who made promises to Jacob centuries before, promises he is still faithful to today. God has been making and keeping promises to his people for centuries, going all the way back to Abraham, Isaac, and Jacob.

God is a source of light and life to his people. Besides verse 11, nowhere else is God explicitly called a sun in Scripture (Boice, *Psalms*, vol. 2, 693). Scripture does not typically identify God with the sun because of pagan religions that worshiped the sun (Goldingay, *Psalms 42–89*, 598). Nevertheless, the psalmist looks up at the light and life the sun brings, and this is the way he describes being in the presence of God, who shines brightly on his people.

God is a shield of protection and provision for his people. This is a picture of protection for people who find refuge in him.

God showers his people with his grace. He grants "favor and honor" and "good" (v. 11). Though they didn't deserve it, God was gracious to Israel. And though we don't deserve it, God is gracious to his people today.

God surrounds his people with his glory. When verse 11 says the Lord grants "honor" to his people, the phrase might be more literally translated as God bestowing his "glory" on his people (Kidner, *Psalms 73–150*, 307). He surrounds his people with his glory so that they dwell in it. This is what the temple was all about. In Psalm 3:3 David prays, "But you, Lord, are a shield around me, my glory, and the one who lifts up my head." As we come into God's presence, God bestows honor on us, surrounding us with his glory.

God shows his people all his goodness. The effect of being in God's presence is that the psalmist lacks "no good thing" (ESV). With God's grace on him and God's glory around him, the psalmist rests confident in God's goodness to him.

When you put all this together, you realize why the psalmist longs to be in God's presence and why you and I, if we realized who God is, would long to be in God's presence. Think about the God whom we gather to worship. This is our King; this is our God. And it is good to be before him and to sing and shout for joy before him day after day. That is the point of the first blessing in this psalm, the blessing of working in the temple.

It Was a Blessing to Journey to the Temple

The second blessing the psalmist mentions comes in verse 5: "Happy are the people whose strength is in you, whose hearts are set on pilgrimage." Zion (v. 7) is a reference to the place where the tabernacle, and later the temple in Jerusalem, was located. The psalmist is talking about people who are far away from the temple but who find their strength by setting their hearts on the presence of God. Obviously, this was the majority of people in Israel; most people lived far away from Jerusalem, and only a relative few actually worked at the temple. So the psalmist sets his gaze on the people of God scattered throughout the country; and he gives us this picture of the road that leads to Zion, and the strength that people find, though far away, when they set their hearts' hope on the presence of God.

The psalmist describes how **hope in God brings strength amid weakness**, even to those who are far away. In verse 7 he uses the imagery of traveling to the presence of God in Zion, saying, "They go from strength to strength."

"Baca" in verse 6 is a Hebrew word meaning "balsam tree," a tree found in dry landscapes. The resin of this tree oozed out, like tears, and this noun, *Baca*, sounds similar to the Hebrew verb for "weeping." That's why some people refer to the "Valley of Baca" as the "valley of weeping" (Kidner, *Psalms 73–150*, 305). The psalmist is talking about people on a figurative (or maybe a literal) journey from where they live to Zion, to the presence of God. They make this journey by walking through the "Valley of Baca," symbolizing dry and difficult days filled with hardship and hopelessness that causes weeping. In the middle of that valley, what sustains them is the hope of God's presence. When they hold on to that hope, even this dry, desolate place becomes a valley of springs and pools from which they can drink and be satisfied.

The psalmist is also describing how **hope in God brings joy amid weeping**. Tears of sadness become springs of joy when the pilgrim looks to the presence of God. It was a blessing to journey to the temple, the psalmist says, both physically and spiritually.

It Was a Blessing to Live with Trust in God

Right after he talks about walking uprightly before God, the psalmist writes, "Happy is the person who trusts in you, LORD of Armies!" (v. 12). This blessing comes wherever one lives, whether at the temple gates or far away. Blessed are those who walk with all of their trust placed in God.

The three blessings mentioned above are for Old Testament Israel, when God was dwelling in a particular way among his people in Jerusalem (in a tabernacle or a temple). However, this is not where the story of this larger book, the Bible, ends. As Christians, we no longer travel to Jerusalem to worship at a temple. There is another "place" where God's glory now dwells, resulting in at least three blessings for Christians today.

Three Blessings for Christians Today

John 1:14 says, "The Word became flesh and dwelt among us. We observed his glory, the glory as the one and only Son from the Father, full of grace and truth." The Greek word for "dwelt" (*skēnoō*) is the same word used in the Greek version of the Old Testament (the Septuagint) to describe the tabernacle. Literally, God became flesh and "tabernacled" among us. The good news of Jesus's coming was that God had come to dwell in the midst of his people, and in Jesus his people would see his glory.

This theme of Jesus as the temple continues in John 2. Jesus was having a discussion with some Jews at the temple in Jerusalem:

> *Jesus answered, "Destroy this temple, and I will raise it up in three days."*
>
> *Therefore the Jews said, "This temple took forty-six years to build, and will you raise it up in three days?"*
>
> *But he was speaking about the temple of his body.* (John 2:19-21)

Jesus was telling the Jewish people that he was the temple. He was the place where the presence of God dwelt. He was the revelation of God's grace and glory in the flesh. When Philip asked to see the Father, Jesus replied, "Have I been among you all this time and you do not know me,

Philip?" (John 14:9). To be with Jesus is to be in God's presence, for he is God.

When Jesus died, the Bible says that the curtain of the temple that separated man from God was torn in two (Matt 27:51). God was making a way for sinful men to be reconciled to him through faith in Christ. Now, for those who are in Christ, God's presence dwells in us: "Don't you yourselves know that you are God's temple and that the Spirit of God lives in you? If anyone destroys God's temple, God will destroy him; for God's temple is holy, and that is what you are" (1 Cor 3:16-17). God identifies his people corporately as the temple. Then, a few chapters later, Paul says something similar: "Don't you know that your body is a temple of the Holy Spirit who is in you, whom you have from God? You are not your own, for you were bought at a price. So glorify God with your body" (1 Cor 6:19-20).

The temple imagery is both personal and corporate. So, Christian, your body is a temple of the Holy Spirit, and the church, corporately, is the temple of the Holy Spirit. Today we don't go to a designated place of worship like Israel did in the Old Testament because *we* are the place of worship. *You* are the place of worship. If you're a Christian, the Spirit of God dwells in you. For the church gathered, the Spirit of God dwells in us.

For the psalmist, working in the temple was a blessing. But you and I don't work as doorkeepers in the temple. Our situation is far better. Consider three blessings we receive by virtue of our union with Jesus.

It Is a Blessing to Be the Temple

The glory of God's presence now dwells in us, which radically changes how we live. We wake up with the presence of God in us; we walk through every detail of our day with the presence of God in us; we go to bed at night with the presence of God in us. The blessing today is not for those who dwell in God's house; rather, blessed are those whose bodies house the glory of God. Knowing this—that God's glory is manifest through your body—changes the way you use your body. It changes the way you act and think, the way you speak and love. You (literally) walk in the worship of God.

On a corporate level, when we gather as the church, there is indeed something unique about this gathering. God is among us! We gather together as the people of God, as the temple of God, and we sing his praise. Our hearts long for this. This is no casual thing we do once a week. This is a blessing! Blessed are those who gather together as the temple to celebrate the glory of their God.

It Is a Blessing to Journey to Heaven

For the psalmist it was a blessing to journey to the temple. For the Christian now, we're not focused on pilgrimages to Jerusalem, but that does not mean the highways of our hearts have no hope, for we now journey to heaven. While this was true for the psalmist then, we know this in an even greater way today based on what we know in the rest of the Bible.

The Bible talks about Christians as "strangers and exiles" (1 Pet 2:11). Along with faithful men and women from the Old Testament who went before us, we are "foreigners and temporary residents on the earth"; we seek "a homeland" and desire "a better place—a heavenly one" (Heb 11:13-16). Revelation 21 describes that heavenly country, that homeland:

> *Then I saw a new heaven and a new earth; for the first heaven and the first earth had passed away, and the sea was no more. I also saw the holy city, the new Jerusalem, coming down out of heaven from God, prepared like a bride adorned for her husband.*
>
> *Then I heard a loud voice from the throne: Look, God's dwelling is with humanity, and he will live with them. They will be his peoples, and God himself will be with them and will be their God. He will wipe away every tear from their eyes. Death will be no more; grief, crying, and pain will be no more, because the previous things have passed away.* (Rev 21:1-4)

Over and above physical descriptions of its beauty and all that will be there, the most important thing about heaven is not *what* is there but *who* is there. The dwelling of God will be with man in this holy city.

Later in the chapter heaven is described with measurements that match the shape of the temple (Rev 21:15-17). The point of this imagery is that all those who have trusted in Christ are secure and will be fully reconciled to God. Yes, God is with us now, and his presence dwells in Christians, but we are longing for more, aren't we? The highways of our hearts are set on the hope of a day when sin and suffering will be no more, and we will be with God in perfect, pure, endless joy forever and ever.

Now, in the meantime, we often find ourselves walking through the Valley of Baca, for on this earth there is weeping and dryness and, at times, darkness. Many of God's people find themselves traveling "most of the way to heaven by night" (Spurgeon, "The Child of Light Walking in Darkness," 542). There is struggle in this world. There is a fight for joy on some days. So what do you do on those days? The answer Psalm 84 gives is to keep your heart fixed and fastened on your hope in God. Even when the journey in the present seems bleak, lift your eyes to the hope you have in God.

Darkness and difficulty often come when we feel alone or isolated. Psalm 84 says to such people, "You have a home with God." For those with feelings of restlessness, Psalm 84 says, "There is refuge in God." To the worthless, Psalm 84 says, "You have worth before God." In the midst of darkness, our greatest need is for a source of light and life, for a shield of protection and provision. And all of these things are found in God. Oh, set your heart's hope on him!

It Is a Blessing to Live with Trust in Christ

It is a blessing to live with trust in God (v. 12), even amid darkness and difficulty. And for the Christian today, it is a blessing to live with trust in Christ. For God has sent his Son, the Word made flesh (John 1:14), to us, and he has identified with us.

He hurt as we hurt. He experienced sorrow as we experience sorrow. He knows what it's like to be abandoned, and he knows what it's like to feel alone. He knows what it's like to look to God the Father in the midst of total darkness and ask, "Why?" He identifies with you, and he says to you, "Trust in me."

Trust in the one who has walked through the dark night and has come out on the other side in victorious light. He has conquered sin and sorrow. He has defeated death and hell. And he is coming back to bring all who trust in him on this earth to glory with him in eternity, where he will wipe away every single tear from your eyes. He will heal every ache in your heart. So put your hope in Christ! Piper put it best:

> Every Christian who struggles with depression struggles
> to keep their hope clear. There is nothing wrong with the
> object of their hope—Jesus Christ is not defective in any way
> whatsoever. But the view from the struggling Christian's heart
> of their objective hope could be obscured by disease and pain,
> the pressures of life, and by Satanic fiery darts shot against
> them. . . . All discouragement and depression is related to the

obscuring of our hope, and we need to get those clouds out of the way and fight like crazy to see clearly how precious Christ is. ("Can Christians Be Depressed?")

The psalmist knew that God's protection of his people was tied to God's protection of the king who led them. **Then the psalmist prayed for God's favor on an earthly king** (v. 9), but that earthly king in Israel was ultimately set up by God to point us to an eternal King over all. **Now the Christian enjoys God's favor through our eternal King.** Whether things are going well for you right now or you find yourself amid difficulty and darkness, you, Christian, have a King who keeps his commitment to you, who has made a covenant of love with you that he will not break. He is the commander of heavenly armies, and he is a source of light and life to you, a shield of protection and provision for you amid whatever you are walking through. His name is Jesus. Spurgeon said,

> I know, perhaps, as well as anyone here, what depression of spirit means—and what it is to feel myself sinking lower and lower—yet, at the worst, when I reach the lowest depths, I have an inward peace which no pain or depression can in the least disturb! Trusting in Jesus Christ, my Savior, there is still a blessed quietness in the deep caverns of my soul, though, upon the surface, a rough tempest may be raging, and there may be little apparent calm. (Spurgeon, "Rest as a Test," 483)

Reflect and Discuss

1. Have you or someone you've known experienced depression? Given that we don't always know the causes, were you able to discern any factors that led to the depression?
2. What would you say to someone who claimed that true Christians should never experience depression?
3. How can the example of the psalmist in Psalm 84 and of Christ's own sorrow give us comfort?
4. Why was the temple so significant for God's people in the Old Testament?
5. What are some things that keep you from longing for communion with God?
6. Is a church building today the equivalent of the Old Testament temple? Explain your answer.

7. How can our future reward strengthen us during times of sorrow, depression, and opposition today?
8. What are some ways churches can minister to those who are depressed or grieving?
9. Why is it important for us to dwell on the promises of Scripture and the character of God rather than looking inward or basing our hope on our feelings and emotions?
10. What promises of Scripture would you share with someone who is depressed? Make a list.

Longing for a New Normal

PSALM 85

Main Idea: God invites his people to ask him to work in ways that upset the status quo and display his glorious power and grace.

I. Recall (85:1-3).
II. Pray (85:4-7).
III. Trust and Obey (85:8-13).

Sometimes it can feel like the Bible is pulling you in two different directions. Take contentment, for example. There are places in Scripture that encourage us to be content with *normal* life—not to fixate or panic about things that are less than ideal.

> *I don't say this out of need, for I have learned to be content in whatever circumstances I find myself. I know both how to make do with little, and I know how to make do with a lot. In any and all circumstances I have learned the secret of being content—whether well fed or hungry, whether in abundance or in need.* (Phil 4:11-12)

Paul seems to be saying that not having everything is an inevitable part of normal life.

But think about your spiritual life. Is it OK that it largely feels normal? I suspect that for many of us, our prayer times this week were normal. No angels singing. No burning bushes or audible voices. No. You prayed, sipped your coffee, read some Scripture, and went to work. It was meaningful but relatively unmiraculous. So there's a lot of normal in our spiritual lives.

There's a lot of normal when it comes to ministry we're involved in. Paul told Timothy to be ready to minister "in season and out of season" (2 Tim 4:2). In other words, Timothy, the pattern of ministry is not a steadily rising curve throughout life. It has "average" in it.

Well, here are a few updates on normal life in a fallen world. Hard-to-reach places Christians and churches have been praying for are, by and large, still hard-to-reach places. The number of professing Christians in this country is huge, and yet it is difficult to find a clear line between the church and the world when it comes to lifestyle choices, spending habits, sexual purity, and healthy marriages. Welcome to life in the normal world, under the fall. What'd you expect? This is what happens here, right?

But Psalm 85 is about revival. It's about a new normal. It's filled with an expectation of something beyond the realm of what we see every day. This psalm was not written in a time of spiritual awakening, yet here we will pick up on a holy discontentment with the way things are. We see someone asking for God to usher in a new set of conditions and realities. And I pray it makes us long for a new normal as well.

Verse 6 captures the deep longing of the psalmist: "Will you not revive us again?" The revival spoken of here is not a sign in front of a church building announcing, "Revival services beginning next week." It's something God sovereignly does when he sovereignly wants to. Yet it's something the psalmist asks for.

Psalm 85 urges us to a kind of holy discontentment with the status quo. The psalmist is not saying, "It is what it is." He's saying, "No, it needs to change. God, come!" And he starts asking for big things. We need renewal. We need joy in God. We're lifeless.

In verse 9 he's asking for a work of God so unique that it can only be described as salvation coming near and glory dwelling in the land. Against a backdrop of widespread unrighteousness, righteousness and peace embrace (v. 10). Rampant idolatry marked the whole of Israel's history, but here is the prospect of truth (or faithfulness, ESV) springing up from the ground (v. 11).

There are moments in biblical history where we see this sort of thing happen. The New Testament book of Acts chronicles the extraordinary work of God through his Word and Spirit in the first century. But this kind of work isn't just confined to the pages of biblical history.

We read summary accounts like this one, which describes what happened in the 1640s in Kidderminster, England, under the ministry of Richard Baxter:

> When [Baxter] came to Kidderminster he found it a dark,
> ignorant, immoral, irreligious place, containing, perhaps, 3000
> inhabitants. When he left it, at the end of fourteen years, he
> had completely turned the parish upside down. 'The place
> before his coming,' says Dr. Bates, 'what like a piece of dry and

barren earth; but, by the blessing of heaven upon his labor,
the face of Paradise appeared there. . . ." The number of his
regular communicants averaged 600. 'Of these,' Baxter tells
us, 'there were not twelve of whom I had not good hope as
to their sincerity.' The Lord's Day was thoroughly reverenced
and observed. It was said, 'You might hear a hundred families
singing psalms and repeating sermons as you passed through
the streets' When he came there, there was about one family in
a street which worshipped God at home. When he went away,
there were some streets in which there was not more than one
family on a side that did not do it. (Ryle, *Facts and Men*, 278)

During those years, Baxter called Kidderminster a colony of heaven.

That's not normal. The psalmist isn't seeing this in his day, but that
doesn't keep him from asking. Have you ever asked for things like this?
Things this big?

The great preacher Charles Spurgeon talked much about praying
prayers that are commensurate with God's almighty power and abundant generosity:

We do not come in prayer . . . to God's poorhouse where He
dispenses His favors to the poor, nor do we come to the back
door of the house of mercy to receive the leftover scraps,
though that would be more than we deserve. . . . But when
we pray, we are standing in the palace on the glittering floor
of the Great King's own reception room. . . . And should we
come there with stunted requests and narrow and contracted
faith? No, it does not become a King to be giving away pennies
and nickels; He distributes pieces of gold. (Spurgeon, *Spurgeon
on Prayer and Spiritual Warfare*, 72)

Legend has it that Alexander the Great wanted to marry a certain
man's daughter. The father demanded a large dowry in exchange for
his daughter. Alexander said, "Just tell my treasurer, and he'll take care
of it." The treasurer came back to him saying that the price this man
asked is way too much. A fraction of that price would be more than sufficient. And Alexander is said to have replied, "He does me honor. He
treats me like a king and proves *by what he asks* that he believes me to
be both rich and generous" (Gray and Adams, *Biblical Encyclopedia*, 547;
emphasis added).

Church, what do our prayers say about our belief in the character of God? That he is rich and generous, or that he is reluctant and economical? What a phrase Paul uses in Ephesians 3! Look how he stacks the descriptive modifiers: "Now to him who is able to do *above and beyond* all that we ask or think according to the power that works in us" (Eph 3:20; emphasis added).

This psalm is meant to cultivate in us a longing for a new normal—a longing for the inbreaking of God's mercy and power in our lives, in the church, and in the world. One of the ways we cultivate this longing and anticipation of God's reviving work is by recalling the past.

Recall
PSALM 85:1-3

These verses are pointing back to a time the psalmist wants to experience in his own day—a time in which there were clear demonstrations of God's power, mercy, and grace. We can read the Bible and get the impression that the front page of the Jerusalem paper always had a miracle on it, but that's not the way it was. The majority of miracles clustered around a few particular moments of biblical history: Moses, Elijah, the ministry of Jesus, and the outpouring of the Holy Spirit on the early church.

Consider Moses and the exodus. That's a unique period of time. God speaks through a burning bush. The staff turns to a snake. The water turns to blood. Then you have Red Sea partings, a pillar of cloud and fire for a GPS device, water from rocks, meals falling from the sky. Much of that happened in the space of about a year. What a year! Here's the thing. Not every generation in Israel was there to see God do that, but every generation was meant to recall these spectacular demonstrations of God's saving power. And when Israel falls into unbelief and idolatry, it is often linked with forgetting the saving intervention of God in their midst.

So the psalmist here resolves not to forget. He calls to mind the saving activity of God on Israel's behalf. Verses 1-3 show God in action. He showed favor; he restored (v. 1). He forgave guilt and covered sin (v. 2). He withdrew wrath and turned from burning anger (v. 3). The God of Israel didn't put his attributes on a chart to be analyzed. He said, "You want to know me? Watch this." He acted in history. The Old Testament is theology in action. God works, speaks, feeds, subdues, lifts up, brings down, leads, loves, saves! This wasn't a distant God who, as some modern theologians say, established a policy of noninterference with the world. God has his hands all over history. He turns even the hearts of kings in order to accomplish his will (Prov 21:1). When Israel recalled God's mighty acts, this was meant to instill a deep-running hope in the power of God. And, as we read Psalm 85, it seems Israel needed that hope right about now. The dark backdrop of this passage becomes more obvious when we move from a remembrance of the past to prayers for the present.

Pray
PSALM 85:4-7

Some commentators think this psalm may have been written during the exile, when Israel had been conquered and the people were kicked out of their homeland. Others believe it may have been the period after, where some of God's people were allowed to go back home to Jerusalem, but they were still under the thumb of foreign rulers, and unbelief and idolatry continued. In either case the move didn't change their hearts, just their zip code. It didn't revive the people spiritually. So the psalmist cries out for revival (v. 4). The prayer could be translated, "Turn us." I love how big a prayer that is.

In one sense the ultimate judgment would be for a sovereign God to refuse to overcome that which is most normal about life here, namely, global and personal idolatry—for God to give us over to our cravings. Romans 1 describes God's judgment this way. Three times it says that he gave them over. It is God taking his hands of mercy off and letting fallen humanity run, unhindered, charging in the direction of our idols. The psalmist is saying, "Don't let that happen. God, turn us."

However, if you know Christ, if you've been revived (made alive) by God's grace, it's not because he merely *said*, "Turn!" because he would've been saying "turn" to someone who by nature does not seek God (Rom 3:11). He would've been shouting "turn" to someone who was "dead in trespasses and sins" (Eph 2:1). But Ephesians 2 tells us what God did to counteract our unresponsiveness. He turned us! He answered this prayer in Psalm 85; he straight up turned you to himself!

> But God, who is rich in mercy, because of his great love that he had for us, made us alive with Christ even though we were dead in trespasses.

You are saved by grace! He also raised us up with him and seated us with him in the heavens in Christ Jesus. (Eph 2:4-6)

If you have a hard time believing in the possibility of revival, look no further than your own personal testimony! You were dead, and he made you alive. You were running for your idols, and he turned you.

The psalmist doesn't merely pray, "Help us to turn." He says, "Turn us! Revive us again so that your people may rejoice in you" (vv. 4,6 author's paraphrase).

This is not a God who is locked outside. This is no Deism. This is gospel-charged theism. It features a God who breaks in on planet earth, who breaks into living rooms, college dorms, bedtime prayers, dark nights of the soul. He breaks in among unreached peoples. He does things that are not normal.

I love the result of this reviving work of God in verse 6. This is a revival unto joy! And verse 7 seems to be the means God often uses in reviving his people. God revives his church by revealing himself afresh. He shows us his faithful love. Paul talked about Christian transformation this way: "We all, with unveiled faces, are looking as in a mirror at the glory of the Lord and are being transformed into the same image from glory to glory; this is from the Lord who is the Spirit" (2 Cor 3:18). Moses's life-changing request in prayer wasn't "Change me." It was "Let me see your glory" (Exod 33:18).

This faith-filled prayer for a new normal is a kind of rebuke. It's as though it's saying that if you don't believe personal, societal, national, even global revival is possible, you have forgotten the power of God.

Christian friends, if we don't pray for things that might set us up for disappointment, we're not doing it right. We are not called to merely pray safe, self-protecting, "realistic," face-saving prayers. So often I pray prayers that match the normal patterns I see in life. In my everyday life, hard-to-reach people continue to be hard to reach. In my everyday life, the church exerts little influence on the world around us. But on page after page of Scripture, God is seeking to convince us that he has options! He intervenes. He brings life where there was death. He brings beauty from ashes. He removes fear while we walk through the valley of the shadow of death. He can cause his word to not return void. He can bring reviving grace to any person you know, any resistant people group, and he could do it by the end of the week.

Charles Spurgeon spoke of the poor condition of the church one hundred years prior. The Church of England, Spurgeon said, was asleep.

It looked as if the living church of God would be extinguished altogether; but it was not so, for God did but stamp his foot, and, from all parts of the country, men like Mr. Wesley and Mr. Whitefield, came to the front, and hundreds of others, mighty men of valor, proclaimed the gospel with unusual power, and away went the bats and the owls back to their proper dwelling-place. ("On Expectations")

When is the last time we were audacious enough to ask God to stamp his feet? We are to pray and hope as though God had options!

Trust and Obey
PSALM 85:8-13

Do you hear this note of trust in verses 8-13? He *will* speak. He *will* give peace. Salvation *is* near. Truth *springs* up. The Lord *will provide* what is good. Trust is all over these verses. But there's also a call to obedience. Verse 8 warns us not to go back to foolish ways. Whatever this reviving work of God is, it's *not* something that renders the believer passive. There's an assertive stance, a posture of readiness we're called to. There's a preparation for God's work. Recall. That is, stay in his Word. Let it frame our expectations. Pray. Ask, seek, and knock, and keep knocking. Strive for godliness. Don't turn back to foolishness.

I read a great book on revival several years ago, called *When God Comes to Church* by Ray Ortlund Jr. I love it because it makes sense of all God's Word has to say about what to expect in life and ministry. Listen to how he describes revival:

> Revival is a season in the life of the church when God causes the normal ministry of the gospel to surge forward with extraordinary spiritual power. . . . Revival is seasonal, not perennial. God causes it; we do not. It is the normal ministry of the gospel, not something eccentric or even different from what the church is always charged to do. What sets revival apart is simply that our usual efforts greatly accelerate in their spiritual effects. (Ortlund, *When God Comes to Church*, 9)

Don't you long for that? Wouldn't it be awesome if we didn't alter the method? If we shunned gimmicks of every kind? If we instead continued to lean in to the normal ministry of the gospel and, suddenly, our usual "efforts greatly accelerate in their spiritual effects"? What might it look like to ask God to greatly accelerate the spiritual effects of his ministry through our lives and our witness?

Turn to Psalm 126. Verse 1 in each text points to the same thing. In Psalm 85 he's longing for God to restore the fortunes of Jacob, as though he's never experienced it. The author of Psalm 126 talks about having seen God restore the fortunes of Jacob; then he tells us some of the effects:

> *When the Lord restored the fortunes of Zion, we were like those who dream. Our mouths were filled with laughter then, and our tongues with shouts of joy. Then they said among the nations, "The Lord has done great things for them."* (126:1-2)

Church, what do you want? I'm not talking about what you can live with and be content with. What's the dream?

We want to see lives marked by such love and faith and joy that there's an impact beyond our own lives, relationships, marriages. Then this city and the nations of the world will say, "The LORD has done great things for them." That's a scale big enough for God to be honored, for God to say, "They must believe I'm awesome. Here's what they asked: They asked for the 'earth [to] be filled with the knowledge of the LORD's glory, as the water covers the sea' (Hab 2:14). They must believe I'm both rich and generous." When believers live with hope and boldness in the face of impossible circumstances, we demonstrate our belief in the bigness of God.

Concerning the vision of Isaiah 64, Raymond Ortlund Jr. writes:

> The prophet envisions God taking the sky, which he has spread out like a curtain, taking that cosmic veil, which hides him from our view, grabbing it in his strong hands, ripping it apart from top to bottom, and stepping down into our world! It's a thought to make every believer tremble with joy. . . . But the prophet is not thinking of a literal earthquake. The "mountains" symbolize long-established, well-positioned, difficult-to-remove resistance to God. That's the world we live in. And that's what the church cannot change by her own efforts and programs and good intentions. But the Lord's presence ("before You") changes everything. The evil that we cannot budge is, to God, like mere twigs before a fire or water set to boil. It has no power to resist. (*When God Comes to Church*, 30)

322   Christ-Centered Exposition Commentary

The presence of fallenness in this world assaults our senses every day. We see it, we hear it. It's all around us. Will we recall the power of God? Will we pray reckless prayers to a God who is "rich and generous"? Will we trust and obey, not only with our personal lives in view, or our local church life in view, but with a scope that is big enough to demonstrate that God's global mission is in our hearts?

We don't need some new initiative, *as if* that would trigger revival. What we need is renewed confidence in the power of God's Spirit working through the gospel.

Reflect and Discuss

1. What is the difference between being content with your life and being apathetic toward spiritual growth and calling?
2. How can we keep a desire for more of God's work in our lives without becoming burned out in efforts and affections?
3. How can we allow the things that make us weary in this world to drive us to a desire for more with God?
4. What keeps us from asking God for "big" things in our lives?
5. What do our prayers and attitude toward prayer reveal about our beliefs in the character of God?
6. How can we practically remember the ways God has worked in our lives? How can we lead our families to be a people of remembrance?
7. About what issues of idolatry and sin in our lives do you need to pray, "God, turn me"?
8. How would your prayers change if you prayed with respectful assertiveness to the God who is sovereign over all and good in character? How do we not get weary in praying those prayers, even if they aren't answered as we wanted?
9. How can prayers to a rich and generous God renew our confidence in the power of the gospel?

Behold His Grace

PSALM 86

Main Idea: God's grace is sufficient to meet our every need, and we should respond by giving him glory and trusting his Word.

I. We Rely on God's Grace to Meet Our Needs (86:1-7).
II. We Respond to God's Grace by Declaring His Glory (86:8-13).
III. We Appeal to God's Grace Based on His Word (86:14-17).

Psalm 86 is a prayer that King David prayed when he was in trouble. After asking for God's protection at the beginning of the psalm (v. 2), David later tells us what kind of trouble he was in. He says that "arrogant people" had attacked him and that a "gang of ruthless men" was out to kill him (v. 14). This psalm reminds us of our greatest need as well as our greatest source of hope—the grace of God.

Christians talk about God's grace all the time, and rightly so. It is the basis for every blessing we have in Christ, including our salvation (Eph 1:3-14; 2:8). However, there's a danger of becoming so familiar with the *term* "grace" that we lose any sense of wonder over what the Bible actually *teaches* about God's grace. The fact that a God who is perfectly holy, righteous, and just would show favor to undeserving sinners like us should never cease to amaze us. And it should shape the way we relate to God and to the world around us. This is where Psalm 86 has so much to teach us. We'll consider three important ways God's grace should shape the lives of his people.

We Rely on God's Grace to Meet Our Needs

PSALM 86:1-7

In the midst of his trouble, David cries out to God for help in verses 3 and 6 because he knows God's grace and mercy are sufficient to meet his needs. These verses are surrounded by thirteen other petitions for God's grace and mercy. For example, David asks God to hear him, preserve him, save him, unite his heart, gladden his soul, give him strength, teach him, turn to him, and show him favor (Boice, *Psalms 42–106*, 703).

And David is asking for all of these things not because he deserves them but because he needs them from a gracious God.

Verse 2 can be a little confusing to some people. It almost sounds like David is saying he deserves God's blessing because he's "faithful," but that's an unfortunate translation, at least the way it comes off in English. David is essentially saying, "Preserve my life, for I *belong to* you, as a part of your covenant people." We might say it this way: "God, I'm your child, and I need you." In the next verse, David cries out for God's grace (v. 3), which he knows he doesn't deserve. This is the picture of grace that we see all over the Bible: God's grace is his goodness expressed toward sinners who don't deserve his goodness.

In fact, this is *the* central message of the Bible. Every person is a sinner who deserves holy judgment from God. If we received what we deserve, then we would all be in hell right now. Thankfully, God is gracious, and he has sent Jesus, his Son, to die on a cross for *our* sin. Therefore, anyone in the world who turns from his sin and cries out for grace from God through Jesus can be forgiven of all his sins and reconciled to God—now on earth and forever in heaven.

This kind of grace totally transforms the way we live, as well as our desires. Like David, we begin to pray, "Teach me your way, Lord, and I will live by your truth" (v. 11). And the good news of the Bible is that God wants to give this grace to us!

Sometimes we fall into the error of thinking we can pay God back for his grace. However, the Christian life is not Jesus giving his life for you, and then you paying him back with your money and time and talents. As soon as you try to pay Jesus back for all he has done for you, you are undercutting the foundation of grace that saved you in the first place. It's not grace if you pay it back.

Many Christians have fallen into the error of thinking their church attendance and Bible reading and prayer and offerings are somehow going to pay Jesus back, like a monthly mortgage. That misses the point. Jesus didn't just give you life in the past; he is giving you life right now! Every good thing in your life *right now* is because Jesus, by his grace, is giving it to you. When you realize this, it changes the way you live.

We Respond to God's Grace by Declaring His Glory
PSALM 86:8-13

Some people view God's grace as a reason to treat sin casually, but this distorts Scripture's teaching. Those who rightly understand and receive

God's grace desire to praise him. In verses 8-13 a new section of petitions begins in which David declares that there is no god like his God (vv. 8,10). In light of God's supremacy, honor and glory belong exclusively to him. This was not only true for Israel but also for "all the nations you [God] have made" (v. 9). David acknowledged God's supremacy over all creation and all the peoples of the world.

In verse 11 David's desire to glorify God went beyond his words. He wanted his life to reflect the same truth. David asks for an "undivided mind" to fear God because he knows how easy it is to have a divided loyalty between God and other things. Money is one of the biggest stumbling blocks. According to Jesus, your heart will either belong to money or to God: "For where your treasure is, there your heart will be also" (Matt 6:21). If you want to know where your heart is, then look at where you spend your money. On the other hand, a heart that's in love with God will live for God and his glory.

The main reason we seek God's grace is not to make life easier or to impress others. We ask for grace because we are needy and because God alone deserves our praise and honor and glory. Here's how Paul put it in 1 Corinthians 10:31: "So, whether you eat or drink, or whatever you do, do everything for the glory of God."

In the final section of this psalm, verses 14-17, David asks for deliverance from those seeking to kill him (v. 14). Once again David grounds his appeal in God's grace (v. 15). However, it's also worth noting how David ends this appeal for God's glory. It's not simply that he wants to save his own skin, though he certainly hopes to escape death. David wants his enemies to see God's hand at work and so "be put to shame" (v. 17). In other words, David wants his enemies to see the supremacy of God. We're reminded of the Lord's purpose in sending the plagues on Egypt:

> Then the LORD said to Moses, "Go to Pharaoh, for I have hardened his heart and the hearts of his officials so that I may do these miraculous signs of mine among them, and so that you may tell your son and grandson how severely I dealt with the Egyptians and performed miraculous signs among them, and you will know that I am the LORD." (Exod 10:1-2)

God is chiefly concerned with his own glory (Isa 42:8; Ezek 20:22), so it is fitting that David would be concerned with God's glory, even when he feared for his own life.

We Appeal to God's Grace Based on His Word
PSALM 86:14-17

In the final section of this psalm, David continues to appeal to God's grace. However, David's pleas are not merely cries of desperation to an unknown deity. They are appeals to God's character and promises *as revealed through his words*. Even though David was being attacked and hunted (v. 14), he could rely on God's character as revealed in Exodus 34:6-7:

> The Lord—the Lord is a compassionate and gracious God, slow to anger and abounding in faithful love and truth, maintaining faithful love to a thousand generations, forgiving iniquity, rebellion, and sin. But he will not leave the guilty unpunished, bringing the fathers' iniquity on the children and grandchildren to the third and fourth generation.

This passage seems to have had a massive influence on the way David thinks about God in Psalm 86. Verse 15 is one of the clearest examples of this (see also v. 5). Based on who God had revealed himself to be through his words, David had not given up hope. However, as we saw earlier, David's concern was not limited to his own well-being. He was also looking forward to the day when all nations will "come and bow down before you, Lord, and will honor your name" (v. 9). This hope was also based on God's words, for God's worldwide purposes of redemption are interspersed throughout the Old Testament (VanGemeren, *Psalms*, 650):

> The Lord said to Abram:
> Go out from your land, your relatives, and your father's house to the land that I will show you.
> I will make you into a great nation, I will bless you, I will make your name great, and you will be a blessing.
> I will bless those who bless you, I will curse anyone who treats you with contempt, and all the peoples on earth will be blessed through you. (Gen 12:1-3)

> Praise the Lord, all nations!
> Glorify him, all peoples! (Ps 117:1)

> In the last days the mountain of the Lord's house will be established at the top of the mountains and will be raised above the hills. All nations will stream to it, and many peoples will come and say, "Come, let us go up to the mountain of the Lord, to the house of the God of Jacob.

He will teach us about his ways so that we may walk in his paths.
*For instruction will go out of Zion and the word of the L*ORD *from*
Jerusalem. (Isa 2:2-3)

Today our hope for the spread of the gospel and the success of Christ's mission (Matt 28:18-20) is not based on our own wisdom or abilities, or even our own faithfulness. Our hope is based on God's faithfulness to keep his promises. We believe, for instance, that death will not prevail against Christ's church (Matt 16:18) and that God has purchased people from every tribe, language, people, and nation (Rev 5:9). Knowing and believing these promises is critical in light of the opposition we face from sin, Satan, and the world. We can rely on God's grace and the fulfillment of his gracious promises because God always keeps his word.

Reflect and Discuss

1. How is the word *grace* typically used in our culture?
2. How should a right view of God's character lead us to be in awe of his grace?
3. How would you define God's grace to someone who is unfamiliar with the Bible?
4. What's wrong with the idea of trying to "pay Jesus back" for all that he has done for us?
5. Does God's free and lavish grace mean our sin is not that big of a deal? Why not?
6. If we can't pay Jesus back for his grace, then how should we respond to him?
7. Why must grace be a prominent theme in the church's corporate worship?
8. How does knowing God's Word give us confidence in our weaknesses?
9. What are some promises in Scripture related to God's grace toward his people? Make a list.
10. Explain the following statement: "Grace should lead us to be focused on the good of others."

The City of God

PSALM 87

Main Idea: God has established a city to be the eternal hub of his worship and the habitation of his children.

I. The Consecration of God's City (87:1-3)
II. The Citizens of God's City (87:4-6)
III. The Celebration of God's City (87:7)

Have you ever heard someone say, "I can't get that song out of my head!"? You're going to hate me for this, but I'm willing to bet that at least one of the times you've heard someone say that, they were referring to the Disney theme park ride, "It's a Small World." The attraction features more than three hundred audio-animatronic children in traditional costumes from cultures around the world. As you make your way through the ride, you're overwhelmed by a diverse multitude of children frolicking in a spirit of international unity, singing that title song.

That ride seared the words and melody of its theme song indelibly into many of our minds. That's exactly what its creators wanted to happen. The entire exhibit is a microcosmic representation of an agenda its originators wanted to champion: world peace. All of the robotic children in the feature are indicative of the multitude of tribes, nations, and languages on the earth living together in harmony. The ride is fantasy, but its message has been a real hope of a lot of people throughout history.

In similar fashion, Psalm 87 describes a microcosm that God established to whet his people's appetites for real hope as well but one that's far more certain than world peace. And he wants this miniature model to make this hope ring in our ears and remain firmly established in our minds so we won't ever forget it! What is this hope? It's the predetermined metropolis of Jew and Gentile alike, the place of the coming conversion of old enemies and their full incorporation into the city of God, the spiritual home for the redeemed from every tribe, nation, and tongue. God has established this city to be the eternal hub of his worship and the habitation of his children.

God's microcosm is the city of Zion, a place in the Old Testament variously called Jerusalem, Salem, Mount Moriah, the city of God, the city of David, and the city of the great king. While it has served as the historical center of Israel's life and worship, God destined it for so much more. It was to prefigure a better city than its earthly precursor ever has been or ever will be. The author of Hebrews tells Christians as much:

> *Instead, you have come to Mount Zion, to the city of the living God*
> *(the heavenly Jerusalem), to myriads of angels, a festive gathering,*
> *to the assembly of the firstborn whose names have been written in*
> *heaven, to a Judge, who is God of all, to the spirits of righteous people*
> *made perfect, and to Jesus, the mediator of a new covenant, and to*
> *the sprinkled blood, which says better things than the blood of Abel.*
> (Heb 12:22-24)

Like Disney's "It's a Small World" ride, the earthly city of Zion is an imperfect miniature. But unlike the popular theme park ride, the city of Jerusalem represents something that actually will come to pass as a result of the redeeming work of Jesus Christ. Zion—the city of God—is a little slice of the hope of heaven that reminds us how small the world really is after all. This psalm shows us this city and its purpose in three simple divisions.

The Consecration of God's City
PSALM 87:1-3

The psalm begins by describing Zion, the historical city God set apart to be the hub of his worship. The writer leaves no doubt that he's talking about that special place God consecrated from all other locales throughout all of history—past, present, and future. It's the city Israel's God chose as his residence (2 Chr 6:5-6), that served as a constant source of delight to Israel's songwriters (e.g., Pss 48:1; 78:68-70; 132:13), and that became a consistent source of envy for Israel's opposers (68:15-16). Here the psalmist specifically notes three reasons for this city's uniqueness.

First, this city is set apart because **God established it** (v. 1). In Hebrew the word *founded* actually opens the psalm and provides an emphatic introduction. It's the work of God, not of men. And as a result of God's establishment, its location is rightly called "the holy mountains" because he's there. God is holy, and his dwelling place has taken on his nature. "Mountains," plural, refer either to the multitude of hills in the Jerusalem area or simply to the magnification of the place where God dwells. The Lord chose this spot for his dwelling place, and that sets it apart forever from all other hills on the planet.

Second, the city of God is consecrated because **God esteems it** (v. 2). The verb *loves* is an active participle and connects God's establishment with his endless affection (cf. Deut 7:6-8). Ross says, "He established Zion as his dwelling-place by elective love, and his love for it as his dwelling-place remained constant" (Ross, *Psalms*, vol. 2, 794). While the word translated "dwellings" certainly is metaphorical for all other possible abodes, it is a common designation for the Lord's sanctuary. So the psalmist may be contrasting this city with other sanctuary cities (e.g., Gilgal, Bethel, Shiloh). God didn't choose other religious centers for his dwelling place. He chose this one as the center of his worship.

The object of God's love for Jerusalem is specifically identified as "Zion's city gates" (v. 2), a metaphorical substitution that represents the city as a whole. The gates of the city not only provided protection from enemies but also served as the primary pathway of entrance, where both visitors and citizens gained access. Inside the gates usually was a plaza where friends met together, the people bought and sold their goods, city officials pronounced legal decisions, and preparations were made for entering the place of worship. In essence, Zion's gates represented Israel's heart and soul (Ross, *Psalms*, vol. 2, 794). God set his delight on the essence of their very being.

Third, the city of Zion is set apart because **God exalts it**. The general commentary on what he's done in choosing Jerusalem is in verse 3. The word *said* designates the introduction to an oracle from God. While praise for the city—both spoken and sung—is offered by those who experience and observe its wonder, their words actually articulate God's perspective. Through their voices he lauds all that has happened in the holy city that attests to his divine presence. He founded it. He loves it. He has established it as the hub of his worship in all the world. He has made it a place where his glory is witnessed and proclaimed!

God's establishment, esteem, and exaltation of the historical and physical city of Jerusalem was not his end game, however. In the songs of Zion, praise is due the city of God, not just because of its physical and earthly splendor but for its spiritual and eternal significance. Even in other psalms the writer is clear to equate God's favor on the holy city to someplace that is beyond the earthly realm. He connects it with the heavenly realm—"The Lord is in his holy temple; the Lord—his throne is in heaven" (Ps 11:4)—and designates it as God's dwelling place for eternity—"For the LORD has chosen Zion; he has desired it for his home: 'This is my resting place forever; I will make my home here because I have desired it" (Ps 132:13-14).

In Revelation 21–22 John sees this larger purpose in vivid detail when God unfolds for him the vision of what believers often refer to as heaven, God's eternal kingdom. It's here where the earthly city finds its ultimate purpose. The "new Jerusalem" (Rev 21:2; cf. 21:10)—as it's called here—is described as "coming down out of heaven from God, prepared like a bride adorned for her husband" (Rev 21:2). This picture likely isn't a reference to the church as the bride of Christ as in some other places in the New Testament (John 3:29; 2 Cor 11:2; Eph 5:25-27,30-32; Rev 19:7-8; 22:17) but merely a simile that portrays something of great value being presented to another.

The voice emanating "from the throne" (Rev 21:3) of God introduces the heavenly city as the place he has been preparing for his children, much like a bride would be prepared for her husband. This reality becomes clear as God declares, "Look, God's dwelling is with humanity, and he will live with them. They will be his peoples, and God himself will be with them and will be their God" (Rev 21:3). God determined long ago to make this city his final and eternal abode with redeemed mankind. When God came to earth, he dwelt temporarily with mankind in the flesh of Christ Jesus (John 1:14). When mankind goes to heaven, they will dwell eternally with God through ultimate union with Christ Jesus.

A number of things will be noticeably different about this new city, demonstrating its obvious superiority over the earthly model. For example, unlike the historical Jerusalem, God "will wipe away every tear from their eyes. Death will be no more; grief, crying, and pain will be no more, because the previous things have passed away" (Rev 21:4). This verse contains one of the most glorious truths in the whole Bible! As believers in Christ Jesus, we long for this day when there will be no more cancer, broken relationships, loss of loved ones, domestic violence, sexual abuse, loneliness, abandonment, murder, or anything else that causes us to shed tears and harbor broken hearts. Certainly, in all of its conflict through the years, this is something that can't be said of the present-day earthly city. Nor can it be said of any human being's current status. But it is the certain hope to which we now cling.

Another difference is that there will be no "temple in it, because the Lord God the Almighty and the Lamb are its temple" (Rev 21:22).

This was God's ultimate intention of his instructions to build a physical temple in the Old Testament—to whet his people's appetite for eternal communion with him! While there's no temple currently located in Jerusalem, it remains the desire, dream, and delight of the Jewish people to see it rebuilt. However, in heaven there won't be any need for it. A physical temple will be irrelevant because God's people will experience perfect, intimate, and perennial communion with him through Christ Jesus. And there will no longer be any chance of mistakenly substituting a physical location for the intended end!

Another difference between the two cities is that the heavenly one "does not need the sun or the moon to shine on it, because the glory of God illuminates it, and its lamp is the Lamb" (Rev 21:23; cf. 21:11). Again, this can't be said for the earthly city. Like every place on the planet, they still need the sun. In fact, life as we know it depends on it! But the hub of God's ultimate worship and the locus of the radiance of his glory won't be a physical structure or a celestial body. Instead, it will be a spiritual reality in the heavenly sphere. The ultimate object of God's worship will be himself as he's manifested in his Lamb-Son, Jesus Christ. When Jesus dwelt with people on earth, they saw "his glory, the glory as the one and only Son from the Father" (John 1:14). When he dwells with us in heaven, we will see that glory to its fullest degree, and it will compel us to worship the Father forever!

The forever dwelling place of God with man. The true temple of God. The full and brilliant radiance of God's glory. Finally, all that God intended for his children—when he consecrated an earthly city to be a foretaste of his glory—will be realized in the new Jerusalem.

The Citizens of God's City
PSALM 87:4-6

Much like the festive atmosphere of riding on a boat through the "It's a Small World" ride at a Disney park, the setting of Psalm 87 may have been one of the festivals in Jerusalem when both Israelites and proselytes would have been present. On such an occasion the worship leaders likely would have started by declaring the glories of Zion, but their words would have extended far beyond the microcosmic earthly city to anticipate the fulfillment of its intended goal. That goal was for the city to be the eternal dwelling place of God where he would finally gather his redeemed of both Jew and Gentile people.

The "glorious things" (v. 3) that make up Jerusalem's high reputation aren't all left to the reader's or singer's imagination or knowledge of history. Some particulars are provided in verses 4-6. The bottom line is that Zion's grandeur largely will be seen in the diversity of those citizens of the city who were not naturally born there. Moreover, this diversity will be the prophetic fulfillment of the gathering of people from all nations who will make up the city's membership register. As Isaiah prophesied,

> *In the last days the mountain of the LORD's house will be established at the top of the mountains and will be raised above the hills. All nations will stream to it, and many peoples will come and say, "Come, let us go up to the mountain of the LORD, to the house of the God of Jacob. He will teach us about his ways so that we may walk in his paths." For instruction will go out of Zion and the word of the LORD from Jerusalem.* (Isa 2:2-3; cf. Isa 26:1-2; 60:15-22; 61:1-7)

This city is not just for Israelites but for people from "all nations" and tribes and tongues under the sun. God is worthy of the worship of every person on the planet, and the glory of his city was always intended to reflect that merit.

The psalmist, therefore, begins in verse 4 to cite God's oracle that was introduced in verse 3. The first-person pronouns *me* and *I* (v. 4) refer to him as the speaker. God is about to point out some examples of people of whom it will be said that—regardless of the place of their natural birth—they were "born there." Such is the common thread that ties verses 4-6 together. Citizenship in Zion isn't determined by location of physical birth or identification of ethnic heritage. If you're a citizen of God's city, it's as if you were born there!

Verse 4 is a roll call of the people groups in God's city, and it's somewhat of an unlikely catalog! The representative list is made up of nations that played menacing roles in Israel's history. "Rahab"—or Egypt (cf. Ps 89:10; Isa 30:7)—and "Babylon" were arguably Israel's greatest oppressors. "Philistia and Tyre" were at the very least the nation's regular troublers. And "Cush"—of the upper Nile—consistently enticed Israel to chase after the things of this world. None of these Gentile nations makes the cut in a political sense, for they were all Israel's enemies. Instead, select individuals from among each one will participate by faith in God's worship as "reborn" citizens of Jerusalem, just as if they were native born in his holy city (cf. Isa 19:19-25; Zech 2:11-12; Mal 1:11).

The official and permanent status of these foreign-born citizens in God's city is stated strongly in three ways in these verses. First, God identifies each one as being "of those who know me" (v. 4). These Gentiles are ones who—by faith—trust in him, acknowledge his words, and worship him in obedience because they've now been adopted by him. Although they were born as citizens of nations that worshiped a myriad of false gods, they now know the one true God, Yahweh of Israel.

Second, God says, "The Most High himself will establish her" (v. 5). This composition of such a diverse and undeserved privilege of citizenship in Zion is his doing. While the great city was founded as a literal and historical city, God says he's orchestrating its true establishment and will ultimately open its gates to the nations and "peoples will stream to it" (Mic 4:1; cf. Isa 54:1-2; 62:4-5; 65:18-24). That's when Jerusalem will fulfill its ultimate purpose (Goldingay, *Psalms 42–89*, 639).

Third, God claims himself to be the one that's actually recording names in the citizenship registry (vv. 5-6; cf. v. 4). It's the cosmic clerk of the universe who's logging people into the archives (see Exod 32:32-33; Ezek 13:9; Mal 3:16), and he's the one who's guaranteeing these foreigners their rightful position as citizens. Because God is the one keeping the roll, they will be as natural-born citizens forever, as if they had been so from the beginning.

The obvious emphasis in these verses is the citizenship that results from one's newly declared birth. Regardless of the location and nationality of a person's physical birth, citizenship in Jerusalem comes about when God declares him or her to have been born there. This declaration is similar to the conversation Jesus had with Nicodemus, who came to Jesus apparently wanting to know how someone gained citizenship in God's kingdom (John 3:1-21). Jesus said you had to be "born again," or "born from above" (CEV). In other words, you have to have two births—one that's physical and one that's spiritual. The physical birth comes about by "water" and is fleshly. The spiritual birth comes about by "the Spirit" and is spiritual. The physical birth grants one citizenship in an earthly kingdom. The spiritual birth makes one a citizen of God's heavenly kingdom.

Nicodemus had a hard time processing this dual citizenship about which Jesus spoke. So Jesus told him,

> *"Do not be amazed that I told you that you must be born again. The wind blows where it pleases, and you hear its sound, but you don't*

*know where it comes from or where it is going. So it is with everyone
born of the Spirit."* (John 3:7-8)

In other words, people don't question where the wind comes from
when they see, hear, and feel its effects. Any good Jew simply attributed it to Yahweh, the Creator of the universe. So it is with spiritual
birth, Jesus told Nicodemus. We see its effects, but we can't necessarily
wrap our limited mind around its divine mystery. Years later Peter would
declare this sovereign and mysterious work of God:

> *Blessed be the God and Father of our Lord Jesus Christ. Because of his
> great mercy he has given us new birth into a living hope through the
> resurrection of Jesus Christ from the dead and into an inheritance that
> is imperishable, undefiled, and unfading, kept in heaven for you. You
> are being guarded by God's power through faith for a salvation that is
> ready to be revealed in the last time.* (1 Pet 1:3-5)

The new birth is the effect of the sovereign and mysterious grace of God
on humanity, and that effect gives us a glorious hope!

A second birth is the only way a person can become a citizen of God's
heavenly city. God must declare a person to have been born there. He
has to record their name in his registry. That's what John said about "the
holy city, Jerusalem, coming down out of heaven from God" (Rev 21:10;
cf. 21:2). He said, "Nothing unclean will ever enter it, nor anyone who
does what is detestable or false, but only those written in the Lamb's
book of life" (Rev 21:27; cf. Phil 4:3; Rev 3:5; 13:8; 20:12,15). God's book
is called "the Lamb's book of life" because therein are recorded the
names of those who have become citizens through the shed blood of
Jesus Christ, "the Lamb who was slaughtered" (Rev 13:8; cf. Gen 22:7-8;
Exod 12:3; Num 28:3-10; Isa 53:7; John 1:29,36) for the sins of the world.
Acknowledging Jesus as this Lamb and throwing yourself at his mercy is
the only way for your name to be written in this book.

True to God's promise to Abraham (Gen 12:1-3) and true to Israel's
stated assignment as God's nation of priests who were to lead all people
to worship him (Exod 19:5-6), the population of the New Jerusalem will
comprise natural-born citizens from every nation on the planet. John
says, "The nations will walk by its light, and the kings of the earth will
bring their glory into it. . . . They will bring the glory and honor of the
nations into it" (Rev 21:24,26). Into this heavenly city people from every
nation will come with their gifts and sacrifices of praise to our Lord.
This will be the gathering John saw earlier: "a vast multitude from every

nation, tribe, people, and language, which no one could number, standing before the throne and before the Lamb. They were clothed in white robes with palm branches in their hands" (Rev 7:9). Finally, God's plan for a far more glorious Zion will be a reality, and his holy city will be the center of life and worship for all humanity.

The Septuagint includes the word *mother* in the first part of Psalm 87:5, the translation of an additional two-letter Hebrew word that may have been eliminated accidentally. The NEB renders it, "Zion shall be called a mother in whom men of every race are born." Paul seems to have this understanding in mind when contrasting slavery to the law and freedom in Christ: "Now Hagar represents Mount Sinai in Arabia and corresponds to the present Jerusalem, for she is in slavery with her children. But the Jerusalem above is free, and she is our mother" (Gal 4:25-26). Citizenship merely in the earthly Jerusalem leaves one in bondage to sin, while citizenship in the heavenly Jerusalem through Christ Jesus means one has been set free. This citizenship is no longer defined by circumcision (Gal 6:12-16) or limited to those who are from the bloodline of Abraham (Gal 3:7-9). It's now available to all who will trust Christ, regardless of where they were born or their ethnic heritage.

As believers, this truth compels us to several responses. First, this text should make us—of all people—most thankful. We are these outsiders! We are the people of Egypt and Babylon, the citizens of Philistia and Tyre and Cush. The easiest thing to do in this passage is to see ourselves as the natural-born citizens of Jerusalem and to see everyone else as people who need to experience the grace of God. Remember, however, the Jews are the natural-born citizens. They are God's chosen people. Everyone else—including most every one of us reading this passage—are the Gentiles. We are the outsiders, the enemies of God. Paul reminds us that

> *God proves his own love for us in that while we were still sinners, Christ died for us. How much more then, since we have now been declared righteous by his blood, will we be saved through him from wrath. For if, while we were enemies, we were reconciled to God through the death of his Son, then how much more, having been reconciled, will we be saved by his life.* (Rom 5:8-10)

We were God's adversaries, standing on the outside of his kingdom and defiantly looking in. Yet through Christ and the grace of the gospel, we're "born again" into the citizenship of his kingdom. This passage should prompt a gush of gratitude in all of us.

A second response to this glorious truth should be for us—as newborn citizens of God's kingdom—to leverage our entire lives to get this gospel to every person on the planet, regardless of geographic location or skin color. This demands that we see immigration issues as more than political policies that benefit us. This motivates us to fight hard against racism and social injustice. The gospel is for everybody, and our Lord has called us to make disciples from among all people groups (Matt 28:19-20) because that's what's going to characterize his holy city. Heaven is going to be made up of all kinds of people because our God is worthy of their worship. So we'd better start practicing for that kind of diversity by making the church on earth look like it's going to look in heaven.

The Celebration of God's City
PSALM 87:7

The adoption of people from every tribe, nation, and tongue into the citizenship of God's glorious city will prompt a big party! This festivity is represented by "singers and dancers," icons of two of Israel's most cheerful forms of celebration (cf. 68:25; 150:4). The city will pull out all the stops to rejoice in this amalgamation of individuals from so many different backgrounds into the makeup of God's people.

This celebration, however, isn't prompted merely by the diversity of people in God's city. The gladness ultimately is the result of the sustenance and blessing these citizens get to experience as a result of being in God's presence. In the Old Testament springs are metaphorical images for true life, the life that only God can give (e.g., 36:9; Jer 2:13). Here the psalmist acknowledges Zion as the "source" of both physical and spiritual sustenance that comes from him. The psalmist previously said of the city, "There is a river—its streams delight the city of God, the holy dwelling place of the Most High. God is within her; she will not be toppled. God will help her when the morning dawns" (Ps 46:4-5; cf. Ezek 47:1-12). The true reason for celebration is that people from every nation get to experience the true life that only God can give!

The image of a water source and fountains as representing the true, eternal life that comes only from God continues in the New Testament with our Lord. Jesus tells the Samaritan woman at the well, "If you knew the gift of God, and who is saying to you, 'Give me a drink,' you would

ask him, and he would give you living water" (John 4:10). Then a while
later, on the last day of one of the Jews' treasured feasts, Jesus inter-
rupts the festivities by standing up in the middle of the crowd and crying out, "If anyone is thirsty, let him come to me and drink. The one
who believes in me, as the Scripture has said, will have streams of living
water flow from deep within him" (John 7:37-38). Jesus clearly and confidently claims to be the source and supplier of the true life from God.

The description of these events that the psalmist declares of the
earthly Jerusalem find their ultimate fulfillment in the New Jerusalem,
God's heavenly city. Revelation 4–5 contains mysterious descriptions of
the awe-inspiring praise God will receive from elders, living creatures,
tens of thousands of angels, and every creature in the universe. Then in
Revelation 7 John sees,

> . . . a vast multitude from every nation, tribe, people, and language,
> which no one could number, standing before the throne and before the
> Lamb. They were clothed in white robes with palm branches in their
> hands. And they cried out in a loud voice: Salvation belongs to our
> God, who is seated on the throne, and to the Lamb!
> All the angels stood around the throne, and along with the elders
> and the four living creatures they fell facedown before the throne and
> worshiped God, saying, Amen! Blessing and glory and wisdom and
> thanksgiving and honor and power and strength be to our God forever
> and ever. Amen. (Rev 7:9-12)

As with the "singers and dancers" (Ps 87:7) in historic Jerusalem, there
will be a great celebration of worship at the throne of God and of our
Lord Jesus Christ in the heavenly city.

Furthermore, as in the earthly Jerusalem, the celebration in the
celestial city will be fostered by the new life the redeemed of mankind
get to experience in God's presence. This time the life is forever. Here
God's children will experience his redemption and restoration in Christ
in its fullness. Not only will he "wipe away every tear from their eyes.
Death will be no more; grief, crying, and pain will be no more" (Rev 21:4),
but he will provide them with something that is curiously reminiscent of
the psalmist's reference to a "source" in Psalm 87:7. John says,

> Then the one seated on the throne said, "Look, I am making
> everything new." He also said, "Write, because these words are faithful
> and true." Then he said to me, "It is done! I am the Alpha and the

*Omega, the beginning and the end. I will freely give to the thirsty from
the spring of the water of life."* (Rev 21:5-6)

In Jesus Christ, God freely restores to his children the life he created them to have (Gen 1:25-26), a life that had been forfeited because
of sin, and a life that none of us deserved to get back.

God isn't finished. John says,

*Then he showed me the river of the water of life, clear as crystal,
flowing from the throne of God and of the Lamb down the middle
of the city's main street. The tree of life was on each side of the river,
bearing twelve kinds of fruit, producing its fruit every month. The
leaves of the tree are for healing the nations, and there will no longer be
any curse. The throne of God and of the Lamb will be in the city, and
his servants will worship him.* (Rev 22:1-3)

The eradication of sin and its effects among people from every tribe,
nation, and tongue will mark the DNA of the New Jerusalem, a nature
the old Jerusalem could only foreshadow. In God's heavenly city people
from every nation will experience healing from sin forever, and they will
worship him accordingly.

Conclusion

John appropriately concludes the record of his glimpse into eternity
with a passionate invitation: "Both the Spirit and the bride say, 'Come!'
Let anyone who hears, say, 'Come!' Let the one who is thirsty come. Let
the one who desires take the water of life freely" (Rev 22:17). That's what
the gospel does. It gives all people—regardless of ethnicity, geographic
location, track record, family upbringing, skeletons in the closet, or any
other thing that characterizes their physical birth or life history—the
opportunity to drink from the fountain of God's true life. The gospel
provides the only sure hope of the forgiveness of sins and true life forever in God's presence. It makes heavenly citizens out of all kinds of
people from all kinds of earthly kingdoms.

One line in Psalm 87—"Glorious things are spoken of thee, O city
of God" (v. 3 KJV)—was the inspiration for John Newton's great hymn,
"Glorious Things of Thee Are Spoken," which he published in 1779 as
part of the *Olney Hymns* hymnal. Although Newton wrote other great
hymns like "Amazing Grace," this particular one is considered by many
to be his best composition. Why? The songs in that hymnal were written

for use in the Anglican clergyman's rural parish, which was made up of relatively poor and uneducated congregants. "Glorious Things of Thee Are Spoken" is the only joyful hymn in the hymnal. Newton apparently understood that expressing the wonders of God's city and anticipating its habitation served a special purpose in lifting the spirits of the hopeless. That same hope of the New Jerusalem gives us a song to sing that God doesn't ever want us to get out of our heads. He doesn't ever want us to forget that our citizenship is not on earth but in heaven. So with that tune stuck in our heads, let's spend our lives telling others the good news that participation in this heavenly city of God is not by ethnicity or socioeconomic status but by faith.

Reflect and Discuss

1. God has had, and may still have, grand plans for the city of Zion. Is the earthly Jerusalem the end goal, or does the current city foreshadow something greater?
2. What is the connection between the city of God in Psalm 87 and Revelation 21–22? Compare and contrast these two cities.
3. How does a vision of the new city of God fuel missions to the nations?
4. Should every believer/local church be concerned with the nations? What are practical ways a local church can get involved in the global context of the Great Commission?
5. How do new covenant, Gentile Christians relate to God's covenant people? In other words, what status did Gentiles have in the old covenant, and has that status changed in the new?
6. We live in an age of racial tension, both at home and all over the world. How does the Christian hope of a New Jerusalem speak powerfully into the issue of racism?
7. How should the vision of the New Jerusalem at the end of Revelation spur on the local church to seek diversity? How should the local church reflect the community?
8. How can the language of "each one was born there" be connected to Jesus's conversation with Nicodemus regarding the true nature of kingdom citizenry?
9. What are some biblical examples of warnings given to those who would rely on their natural birth, as opposed to their spiritual birth?
10. According to the end of Revelation, what are the key characteristics about life in the new city of God?

Songs in the Night

PSALM 88

Main Idea: It is possible to be greatly shaken and yet still trust in God.

I.   Desperation: I Have Had Enough Troubles (88:1-8).
II. Disputation: Do You Work Wonders for the Dead (88:9-12)?
III. Isolation: Why Do You Hide Your Face from Me (88:13-18)?
IV. Restoration: How the Story Ends and How We Help One Another

---

Psalms is a book filled with the kind of singing that prepares us for living in a real world with an unshakable hope in God. We'll see today that unshakable hope doesn't always feel unshakable. This psalm lets us in on what it sounds like to be greatly shaken and yet still trust God.

The late pastor and Bible commentator James Montgomery Boice said, "It is good that we have a psalm like this, but it is also good that we have just one" ("Monday: Dark Night of the Soul"). Thankfully, the experience underneath Psalm 88 isn't your everyday, garden-variety trial. But if you find yourself in the cellar of affliction, it's good to know there's stuff like this down there. This is the darkest psalm in the Bible. Literally, the last word in the original Hebrew is *darkness*.

A subtle version of the prosperity gospel lives in churches that are otherwise quick to denounce the error. We may rightly point out that real believers might be poor and might get sick; faith doesn't guarantee those things. But then we might add, "Still, they're never depressed. Believers by definition never feel hopeless. Even when they face severe trials, they always have this unexplainable peace and calm." Psalm 88 wants a word because not only does that position reflect a selective reading of the Bible that edits out chapters like this one, but saying things like that is a great way to create a church where everybody acts happy even if they're falling apart.

Theologian Robert Dabney knew pain. Born in 1820, his father died when he was thirteen. As chief of staff to General Stonewall Jackson, he witnessed the carnage of the Civil War. On the home front he was beset by illness most of his life and lost his sight toward the end. He had six sons. Three of them died before they were old enough to leave the house. Two of them passed away within a month of each other. He describes that month this way: "When my Jimmy died, the grief was painfully sharp, but the actings of faith, the embracing of consolation, and all the cheering truths which ministered comfort to me were just as vivid" (Dabney, as quoted in Piper and Taylor, *Suffering and the Sovereignty of God*, 179). Those are the stories we like to hear. However, he goes on to say something that we, for some reason, are more reluctant to quote:

> But when the stroke was repeated, and thereby doubled,
> I seem to be paralyzed and stunned. I know that my loss is
> doubled, and I know also that the same cheering truths apply
> to the second as to the first, but I remain numb, downcast,
> almost without hope or interest. (Ibid.)

Have you ever felt that things you knew about God were failing to leverage their soul-stabilizing effect in your actual experience? In other words, your pain eclipsed, or outran, your theology for a day, or a month, or longer? What do you do from that place of darkness? How do you sing your pain in the presence of God? How do you sing when you've lost a child? When depression grabs your mind with both hands to where you wake up in the morning and you don't have the energy to get dressed? How do you sing when the enemy of your soul reminds you of things you keep trying to forget? If Christian faith doesn't speak to these places, the hard realities of life in this world, then we shouldn't be surprised when the world says, "No thanks." And even as a local church, we can't just speak upbeat truths to upbeat people. Why? Because on any given Sunday there are people in that sanctuary who are barely hanging on, and if our worship pretends everything is awesome, it's painting a false picture of reality. When we do this, we leave embattled Christians with no resources to help them endure. The truth of Psalm 88 is that God gives his people songs in the night. Songs they can sing, we can sing, when darkness closes in.

The author of this psalm loves the Lord. He was a worship leader in Israel, appointed by King David himself to train and direct a guild of 288 skillful musicians who served at the temple. This is not the journal of a cynic. Cynicism pulls away from God. The psalmist is not running from God; he's running to God. He's not backing away. If anything, he's in God's face.

As a matter of fact, the passage opens up when you notice this little, recurring refrain—in verses 1, 9, and 13—"I cry out" or "I call to you." This brings us to the first movement in this passage.

Desperation: I Have Had Enough Troubles
PSALM 88:1-8

"I cry out, I cry out, I call." He doesn't have time for pious pleasantries and cliché prayers. The gist of Psalm 88 is, "Lord, you have to answer to me. And it has to be today." Do you ever pray like this? Do you ever bring your sorrows to God without dressing them up in church clothes? Here's the sad truth about so much of evangelical piety in the modern church. We've learned to pray presentable prayers rather than real ones. By contrast, notice the language of feeling here.

> *I cry out* (v. 1)
> *I have had enough* (v. 3)
> *going down . . . without strength* (v. 4)
> *abandoned . . . lying in the grave, . . . cut off from your care* (v. 5)
> *darkest places* (v. 6)
> *weighs heavily . . . overwhelmed* (v. 7)
> *distanced . . . shut in* (v. 8)
> *worn out . . . I cry out . . . I spread out my hands* (v. 9)
> *I call* (v. 13)
> *I have been suffering, . . . I am desperate* (v. 15)
> *They surround me . . . they close in on me* (v. 17)
> *distanced . . . darkness* (v. 18)

Having grown up in New Orleans, I can't tell you how many times we've tuned in to the Weather Channel during hurricane season. And there's Jim Cantore with the rain jacket leaning against the wind, screaming in the mic. Sheets of corrugated metal flying past. A small horse. They always seemed to send Cantore into the eye of the storm. He's not in the studio, crisp shirt, full Windsor, witty banter with colleagues. He's giving a live report on location while trying to not die.

Same here. This isn't Heman the Ezrahite on a podcast with The Gospel Coalition, every hair in place. "Heman, glad to have you in the studio today. So tell us about hardship and the songwriting process." No, this is a live report from landfall. Sideways rain. Screaming into the mic.

And this is where the psalm starts to get real—these I/you descriptions, mainly in verses 3-8: "I have had enough" (v. 3); "I am . . . going down" (v. 4); "I am like a man without strength" (v. 4); "I am . . . abandoned . . . lying in the grave" (v. 5). And you: "You no longer remember [me favorably . . . I am] cut off from your care" (v. 5); "You have put me in the lowest part of the Pit" (v. 6); "Your wrath weighs heavily on me; you have overwhelmed me with all your waves" (v. 7); "You have distanced my friends from me; you have made me repulsive to them" (v. 8).

Christian friend, God doesn't run in to make sure all your statements in prayer are theologically tidy and properly nuanced. God is not put off by your desperation.

This psalm doesn't give us enough information to determine whether he is actually experiencing the wrath of God, whether God is actively pushing Heman's friends away, and so on. That's not the point. He's not writing a seminary thesis. He's telling God how he feels.

Psalm 88 isn't a license to spit bitter accusations at God. This is a man wrestling with the tension between what he knows and what he feels. What he knows he expresses in the first five words of the psalm: "Lord, God of my salvation." That's the tidiest theology in the whole psalm. But his feelings aren't buying it. In other words, "I know you are the God of my salvation, but my experience is telling me there won't be any saving today."

Christian friend, it is possible to have faith yet feel cut off from God's favor and blessing. Some of the greatest heroes of the faith have felt that. The great hymn writer, William Cowper, author of "There Is a Fountain Filled with Blood." Luther, Bunyan, Spurgeon. Many others.

The great preacher Charles Spurgeon experienced tremendous hardship. Nine years into his marriage to Susannah, she became virtually homebound. They couldn't figure out what was wrong. For the next twenty-seven years, she hardly ever heard him preach. Spurgeon himself was greatly afflicted with all kinds of trials. For the last twenty-two years of his ministry, one-third of it was out of the pulpit, sick or recovering. He writes of one Sunday when he preached Psalm 22—"My God, my God, why have you abandoned me?" (v. 1). He said, "Though I did not say so, yet I preached my own experience. I heard my own chains clank while I tried to preach to my fellow prisoners in the dark" (Spurgeon, *An All-Round Ministry*, 221–22).

The psalmist is desperate, and there's no reason to hide that in the presence of God. The text then changes direction to argument.

Disputation: Do You Work Wonders for the Dead?
PSALM 88:9-12

The psalmist stockpiles questions that, to the Old Testament way of thinking, demand the answer no, and then he calls for action to remedy the situation.

Now we need to bear in mind that when it comes to what happens after death, the Old Testament saints were largely in the dark. The blessed hope (if you will) of the Old Testament patriarchs wasn't to "die and go to heaven." It was to live to see your children's children. To live out your days in the promised land. And they didn't mean the one up there. They meant the one they were standing on.

Yes, there are hints of resurrection or life after death in Psalm 16, two verses in Isaiah, and a few other places. However, we shouldn't force Old Testament saints to pass New Testament exams. Being an inspired biblical writer didn't mean you had this "matrix plug" with a full download of future names, places, and events, so that somewhere in 750 BC you wake up and tell your friends, "The tomb is empty," and you quote words Paul will write much later: "Jesus has brought life and immortality to light through the gospel!" (see 2 Tim 1:10). Awesome! So it shouldn't surprise us when we don't hear Old Testament saints say, "To live is Christ and to die is gain" (Phil 1:21).

Even in the New Testament, it shouldn't surprise us when we read Mark 9. Jesus is coming from the Mount of Transfiguration event with Peter, James, and John, and he orders them to tell no one what they had seen "until the Son of Man had risen from the dead." Then the text says, "They kept this word to themselves, questioning what 'rising from the dead' meant" (Mark 9:9-10). So again, let's not require pre-resurrection believers to pass post-resurrection exams.

That said, even though the New Testament sheds new light on this, there is still truth tucked into these questions—namely, that God gets unique glory and praise when he rescues his people in this life, in the sight of the nations. The psalmist asks, "Will your wonders be known in the darkness?" (v. 12).

Think about the great rescuing act of God in the Old Testament. What if it never happened? What if Israel never left Egypt? Never crossed the Red Sea? Instead, they died in captivity. What becomes of that great outburst of praise on the far side of the Red Sea? It never happens. The Song of Moses never gets written. Miriam's tambourine never gets played. Church, we do well to remember, God receives glory when he saves us *from* death, not just *through* it. When he takes away ashes and gives us garments of praise here. When he rescues a marriage and writes a new story.

In that way the psalmist may lack a full understanding of the doctrine of resurrection as it comes into focus in the New Testament. But in another way he's onto something important. God gets glory when he rescues his people not just "then and there" but "here and now."

This brings us to the third refrain.

Isolation: Why Do You Hide Your Face from Me?
PSALM 88:13-18

This is the deepest pain a believer can experience—the pain of feeling God is absent. We don't know exactly what kind of experience he is facing. Is it mental anguish? Is it spiritual attack? Is it primarily physical? Maybe it's all of it mixed in together. Whatever it is, the final straw, the specific thing that makes life unlivable is that he's alone. He's dying. Heaven is painfully silent. And he's alone.

I don't know where all of you are right now, what you're going through, but Psalm 88 has welcome realism should you find yourself in a place of deep spiritual darkness. Friend, it's possible to have faith and feel burdened beyond your strength. It's possible to have faith and feel like God is hiding from you. It's possible to have faith and wrestle with hard questions. It's possible to have faith, and yet every day with Jesus isn't sweeter than the day before. It's possible to know him as the God of your salvation and yet feel convinced there will be "no saving today." It's possible to have a right knowledge of God and yet for that knowledge to not yield its full, soul-stabilizing effect at every point of your life.

You ask, "Where is faith in the most misery-laden song in the Bible?" Don't forget the little chorus he sings three times: "I cry out, I cry out, I call." Consider it. What keeps this man talking to God when his experience tells him no one is listening? What keeps him asking for help? What makes him want to declare God's praise when his prayers still go unanswered? Don't miss what we're seeing here. We see someone calling and crying out to God in the midst of total devastation, and the Bible has a word for that: *faith.*

That's the end of Psalm 88, but Psalm 88 isn't the end of the story.

Restoration: How the Story Ends and How We Help One Another

The 150 psalms are divided up into five books or mini-hymnals. Flip the page and look at Psalm 90, which begins Book IV. They're not organized chronologically; Psalm 90 is a Psalm of Moses. They're arranged to tell the story of the pilgrimage through which God is taking his people, a pilgrimage from suffering to glory. We're coming to the end of Book III. Beginning in Book IV, the tone begins to change. It even bears out statistically. In Books I through III (Pss 1–89) lament psalms outnumber hymns of praise by more than two to one. In Books IV and V (Pss 90–150) the proportion is reversed plus some (Kidd, *With One Voice*, 29).

What does this mean? As this big, sweeping story of God and his people comes full circle, we discover that what begins in personal anguish ends in global praise (Ps 150). That whole story pivots on Jesus Christ coming into the world. He took up (fully) the anguish of Psalm 88. He was the only truly God-forsaken person who ever lived. When he hung on the cross, God's wrath truly swept over him. He said, "Why have you abandoned me?" (Matt 27:46). And because we've read the New Testament, we know why. He was forsaken so that we who trust in him would never be forsaken. He was abandoned by his friends so that we could know unbroken friendship with God.

A happy ending awaits all who have trusted in Christ. We have confidence in future grace. But we still need Psalm 88 because this world hasn't become any more like heaven in the three thousand years since this psalm was composed. We still need songs in the night, and God gives them to us.

Reflect and Discuss

1. Why is there often a disconnect between what we know about God and how we feel and act?
2. Consider the psalmist's exchanges with God—the "I/you" statements. How do these statements reveal what is happening in the writer's soul? If you were to make a list of "I/you" statements, what would they be during this season of your life? During a dark season of your life?
3. What does it look like to "sing your pain" to God from the perspective of the cross?

4. How was the deafening silence of God making life unsustainable for the psalmist?

5. Is it possible to have faith and feel that God is hiding his face from you? Why? Does right knowledge about God always yield sustaining belief? What makes the psalmist keep asking when his prayers were going unanswered?

6. What happens when we use our feelings (instead of our knowledge of God through his Word) as an indicator of our faith and trust in God?

7. How have you seen your feelings deceive you?

8. When you feel like God has hidden himself from you, what choices are in front of you? Why should you choose to turn to him in prayer even though you may feel like he is not listening?

9. If your faith is weak right now, how does the truth that Jesus was forsaken so you never will be forsaken encourage you to pray? Is there someone with whom you can share what you're going through so that he or she can pray with you over your suffering? When will you share your struggles with them?

The God Who Is Faithful

PSALM 89

Main Idea: The most important time to believe that God's promises never fail are when they seem to have failed.

I.   **Faithful in Love (89:1-4)**
II. **Faithful in Power (89:5-18)**
    A.   Heavenly hosts revere him (89:5-8).
    B.   The raging sea obeys him (89:9).
    C.   Earthly powers tremble (89:10).
    D.   Creation shouts his praise (89:11-16).
    E.   This God is for us (89:17-18).
III. **Faithful to Save (89:19-37)**
    A.   It's a promise of total salvation.
    B.   It's a promise pointing to the Messiah.
IV. **Faithful When We're Faithless (89:38-52)**

The historical background of this, the third-longest psalm, is likely the Babylonian exile. Babylon came in 586 BC and destroyed Jerusalem and carried the people of Judah away to Babylon. Perhaps two clues that suggest the exile are what we find in verse 40—the fortified city is in ruins—and verse 44—the throne of David had been overturned.

In the United States we sometimes mark time by 9/11. This or that thing was before or after 9/11. Everybody knows where they were when it happened. For the Old Testament people of God, 586 BC was the darkest of days. They marked time by it. Yet we hear this man singing from exile.

There are some primary turning points in the text. Verses 1-4 sing about the Lord's faithful love and God's promise to King David. Verses 5-18 speak of God's sovereignty and grace. Verses 19-37 zoom in further on the Davidic covenant. Then verse 38 sounds a different note. It's as though we've driven past Jerusalem the day after Babylon swept through, and the psalmist is basically saying, "Wait, why? How did this happen?" Verses 49-51 move from a question about God's faithful love to appeals for God to act in judgment, and verse 52 closes with Godward praise.

Sometimes we find ourselves living in this tension between glorious promises and present darkness. If you want to feel some of force of his questions, go back and listen to what God promised David centuries earlier:

> The LORD declares to you: The LORD himself will make a house for you. When your time comes and you rest with your fathers, I will raise up after you your descendant, who will come from your body, and I will establish his kingdom. . . . Your house and kingdom will endure before me forever, and your throne will be established forever. (2 Sam 7:11-12,16)

"But you promised!" Do you ever feel like saying that? You hear the psalmist in verse 49 ask, "Lord, where are the former acts of your faithful love that you swore to David in your faithfulness?" It's like he's saying, "I don't have a theology for this." He's got 2 Samuel 7 on his lap and exile all over the evening news, and he's saying, "How is this happening?" We can struggle in the same way. Christian friend, the most important time to believe that God's promises never fail is when they *seem* to have failed.

But there's something instructive for us here. The first words in this psalm are, "I will sing about the LORD's faithful love forever." And despite all the questions in the middle, the last words are "Blessed be the LORD forever." This psalm is bookended with worship. This psalm reminds us of the character of God—the God who is faithful.

Faithful in Love
PSALM 89:1-4

The psalmist begins by announcing his intention to sing (v. 1). The theme on his lips is the faithful love—or it could be translated the "mercies"—of the Lord. It's in the plural. He's counting them up, and there are so many he just keeps counting.

Believers, this is true for us as well. I could sit down with you for an hour and walk you through my life (the ups and downs) and tell story after story. In a way, the one word over it all would be *mercies.* Mercies in the form of comfort in a time of loss. Mercies in the form of discipline, peeling me away from things that were destroying me. Mercies in the form of relocating me away from high school friends who were influencing me more than I was them. Times where God's Word leaped off the page with transforming power. I could put you in specific places where I read, for the first time, Philippians 3:7-11; Psalm 63; Isaiah 35; Romans 8; and John 15, where God turned lights on in my heart. Relentless mercy.

I don't know if you've ever seen Niagara Falls, or any of the world's great waterfalls. I saw Niagara Falls when I was in college. I was spellbound. I don't know that I've ever seen anything in nature more deserving of the word *relentless* than a waterfall.

In Scripture there is nothing more relentless than the love of God. You see it in several places in Scripture. Romans 8, for example, is a Niagara Falls text. The raging river of God's almighty love bursts forth from Calvary. It is relentless. You get too close, and it'll pull you in and drag you over the ledge, and it'll be wonderful.

What we see in verse 1 is more than a resolve to sing but to keep singing. This song will never be outdated because God's faithfulness is unchanging. However, it's not just musical singing because the parallel is "I will proclaim your faithfulness to all generations with my mouth" (v. 1). So you ask, Wait, is he singing or sharing the gospel? Yes! This "singing" isn't *less* than singing, but it's more. For Christians, this is a summons into a *life* of making much of Christ in all things.

Faithful in Power
PSALM 89:5-18

Heavenly Hosts Revere Him (89:5-8)

The psalmist is talking about the innumerable angels who worship before God. He calls them "the assembly of the holy ones" (v. 5). The word *assembly* in the New Testament is often translated "church." This is "having church" in heaven.

Did you ever stop to think that, as we gather as a church, we aren't the only ones singing the praises of God? There are innumerable angels, the hosts of heaven, and those who have crossed the finish line of faith, together with the cherubim and seraphim, falling down before the holy, almighty Lord of heaven. Worship in the local church is meant to be a foretaste, a preview, of heaven.

Angels in the Bible are not like their porcelain gift-shop depictions, holding harps and wearing diapers. No, Scripture calls them "angels of great strength, who do his word" (Ps 103:20). They're called fiery messengers (see Ps 104:4). They show up, and the holiest people in the Bible hit the dirt. The angels frequently have to say, "Fear not," because people's first instinct is to fear. You can hardly pay attention to what the angelic messenger is about to say because you're too busy trying not to die. Consider this: Humans in the Bible tremble in the presence of the holy angels. Angels tremble in the presence of the holiness of God (v. 7).

The Raging Sea Obeys Him (89:9)

What is more untamable in nature than the sea? You watch these tsunami videos, and the sea just comes in and does whatever it wants. It moves cars like they're plastic toys. It takes an ocean liner and rams it into a building. But verse 9 says that God tames and rules the sea. Charles Spurgeon said, "As a mother stills her babe to sleep, so the Lord calms the fury of the sea, the anger of men, the tempest of adversity, the despair of the soul, and the rage of hell" (*Treasury of David*, 27).

Earthly Powers Tremble (89:10)

"Rahab" in the Old Testament often symbolizes Egypt. At an earlier point in Israel's history, Egypt was the superpower of the world. The ESV translates verse 10, "You crushed Rahab like a carcass." The one true and living God is fearfully holy. He is a consuming fire (Heb 12:29). He opposes the proud but gives grace to the humble (Jas 4:6).

Sometimes in the Bible when God comes to town, it's a bad day for the town. He is a God of justice. There is mercy for any broken sinner who runs to Jesus Christ for rescue, no matter what you've done. But those who shake their fists at heaven, those who inflict violence on the weak and multiply oppression in this world, will, at the end of it all, find Jesus, and they'll wish they hadn't.

God's power to execute justice has been a word of assurance and consolation for his embattled people through the ages. God's people throughout history have taken comfort in knowing no collaboration of human intellect or military might can stop the Lord from bringing his promises to pass.

Creation Shouts His Praise (89:11-16)

I lived to experience one of the greatest inventions (maybe of all time): the Walkman. You could listen to music and walk places. I wore out a few tapes that brought together some musical highpoints (or not so much) for children of the '80s: Michael Jackson, a Christian rock band called Stryper, Ray Boltz (some of you know the song I'm talking about), and a trio called 2nd Chapter of Acts. That last group introduced me to a hymn I had never heard before.

> This is my father's world, And to my listening ears
> All nature sings, and round me rings the music of the spheres.
>   (Babcock, "This Is My Father's World")

Scripture often personifies creation as delighting in the Creator. The trees of the field clap their hands (Isa 55:12), and here Mount Hermon and Mount Tabor shout for joy at God's name (Ps 89:12).

The theme of joy continues in verses 15-16, but it's not just *mountains* shouting for joy; it's people. What a song to sing in the midst of hardship and questions! To remember that heavenly hosts revere him, the raging sea obeys him, earthly powers tremble, creation shouts his praise—and to think: this God is for us!

This God Is for Us (89:17-18)

Verses 17-18 answer the question of why God's people are joyful in verses 15-16. I heard a well-known author and biblical scholar relate a personal story of how he was driving his son to his first semester of college, and his son was clearly stressed and anxious. No encouragement was sticking. The father decided to pull over, and he told his son he loved him and was proud of him, no matter what happened this semester. And that somehow broke through the flood of anxious thoughts in his son's heart.

I remember hearing a pastor describe a moment in his ministry in which he was wrestling with deep discouragement. Tragedies and difficult decisions all seemed to be converging in the same moment. He went to bed one night so heavy of soul and feeling "done." He woke up eighteen hours later. All the same realities were facing him. In desperate prayer he said he sensed the Lord telling him, "If you preach weak sermons, I love you. If this church tanks, I love you." And the fog began to lift.

Story after story unpacks this glorious truth: perfect love drives out fear (1 John 4:18). He is "for us." And his "for us-ness" produces a kind of strength, an ability to persevere.

Faithful to Save

PSALM 89:19-37

All those promises concerning David's kingship were seen in the Old Testament as the inheritance of people as well. Consider God's great promises to King David in verses 21-24. Israel didn't hear that and say, "Man, wouldn't it be awesome to be in David's family?" They heard it and said, "He's our king. Those promises fall to us!" The same thing is true about the "in Christ" language of the New Testament. United to him by faith, we are coheirs with him. We see in these verses the nature of God's promises to save.

It's a Promise of Total Salvation

God's promises of rescue in Psalm 89 include constant presence (v. 21), defeating enemies (vv. 22-23), faithful love (v. 23), extended borders (v. 25), chasing them when they stray (vv. 30-35), and everlasting dominion (vv. 29,36-37). These promises to David, and ultimately to Jesus Christ, were promises that rest not only on the king but on the people of the kingdom.

God's promises to us in Christ are comprehensive. It's a life-abundantly promise (John 10:10). A sin-will-not-rule-over-you promise (Rom 6:14). An I-will-give-you-a-new-heart promise (Ezek 36:26). A there-is-therefore-now-no-condemnation promise (Rom 8:1). A pleasures-evermore (Ps 16:11), rest-for-the-weary-and-heavy-laden (Matt 11:28), grace-the-hour-you-first-believed and grace-that-leads-you-home promise.

It's a Promise Pointing to the Messiah

> I will extend his power to the sea
> and his right hand to the rivers.
> He will call to me, "You are my Father,
> my God, the rock of my salvation."
> I will also make him my firstborn,
> greatest of the kings of the earth. (vv. 25-27)

It turns out there are two ways God's promise to David could have been fulfilled. The psalmist only seems to anticipate one—namely, David's house will sit on the throne forever. That is, one son will rule then die, then another will rule then die, on and on, for all generations. That's certainly one way of looking at it. Or maybe God was intending to raise up a Son from David's line and put him on the throne forever, world without end. That's what ended up happening.

When Jesus rose again from the dead, God gave him the name above every name. Jesus ascended on high and was crowned King over all the kings and Lord over all the lords. And Jesus Christ is the ruling, reigning, and coming King who will bring righteousness, peace, and joy in fullness forever, to be enjoyed by all who have trusted in him.

This leads us to one more reason to worship God while we wait for all of his promises to be fulfilled. We worship because he is faithful in love, faithful in power, faithful to save, and faithful when we are faithless.

Faithful When We're Faithless
PSALM 89:38-52

I read psalms like this, and in one way I so wish I could travel back there. We see things the psalmist couldn't see. Ethan the Ezrahite hasn't read the New Testament. Given where we live in history, when we hear him asking questions that imply God has abandoned his promise, we wish we could travel back and say, *"Wait, there's more!* Listen, in about five hundred years, the skies above Bethlehem are going to light up. Angels will announce that the wait is over and a King has been born. He will rule the raging sea. He says, 'Peace be still,' and the waves obey him! He will take our sin on himself (just as Isaiah predicted!). He'll rise again from the dead. And God will put Jesus Christ, the Son of David, on an eternal throne." We could tell him that in our time we are seeing the kingdom and rule of Jesus expanding through the church of Jesus Christ. Nations are being drawn to him right now. We could say that because we see things the psalmist couldn't see.

But at the same time, we wait with the psalmist for what we still don't see. Just as we could go back and tell Ethan, "Hang on, there's more," Hebrews 12 tells us a great cloud of witnesses have gone before us, and if we could hear them, they would be saying to us, "Hang on. There's more." The problem is that waiting isn't always easy.

I don't know if they still have this, but in some places when you waited in line, you pulled a ticket number. So for example, you might walk inside and pull the number 43, and then you hear someone yell out, "Serving number five," and you want to give up and leave. But what happens when you pull number 43, and you immediately hear them call, "Number forty-two"? Feels different, right?

The Bible has four tickets to pull. Ticket 1 was called in Genesis 1 (creation). Ticket 2 was called in Genesis 3 (fall). Ticket 3 was called in Matthew 1 when Jesus came to be our Redeemer (redemption). Believer in Christ, in your hand right now is ticket 4. The next thing on the calendar of redemption is pleasures evermore (glory).

The reason the ancient believers called this truth the "blessed hope" (Titus 2:13) is because if we knew this and lived life in light of eternity, though it wouldn't give us heaven on earth, it would give us something we desperately need: *hope*. Hope in the knowledge and certainty that Jesus is ruling, Jesus is reigning, and Jesus is coming.

While we wait for the fulfilment of the promise, what do we do? We sing of the Lord's faithful love. We call to mind his promises of salvation. We proclaim his glory to the nations.

A hymn was composed in the middle of the Civil War. Like Psalm 89, it brings together the themes of God's sovereignty, our trials, and his promises.

> My life goes on in endless song, above earth's lamentations.
> I hear the real, though far-off hymn, that hails a new creation.
> Above the tumult and the strife, I hear its music ringing.
> It sounds an echo in my soul. How can I keep from singing?
> What though my joys and comforts die, the Lord my Savior liveth.
> And though the darkness round me close, songs in the night he giveth.
> No storm can shake my inmost calm while to that Rock I'm clinging.
> Since Christ is Lord of heaven and earth, how can I keep from singing?
> (Lowry, "How Can I Keep from Singing?")

What does faith sound like when we're still waiting for God's promises to land in our experience? It sounds like a life bookended by worship, where we open our eyes on the day of our conversion with, "I will sing about the LORD's faithful love forever" (v. 1). And by God's grace we close our eyes at the end of this life saying, "Blessed be the LORD forever" (v. 52).

Reflect and Discuss

1. What does it feel like to live as a Christian in the tension between God's glorious promises of redemption and the current reality of the world's brokenness?
2. How do we guard our hearts from allowing our circumstantial feelings to influence the truth we know about God? What role does God's Word have in anchoring our hearts to the truth of God's character?
3. Even in his time of pain and doubt, the psalmist begins and ends this psalm with worship. What does this say about the value of worship in times of pain?
4. Think of how God has shown his mercies to you throughout your life. What demonstrations of his love have made you the person you are today?
5. How can we trust God when he has the power to intervene in situations but doesn't? Why is our trust in his faithfulness and love so important in circumstances like these?
6. What does it mean about our understanding of ourselves to be able to trust in a God who knows more than we do and won't always tell us everything we want to know?
7. What does it mean to fight for our faith? How can we do this on a daily or weekly basis?
8. How can we steward the circumstances we have experienced or are experiencing to proclaim the faithfulness of God to others?
9. How can we steward our waiting time to grow in our relationship with him?

Behold His Grace

PSALM 90

Main Idea: God's grace is sufficient to meet our every need, and we should respond by giving him glory and trusting his Word.

I. **Four Truths**
   A. God is eternally glorious.
      1. God has no beginning.
      2. God has no end.
      3. God is Lord over time.
      4. God is unchanging throughout time.
   B. Sin is eternally serious.
      1. Sin robs us of life.
      2. Sin results in death.
   C. The wrath of God is eternally real.
   D. The salvation of God is eternally satisfying.
II. **Two Exhortations**
   A. Live today for what lasts forever.
   B. Hold on to hope because you know God is your home.

Psalm 90 gives us one of the clearest pictures in God's Word of God's eternal nature. It is the oldest psalm we have, written by Moses when the people of God were wandering in the wilderness. The contrast between Psalm 90 and our own perspective on time is striking.

Our lives are so consumed with the temporary, with what matters today. We're focused on *this* moment, and we live in a culture that lauds pleasure in the moment. We want immediate, instant gratification. We're so intoxicated by the temporary that we become blind to what's going to matter ten trillion years from now. But life changes when you open your eyes to that reality, and the nature of God beckons us to see that.

I see four truths in Psalm 90; each one builds on the others. These truths lead to some massive implications for our lives.

Four Truths

God Is Eternally Glorious

Rather than speaking of something lasting "from eternity to eternity" (v. 2), we normally say, "from beginning to end." However, **God has no beginning**. How old is God? is a wholly inappropriate question. God is different from us, for there was a day when we weren't; then one day we were born. But God isn't a certain age because he was never born. Even more mind-boggling than that is the fact that **God has no end**. Verse 3 says that man returns to dust but not God.

Verse 4 talks about God's relation to time, and this will really give you a headache if you think about it! Psalm 90 teaches that **God is Lord over time**. Whereas we exist *in* time, God exists *over* time. Isaiah 57:15 says that God "inhabits eternity" (ESV). For him a thousand years are like a day, or like a "few hours of the night" (Ps 90:4). Think about all that happens in a thousand years: generations come and go, empires rise and fall, and to God it's all like a short watch in the night. The United States of America has existed for 240 years, which is a matter of mere minutes in God's perspective.

God is unchanging throughout time. From "eternity to eternity," God is God. Unlike us, his attributes do not change with time. The way we look changes over time. The way we think changes over time. We grow in knowledge, and we change in skill over time. We're able to do things at age forty that we weren't able to do at fourteen—and vice versa. But God is totally different from us.

God is omniscient, which means he knows all things. God doesn't forget anything over time, and he doesn't learn anything over time because he has all knowledge at all times. And God is omnipotent—he has all power—which means God doesn't weaken or strengthen over time. He has all power at all times.

The fact that God is unchanging throughout time is good news when you think about it. We don't ever have to worry about God changing for the worse. Who God is today is who God will be tomorrow. *But, we may think, wouldn't it be good for God to change for the better?* No, because if God changed for the better in any way, then that would mean God previously wasn't the best possible being. And he is. God in all of his attributes is perfect at all times. He is just as perfect today as he was a billion years ago, and he will be just as perfect a billion years from now as he is today. God is eternally glorious!

If God is eternally glorious, then think about the awesome, even alarming, truths in Psalm 90 that flow from this reality.

Sin Is Eternally Serious

Moses reflects on God's eternality in the first six verses, and then he turns immediately to man's frailty in the next five verses. Why are we terrified by God's wrath (v. 7)? Because none of our sins are hidden from God (v. 8), and each of those sins is eternally serious.

Psalm 90 is a potent reminder that **sin robs us of life**. This psalm takes us all the way back to the opening chapters of Genesis and the first sin. God created man and woman to live with him forever, but man and woman turned from God. According to Genesis 3, this rebellion led to God's curse on creation, a truth that is reiterated in the "struggle and sorrow" resulting from sin mentioned in Psalm 90:10. This is the way sin works in our lives: it robs us of the life God has intended us to live.

Remember that Moses wrote this psalm during the Israelites' wandering in the desert. The people of God had stood on the edge of the promised land, but then they turned back in sin. They didn't trust God, and they disobeyed him because they didn't think they could take the land. As a result, God told an entire generation of Israelites that they would wander in the wilderness until they died (Num 14:20-35). Thousands upon thousands of people missed out on the blessing of God in the promised land because of their sin.

Israel's example serves as a warning to us. We should look at any sin we're holding on to, particularly secret sin we're trying to hide, and realize two things. First, it's utter foolishness to try to hide your sin from an eternally omniscient God. Second, that sin, any sin we're holding on to, is serious. It is robbing us of the life God has given us to live. Sin is robbing us of the hopes and plans and dreams and love and peace and satisfaction the God of the universe has designed for us to know.

Don't treat sin lightly because ultimately **sin results in death**. Again, think about the context of Israel's wandering in the wilderness for *forty* years. They wandered until an entire generation had passed away. Can you imagine that? Every day, another death. Funeral after funeral after funeral. So it makes sense for Moses to write, "We are consumed by your anger" (v. 7); "We end our years like a sigh" (v. 9); "They [our years] pass quickly" (v. 10).

Why are we consumed by God's anger? Why do we end our years like a sigh? Why do we have only a relatively small number of years on this earth—whether it's seventy or eighty or seventeen? Why do we experience such pain and hurt and heartache through death in this world? The definitive answer the Bible gives is sin. We all die because we're all sinners.

Do we realize how serious sin is? If sin robs us of life, and if sin results in death, then why do we treat it so casually? May God help us realize that he is eternally glorious, which means sin against him is eternally serious. This realization leads to the third truth in Psalm 90.

The Wrath of God Is Eternally Real

Over and over again, Moses speaks of God's wrath and anger: "For we are consumed by your anger; we are terrified by your wrath" (v. 7); "For all our days ebb away under your wrath" (v. 9); "Who understands the power of your anger? Your wrath matches the fear that is due you" (v. 11). In verse 11 the psalmist is basically asking the question, "God, if you are eternal in all of your attributes, then who can imagine the eternality of your wrath?" If God is eternally glorious, then all of his attributes, including his wrath, are eternal.

Whenever we see hell described in God's Word, it is never described as a temporary place. God's wrath is described as lasting "forever and ever" (see Rev 14:11; 19:3; 20:10). It's as if "forever" was not sufficient to get the point across, so God adds the words *and ever*. Hell is never-ending. George Whitefield used to speak with tears in his eyes of

> the torment of burning like a livid coal not for an instant or
> for a day, but for millions and millions of ages, at the end
> of which people will realize that they are no closer to the
> end than when they first begun, and they will never ever be
> delivered from that place. (Hofstadter, *America at 1750*, 240)

I can't even begin to comprehend what hell is like, but according to the Word of God, it is real. The fact that there is eternal wrath awaiting sinners confronted by a holy God helps us understand Moses's words in verse 13: "Lord—how long? Turn and have compassion on your servants." In other words, "Have mercy!"

Notice the contrast between verse 14 and the previous verses. Moses has contemplated the eternal wrath of God, so now he pleads for the eternal love of God. He asks to be satisfied with God's "faithful love" (*chesed*), which, because of God's covenant, never comes to an end. This leads to a fourth and final truth in Psalm 90.

The Salvation of God Is Eternally Satisfying

The mercy, grace, and love of God are eternally satisfying for all who turn from sin and trust in God, and this is only possible through the gospel. This is where Psalm 90 points us forward to Jesus, for this eternal God has made a way for us to be saved from the eternal consequence of our sin through the life, death, and resurrection of his Son. And the love of God toward all who trust in him will never end. It is *eternally* satisfying.

Many Christians have a view of heaven that's pretty boring. They picture believers just sitting around for all eternity singing on clouds. If that's what you think, then I have good news for you—heaven is *not* a never-ending choir practice in the clouds! No, heaven is a physical place where we will dwell with one another in God's presence forever. There are a lot of things we don't know about heaven, but this we do know: for all of eternity, we are going to enjoy more and more and more goodness in God. For if the goodness of God is eternal and infinite, then a thousand years from now there will still be more goodness in God for you and me to experience and enjoy. The same will be true ten trillion years from now—there will still be more goodness to explore, more satisfaction to experience in God. This means our joy will increase more and more with each passing day, and this will go on forever. There will never be an end to more and more joy in God!

Have you ever enjoyed a new gift, but then after a while it starts to get old and not as enjoyable? It's similar to when my kids get a new toy and play with it all the time for about a week. Then they ask, "Can I get a new toy?" We do the same thing as adults. We're constantly on the quest for something newer, better, or nicer, and it's because everything in this world eventually fades. But not God. He never fades; he is eternal. You will never be bored by an eternally good God. Stephen Charnock put it this way:

> When we enjoy God, we enjoy him in his eternity without any flux. . . . Time is fluid, but eternity is stable; and after many ages, the joys will be as savory and satisfying as if they had been but that moment first tasted by our hungry appetites. When the glory of the Lord shall rise upon you, it shall be so far from ever setting, that after millions of years are expired, as numerous as the sands on the seashore, the sun, in the light of

whose countenance you shall live, shall be as bright as at the
first appearance; he will be so far from ceasing to flow, that
he will flow as strong, as full, as at the first communication of
himself in glory to the creature. God is always vigorous and
flourishing; a pure act of life, sparkling new and fresh rays
of life and light to the creature, flourishing with a perpetual
spring, and contenting the most capacious desire; forming
your interest, pleasure, and satisfaction; with an infinite
variety, without any change or succession; he will have variety
to increase delights, and eternity to perpetuate them; this
will be the fruit of the enjoyment of an infinite and eternal
God. (*The Existence and Attributes of God,* Discourse V: On the
Eternity of God, part IV, Use 2, paragraph 3)

Because God is eternal, our delight in him will be eternal and our
lives will be marked by infinite enjoyment of him!

Two Exhortations

Based on the four eternally important truths we've looked at in Psalm 90,
we should be asking how these truths change our lives today.

Live Today for What Lasts Forever

Psalm 90:12 says, "Teach us to number our days carefully so that we may
develop wisdom in our hearts." When you know God is eternal and you
know your time on earth is limited, then you make each day count for
that which will last in eternity. You realize that how much money you
make doesn't matter; what matters is what you do with the money you
make. You realize that the *people* around you are far more important
than the things on your to-do list. You realize that, as a parent, the most
important thing in the lives of your children is not the clothes they wear
or the sports they play or even the grades they get; what's most important is that they know God.

In your own life you realize that knowledge of God and obedience
to God are far more important than the achievements you accomplish
and the positions you attain. You also realize that every person in your
life—at home, at work, in your neighborhood, in your city, and around
the world—is either headed to an everlasting heaven or an everlasting
hell, and the only difference is what they do with Jesus. So you speak
about Jesus. That's how you live today for what lasts forever.

Hold on to Hope Because You Know God Is Your Home

Even in a world of sin and suffering, or as the psalmist puts it, "struggle and sorrow" (v. 10), we can live with hope. Recall that Moses, the author of this psalm, was wandering in the wilderness, and he began with these words: "Lord, you have been our refuge in every generation" (v. 1).

Christian brother or sister, the eternal God of the universe is your dwelling place forever. Moses didn't have a physical home, so he looked up to the eternal God and said, "God is my home, both now and forever." For all who trust in Christ and what he did at the cross, know this: pain, sorrow, trials, and trouble in this world are always temporary. The eternal God of the universe loves you, and nothing can separate you from his love. A day is coming when he will remove all your pain, sorrow, trials, and trouble. This eternal God is going to personally wipe every tear from your eyes (Rev 21:4); his love toward you is never going to end.

Reflect and Discuss

1. What temporary needs seem most pressing in your life right now?
2. Why is the fact that God has no beginning or end good news for us?
3. List some ways God's unchangeableness can be a comfort for Christians.
4. What are some examples from Scripture that teach us about the seriousness of sin?
5. Many Christians treat sin casually. Why is this so dangerous?
6. "God is loving, so he would never be angry." What's wrong with that statement?
7. Why do you think many Christians are not thrilled at the prospect of heaven?
8. What are some specific areas of your life that might change if you took an eternal, God-centered view of life?
9. It's inevitable that we have to focus on temporary things in this life. At the same time, what are some signs you might be focusing *solely* on things that are temporary?
10. How can God's eternality give us hope in the midst of suffering and opposition? How could you use this truth to counsel a fellow church member?

The God Who Delivers from Fear

PSALM 91

Main Idea: God is bigger than whatever keeps us up at night, and he will deliver us.

I.   **The Strength of the Deliverer (91:1-13)**
II. **The People He Delivers (91:14-16)**
III. **The Nature of Deliverance**

There's not a person reading this who doesn't know what it's like to be afraid. I'll confess I have some embarrassing fears. If a cockroach crawled up on me right now, I can't predict what exactly I would do, but it would be embarrassing. You may or may not identify with my small, petty fears, but I'm confident you'll identify with my big ones.

I'm afraid of rejection and failure. I'm afraid of apostasy, especially when I see or hear of a professing believer denying the faith. In those moments I can worry about the future and about my own perseverance. The word *cancer* scares me. I've seen what it can do. I'm afraid of losing loved ones. I've experienced it before. The thought that, with time, I'll go through that again is deeply troubling. What Scripture calls the last enemy: death. That's scary. Not what happens after death but the dying part.

The world is full of people controlled by fear, worry, and anxiety. We're constantly sizing up the world around us. Nobody tells us to do this. We look at our fears—the things that threaten our peace and security. We look at our hopes—the things that promise us security. Depending on which one seems bigger at a given moment, we either come out of that exercise with a sense of peace, or it creates turmoil and anxiety.

The thing that's so frustrating about fear and anxiety is how incredibly resilient they are. They can grow in all climates, all seasons of life. So on the one hand, when catastrophe strikes and I discover that my sense of controlling my world was a myth, what happens? Fear and anxiety move in. On the other hand, when I gain a sense of control

365

over my circumstances, fear and anxiety grow there as well because I immediately begin to wonder how long I'll be able to sustain that set of conditions.

This is a big part of the reason the self-help section of the bookstore is its largest section. We want handles on the world, and we can't quite seem to find our way to peace. We can't seem to find a fail-safe, lasting escape from fear and worry.

Enter Psalm 91. God wants to help us size the world accurately. I believe the divinely intended effect of this chapter on our souls is to create a deep-seated, unshakable security and confidence in God. The psalmist states the primary truth right up front. This is a word to the fearful, and God wastes no time getting to the point. He just comes right out in verse 1 and says, "You are safe!" He tells us why, and it has everything to do with who he is.

We're not even into verse 2 before we're confronted by the strength of the deliverer.

The Strength of the Deliverer
PSALM 91:1-13

God confronts our greatest fears firstly by letting us see how big he is. He stands all the way up in verse 1. He is God "Most High." He is God "Almighty." These descriptions in a passage filled with a world of fears are clearly chosen on purpose.

I love the way our ancestors in faith, the Hebrew people, thought and spoke about God. Oftentimes Hebraic ways of thinking are contrasted with Greek ways of thinking. The ancient Greeks loved to speak of God in abstract terms. Aristotle thought of God as the "unmoved or self-moved Mover." Plato thought of God as the "first Cause." Philosophers love this stuff. More recently, existentialist philosopher Paul Tillich called God "the Ground of Being." If I were smarter, maybe this would strike me as helpful and profound. But for now I'm just glad the authors of the Bible were better connected to life. They preferred concrete imagery.

So, for example, the psalmist speaks of God as owning the "cattle on a thousand hills" (Ps 50:10). The prophet Isaiah seeks to give a sense of God's immensity by saying, "Heaven is [his] throne, and earth is [his] footstool" (Isa 66:1). It's an image of God sitting down in heaven and propping his feet up on earth. That's much easier to picture and connect with than self-moved mover and first cause. Here in verse 4 God is portrayed as a raptor who spreads his wings of protection over his people.

Verse 4 goes on to speak of God as a "protective shield," or, as older translations render it, "shield and buckler." The shield in ancient times was large and stationary. It could protect two or three soldiers crouching behind it. The buckler was strapped around the arm for mobility in battle. This is an earthy image for how God is able to cover us both when we are in a defensive position and when we are advancing in battle.

Throughout this chapter God is sized up against the greatest threats and fears of the ancient world. So in verse 3 we see God against the traps of the enemy and the destructive plague. In verses 5-6 it's God against the things that terrorize both at night and during the day. In verse 7 it's God against a thousand on your left and ten thousand on your right. In verse 10 it's God against all harm and all plagues. In verse 13 it's God against lion and adder. In verses 11-12 it's God against the laws of physics.

If you're familiar with the New Testament, verses 11-12 feature in the temptation of Jesus in the wilderness. As one of his temptations, Jesus is taken up to the pinnacle of the temple to be tempted by Satan, and Satan calls into question Jesus's trust in God. "If you are the Son of God," he says, "jump off." Then Satan quotes these verses back to Jesus. "You know Psalm 91 promises that God will give his angels orders concerning you. They will support you so that you will not strike your foot against a stone. Surely, if you're the Son of God, he won't sit by and watch you splatter on the rocks. You have an easy opportunity here to prove your stature as the one and only Son. You believe God's promises, right, Jesus? Prove your faith, and I'll be prepared to swallow my words when the Father protects you from harm." Of course, Jesus didn't jump. He took issue with Satan's superficial reading and selfish application of God's promise. We'll come back to that in a moment.

In all these contests between God and human fears, you notice a pattern. These contests are completely one-sided. God is in total domination mode. This is a comprehensive list of the greatest fears of the then-known world. It seems these terms are doing double duty. They can refer to literal plagues and actual lions and snakes, but there's no need to limit it merely to snakes, lions, diseases, and armies. The four dangers listed in verses 5-6 (terror of night, arrow of day, pestilence at night, destruction of day), it seems, come together as a collective placeholder for the greatest threats of life.

I had an interesting experience of fear as a teenager. God brought a father figure into my brother's and my life when we were teenagers. Joe Champion was pretty much the biggest guy I had ever seen. He played football in college at LSU. For me and my brother, having lost our dad not long before, Joe came on the scene at a pivotal point in our lives. Joe was godly. He was hilariously funny. He combined boldness with personal care.

Well, I remember riding in the back of his car as we drove down my street one day. Some boys who were older and bigger pointed at me as we passed, taunting and shouting profanities. For the next thirty feet, my brother-in-law was deciding whether to shrug it off and be godly or to make a scene. He decided he'd make a scene. Slammed on the brakes. Opened the car door. His size sixteen cowboy boot touched the pavement, and he stood all the way up and shouted, "Hey!" I don't remember what Joe said after that, but it didn't matter because the boys weren't there to hear it. They ran away as soon as they saw him. Within a period of seconds, I experienced a dramatic range of emotions. When I was taunted by those big boys, I felt tremendous fear. It was immediate pressure. An instant boil of anxiety. When Joe stood and the boys ran, the relief was virtually instantaneous as well.

What happened? My fears sized up against my help, and my help was bigger. This passage doesn't make fears look small. The animals chosen to represent the things we fear in this passage are not rabbits. They're lions and snakes. The army arrayed against us numbers in the thousands. This passage doesn't belittle our fears. The reason it doesn't need to is because of the size of our Help!

So much of the remedy of the Bible for our fears is this: our small fears are cancelled out by a bigger fear. Big fears can cancel out smaller fears. For example, I know someone who would put "going under water" on her list of fears. She also happens to be a mother, so losing a child would be on her list of fears as well. What happens when junior jumps into the deep end of the pool? She doesn't even think about her fear of water. She jumps in. The power of her fear of losing a child trumps her fear of going under water.

Think about this. The most frequent command from God in the Bible is, "Do not be afraid" (e.g., Isa 41:10). At the same time, the Bible's first lesson for life wisdom is, "The fear of the LORD is the beginning of wisdom" (Prov 9:10). If you sit down with the ancients and say, "Teach me theology," they say, "OK, let's start here: fear God." So how does this come together? God sets us free from a world of fears by giving us a bigger fear. There's a fascinating statement in Luke 12:

> I say to you, my friends, don't fear those who kill the body, and after that can do nothing more. But I will show you the one to fear: Fear him who has authority to throw people into hell after death. Yes, I say to you, this is the one to fear! Aren't five sparrows sold for two pennies? Yet not one of them is forgotten in God's sight. Indeed, the hairs of your head are all counted. Don't be afraid; you are worth more than many sparrows. (Luke 12:4-7)

Notice the progression: Point 1: Do not fear your persecutors. They're a small threat. Point 2: Fear God. He's a big threat. Point 3: God cares for you. Point 4: Fear not.

What was the purpose of this gymnastics exercise: don't fear, fear, OK, don't fear? If you're going to be freed from the fear of man, it's not going to happen because you took a course on assertiveness. Jesus said you need a bigger fear to drive out the little ones. The fear of God drives away not only the fear of man but also every other fear. Because as we just read from Jesus, this God is personal. He values his children.

Psalm 91 views God the same way. God is not just powerful; he's personal. The psalmist speaks of God in verse 2 as "my refuge and my fortress, my God." This relational connection brings us to the second element highlighted in this passage.

The People He Delivers
PSALM 91:14-16

We pick up on a story in Acts 9. Paul hasn't been converted yet. If we're not allowed to read ahead in the account, his conversion doesn't look likely since he is leading the charge in snuffing out this new movement of Christ followers. He is having them beaten and thrown in jail. He's presiding over their executions, holding coats so his friends can throw rocks without ripping their jackets.

Then the risen Jesus confronts Saul of Tarsus on the road to Damascus. Jesus doesn't say, "Saul, Saul, why are you persecuting these believers?" He doesn't say, "Saul, Saul, why are you persecuting your fellow man?" He says, "Saul, Saul, why are you persecuting me?" (Acts 9:4).

This is not a Jesus who is merely empathizing with victims of oppression. This is Jesus identifying with his people. This is Jesus, if you will, getting out of the car and saying, "Hey! They're mine. I'm with them." Jesus is simultaneously revealing himself to Saul and identifying with his persecuted people.

Are you joined to Jesus in this way? Are you part of his people?

Psalm 91 describes God's people as those who dwell or abide under God's protection. In light of New Testament truth, we know more fully now that God's protection is found and experienced only by those who trust in Jesus Christ, the Savior whom God has sent. Jesus came to rescue us from our most fearsome enemies: death, hell, Satan, and the judgment of a holy God. Jesus accomplished this rescue through his perfect life, his sacrificial death as our substitute, and his triumphant resurrection. And now all who believe on him—all who run to him for refuge—are safe forever. This is the Christian gospel.

Apart from faith in Jesus Christ, we are without ultimate shelter. This is why the phrase *in Christ* has so much meaning in the Bible. When we turn to Christ in faith, we are considered to be "in him"—that is, all that belongs to Jesus is ours. All the favor he enjoys at the hands of the Father is ours. The moment we believe, Christ becomes our shelter, our refuge, our fortress, our salvation.

Think with me about the Christian symbolism of water baptism. Verse 2, if you will, is the confession of every believer at their baptism. They're saying, in a word, "The God I have trusted has become a refuge for me. I'm in this water to say to the church and to the world, there is one refuge for sinners and his name is Jesus Christ!" This is the gospel, friends.

There's a sobering and wondrous tension here. The fear of facing a holy God may not make the top of people's list of fears right now, but there will be a day when it will immediately rise to the top of the list. But this is the wonder of the gospel: the God of holiness and righteousness—the one whom we ought to fear more than anything in this world—that God is the one who has provided us a refuge. He has given us the shield by which we are protected from his just wrath. And in his mercy he says, "My justice will be poured out in full. But hide here. Hide in Christ."

I love how this psalm goes on to describe God's people. Their hearts are set on the Lord, and they know his name (v. 14). They call to God, and he answers (v. 15). They are rescued and honored by God (v. 15). They are satisfied by God and shown his salvation (v. 16).

Christian friend, God doesn't just tolerate you. He is a loving Father. Sadly, the idea of God being a Father can be a problem because our families are flawed. We parents say things that are far from constructive. We lash out, and we tear our children down. However, on our best days, we look for opportunities to bestow honor on our children, don't we? We'll say, I know you get mixed signals from me, but please don't miss this: I'm proud of you. I'm honored to be called your dad.

The idea that we are to honor *God* is familiar to anyone who reads the Bible. It strikes us as perfectly fitting that we should honor him. He's the only God, and he's supremely worthy. What comes as a surprise is that God would honor *us*. Is that not staggering? Don't tell me God is hard-nosed in the Old Testament and softens up once Jesus arrives. Here is God bestowing honor on his people.

Before we're done, we need to look at one more thing. How do we fit the promises of this passage with our experience? In the real world Christians go hungry and face persecution and die prematurely and face all manner of hardships.

The Nature of Deliverance

I was working on this passage on a Wednesday when an email came from a fellow pastor. He told me that a close friend had just discovered their son's body. He had been thrown off his motorcycle and was found in the lake near their home. In that moment I looked back down at Psalm 91 and read, "For he will give his angels orders concerning you, to protect you in all your ways" (v. 11). Seems like a disconnect, right? How can Psalm 91 be true when that funeral is currently being planned in Mississippi?

This might seem anticlimactic, but it's the truth, and it needs to be said: the protection God brings doesn't mean a trouble-free life. This is why the prosperity gospel is so cruel.

I can tell you the name of the man who, as a young believer, was taught that sickness is never God's will. Healing is always God's will. His wife was diagnosed with brain cancer early in their marriage, and he believed. He claimed the victory. He did all the stuff. He spoke healing. And his wife died. He was left to conclude that his lack of faith was the reason she died. What else was he to conclude, given what he was taught. "God always wills healing. We just have to activate it by faith." He was shattered by the tragically mistaken idea that God was trying to heal his wife, but his imperfect faith tied God's hands, so she died. That is a horrific abuse of what God's Word says about faith and victory and protection. It's emotionally and psychologically devastating to be told that if you have enough faith, if you use the right self-talk, your life will be brimming with health and wealth.

When we read the Bible looking for what it says about fear, trials, and faith, it says the same thing on virtually every page. This life is filled with pain. We are greeted by a thousand fears on our left and ten thousand fears on our right, but a day will come when all our fears will be completely and totally conquered by God Almighty. Listen to the way this is described in the "faith chapter":

> *For he was looking forward to the city that has foundations, whose architect and builder is God. . . .*
>
> *These all died in faith, although they had not received the things that were promised. But they saw them from a distance, greeted them, and confessed that they were foreigners and temporary residents on the earth. Now those who say such things make it clear that they are seeking a homeland. If they were thinking about where they came from, they would have had an opportunity to return. But they now desire a better place—a heavenly one. Therefore, God is not ashamed to be called their God, for he has prepared a city for them.*
> (Heb 11:10,13-16)

The Bible has great news for people of faith. Your best life comes later. It comes later, but it lasts forever. That's great news for people of faith, both then and now.

The tragedy is that we are so fixated on getting heaven here and now that we view eternal joy as a downer. People reason, "So my best life starts when Jesus comes back? Or when I die, and then joy lasts a billion years? That's stinks! I want it all now!"

Several years ago a friend of mine had dinner at the home of a famous author. His wife came around with a few slices of pie, and the host himself asked his wife to give him the larger slice. My friend thought the author was kidding until he ate the entire piece without batting an eye.

When we think about fear and faith, we can reach for two options. There's a big piece and a small piece. We can think mainly about **this life**. That *feels* like reaching for the big piece—the best piece—but it's actually the small piece. You'll get eighty to ninety years here, and you won't even fully enjoy the small piece. No amount of money, power, technology, or faith-speak can make this world a paradise. Or you can think like the people in Hebrews 11. You can process blessings with the **long view** in mind. The irony is when we reach toward God in faith, we don't just get eternal joy then and there; we get help here and now.

My dad died while preaching a sermon on Palm Sunday in 1988. I was twelve years old, on the second pew when it happened. When this passage speaks of the arrow that flies by day and the pain that stalks in darkness, I knew both of those intimately. I felt the turmoil of being pulled in two directions. I felt an inner voice of the enemy saying, "So much for God's faithfulness." There was a real temptation to say, "You know what, I'm done with this Christianity thing. This is stupid." At the same time I felt like, despite myself, something was keeping my faith alive. There were moments when I knew God was near.

The believers in Romans 8 affirmed they were more than conquerors through Christ, and yet at the same time they said, "Because of you we are being put to death all day long" (v. 36). Those phrases lived side by side. How can it be that God's protection is comprehensive when we see death all around us? Romans 8 answers that question by saying there's a greater problem in the world than cancer, heart attacks, rejection, and pestilence and sword. We need a God who drowns our guilt and shame. We need a shelter. Psalm 91 and Romans 8 are shouting in unison, "You've got one!"

Believer, rest here. This is your security amid the perils of this world. You are loved by God! In taking Christ by faith, you chose the better part. You chose the bigger joy, the one that lasts forever. In getting him, here's what you got: you got eternal joy a billion years after this life is over, but you also got God himself. He is with you, even in your darkness. You will never be alone.

Sometimes in his mercy God rescues us *from* suffering. We can pray for grace, for help in all forms. Sometimes, in his mercy, God rescues us *in* suffering. He keeps us, holds us, keeps faith alive. However, in a little while, God will yet rescue us from *all* suffering. This is when we experience in fullness what Psalm 91:16 is all about. With long life, for ages on ages, God will satisfy his people.

It makes me think about a conversation God had with Solomon. God asked Solomon what he wanted the most. Solomon reached for something bigger and deeper than earthly blessings. He asked for wisdom. God loved that Solomon asked for wisdom. He gave him the wisdom he asked for and the earthly blessings as well.

Think about your fears. What do you want most? I hope God is going to teach us to say, "I want a shelter. I want final salvation. I want eternal joy." The beautiful thing is that God says, "Wonderful. I'll give you eternal joy, and I'll also come and meet you now. I'll give you eternal satisfaction, and I'll be a present help in trouble now."

The climactic day of absolute triumph is coming: The blessed hope! The return of the King! Our great fear arrives, and he conquers all other fears once and for all. Our fears won't have the last word. Death won't have the last word. Jesus is the shelter of the Most High, Jesus has conquered death, and Jesus will never leave us.

Reflect and Discuss

1. What do you do with anxious thoughts? Have you noticed any patterns of response, healthy or unhealthy? Prayerfully reflect on this.
2. How would you describe the prosperity gospel?
3. In what ways does prosperity teaching set people up for discouragement?
4. How does the fear of the Lord drive out other fears?
5. What are some ways we can cultivate the fear of the Lord?
6. How does remembering the gospel enable the Christian to battle fear?
7. How does the truth of Christ's return sustain us in present trials?

A Song for the Battle Weary

PSALM 92

Main Idea: Our faith is energized by remembering God's Word and his work on our behalf.

I. **Remember the Rescue of Grace (92:1-5).**
II. **Remember the Way of Wisdom (92:6-9).**
III. **Remember the Hope of the Gospel (92:10-15).**

God's Word always addresses people. It's always personal, and it always speaks to real need. And there's always help.

One of many questions I encourage you to ask before you've finished studying a passage is, God, who are you reaching for in this passage? What state of heart are you addressing here? For example, in this passage I find application for at least three kinds of people.

The Joyless

Some tend to think God's grace is like your cell phone battery. It seemed to last longer in the early days, but now you feel like every time you turn around it's about to die. You have to keep it powered up, and you power it up by doing your spiritual chores on time, but it's feeling like drudgery—just piles of rules.

The Foolish

Some are running after sin, coddling it, believing an unbroken series of good times and good feelings, as defined by this world, is the path to life and happiness. This psalm speaks to you as well.

The Hopeless

Some believers are so constantly under attack that they struggle to see any fruit. God's promises seem to apply to others but not to them.

You might think, *What does "remembering" have to do with my stepping toward joy and wisdom and hope?* Everything. The Christian life is fueled by remembrance. Our passage shows this to us from a few different angles.

Remember the Rescue of Grace
PSALM 92:1-5

The word *remember* doesn't actually occur in Psalm 92, but one of the reasons this word can act as a bonding agent, holding various themes together, is because of the superscription: "A psalm. A song for the Sabbath day."

God established holy days. They were reminders. Passover was a reminder. The Festival of Shelters was a reminder. And Sabbath was a regular, weekly reminder. This psalm was written for this occasion. It is a song best sung on the day God's people are remembering his work on their behalf. The accent in these opening verses is not this believer's sacrifices for God. It's not a song about the believer's work, labor, and love. It's pointing to God: "*your* faithful love . . . *you* have made me rejoice . . . what *you* have done . . . *your* hands . . . *your* works . . . *your* thoughts." There's a pronounced emphasis throughout this chapter on God and his saving grace. This fits with what we know about the Sabbath.

God established the Sabbath pattern in creation. In Genesis 2 he made the world in six days and rested on the seventh day. When we come to Exodus 12, God's people have not been resting—they've been slaves in Egypt. But God tells Moses that's all about to change. God has one more act of judgment to bring down on the pride of Egypt, and then his people will be free to leave Egypt and head toward the promised land to rest in God's provision for them. He rescued them from slavery, and Sabbath was instituted to keep them from forgetting what God had done. Moses instructed the people to

> "*remember that you were a slave in the land of Egypt, and the Lord your God brought you out of there with a strong hand and an outstretched arm. That is why the Lord your God has commanded you to keep the Sabbath day.*" (Deut 5:15)

And in Exodus 31 the Lord tells Moses exactly what he should think about the Sabbath.

> *And the Lord said to Moses, "You are to speak to the people of Israel and say, 'Above all you shall keep my Sabbaths, for this is a sign between me and you throughout your generations, that you may know that I, the Lord, sanctify you.'"* (Exod 31:12-13 ESV; emphasis added)

I, the Lord, sanctify you. I rescued you. The exodus wasn't a cooperative effort where God did 50 percent and the people did the other 50 percent. This is symbolized in the way they were to celebrate the Sabbath. Put down all the tools of labor. Don't do anything that even looks like work on the Sabbath. Why? So that you remember what it looked like when I saved you. You had no power against Egypt. You had no weapons to stand up to your oppressors. You were, to borrow a phrase from Jesus in the gospels, "weary and burdened" (Matt 11:28), and I gave you rest.

As a Christian, when you think of things that light you up the most about the Christian faith, what comes to mind—the things you're currently doing or the things Jesus has done? Friend, the Christian gospel isn't fundamentally an exhortation. It is a report of what God has done to rescue sinners.

Let me try to illustrate this from marriage. Imagine a husband married to a woman who is absolutely radiant inside and out. Now imagine that husband works at the office with men and women who have never seen his beautiful wife. All he tells them are stories of his devotion to his wife. He trots out the poems he's written for her. He brings his guitar to the break room and plays the song he's been working on, which covers the turning points in their ten years of marriage. All his coworkers are amazed at *the devotion and sacrifices of this husband.* Then, let's imagine, one day his wife drops by the office to bring him a box lunch from his favorite restaurant, and there she is. Immediately she strikes them as the absolute epitome of grace, elegance, and beauty. Suddenly the husband's sacrificial devotion isn't the best explanation for all that he's been doing these past ten years. *She* is!

You see the difference? Christian faith is not primarily devotion driven or discipline driven. No, it's beauty driven.

Where do we see this in the Bible? We catch up to a man in Matthew 13 and see him selling everything he has, and then he goes and buys a field with treasure in it. He sold all that he had; can you believe that? That's not the point though. We're not supposed to think, *Wow, what amazing sacrifice! I wish I could be that unselfish, that detached from the blessings I have.* No, we're supposed to see the treasure in the field he just bought and say, "Of course he sold everything! He's found greater treasure!"

The story of the prodigal son is in Luke 15. He squanders all of his inheritance and finds himself friendless, covered in mud, and eating with pigs. What thought led him home? It was the thought of the generosity of his father. Yet, he even underestimated that. He thought his dad might be gracious enough to let him work as a hired hand. Of course, what happened was the father saw his penitent son from a distance and tore off toward him. He hugged him and kissed him and started snapping orders. I need a ring, some shoes, a barbeque pit, and a DJ, stat! My son who I thought was dead is alive!

Don't domesticate God's grace. It is so much better than we realize. Look at how Psalm 92 describes the believer. Clearly this person has encountered good news: He's giving thanks and singing (v. 1). He's declaring God's faithfulness morning and night (v. 2). He's grabbing instruments (v. 3). He's rejoicing and shouting for joy (v. 4). He's talking about the greatness of God's works and thoughts (v. 5). There's an overflow of joy in the love and grace of God.

Our joy as believers runs deeper than circumstances. It doesn't depend on happy events or emotional highs. Ours is a joy that drinks deeply from the fountain of the gospel—the perfect work of God on our behalf.

Remember the Way of Wisdom
PSALM 92:6-9

This psalm moves from a vision of how the past shapes present faith to how the *present* informs the *future*. The Psalms, in particular, sometimes go about this in a positive way, pointing out the blessings that await the believer in the future. However, at times they come at it from the warning angle. Wisdom sayings in the Bible often distinguish between the way things appear now and the way things finally turn out in the end. For example, Proverbs says, "There is a way that seems right to a person, but its end is the way of death" (Prov 14:12). Further, in Proverbs the writer uses stories to bring this message across—for instance, a seductress who calls out to a naïve young man. Lacking understanding, he sees and follows her (thinking this is going to be a great experience), but the evening doesn't turn out as he expected, for "her house sinks down to death and her ways to the land of the departed spirits. None return who go to her; none reach the paths of life" (Prov 2:18-19).

Similarly here, the psalmist is saying, things aren't what they seem. It may *look like* the wicked sprout like grass (v. 7), and it may *look like* they are flourishing, but this psalm urges us: don't ever forget that sin destroys.

Christian friend, sin deceives and destroys. When we coddle it, rather than turn from it, it dulls our senses. Secret sin in our lives is promising exciting life, but is actually killing us. If you're married, secret sexual sin is ruining your marriage. You might say, "But she doesn't know." It is already doing its damage, even now.

This is why repentance is to be a way of life. Christians are always fighting against sin, walking toward light, confessing, and turning away from sin. Turn to the wisdom of God's Word. Confess your sin to him. Invite others to keep you accountable and help you move toward freedom.

This psalm rejoices in grace. It's a Sabbath psalm! However, it is not without warning. Verses 6-9 warn the believer, not convert the pagan. The pagans weren't reading this. The primary purpose is similar to what Asaph did for the readers of Psalm 73: "But as for me, my feet almost slipped; my steps nearly went astray. For I envied the arrogant; I saw the prosperity of the wicked" (vv. 2-3). He speaks honestly about this struggle, then expresses his frustration: "Look at them—the wicked! They are always at ease, and they increase their wealth. Did I purify my heart and wash my hands in innocence for nothing?" (vv. 12-13). If you stop here, you're left wondering if he is about to forsake the faith. But notice what turns him back toward God. "When I tried to understand all this, it seemed hopeless until I entered God's sanctuary. Then I understood their destiny" (vv. 16-17). Then he says in verse 19, "How suddenly they become a desolation!"

Wisdom literature in the Bible is constantly saying, "Things aren't always what they seem." Sometimes God haters look like they're flourishing, but it doesn't end well. Sometimes the righteous look like they're withering, but check them out later as they approach the end. That's where the psalmist looks next. The endnote of this psalm is not gloomy. In fact, this is a powerful song of assurance. Despite its implicit warning about the way of the fool, it speaks of the future of the believer with total confidence.

Remember the Hope of the Gospel
PSALM 92:10-15

One of my favorite hymns is a lesser known lyric by Augustus Toplady. It's about assurance.

> The work which Your goodness began, The arm of Your
> strength will complete;

Your promise is Yes and Amen, And never was forfeited yet.
The future or things that are now, No power below or above,
Can make You Your purpose forego, Or sever my soul from
    Your love.

It finishes this way:

> *Yes! I to the end will endure, As sure as the promise is given;*
> More happy, but not more secure, The glorified spirits in
>   heaven. (Toplady, "A Debtor to Mercy Alone"; emphasis
>   added)

What God's grace begins, God's faithfulness completes. Psalm 92 is a
sort of Old Testament preview of what Paul says in the New Testament:
"I am sure of this, that he who started a good work in you will carry it on
to completion until the day of Christ Jesus" (Phil 1:6). It's a promise of
future flourishing for the believer.

This psalm, if you will, fast-forwards through life. The one who was
praising God in the opening verses is old in verses 12-15. This old man
or woman is flourishing like a palm tree. She's growing like a cedar in
Lebanon. In other words, she's strong in the faith! Early on she was
planted in the house of the Lord, and she hasn't withered. No, in fact
she is flourishing in the courts of our God. Earlier it looked like the
wicked were flourishing. It turns out they weren't. And at various times
in the life of the believer, it may have looked as though the righteous
were not flourishing, but they were.

Look at her in verse 14, bearing fruit in old age; healthy and
green, declaring that the Lord is just, he is my rock, and there is no
unrighteousness in him (v. 15). What a story she's telling! This is the
life of grace. This is what the gospel, working in our souls by God's
Spirit, produces.

How do we grow healthy and green? Psalm 92 tells us we look to
God's grace in the past to fuel perseverance in the present, toward the
confident hope of flourishing in the future.

There are no imperatives in this passage. There's no application
to-do list. It is a Sabbath song through and through. It's taken up *not*
with evidences of *our* faithful love for God but *his* faithful love for us.

Christian, you're not the author and the finisher of your faith. And
it's not that he's the author and you're the finisher. He's the author *and*
the finisher of your faith. Psalm 92 does a happy dance to that truth.
This psalm describes the perseverance of the believer, but even more

it highlights the preserving grace of God to keep us to the end. It's a Sabbath song.

It's a word to the joyless, the foolish, and the hopeless. It's an invitation not to work but to believe, to remember, to rest in God's work on our behalf!

Reflect and Discuss

1. How does a time of rest help us reflect on God's work in our lives? Why is Sabbath not only important for our physical bodies but also for our faith?

2. What are some key moments in your life where you have seen God's faithfulness, goodness, or love? How can you practically record and remember God's work—events such as these—in your life?

3. Take a moment to name some one-word adjectives for God. How can you incorporate praise of God into the time you spend with him? How can you find joy and treasure in God for who he is?

4. How should we react, as followers of Christ, to the truth of sin's destruction? Why should it drive us to repentance, humility, and mission?

5. When are we most likely to feel discouraged or hopeless while facing the future? What are the dangers of basing God's truths in our lives on the circumstances surrounding us?

6. Similar to looking to the future for the ultimate outcome of sin, we sometimes have to look to the future of God's people to find hope in the midst of the present. How do verses 12-15 give us a picture of what is to come (ultimately) for those who pursue God's righteousness?

7. What does it say about our belief in God when we dismiss his promises for us?

8. How can we encourage one another with hope when we are in the midst of despair and pain? How can we sensitively share the journey of remembering and looking forward when we are in the midst of anguish?

Our God Reigns

PSALM 93

Main Idea: Because God is sovereign and keeps his promises, we can be assured of final rescue from powers too strong for us.

I.   **The Lord Reigns (93:1-2).**
II. **The Floods Roar (93:3).**
III. **The Lord Is Mightier (93:4-5).**

We can never overdose on hope. We need more hope than we can handle because there will be moments in our lives when we feel like we have more trouble than we can handle. The psalmist writes to those who need hope. The first three words of the psalm are the first point.

The Lord Reigns

PSALM 93:1-2

This psalm just begins by stating this as a universal fact, and there is tremendous power in this statement. In Scripture, God's sovereignty is not the stuff of controversy; it's the stuff of worship.

At the absolute bottom, what are those bedrock truths on which everything else stands? God's self-existence. His "I AM-ness" (see Exod 3:14-15). That's a big and important truth in Scripture. Having established that God *is*, the next thing we might say is that God *reigns*. A massively comprehensive statement about the message of the entire Bible might go like this: "The God who is, reigns." There's certainly more to it, but we're onto something really big in that simple statement.

This was, in a word, Moses's message to Pharaoh: "The Lord reigns, you've got his people, and he wants his people back." He preaches that message with words in Pharaoh's court. Then he preaches it with gnats. Frogs. Cow-tipping. In plague after plague God is saying, "Pharaoh, you really should just let the people go. I'm not getting tired. It's my world. They're my flies. They're my gnats. The breath in the lungs of the firstborn of every child in Egypt—that's mine too." Moses is warning

Pharaoh, trying to get Pharaoh to grasp that he is contending against the Lord and, in case Pharaoh was unaware, the Lord reigns.

As Christians we know that in the fullness of time God sent his Son into the world. Paul speaks of the progression from Jesus's incarnation, to his suffering and death on the cross, to his triumphant resurrection and ascension to God's right hand.

> *For this reason God highly exalted him and gave him the name that is above every name, so that at the name of Jesus every knee will bow—in heaven and on earth and under the earth—and every tongue will confess that Jesus Christ is Lord, to the glory of God the Father.* (Phil 2:9-11)

There will be a worldwide, almost liturgical response on the day of Christ's return; a confession will rise from the lips of every creature. The angels—along with every human being on earth, every person who has ever lived, and even the demons in hell—all with one voice, acknowledge, "Jesus Christ is Lord." And Psalm 93 tells us, "The Lord reigns!"

The psalm goes on to say more about this reign of God (v. 2). In a way you can see the stability of a kingdom by looking at the stability of the throne of that kingdom. For example, the first three kings in Israel (Saul, David, Solomon) each reigned for roughly forty years. When the kingdom was divided under Rehoboam, you can see the instability by simply looking at the number of years the subsequent kings occupied the throne: 17, 3, 41, 25, 8, 1, 40, 29, 52, 16, 16, 29, 55, 2, 31, 3 months, 11 years, 3 months, and 11 years. In almost every case those big numbers were the good kings: Asa, Jehoshaphat, Joash, Amaziah, Uzziah, and Hezekiah. It's not an absolute rule, but generally a righteous throne is an enduring throne. So when the psalmist speaks of God's throne, he ties the endurance of God's reign to the perfection of God's righteousness.

Note the foundation of God's throne: "Righteousness and justice are the foundation of your throne" (Ps 89:14). Note the reach of God's throne: "The Lord has established his throne in heaven, and his kingdom rules over all" (103:19). Note the endurance of God's throne: "Your throne, God, is forever and ever; the scepter of your kingdom is a scepter of justice" (45:6). If you want to see the stability of God's kingdom, walk through the course of history and look at how many sit on the sovereign throne: one. His throne is established "from the beginning."

When the psalmist thinks of the reign of God, he goes back further than the great displays of God's power in the exodus. Verse 1 takes us all

84 Christ-Centered Exposition Commentary

the way back to the first page of the Bible, where in an act of unrivaled power the Lord established the world. Having established it, it will never be moved.

It's not as if God's throne came with creation. God didn't say, "Let there be grass, trees, and I'd like a throne." No. God didn't *become* sovereign in Genesis 1. Genesis 1 happened because God *was* sovereign. God's throne is identified with his eternality. That's a fancy way of saying, "As long as God has been, God has reigned." Many years ago I heard a Christian theologian say, "The sovereignty of God is God's favorite doctrine. If you were God, it'd be your favorite doctrine as well because it means you get to be *God*."

In Isaiah 46 God lays down a test to apply to any so-called rival gods. He told Israel to ask the supposed god if he knows the end from the beginning and if all of his purposes are fulfilled (Isa 46:10). In other words, see if the god candidate can demonstrate sovereign power because, as God says through the prophet, when I call a bird of prey from the east, a bird of prey comes, and it doesn't come from the west (Isa 46:11). And if I say a kingdom will fall on Tuesday morning, it won't fall on Wednesday. It won't fall on Tuesday afternoon. It falls on Tuesday morning.

In the grand scheme of things, the one who has ultimate sovereignty gets to be called God. I am not sovereign, as often as I try to be. Luck or fate is not sovereign. Mother nature is not sovereign. The devil is not sovereign. America is not sovereign. God alone is sovereign, which is another way of saying, God alone is God.

So the psalmist here proclaims two things: God reigns in majesty and in power, and God's throne is as old as he is.

The Floods Roar
PSALM 93:3

The sovereignty of God is not a challenge for Christians to affirm when all is well.

You think about the history of Israel. From the call of Abraham in Genesis 12 through the birth of Jesus, you've got about two thousand years of history. They're sojourners for a while. They put down roots in Egypt—started well but mostly horrific. God rescued them through Moses, and they wandered through the desert and tested God's patience for forty years before finally moving into the promised land.

That led to the period of the judges, which was one of the worst eras in all of Old Testament history. Then Saul takes the throne, becoming Israel's first king. The monarchy period is off to a bumpy start. David takes the throne and rules for forty years! David's son Solomon takes the throne, builds the temple, and rules for forty years! That was the golden age of Old Testament history. Hope you didn't blink. Everything unravels after Solomon. The kingdom is divided. The northern kingdom is eventually conquered by Assyria—terrible. The southern kingdom lasts a little longer but is conquered by Babylon—absolutely horrific. Then come a series of occupations: after Babylon it's Persia, then Greece, then Rome. This is the history of God's Old Testament people. Two thousand years of embattled history: sin and suffering. Eighty years of relative peace (also lots of sin). Which is to say, these people knew the sound of the floods lifting up their voice (v. 3). They were all too familiar with this sound. No wonder so much of the Psalter is lamentation songs.

There are a hundred modern equivalents. There are probably people reading this right now who could cry at the drop of a hat, life is so overwhelming for them.

I went to the bank recently to help get our son set up with online banking. A professional woman called us over, and we sat down. She was wonderfully friendly. We made some small talk while she looked everything up. She saw evidence that we had lived in New Orleans, and so she told us a story about almost moving there, but, the story went, she ended up getting engaged to a guy here. In passing she mentioned a health issue, then said, "Well, I'm rambling. You're here to get a checking account."

My oldest son said, "No, it's a great story. Tell us more."

She continued and had to stop five seconds later. She turned her face, apologized, and flapped an envelope in front of her eyes. She took us through her cancer diagnosis and how the doctor, lacking gentleness, said, "This could be a situation where we would," and she quoted him exactly at this point, "just *try to keep you comfortable.*" And she said, "I didn't hear anything after that."

This was the eye-opening thing—to realize I walk past people like that every day. To realize afresh that my church is full of people having similar experiences. People who could cry at the drop of a hat. An unsuspecting stranger says, "Tell me more," and they fall apart right there in front of you.

Have you heard the floods lifting up their voice? Are you hearing the floods even now? Loneliness. Infertility. The stubborn darkness of depression. The doctors say to someone you love, "There's nothing more we can do." An adult child won't go into the same room with you. It's official, you're going to lose the house. The floods have lifted up their voice. One of the primary reasons we sing and preach the sovereignty of God is because no truth settles a heart in turmoil more than the truth that "the LORD reigns."

Yes, the floods are noisy and tumultuous, but that is not the last word of this psalm. It began with hope, and it will end with hope!

The Lord Is Mightier
PSALM 93:4-5

The whole psalm now comes into view for us. The Lord reigns, the floods roar, but the Lord is "greater" (v. 4). And the assurance we have that God will still the waves that are too strong for us is the knowledge that his "testimonies are completely reliable" (v. 5).

Let me say something about the structure and arrangement of the book of Psalms. The psalms are arranged in five collections—if you will, five mini-hymnals. They are not arranged chronologically. See, for example, Psalm 90 is written by Moses. No, they are arranged to tell a story.

> The organization of the Psalter reminds us not only of the law of Moses but of a pilgrimage through which God is taking his people. The Psalter helps to tell the story of a journey from suffering to glory and from lament to praise. One statistical detail tells the tale: in Books One through Three (Psalms 1–89), so-called "laments" outnumber "hymns" of praise by a little more than two-to-one, while in Books Four and Five (Psalms 90–150), the proportion is reversed, and actually amplified—here "hymns" of praise outnumber "laments" seven-to-three. (Kidd, *With One Voice*, 29)

God is unfolding a story for his people—a story that moves from the wreckage of the fall to the restoration of creation. What begins in anguish ends in Psalm 150 where we break out the trumpets and tambourines, and everything that has breath praises the Lord. We're right here toward the beginning of Book IV (Pss 90–106). There's no question about the capacity of God in Psalm 93. The Lord reigns. We know he can quiet the waves, but how? How will he deliver us from the troubles that vex us in this life? Even more significantly, how will he save us from our most fearsome enemies, the loudest floodwaters: death and the righteous judgment of God against our many sins? The answer has everything to do with the reliability of God's promises (v. 5).

Psalm 93 leverages comfort in two ways. Be comforted, people of God, because God is sovereign (vv. 1-4). And be comforted because God will keep his promise (v. 5). God had made promises to his people about a King, a Son of David, who would sit on an eternal throne. He would usher in a reign of righteousness, peace, and joy. He would conquer the enemies they could not conquer. The people would live in God's place under his rule and blessing forever.

Book III (Pss 73–89) ended with a reminder of the promises God made about this Son of David. Psalm 89:19-25 tells about God being with his chosen one, an exalted warrior, and about his power over the sea. In the fullness of time, Jesus Christ, the Son of David, arrives, and the disciples realize he is no ordinary man. He is God in the flesh. At one point they are in a boat, being thrashed by the waves (literal waves!), having a near-death experience, and Jesus quiets the waves of the sea with a word (Mark 4:35-41). If they had eyes to see it, the great story peeked through for just a moment. God's reliable promise. He said he would send a Son of David who would still the raging sea, and that one is here.

Jesus goes to the cross and dies in our place, and rises again, conquering our most fearsome enemies: sin, death, and Satan. Everyone who looks to Jesus Christ for refuge, for salvation, is secure forever. He promises to come again and make everything right—all the floodwaters of life in a broken, cursed, and fallen world.

The challenge of Psalm 93 is that two things are set side by side. The throne and the sea—the throne representing God's sovereignty, the sea representing evil powers too strong for us to control. Both the throne and the sea appear again, together, in Revelation 4:5-6, but the sea doesn't sound like Psalm 93 anymore: "Flashes of lightning and rumblings and peals of thunder came from the throne. Seven fiery torches were burning before the throne, which are the seven spirits of God. Something like a sea of glass, similar to crystal, was also before the throne."

What happened? In Revelation 4 we see the final realization and fulfillment of the promise at the end of Psalms Book III. We see Jesus, the Son of David, set his mighty right hand on the sea, and there he stills it forever. No more foaming waves lifting up their voices. No, he wipes away all tears and stills every wave. "The dominion will be vast, and its prosperity will never end. He will reign on the throne of David and over his kingdom, to establish and sustain it with justice and righteousness from now on and forever. The zeal of the LORD of Armies will accomplish this" (Isa 9:7).

In this way our passage tells the story of the world. God will bring his people into his place under his rule and blessing. God has promised this, and his promises are reliable. God can make good on his promises because he is the Lord, and the Lord reigns!

Reflect and Discuss

1. How does God's sovereignty in the life of his people give us hope in our own life stories?

2. Some people condescendingly say that belief in God is a crutch to support believers in times of weakness. However, how can belief in a sovereign God bring doubt of his goodness in times of weakness?

3. Think about a time in your life when you questioned God's sovereignty. Why is trusting his character essential in times of doubt? How can we lay a foundation secured in the character of God?

4. Why do we want to give God credit for his blessed sovereignty when things are well but question him when circumstances are painful?

5. How can you document the faithful sovereignty of God throughout circumstances in your life? Consider making a timeline and marking significant times when God's sovereign hand was clearly at work in your life.

6. Even when our circumstances do not change, why can we still trust in God's sovereign promises to deliver us eternally?

Praying for God's Vengeance

PSALM 94

Main Idea: Believers can pray confidently for God to exercise vengeance on his enemies in light of his nature.

I. Appeal to God's Character (94:1-2).
II. Appeal to God's Covenant (94:3-7).
III. Appeal to God's Creation (94:8-11).
IV. Appeal to God's Commands (94:12-15).
V. Appeal to God's Comfort (94:16-23).

While I certainly wasn't the toughest kid in school growing up, I never considered myself to be what we referred to as a pansy, sissy, or wimp. I was a quarterback in football all the way through college, so I didn't mind getting hit . . . when I had shoulder pads and a helmet on. However, off the football field, I wasn't a big fan of street fights or locker-room brawls. I hated (and still do!) the prospects of someone hitting what I thought was this pretty little face of mine. So I grew up despising any kind of bullying. Whenever I witnessed it—whether it was directed at me or someone else—I always fantasized about being one of the Avengers! I wanted to be the good guy who came out of nowhere at just the right moment and whipped the bad guys. I always wanted to be Cordell Walker in *Walker, Texas Ranger*, Kwai Chang Caine in *Kung Fu*, John Reese in *Person of Interest*, and Robert McCall in *The Equalizer*.

There's something natural about wanting to see the little guy defended, the innocent vindicated, and justice served. I think that's part of the reason behind the contemporary movement to eliminate bullying. Bullying is when somebody uses force, threat, or coercion to abuse, intimidate, or dominate someone else. The 2017 Youth Risk Behavior Surveillance System revealed that, nationwide, 19 percent of students in grades 9–12 reported being bullied on school property in the twelve months preceding the survey (CDC, 31). That's not OK.

Nowhere is bullying more intolerable than when it's levied at God's children and the gospel they embrace. Psalm 94 is a case in point. The song is constructed in an inclusio that capsulizes its clear message. The verbs translated "repay" in verse 2 and "pay them back" in verse 23 are from the same root, forming the song's bookends and giving direction to everything in between. Furthermore, the repeated phrase *destroy them* (v. 23) reaches back to the repetitive introduction of the "God of vengeance—God of vengeance" in verse 1 (Ross, Vol. 3, 108). So the psalmist closes the loop of the initial heart cry by cementing the truth that God ultimately will destroy his enemies for all their willful wickedness, self-serving speech, and dictatorial and domineering deeds. The psalmist ends where he began—with a solid confidence that God will act according to his nature on behalf of those for whom he cares.

The bottom line is that God cannot and will not put up with "proud" (v. 2) bullies who act on their own accord without any regard for him, his people, or his orderly rule (cf. Pss 10:2; 31:18; Prov 29:23; Isa 2:12). Consequently, he will exercise his vengeance in his time. Whether it's an atheistic special interest group that sues a Christian baker for refusing to bake a cake for a transgender celebration, a student who gets pushed around on a playground for her faith, a family who's forced to remove a nativity scene from the yard because of the pressure from a homeowners' association, or a people group who are the victims of genocide at the hands of an evil regime, God promises to hear and see and respond.

Christians are never to take the pursuit of justice into their own hands and presume to be the instruments of God's vengeance. Paul reminds us, "Friends, do not avenge yourselves; instead, leave room for God's wrath, because it is written, Vengeance belongs to me; I will repay, says the Lord" (Rom 12:19). On the contrary, Jesus instructs us to "love your enemies and pray for those who persecute you" (Matt 5:44). Scripture compels us to live in the mysterious tension between leaving vengeance to God and praying for him to exercise it. So, while gripped by a burden for all to believe the gospel, believers should aggressively appeal to God to exercise his vengeance on bullies and to bring about his justice. To that end the psalmist gives us five appeals we can make to God.

Appeal to God's Character
PSALM 94:1-2

The writer knows that God is always faithful to himself and, therefore, that the most potent prayer is one that appeals to his character. So he addresses his plea to the "God of vengeance" twice in verse 1, and then to the "Judge of the earth" in verse 2. Moses attributed the first title to God's assertion about himself when he included in his song the claim "Vengeance belongs to me; I will repay" (Deut 32:35). Abraham used the second title to question God about his judgment of Sodom: "Won't the Judge of the whole earth do what is just?" (Gen 18:25). This is God's character as recognized by his people.

The specific nature of the psalmist's request is that this God of vengeance and judge of the earth would "shine! Rise up" (vv. 1-2). He wants the Lord to make a grand entrance in his royal splendor and bring justice to the anarchy caused by all the people who've intimidated God's people and exalted themselves as their rulers (cf. Deut 33:2; Ps 80:1; Isa 2:20-21; 3:13-14; 6:1). He wants God to explode on the scene, wield his just sword, and lower the boom on these arrogant bullies.

It's not a vindictive response that the psalmist wants from the earth's Judge. He wants him to give them "what they deserve!" God's vengeance is never vindictive but merely a response to the evil that wicked people incite (Ps 28:4; Lam 3:64; Rom 12:19; 1 Thess 4:6). The psalmist's prayer here is consistent with the character of God that's reflected in other psalms that call for divine recompense of wrongs (Pss 35:23-24; 58:11; 76:8-9; 82:8; see also Isa 51:1).

Once again we're reminded in this passage that it's more than wishful thinking when we appeal to what God claims about his own character. It's solid intercessory ground. Believers can and should ask God to respond to those who bully the gospel and its adherents, and we should ask on the grounds that this is who he is. He is the "God of vengeance . . . [and] Judge of the earth." Therefore, it follows that he can and will act accordingly.

Appeal to God's Covenant
PSALM 94:3-7

After appealing to God's character, the psalmist turns his attention to God's covenant with his people. The key to understanding this section is found at the end of verse 7 when the songwriter points out the enemies' identification of God as "the LORD . . . the God of Jacob." Both of these names reach back to God's covenantal relationship with Israel and essentially form the basis of the psalmist's complaint in this section. Basically, he's calling attention to the fact that the evildoers are mocking God for not responding to the plight of the people with whom he made his covenant promises. In fact, his enemies are claiming that he "doesn't see . . . [or] pay attention" to their slaughter. Their obvious insinuation is that God doesn't care.

The psalmist's appeal to God's covenant with his people is strengthened by his references to "your people . . . your heritage" (v. 5) for whom God had promised to care (Deut 4:20; Ps 28:9). The songwriter knows that whenever the wicked assault God's people, they arrogantly attack the Lord himself. He specifically calls attention to "the widow and the resident alien . . . [and] the fatherless" (v. 6), all of whom need God's particular protection because of their vulnerability, and all of whom he had promised to defend (Exod 22:21-22; Deut 10:18; 24:19; Ps 10:14; Mal 3:5; Jas 1:27). Yet these evildoers "crush . . . oppress . . . kill . . . and murder" them (vv. 5-6), while the God who had promised to be their defender appears to ignore their trouble.

This appeal forms the basis for the basic question on the table: "How long will the wicked celebrate?" (v. 3). The psalmist isn't questioning God's nature or ability. He's just noting that the night is dragging on and the knees of his covenant people are buckling while the wicked are having a party. They "pour out arrogant words . . . [and] boast" (v. 4) in a continual tirade of superior speech and rude rhetoric (cf. Pss 31:18; 59:7; 75:4; 1 Sam 2:3). They're taunting the people of God, like a victorious boxer standing over his fallen opponent and mocking his defeat.

On this side of the cross, believers sometimes feel the same way. It seems that God often turns a deaf ear to the worldwide persecution of his people, the escalation of terrorists against the Christian faith, and the growing bias against evangelicals even in America. Yet we can be sure that God is sovereignly working on behalf of his people through the gospel. Quoting from Jeremiah 31:33, the author of Hebrews reminds believers that God said,

For this is the covenant that I will make with the house of Israel after those days, says the Lord: I will put my laws into their minds and write them on their hearts. I will be their God, and they will be my people. (Heb 8:10)

God wrote his law on our hearts and minds through the gospel. Because we are his people, we can appeal to his covenant with us in Christ Jesus, a covenant in which he's promised to love and care for us (Rom 8:31-39; Heb 13:5-6), to orchestrate our suffering to shape us into Christ's image

(Rom 8:28-30), and to bring vengeance on the enemies of the gospel (Rom 12:19; 2 Thess 1:5-10).

Appeal to God's Creation
PSALM 94:8-11

The psalmist next turns the evildoers' taunts back on them by appealing to God's role as Creator. In response to their derision that God is imperceptive (v. 7), he rebukes them as being the ones who are "stupid people" (v. 8). The English adjective here is a verb in Hebrew, putting the emphasis on behavior instead of ability (Kidner, Vol. 16, 373). The writer basically says they're acting like senseless and irrational animals, "fools" who lack the ability to comprehend. So he counters with the demand for them to "pay attention" to the real truth about God's nature and rhetorically inquires when they will "be wise" enough to do so.

To support his retort, the songwriter uses three rhetorical questions (see vv. 9-10a) and one strong declaration (see vv. 10b-11) to highlight God's nature as Creator and, therefore, the one who is more than capable of vindicating his people. God actually is the one who "shaped the ear . . . formed the eye . . . instructs nations . . . [and] teaches mankind knowledge" (vv. 9-10). Consequently—and in contrast to the claim in verse 7—he does in fact "hear . . . see . . . discipline . . . [and know] the thoughts of mankind" (vv. 9-11). The final qualification that man's thoughts "are futile" (v. 11) is intended to be a particular rebuke of these wicked opponents. Even though they think they are powers to be reckoned with, like all of humanity their faulty feelings are futile in the court of the one who created them (cf. Pss 39:5; 78:33; Eccl 1:1).

The psalmist understood that an appeal to God's creative activity is irrefutable. If God created us, then surely he's capable of hearing the cries of his people and responding to them. Not only that, he merits our lifelong pursuit and allegiance. This is at least one of the reasons the host of heaven in John's revelation cries out, "Our Lord and God, you are worthy to receive glory and honor and power, because you have created all things, and by your will they exist and were created" (Rev 4:11). He's all-sufficient for our needs and all-deserving of our worship.

Believers in Christ today have the same basis of appeal when we're bullied for our faith. Speaking of our Lord Jesus Christ, Paul says,

He is the image of the invisible God, the firstborn over all creation. For everything was created by him, in heaven and on earth, the visible and

the invisible, whether thrones or dominions or rulers or authorities—
all things have been created through him and for him. (Col 1:15-16)

Jesus was there at the beginning, and he is the beginning of all things (John 1:1). As Creator of the universe, he stands ready to act on behalf of his persecuted followers according to his nature. He hears and sees our dilemma, and he promises to act in response to our appeal to his creative power.

Appeal to God's Commands
PSALM 94:12-15

The psalmist's fourth appeal is to the promised benefit of those who obey God's commands. Contrasting God's wisdom with the foolishness of his enemies, he pronounces everyone who adheres to God's commands to be "happy" (v. 12; cf. 1:1). The verbs *discipline* and *teach* describe the application of God's wisdom, and they're the same verbs as those used in verse 10. All wisdom comes from God, and his common grace makes it available to all people, even the wicked who oppose him. However, God is so desirous that his people not miss it that he wrote it down for them in his "law" (v. 12; cf. Pss 19; 119). And the psalmist exults in the victory God's people experience when they align themselves with his commands in the school of divine wisdom.

The next three verses unpack some of the divine blessings experienced by God's pupils. First, those who obey God's commands are blessed with "relief from troubled times" (v. 13; cf. 49:5), an inward tranquility when times are bad. He promises to provide relief "until a pit is dug for the wicked"—until they get what's coming to them (cf. Pss 7:15; 9:15; 35:7; 57:6; Prov 26:27; Eccl 10:8). In the economy of God, the wicked don't always get their just recompense immediately. But the righteous can rest assured that it's coming, and they can do so with the inner quietness that God provides.

Second, those who obey God's commands are blessed by the confidence that he "will not leave . . . or abandon" (v. 14) them during their seasons of trouble. Why? Because they are "his people . . . his heritage." This is God's answer to the earlier call of distress (v. 5). He never goes back on his pledge (1 Sam 12:22; Rom 11:1-4). Consequently, his children live in the blessed assurance of his imminent justice and vindication because they belong to him.

Third, those who obey God's commands are blessed with the assurance that righteousness ultimately will win the day (v. 15; cf. Ps 72; Isa 11; 32). Like the pit being dug for the wicked in verse 13, God is storing up his vengeance on them and will one day unleash it with unbridled force. On that day the righteous will be vindicated and "all the upright in heart will follow it" (v. 15). Righteousness and justice are the promises of God's kingdom, and those whose hearts are given to his commands seek it with their entire beings.

The kingdom of Christ is characterized by God's righteousness and, therefore, believers should pursue it above all else. Jesus says, "Blessed are those who hunger and thirst for righteousness, for they will be filled" (Matt 5:6) and, "Seek first the kingdom of God and his righteousness, and all these things will be provided for you" (Matt 6:33). True satisfaction of the soul, provision of the necessities of life, and more are the blessings that await those who seek his righteousness. Jesus also said, "Everyone who hears these words of mine and acts on them will be like a wise man who built his house on the rock" (Matt 7:24) and, "If you remain in me and my words remain in you, ask whatever you want and it will be done for you" (John 15:7). When praying for God's vengeance on the enemies of the gospel, we should appeal to God's economy of blessing the citizens of his kingdom as they walk in obedience to Christ's commands and pursue his righteousness.

Appeal to God's Comfort
PSALM 94:16-23

The final appeal the psalmist makes is to the comfort God so faithfully provides. God's steadfast love is introduced with two rhetorical questions that return to the cry for vindication in verses 3-7. The writer rhetorically asks, "Who stands up for me against the wicked? Who takes a stand for me against evildoers?" (v. 16). The next three verses list three when-I-was-X-God-did-Y confessions that reveal the expected answer to the psalmist's loneliness. At every turn the compassionate and caring presence of God was there to bring comfort to his servant (cf. 124:1-5; 139:23).

The final confession, found in verses 20-22, is a pregnant testimony to God's compassionate comfort. The psalmist again rhetorically poses the question as to whether the reign of evildoers and their unjust laws can coexist with God's reign (v. 20). In their unrighteous leadership and legislation, "they band together against the life of the righteous and condemn the innocent to death" (v. 21). Through the darkness of night, it appears as if the oppressors were in power and their mischief was the law of the land (cf. Eccl 4:1). And from all appearances, evil was going to win the day as well.

When the sun rises, however, a different picture emerges. The conjunction *but* at the beginning of verse 22 calls attention to the one who ultimately will win and come to the rescue of his children. Using metaphors consistent with David's songs, the psalmist celebrates something that's even better than the vindication God will bring for his own and the vengeance he will levy on their enemies. God proves himself to be a superior ally over any assault the enemy can muster, and that's a huge comfort to this poet.

Even though he had asked, "How long?" (v. 3), and God's silence seemed to indicate that he didn't care, the unwavering answer to the psalmist's question in verse 16 is that God won't allow evil to have the upper hand for very long. I love the way VanGemeren summarizes the conclusion of this psalm:

> The closure of the psalm restores harmony to an otherwise disturbing psalm. The psalmist has posed many questions and has asked God to respond by bringing in the fullness of his kingdom. In these verses the psalmist calls on the godly to cast their lot with his God, who alone is the fortress of his people and to whom alone belongs vindication. (VanGemeren, *Psalms*, 616)

Although the psalmist prays for vindication, he trusts the Lord to orchestrate the events and timing of his kingdom, including the vindication of his servants and his vengeance on every manifestation of evil. While the wicked seem to go unopposed for a season and their rule appears to be the norm, God is sovereignly in control of it all. Who could ask for a greater comfort than this?

The conclusion of this psalm leaves believers with several clear applications. One, we should find great comfort in him who is our stronghold and the rock of our protection (v. 22), who sovereignly controls the events of our lives, and who will vindicate our suffering in his time. Two, we should do everything in our power to comfort one another in the midst of suffering. God—in Christ—has acted to provide comfort for his suffering children through the gospel, and he uses us as instruments to administer that comfort. In one of the most beautiful passages in the New Testament, Paul writes,

> Blessed be the God and Father of our Lord Jesus Christ, the Father of mercies and the God of all comfort. He comforts us in all our affliction, so that we may be able to comfort those who are in any kind of affliction, through the comfort we ourselves receive from God. For just as the sufferings of Christ overflow to us, so also through Christ our comfort overflows. If we are afflicted, it is for your comfort and salvation. If we are comforted, it is for your comfort, which produces in you patient endurance of the same sufferings that we suffer. And our hope for you is firm, because we know that as you share in the sufferings, so you will also share in the comfort. (2 Cor 1:3-7)

Three, we should ask God to vindicate our suffering by exercising vengeance on our enemies. Christians can and should appeal to God to act with vengeance on those who assault the children for whom he cares. Four, we should leave the matter in the hands of the God of vengeance and Judge of the earth. He will repay the opponents of the gospel and wipe them out in his time (v. 23).

Conclusion

My observation of the contemporary Hollywood renditions of all the comic book heroes I grew up with certainly is limited. However, it seems to me that the writers—and the culture they reflect—have a difficult time embracing good guys who are distinctively good. It appears we now have to bring these superheroes down to a level that is more relatable to our own depravity. Consequently, we pit Batman against Superman, we magnify dissension among the ranks of the Avengers, and we exploit and even magnify the weakness in every one of our heroes. The lines between good and evil and right and wrong seem to be much blurrier than they used to be. When it comes to God's vengeance against those who bully Christians and their gospel, however, the lines won't be blurry. He will show no weakness, and there will be no question about who's in the right. God will win the day, so his children can and should pray with confidence to that end.

Reflect and Discuss

1. Is it godly to pray for God's enemies to get "what they deserve"? Is this consistent with God's character?

2. How do we, as followers of Christ, reconcile this request of the psalmist with the command in the New Testament to love our enemies?
3. The psalmist has no qualms about appealing to God's character in prayer. Do you claim God's character in your prayer life? How does speaking and meditating on God's character in prayer change our prayer life?
4. The psalmist has, in his mind, a valid complaint—that God is late in his vindication of his people. Where can we find both peace and strength when God seems to delay his justice in our lives?
5. How does God's sovereignty over creation give confidence to our prayers?
6. The psalmist in verse 19 states, "Your comfort brings me joy." How should we then view trouble in our lives? Should difficult circumstances drive us to find our hope in God? How should we let them drive us to prayer?
7. Verse 11 reminds us of God's complete and unhindered knowledge of the thoughts of man. How does this comfort us? How does this truth also compel us to live holy lives before him?
8. Verse 12 cites the promise of God to give rest to his people. Does he give rest to our earthly lives or eternal lives? In Christ, how so?
9. The psalmist has absolute certainty that God will fulfill his promise to not abandon his people. How was this promise eternally solidified in Christ?
10. Consider verse 15. How does God's administration of justice spur us on to follow holiness?

Behold His Glory

PSALM 95

Main Idea: In order to glorify God in our worship, we must recognize him for who he is and respond appropriately.

I. **We Need to Remember Whom We're Worshiping.**
   A. He is the self-existent Lord over all.
   B. He is the supreme King above all.
   C. He is the Creator of the universe.
   D. He is the Owner of the universe.
   E. He is the Maker who forms and sustains us.
   F. He is the Shepherd who loves and leads us.
   G. He is the Rock who saves and delivers us.
II. **We Need to Realize How We Worship.**
   A. We sing and shout to him.
   B. We bow down and kneel before him.
   C. We thank him for all he does and praise him for who he is.
   D. We listen to him humbly.
   E. We obey him immediately.
   F. We rest in him completely.
   G. We rejoice in him wholeheartedly.

When God delivered his people out of slavery in Egypt, he did it for a reason. He told Moses to say to Pharaoh, "Let my people go, so that they may hold a festival for me in the wilderness" (Exod 5:1). God freed his people so they could worship him.

God delivered his people out of slavery in Egypt, and he guided them to Mount Sinai, where they gathered for worship before God. Imagine this scene in Exodus 19:16-20.

> On the third day, when morning came, there was thunder and lightning, a thick cloud on the mountain, and a very loud trumpet sound, so that all the people in the camp shuddered. Then Moses brought the people out of the camp to meet God, and they stood at the foot of the mountain. Mount Sinai was completely enveloped in smoke because the LORD came down on it in fire. Its smoke went up like the

> *smoke of a furnace, and the whole mountain shook violently. As the*
> *sound of the trumpet grew louder and louder, Moses spoke and God*
> *answered him in the thunder.*
>
> *The LORD came down on Mount Sinai at the top of the mountain.*
> *Then the LORD summoned Moses to the top of the mountain, and he*
> *went up.*

Right after this, God gave his people the Ten Commandments and the rest of his instruction. What happened there would become a pattern throughout the Old Testament. While it was not always at Mount Sinai and not always in this exact kind of scene, it did serve as a pattern for God's people gathering regularly to worship God and hear his Word. In a sense this is what it meant to be a member of God's people—to have this privilege of standing in the great assembly before God.

In Nehemiah 8 the people of God gathered and stood for hours, worshiping and listening to God's Word. With their hands raised, they cried out, "Amen, Amen!" and they bowed down with "their faces to the ground" (Neh 8:6). God's people gathered to behold his glory and hear his Word.

When you get to the New Testament, the word for "church" (Gk *ekklesia*) literally means "assembly." The church is the gathering of God's people. Thus, we read the author of Hebrews encouraging those who were not assembling together in the church (and probably growing lukewarm in their faith as a result) not to neglect this important means of grace (Heb 10:24-25). His description of the church's gathering has echoes of the scene mentioned above.

> *For you have not come to what could be touched, to a blazing fire, to*
> *darkness, gloom, and storm, to the blast of a trumpet, and the sound*
> *of words. Those who heard it begged that not another word be spoken*
> *to them, for they could not bear what was commanded: If even an*
> *animal touches the mountain, it must be stoned. The appearance*
> *was so terrifying that Moses said, I am trembling with fear. Instead,*
> *you have come to Mount Zion, to the city of the living God (the*
> *heavenly Jerusalem), to myriads of angels, a festive gathering, to the*
> *assembly of the firstborn whose names have been written in heaven,*
> *to a Judge, who is God of all, to the spirits of righteous people made*
> *perfect, and to Jesus, the mediator of a new covenant, and to the*
> *sprinkled blood, which says better things than the blood of Abel.*
> (Heb 12:18-24)

The author of Hebrews reminds us that we are not coming to an earthly mountain like Israel did in the Old Testament. No, we are coming to something greater, for we are joining with a heavenly assembly filled with throngs of angels and saints throughout the ages, and together we are giving glory to God and hearing him speak—not through thunder but through his Word.

We tend to miss the significance of the church's gathering. We come into the gathering casually because, well, this is what we do on Sundays. It doesn't even cross our minds how awesome, mind-boggling, breathtaking, and distinct this is compared to anything else we do throughout the week. When we come together, we are joining in what God's people have done ever since Mount Sinai: we are gathering to behold the glory of God. We are joining with angels in heaven and saints throughout the ages to sing God's praise, to stand in awe of him, and to listen to God speak! This is why John Stott said, "True worship is the highest and noblest activity of which man, by the grace of God, is capable" (*Christ the Conversationalist*, 160, as cited in Boice, *Psalms*, vol. 2, 775).

We should not miss the wonder and the weight of what we're doing. More specifically, we shouldn't miss the wonder and the weight of whom we're worshiping.

> In my opinion, the great single need of the moment is that lighthearted superficial religionists be struck down with a vision of God high and lifted up, with his train filling the temple. The holy art of worship seems to have passed away like the Shekinah glory from the tabernacle. As a result, we are left to our own devices and forced to make up the lack of spontaneous worship by bringing in countless cheap and tawdry activities to hold the attention of the church people. (Tozer, *Tozer on Worship and Entertainment*, 27)

It is not necessary for us to bring in "countless cheap and tawdry activities" to hold the church's attention. The glory of God is more than sufficient to hold our attention, that is, *if* we'll just realize who he is. We desperately need to rediscover the wonder and the weight of worship before God, and I know of no better psalm that expresses that than Psalm 95.

For centuries, going all the way back to Israel's experience in the Old Testament, Psalm 95 has been used among God's people as a call to worship. The first half of Psalm 95 (vv. 1-7) depicts the wonder of worship, while the second half of the psalm (vv. 8-11) depicts the weight (or the seriousness) of worship.

We Need to Remember Whom We're Worshiping

We are tempted to forget whom we are worshiping, though not intentionally. For instance, when someone prays in corporate worship, we close our eyes, but then, before we know it, our minds can start to wander. Within seconds we are thinking about all kinds of other things. If we're not careful, prayer can become a perfunctory exercise that takes place in worship. Meanwhile, you can imagine all of heaven shouting, "Do you realize *whom* you're talking to? Do you realize the wonder and the weight of what you're doing? You're talking to *God!*"

Stop to consider that, even with thousands or even millions of people praying to God at the same time, he is listening to you! Sure, he's upholding Mars at the same time, in addition to trillions of stars that he knows by name and 7.2 billion people on the planet that he's sustaining right now, but you have *God's attention.* So don't let your mind wander!

Psalm 95 lifts our eyes to the wonder of the one we worship. Just think about all the different descriptions of God in this psalm:

He Is the Self-Existent Lord over All

In verse 1 "Lord" is in small capital letters. That's a translation of the Hebrew name for God, *Yahweh*, which is how God revealed himself to Moses in Exodus 3. It means "I AM," which may include a reference to God's self-existence, that is, the reality that God exists, has always existed, and will always exist. The classic children's question, "Who made God?" has one answer: "No one made him." God has always been, and God will always be. We gather to worship before the self-existent Lord over all.

He Is the Supreme King above All

In verse 3 God is the capital "K" King who reigns over all the lowercase "k" kings in the world. He rules them as the supreme King above all.

He Is the Creator of the Universe

Verses 4-5 contain wonderful imagery. The world is hand-shaped and handheld by God.

He Is the Owner of the Universe

God is not only the Creator of the universe but also its Owner. It all belongs to him, including the mountains, the seas, and the land. We think we own possessions and property, but ultimately God alone owns it all.

He Is the Maker Who Forms and Sustains Us

The psalmist gets more personal in verse 6. The psalmist is in awe not just by how God has made everything in the universe but that God has made him. We assemble before the God who formed our hands, our feet, our legs, and our arms. He is the one who is causing our lungs to breathe right now.

He Is the Shepherd Who Loves and Leads Us

According to verse 7, *this* God, the self-existent Lord over all and supreme King above all, is our Shepherd, and we are his sheep! He is protecting us and providing for us and caring for us. But this leads to a question: How is this possible given that we are sinners who have rebelled against God and run away from him in all of his holiness? How can we be sheep in his pasture? That question leads us back to the first verse.

He Is the Rock Who Saves and Delivers Us

We're reminded of God saving his people from slavery in the book of Exodus so that they could worship him in freedom. That's exactly what has happened in the life of every follower of Jesus. Our worship gatherings are full of men and women who were slaves to sin, separated from God, and destined to pay the penalty for sin—eternal death. But God in his mercy made a way for us to be saved from our sin.

Amazingly, the God referred to in Psalm 95 has come to us in the person of Jesus Christ. John's Gospel introduces Jesus as God in the flesh (John 1:14). Then in John 8:58 Jesus echoes God's revelation of himself in Exodus 3, saying, "Truly I tell you, before Abraham was, *I am*" (emphasis added). John writes later in Revelation 19:16 that Jesus is the supreme King above all, for written on his robe and on his thigh is the name, "King of Kings and Lord of Lords." Colossians 1:16-17 says Jesus is the Creator and owner of the universe: "All things have been created through him and for him"; and Jesus is the one who forms and sustains us: "By him all things hold together." Jesus is the "good shepherd" who has laid down his life for us his sheep (John 10:11). Indeed, Jesus is the rock of our salvation, for he has died on the cross for our sin and risen from the grave in victory over sin so that you and I can have the privilege of knowing and worshiping God.

We Need to Realize How We Worship

Once we get a glimpse of whom we worship in Psalm 95, the question becomes, How do we respond to this God?

We Sing and Shout to Him

Verses 1-2 talk about making a lot of noise in worship, which we see in other psalms as well. Psalm 66 begins, "Let the whole earth shout joyfully to God!" Psalm 47:1 says to "shout to God with a jubilant cry." This picture of shouting is like a triumphant war cry that strengthens an army and strikes fear in the enemy. Shouting like this needs to be a part of our worship.[6]

Throughout the first seven verses the phrase *let us* is emphasized. Worship is not a spectator sport; this is a participant's activity. When those leading the congregation in musical worship are up on a stage while you're in a seat, it's so easy to think you're a spectator. That perspective misses the whole point of worship because there are no spectators. God is the audience, and those who lead up front, including pastors, are participants. *We* come together, and *we* sing and shout.

We Bow Down and Kneel before Him

The Hebrew word for "worship" literally means to prostrate oneself. This is a biblical response to God. During times of spiritual awakening in the past, it was common for people, in the middle of singing or in the middle of the sermon, suddenly to come down to the front and just kneel before God in worship. I would even say that if we really realize whom we're worshiping, we will be compelled to do this at points. This kind of response is entirely appropriate in private worship as well. May none of us be so prideful that we wouldn't bow down and kneel before God.

---

[6] For more on the role of shouting in corporate worship, see the comments on Psalm 66:1.

We Thank Him for All He Does and Praise Him for Who He Is

According to verse 2, there's praise *and* thanksgiving in this psalm, and both are involved in worship. We exalt God for his attributes, and we thank God for his actions—in history, around the world, and in our lives.

We Listen to Him Humbly

Many people stop part way through verse 7, but we can actually miss the whole point if we stop there. Worship doesn't only involve our singing and shouting and speaking to God. Worship also involves God's speaking to us, like thunder from heaven, which makes corporate worship even more breathtaking.

Worship involves hearing the voice of God, which is why the proclamation of Scripture is such a large portion of the weekly worship gathering. We worship God by opening up his Word and listening to him. We should bring our Bibles to corporate worship because Scripture is the Word of God, and this is how God—the self-existent Lord over all, supreme King above all, the Creator and owner of the universe—speaks to us.

We Obey Him Immediately

Psalm 95 closes with a weighty warning (vv. 8-11). This is a warning of God's wrath on those who claim to worship him while ignoring his Word. This is what happened at Meribah and Massah: God's people complained and quarreled before him (Exod 17:1-7). They ultimately disobeyed him by not trusting him. An entire generation of God's people were left to wander in the wilderness until they died. They hardened their hearts toward God.

Based on Psalm 95, Hebrews 3–4 urges Christians not to harden their hearts toward God and his Word. We are to have soft hearts that hear God's Word humbly and obey it immediately. We can come into the church's weekly gathering, sing and shout, and even bow and kneel; but if, when it comes to God's Word, we either don't hear it or harden our hearts to it by living however we want, we will miss the point of worship.

It is extremely serious to open up the Word of God and hear what he says. We will be accountable before God for our response. We don't want to be found to be mocking God if we sing some songs, bow our heads for some prayers, and then walk out ignoring God's Word. That kind of response, according to Psalm 95, is a recipe for wrath. This is similar to what Jesus himself warned against in Matthew 15:8-9: "This people honors me with their lips, but their heart is far from me. They worship me in vain."

I think of the number of people who grow up in the church, attending week after week, going through the motions, but their hearts are far from God. There are kids who attend worship to please their parents and husbands who attend worship to appease their wives (or vice versa). Based on the Word of God, it is dangerous to be cold toward God in worship—eternally dangerous.

We Rest in Him Completely

In the Old Testament God's rest was the promised land, an abundant land flowing with milk and honey that he promised to Israel. But an entire generation missed it because they disobeyed God's Word. When you turn to the New Testament, and Hebrews 3–4 in particular, the rest represented by the Old Testament promised land becomes symbolic for the rest that's found in following Jesus. We have abundant life now and abundant life for all of eternity. Hearing and obeying God's Word, then, is the path to life, to rest in God. When we truly worship, it brings glory to God, *and* it is good for us.

We Rejoice in Him Wholeheartedly

Don't miss the logic of heaven in this psalm. We shout "joyfully to the LORD" (v. 1) and "enter his presence with thanksgiving" (v. 2) *because* "the LORD is a great God, a great King above all gods. . . . He is our God, and we are the people of his pasture, the sheep under his care" (vv. 3,7). In other words, we rejoice in God because he is supreme! And when you exalt his supremacy, you will experience his satisfaction.

Do you want to experience satisfaction in your life? I'm talking about a joy that's deeper, higher, and greater than anything money can buy, a joy that supersedes circumstances and cannot be taken away from you. It's a joy that endures through sorrow and suffering. If you want this kind of joy in your life, then, according to Psalm 95, worship God!

Reflect and Discuss

1. What's wrong with a casual, lighthearted approach to worshiping God?

2. How would you respond to someone who said worship should be filled with truth rather than emotion?
3. How does our view of God affect the way we worship?
4. What are some truths about God that should evoke praise and awe in us?
5. According to Psalm 95, what are some appropriate ways to respond to God in worship?
6. What role should Scripture play in our worship? Why is this so important?
7. Why is it dangerous to observe worship with a heart that's cold and unbelieving toward God?
8. How is our worship related to our obedience?
9. God promised Israel "rest" in the promised land. What is the "rest" that God offers to his people today?
10. What are some specific ways you can better prepare your mind and heart to worship God weekly with your local church?

Sing His Praise among the Nations

PSALM 96

Main Idea: To see the glory of God is to respond in joyful worship and witness.

I.   A Singing People (96:1-3)
II. A Glorious God (96:4-6)
III. A Global Summons (96:7-13)

This psalm was composed for a specific event in the Old Testament. We find this psalm back in 1 Chronicles 16 as the ark of the covenant was being transported to the city of Jerusalem. It was a huge moment of celebration because it represented God's coming to Jerusalem to rule and reign. This was not a somber occasion. Trumpets, harps, and lyres were cranked up full volume. People were singing and dancing. This is the moment King David danced so hard his wife was embarrassed.

This psalm points forward as well as backward: backward to the celebration as the ark approached the city of God and forward to the coming reign of Jesus Christ over creation.

I graduated from high school in 1993, and certain things about that year stand out. The TV show *Cheers* ended its eleven-year run. Michael Jordan retired from the NBA. Hollywood generated films from the timelessly significant (*Schindler's List*) to the shamelessly silly (*Robin Hood: Men in Tights*). Bill Clinton became the forty-second president of the United States. Perhaps you remember watching scenes from the siege of the Branch Davidian compound in Waco, Texas. Baseball fans may remember Joe Carter winning the World Series for the Toronto Blue Jays with a three-run homer in game six.

In the Christian corner of the world, 1993 was also the year John Piper wrote a little book called *Let the Nations Be Glad!* in which he said this:

> Missions is not the ultimate goal of the church. Worship is.
> Missions exists because worship doesn't. Worship is ultimate,
> not missions, because God is ultimate, not man. When this age
> is over, and the countless millions of the redeemed fall on their

faces before the throne of God, missions will be no more. . . .
Worship, therefore, is the fuel and goal of missions. It's the
goal of missions because in missions we simply aim to bring the
nations into the white-hot enjoyment of God's glory. (17)

That was a good year indeed. What a truth to recapture! That's
Psalm 96 in one sentence: worship is the fuel and goal of missions. Our
passage unfolds in three stages.

A Singing People
PSALM 96:1-3

Just think about the physical real estate the book of Psalms takes up.
Right in the middle of your Bible is a giant, thirty-thousand-word hym-
nal. It's three times longer than Mark's Gospel, three times longer than
Revelation, four times longer than Romans.

The Scriptures are inspired by God (2 Tim 3:16). Even the balance
of literary styles we have in the Bible came together under God's direction. There are more than five hundred references to singing and more
than one hundred direct commands to sing. So why so much singing?

In Psalm 96 God commands his people to sing. It compels us to
sing to the Lord "a new song." This doesn't mean we shouldn't sing old
songs. The point is it's not enough to just remember the past. Many
psalms point back to God's mighty acts of redemption in history—the
exodus, for example, where God broke the chains of Israel's oppressors.
God instituted Passover so Israel would never forget what he did for
them. Then this same God says to his people in Psalms 33, 40, 96, 98,
144, and 149 to sing new songs. Why? Because God's mercies aren't all
centuries old. "They are new every morning" (Lam 3:23).

Many vital signs are given in Scripture to evaluate the condition of
the church of Jesus Christ. One you might not have considered before
is, Are new songs being written and sung? New mercies call for new
music. We are blessed in our time to have so many songwriters who manifest a love for and firm grasp of the Scriptures—all using their musical
gifts to give the church modern hymns by which believers today may
sing ourselves deeper into the hope of the gospel.

Singing here isn't just singing. Verse 2 expounds, "Sing to the Lord,
bless his name; proclaim his salvation from day to day." In the LXX the
Greek word translated "proclaim" is where we get our word *evangelize*.

Publish it! Make known his salvation! In other words, spreading the gospel is a *means* by which we praise God.

Think about this in marriage, for example. I can praise my wife in two ways: I can tell *her* she's awesome, or I can tell *you* she's awesome. Both praise her. The same is true with God. We sing to *him,* and this is praise. We proclaim his salvation to the *nations,* and this is praise. This idea of calling the nations/outsiders/Gentiles to worship comes up in verses 1, 2, 3, 7, and 10. There is a missionary heartbeat here.

There's a sense in which "sing" can be a metaphor for praising God in nonmusical ways, but it's really important not to skip over the fact that the call to sing isn't *just* a metaphor. It's a call to sing, literally, which leads us to the next point.

Not only are we commanded to sing, three times in the space of two verses, but the command goes on to include a word about who is listening. We are singing "to the LORD" (v. 2). God is the audience as we sing.

Our singing matters for all kinds of reasons—if for no other reason than he commands his people to sing, and since he has captured our hearts and our affections, we delight to do this. However, as it relates to verse 2, do we sing in the awareness that God is listening? It's so easy to approach corporate musical worship thoughtlessly. We underestimate the privilege and honor it is to have a God who actually delights to hear his people sing. His favorite instruments in the world are the collected voices of his singing people. He never gets tired of it. The great apologist G. K. Chesterton expressed this beautifully:

> Because children have abounding vitality . . . they want things repeated and unchanged. They always say, "Do it again"; and the grown-up person does it again until he is nearly dead. For grown-up people are not strong enough to exult in monotony. But perhaps God is strong enough to exult in monotony.
>
> It is possible that God says every morning, "Do it again" to the sun; and every evening, "Do it again" to the moon. It may not be automatic necessity that makes all daisies alike; it may be that God makes every daisy separately, but has never got tired of making them. (*Orthodoxy,* 61)

He listens and he delights. They say it's hard to make a billionaire smile. Why? Because the billionaire has seen better. Now we're talking about God! It's not like God doesn't have better art at his disposal. He put stars into places science won't see for another thousand years. He has art, for now tucked in cosmic closets, that would blow our minds. Yet he delights in our singing!

A Glorious God
PSALM 96:4-6

This psalm doesn't just tell us to sing; it gives us a reason.

God Is the Reason We Sing

The only thing that adequately explains the worship of the church is the glory of her God. "The Lord is great and is highly praised" (v. 4). A great God is to be greatly praised. The praise we offer is to be proportionate to the greatness of the God we praise. You might say, "That's impossible." Of course it is. However, the point is that God's people don't offer half-hearted worship. No, it's heart, soul, mind, strength worship. Lips, life, voice, hands, feet. All his! Nothing held back.

My dad planted a church in New Orleans, and the music was soulful. My mom played the Hammond B3 organ, and she sang riffs into the open spaces of the song. We sang a song growing up; it was so simple, but it was drawn straight from Scripture. We'd clap our hands on beats two and four and sing, "He Has Made Me Glad." I would look around and watch those believers, and here's what I was learning even as a child: The Lord is great and is highly praised! Listen, the nations aren't drawn to praise God if his own people look like they're doing *chores*. I wonder whether unbelievers who happen to come into the gathering of God's people ever leave thinking, *God seemed real! Those people sang as if God was giving them hope—as if God were holding them up, supplying them with strength.*

Every Rival God Leaves Us Empty

That's the reminder of verse 5. "All the gods of the peoples are idols." In the original Hebrew it's a play on words. All the *elohim* of the people are *elilim. Elohim* is the word for "God." *Elilim* is the word for "nothing." In other words, what they treat as a god really has no power, no life. This means you can buy all the cars and houses you ever dreamed of. You can get the trophy spouse and the corner office. You can wrap your fingers around every joy held out by this world, but you'll never know rest a day in this world without Christ. Every trinket, self-help solution, or man-made religion is just one more in an endless line of broken cisterns that hold no water (Jer 2:13). Meanwhile, the living God is in verse 6. All the beauty your soul longs for isn't on the next website. If only we knew where true strength and beauty are found. The *Lord* is the strength of his people. Jesus gives beauty for ashes. Jesus makes all things new. That's why we sing the way we do. The one explanation for the singing of the church is the greatness and strength and beauty of our God.

A Global Summons
PSALM 96:7-13

We call the nations to worship. Think about the work of the church. Why do we send out missionaries, including to places that are hostile to Christian witness, to closed countries where it's illegal to convert to Christianity? We do it because verse 3 commands the people of God to "declare his glory among the nations." It's a global invocation, a global call to worship.

I remember the first time I heard the Muslim call to prayer in the horn of Africa. Suddenly a voice was singing over a loud speaker, and you heard it all over the city at the appointed hours. Unless you've learned the language, you can't tell what they're singing. Here's what's being broadcast all over the city:

God is the greatest!
I bear witness that there is none worthy of worship except
  God.
I bear witness that Mohammed is the messenger of God.
Hasten to prayer.
Hasten to security.
God is the greatest!
There is no god but Allah.

I was sitting on the floor in the home of a gracious Muslim family. We were eating and talking. Then came the call to worship. The men stood and excused themselves to go and pray. They heard the call and answered. In our passage there is a wider call. Verses 7-12 are a call to worship that rings out over the whole cosmos.

As we go with the gospel, we go with verse 10 beating in our hearts. We go to say among the nations, "The LORD reigns!" To declare that Jesus Christ is Lord. To announce that the one and only Savior has come. He lived the life we could not live. He died the death we deserved to die. He rose and conquered the enemy that we could never conquer. This King now reigns over the nations. This King will return to judge the world in righteousness. But whoever trusts him *now*, whoever calls on the name of the Lord, shall be saved. This salvation is gloriously comprehensive: sins forgiven, conscience cleansed, death defeated, adopted into his forever family, and destined for pleasures evermore at his right hand.

As local churches committed to the Great Commission, our praying, giving, going, and sending are all aimed at one thing: global worship! We're saying, "Ascribe to the Lord, you nations, you families of the peoples. You Hui. You Baloch. Kurds. Egyptians. Come sing a new song to the Lord. Let the whole earth sing to the Lord!" And we do this in the confidence that our labor will not be in vain. We call the nations to worship, knowing the nations will join in the singing.

What happens when the nations hear and turn from idols to ascribe glory to the one true and living God? The answer is in verses 11-12. The heavens are glad. The earth rejoices. The sea resounds. The fields celebrate. The trees shout for joy. What beautiful imagery! The gospel leaves joy in its wake. The Great Commission is the awesome prospect of good news spreading around the world. It's a joy project. It's gladness in tennis shoes, joy on the run.

We, God's image bearers, were created for song. Our voices were broken at the fall, but many places in Scripture remind us that the world is waiting for the grand finale of history. Isaiah prophesied that God's people would sing again. Isaiah 51 points to the finale of God's redemptive story, when his redeemed exiles come home: "And the ransomed of the Lord will return and come to Zion with singing, crowned with unending joy. Joy and gladness will overtake them, and sorrow and sighing will flee" (Isa 51:11).

Christians are a singing people. We always have been, and we always will be. Christian, when God saved you, he retuned your voice. He put a new song in your mouth. However, we are not called to sing alone. We are called to sing in a way that invites others to join in the song. And we know the nations will join in the singing because we happen to have a window into the future. If you ever wonder what will become of the nations that are still shrouded in darkness, without the light of the gospel, Revelation 5 says, "I'm glad you asked."

> *When he took the scroll, the four living creatures and the twenty-four elders fell down before the Lamb. Each one had a harp and golden*

bowls filled with incense, which are the prayers of the saints. And they sang a new song:

You are worthy to take the scroll and to open its seals, because you were slaughtered, and you purchased people for God by your blood from every tribe and language and people and nation. You made them a kingdom and priests to our God, and they will reign on the earth.

Then I looked and heard the voice of many angels around the throne, and also of the living creatures and of the elders. Their number was countless thousands, plus thousands of thousands. They said with a loud voice,

Worthy is the Lamb who was slaughtered to receive power and riches and wisdom and strength and honor and glory and blessing!

I heard every creature in heaven, on earth, under the earth, on the sea, and everything in them say,

Blessing and honor and glory and power be to the one seated on the throne, and to the Lamb, forever and ever!

The four living creatures said, "Amen," and the elders fell down and worshiped. (Rev 5:8-14)

Missions exists because worship doesn't. When this age is over and the countless millions of the redeemed fall on their faces before the throne of God, missions will be no more. (Piper, *Let the Nations Be Glad,* 17)

Missions exists because worship doesn't. What kind of church do we want to be? We can live for passing pleasures, or we can spread eternal joy. Christian friend, salvation has retuned your voice. Here's God's call on your newfound voice. Sing. Sing a new song. Sing and bless his name. Sing and tell his salvation. Sing and declare his glory among the nations. Sing for he is great and greatly to be praised.

Reflect and Discuss

1. Have you reflected personally on the many commands in Scripture to sing? How are you answering this call both in your personal life and as a member of the local church?

2. How can we demonstrate a passion for God's glory among the nations? What does that look like practically in your life? In your local church?

3. Think about the connection between joy and global missions. What happens if the Christian loses sight of that and is driven more by duty than delight?

4. When it comes to gathered worship in the local church, are you leaning forward? Are there any words of encouragement that might refresh the hearts of worship leaders and ministers in your church?

5. What are the worthless idols that tempt you the most? When you get your eyes off of Jesus, where are you most inclined to set your hopes? How can you fight this temptation?

6. In what ways are you pursuing a greater knowledge of God? How do you think the spiritual disciplines (prayer, Scripture, local church, evangelism) play a part in the way we see God and the way we live?

God's Grand Entrance

PSALM 97

Main Idea: Believers should live righteously in joyful anticipation of the coming reign of the one true God.

I. **The Revelation of God's Reign (97:1-5)**
II. **The Distinction of God's Reign (97:6-9)**
III. **The Anticipation of God's Reign (97:10-12)**

I can't wait for Jesus to get back. It's going to be awesome! When God ushers in his eternal kingdom, evil will be obliterated and good will win the day. And it's going to be a glorious celebration:

> *After this I heard something like the loud voice of a vast multitude in heaven, saying,*
> *Hallelujah! Salvation, glory, and power belong to our God, because his judgments are true and righteous, because he has judged the notorious prostitute who corrupted the earth with her sexual immorality; and he has avenged the blood of his servants that was on her hands.*
> *A second time they said, Hallelujah! Her smoke ascends forever and ever!*
> *Then the twenty-four elders and the four living creatures fell down and worshiped God, who is seated on the throne, saying, Amen! Hallelujah!*
> *A voice came from the throne, saying, Praise our God, all his servants, and the ones who fear him, both small and great!*
> (Rev 19:1-5)

What John heard and saw in his vision on the island of Patmos causes me to sit up on the edge of my seat, look toward the eastern sky, and join him in praying, "Come, Lord Jesus!"

That's what Psalm 97 is about—the revelation and anticipation of the coming reign of God. While the psalms on either side of it reflect the global gladness that will be experienced by God's people everywhere when he comes, this song incorporates the additional reality of the judgment of his enemies and those who tried to steal his glory. When Jesus comes back to set up his kingdom, his followers can expect both. And when it's time for that simultaneous joy and judgment to happen, everybody will know it. Jesus isn't going to slip in by stealth, flying under the radar. He's going to make a grand entrance! Consider the psalmist's proclamation of the appearance of this universal reign, a reign that compels his followers to holy living as we wait.

The Revelation of God's Reign
PSALM 97:1-5

The psalm begins with a positive declaration, "The LORD reigns!" (cf. Pss 93:1; 96:10; 99:1), an assertion that's characteristic of the companion songs (see Pss 93–100). In these first five verses God is revealed as the King of the universe, and his emergence is anything but routine. The extent of this administration isn't confined to Israel but instead reaches to "the many coasts and islands" (cf. Ps 72:10; Isa 41:1,5; 42:4,10; Jer 31:10; Ezek 27:10; Zeph 2:11) across the earth (cf. Isa 49:13). So the psalmist calls for the only appropriate response to such a grand rule: "Let the earth rejoice . . . [and] be glad!" This revelation of God's rule demands that the entire planet throw a party!

This initial celebratory declaration of God's universal reign is followed by a sobering catalog of theophanies in verses 2-5 (cf. 18:7-11; Isa 6:4; Ezek 1:4-28; Nah 1:5; Hab 3:3-15). The psalmist provides a list of terrifying and awe-inspiring pictures of God condescending into historical and physical existence through nature. The litany takes its cue from similar manifestations at Sinai (Exod 19:16-18; Deut 4:11,22) and in the Song of Deborah (Judg 5:5), and it puts the response to the revelation of God's rule in proper perspective.

In verse 2 this Lord over the universe sits on a throne of "clouds and total darkness," wielding his unapproachable "righteousness and justice." He finally will make godliness be the order of the day on the earth. The consuming "fire" of his holiness shoots out like arrows in verse 3 (cf. 18:8-14; 50:3; 68:2; 77:17; 106:18; 144:6; Hab 3:11; Heb 12:29), devouring his enemies. In verse 4 the power and brightness of his appearance are so pronounced that he "lights up the world" like "lightning" that illuminates the night sky (cf. Ps 77:18), and "the earth sees and trembles" like an earthquake (cf. Ps 77:16; Hab 3:10). Finally, in verse 5 the Lord's terrible presence makes "the mountains melt like wax" (cf. Mic 1:4;

Nah 1:5). There's no escape from his reign, which will cause even the time-tested landmarks and most secure refuges to dissolve into oblivion. The metaphors in these verses are reminiscent of those used by the prophets to describe the awesome nature of the coming day of the Lord (e.g., Joel 2:2; Zeph 1:15). Before his death our Lord Jesus Christ used similar terms to describe his return:

> Immediately after the distress of those days, the sun will be darkened, and the moon will not shed its light; the stars will fall from the sky, and the powers of the heavens will be shaken. Then the sign of the Son of Man will appear in the sky, and then all the peoples of the earth will mourn; and they will see the Son of Man coming on the clouds of heaven with power and great glory. He will send out his angels with a loud trumpet, and they will gather his elect from the four winds, from one end of the sky to the other. (Matt 24:29-31)

After Jesus's ascension back to heaven, Peter—quoting from Joel 2:30-31 on the day of Pentecost—offers God's commentary on the era of Christ's coming:

> "I will display wonders in the heaven above and signs on the earth below: blood and fire and a cloud of smoke. The sun will be turned to darkness and the moon to blood before the great and glorious day of the Lord comes." (Acts 2:19-20)

Later, in his second letter, he writes of this day of God: "Because of that day, the heavens will be dissolved with fire and the elements will melt with heat. But based on his promise, we wait for new heavens and a new earth, where righteousness dwells" (2 Pet 3:12-13).

This prophesied coming reign of the God of the universe will find its ultimate fulfillment in the return of Jesus Christ, who will consume this sin-diseased earth and usher in his eternal kingdom. His reign will be celebrated in like fashion as Psalm 97:1-5 at his glorious wedding:

> Then I heard something like the voice of a vast multitude, like the sound of cascading waters, and like the rumbling of loud thunder, saying,
> Hallelujah, because our Lord God, the Almighty, reigns! Let us be glad, rejoice, and give him glory, because the marriage of the Lamb has come, and his bride has prepared herself. She was given fine linen to wear, bright and pure. For the fine linen represents the righteous acts of the saints. (Rev 19:6-8)

The reign of God over the whole of creation will culminate with the marriage of Jesus Christ to his glorious bride, the church!

The Distinction of God's Reign

PSALM 97:6-9

The next four verses simply show the distinctive nature of God's reign that separates it from all other self-proclaimed regimes. At the heart of this uniqueness is the fact that he's the only true god in the universe. Notice the all-inclusive expressions that set him apart. The psalmist says, "All who serve carved images, those who boast in idols, will be put to shame" (v. 7). It's not just *some* worshipers of false gods who will recognize his sole deity but *all* of them; so the psalmist concludes that there remains only one appropriate response: "All the gods must worship him." This line in the Septuagint could indicate a reference to supernatural beings or angels. Whether futile gods or angelic beings, mankind tends to exalt both above the one true God. This call to homage encompasses both.

This comprehensive and exclusive nature is further seen in the scope of God's reign. This is not just a regional revelation or selective supremacy (v. 9). He's not just *high*, but he's *most high*. He's *exalted* over the whole planet, the entire population, and all of their fabricated deities! Furthermore, this distinctive nature of his reign as the one true god will be evident to everyone. Reflecting back on the phenomenological entrance described in verses 1-5, the psalmist notes that a global audience watches in awe as his reign is supernaturally revealed (v. 6; cf. Isa 40:5). When the dust settles, there won't be any doubt in anybody's mind who's left standing and in charge.

Included in this audience are the people to whom God first made himself known: Israel (v. 8). Israel was the first nation God prohibited from making empty images and bowing down to fictitious gods, but Israel was merely intended to be an example to all people. The prophets later would declare that all nations will be brought to shame because of their images (Isa 42:17; 44:9-11; Jer 10:14) because both they and the gods they symbolize are empty and deceptive nobodies (Ps 96:5). The particular reference to Israel here likely indicates that God is bringing full circle his claim over all nations.

Both "righteousness" in verse 6 and "judgments" in verse 8 pick up the themes in verse 2 and reflect the moral aspects of God's appearing that help set him apart from other supposed gods, aspects that form "the foundation of his throne" (v. 2). The former term is a reference to God's faithfulness. When God manifests himself in the spectacular way described in verses 2-5, it's not just fireworks. Goldingay says, "It is flashing of the actual weapons that fireworks symbolize, and these are weapons exercised for the sake of faithfulness" (Goldingay, *Psalms 90–150*, 114). Similarly, the latter term refers to the authoritative decisions that reflect God's justice that Israel experienced throughout its history. God's distinctiveness lies not merely in his fireworks but in his faithfulness and fairness that make things right in the world. That gives Israel and all nations reason to rejoice.

The distinction of God's reign as the only true god who reigns over the whole universe is fully realized in the person of Jesus Christ. Many scholars believe the author of Hebrews was citing the Septuagint rendition of the end of Psalm 97 when he said, "When [God] brings his firstborn into the world, he says, 'And let all God's angels worship him'" (Heb 1:6; see VanGemeren, Vol. 6, 625; Kidner, Vol. 16, 383). The writer goes on to say,

> *And about the angels he says: He makes his angels winds, and his servants a fiery flame, but to the Son: Your throne, O God, is forever and ever, and the scepter of your kingdom is a scepter of justice. You have loved righteousness and hated lawlessness; this is why God, your God, has anointed you with the oil of joy beyond your companions. And: In the beginning, Lord, you established the earth, and the heavens are the works of your hands; they will perish, but you remain. They will all wear out like clothing; you will roll them up like a cloak, and they will be changed like clothing. But you are the same, and your years will never end. Now to which of the angels has he ever said: Sit at my right hand until I make your enemies your footstool? Are they not all ministering spirits sent out to serve those who are going to inherit salvation?* (Heb 1:7-14)

In the incarnation Jesus was introduced as the one who reigns supreme, not just over all of the spirit world but over all of the enemies of God as well.

The same combination of delight and devastation that characterized Jesus's first coming will also characterize his return. While the people of God rejoice, his enemies will regret. Jesus says that on that day "the sign of the Son of Man will appear in the sky, and then all the peoples of the earth will mourn; and they will see the Son of Man coming on the clouds of heaven with power and great glory" (Matt 24:30). John offers similar testimony: "Look, he is coming with the clouds, and every eye will see him, even those who pierced him. And all the tribes of the earth will mourn over him" (Rev 1:7). No one will need to check Facebook or Twitter to see what's going on or to find out who's in charge. It will be clear to everyone that Jesus Christ reigns supreme.

The Anticipation of God's Reign
PSALM 97:10-12

The psalmist knows that the revelation of this distinct God who bursts dramatically on the scene, crushes the wicked, obliterates the worship of imposter gods, and reigns supreme over all the earth is yet to be fully realized. Until God's kingdom comes in the brightness of his glory, the interim will still be dark and hold its challenges for the godly. So in the three remaining verses, the writer exhorts God's loyal subjects to hold on until the day dawns and his victory is finally accomplished. He leaves them with something to anticipate, something to look forward to.

The hope laid out for God's true worshipers is described as the dawn of the new age of God's reign (v. 11). The parallel descriptions of "light" and "gladness" reflect the benefits of his rule for those who've faithfully waited for him. The idea is the same as the psalmist's declaration that "weeping may stay overnight, but there is joy in the morning" (Ps 30:5), and that "those who sow in tears will reap with shouts of joy. Though one goes along weeping, carrying the bag of seed, he will surely come back with shouts of joy, carrying his sheaves" (Ps 126:5-6). Herein lies the goal of all of history. When the day of God's coming dawns, his light will dissipate the darkness, and the "righteous" and "upright in heart" will enjoy the blessed state of redemption and victory (cf. Isa 60:1-3) in a new age of total restoration (VanGemeren, *Psalms*, 626; cf. Isa 58:8,10; Mal 4:2).

This bright ray of hope is framed up by two appeals, obedience to which will enable God's people to wait for his arrival with patience and faithfulness. The writer encourages those "who love the LORD" (v. 10) to anticipate his coming in two ways—consecration and celebration. Their consecration is reflected in the imperative to "hate evil." God's people are to live in the night in a way that's consistent with the economy of the dawn they're anticipating. Because they're awaiting the arrival of the righteous one (see vv. 2,6), they are to wait with righteous living.

Such a righteous lifestyle of hating evil can be costly when the culture of the night is governed by ungodliness. So the songwriter follows with the reassurance that God will protect and rescue his people. While this is no guarantee that there won't be some casualties throughout the dark battle of night, it does carry the assurance that God's faithful ones don't have to fear his appearing. He will guard those who have demonstrated where their loyalty lies.

The righteous are to await God's arrival with celebration as well (v. 12). The writer has woven this thread of joy in God's reign throughout the tapestry of his poem (see vv. 1,8,11). When the supreme sower sows light into the darkness of gloom and disaster, the inevitable harvest will be the joy of life, deliverance, and blessing (Goldingay, *Psalms 42–89*, 117). Consequently, his loyal subjects are to live their lives in view of his final victory as if it were already an accomplished fact (2 Chr 20:21; Hab 3:17-18).

The last verse of this psalm closes the loop opened in verse 1 where the nations were compelled to rejoice in God's reign. This connection reveals two applications for believers today. First, we should spend our days living righteously because of our delight in what God has done, what he's doing, and what he will do when he finally ushers in the coming kingdom of Jesus Christ. The last word in the psalm—God's "name"—carries the idea of remembrance (Exod 3:15). It signifies a recollection of all of his promises that have been fulfilled throughout the history of redemption, as well as those that are yet to be accomplished in the future. His faithfulness compels Christ followers to live righteously as we anticipate their completion. Peter explains,

> *Since all these things are to be dissolved in this way, it is clear what sort of people you should be in holy conduct and godliness as you wait for the day of God and hasten its coming. Because of that day, the heavens will be dissolved with fire and the elements will melt with heat. But based on his promise, we wait for new heavens and a new earth, where righteousness dwells.* (2 Pet 3:11-13)

God's people are to live righteously, rejoicing in what he's done in the past (cf. v. 8), in how he's ruling and blessing his people even in the present darkness, and in the blissful hope of his reign in Christ that's still to come (VanGemeren, *Psalms*, 626).

A second application is another installment in the clarion call for believers to proclaim "his holy name" to every people group on the planet so they can experience the same joy through the gospel. The clear assignment of God's "righteous ones" is to be a light to all people:

I am the Lord. I have called you for a righteous purpose, and I will hold you by your hand. I will watch over you, and I will appoint you to be a covenant for the people and a light to the nations, in order to open blind eyes, to bring out prisoners from the dungeon, and those sitting in darkness from the prison house. I am the Lord. That is my name, and I will not give my glory to another or my praise to idols. The past events have indeed happened. Now I declare new events; I announce them to you before they occur. (Isa 42:6-9)

The first Christian missionaries embraced this assignment as part of their global enterprise. Citing Isaiah 49:6, they demonstrated how faithfulness to it bears the fruit of joy when the nations receive the light of the gospel:

Paul and Barnabas boldly replied, "It was necessary that the word of God be spoken to you first. Since you reject it and judge yourselves unworthy of eternal life, we are turning to the Gentiles. For this is what the Lord has commanded us: I have made you a light for the Gentiles to bring salvation to the end of the earth." When the Gentiles heard this, they rejoiced and honored the word of the Lord, and all who had been appointed to eternal life believed. The word of the Lord spread through the whole region. (Acts 13:46-49)

As righteous believers await the full revelation of God's reign, our task is faithfully to leverage everything in order to proclaim Jesus Christ to all people as the light of the world (Luke 2:32; John 8:12; Acts 26:23; 1 Pet 2:9). As we do, people from every tribe and nation and tongue will believe the gospel and experience the joy of being appointed to eternal life.

Conclusion

Like most married men, I still remember the moment the doors opened at the back of the church and my precious bride appeared. As I stood at the other end of what seemed to be an eternal aisle, my legs felt like jelly, and my brow was dripping with sweat, but my heart was full of joy! What I had anticipated for so long was finally about to happen. I was about to marry the most beautiful woman in the world! Such anxious waiting is merely indicative of our patient expectation of Christ's return for us. John says,

Then I heard something like the voice of a vast multitude, like the sound of cascading waters, and like the rumbling of loud thunder, saying, Hallelujah, because our Lord God, the Almighty, reigns! Let us be glad, rejoice, and give him glory, because the marriage of the Lamb

has come, and his bride has prepared herself. She was given fine linen to wear, bright and pure. For the fine linen represents the righteous acts of the saints. Then he said to me, "Write: Blessed are those invited to the marriage feast of the Lamb!" He also said to me, "These words of God are true." (Rev 19:6-9)

As the church of Jesus Christ waits to be married to her holy husband, our lives are to be characterized by "righteous acts." Holy living is the only thing worthy of the one who will reign in righteousness. When his reign is revealed, it will be evident to all that he and he alone is the God of the universe and the Savior of his people. Come quickly, Lord Jesus.

Reflect and Discuss

1. How should the images put forth of God's coming and justice put faith, hope, and a healthy fear of him in us as believers?
2. How should these images of God's judgment also drive us to mission?
3. If the heavens proclaim his righteousness, and all the peoples see his glory, what keeps people from knowing and loving God?
4. Although we do not worship the "gods" that the ancient people did, idolatry spans the distance of all cultures. What are some contemporary "gods" that modern people submit to?
5. How does the truth of God being "the Most High" over all the earth impact our prayer lives?
6. How does the truth of God's being "the Most High" impact our efforts in both local and global mission?
7. We who love the Lord are to "hate evil." What is it about God's nature and character that drives us to live consecrated lives?
8. The psalmist is confident in God's rescue, confident that he will preserve the lives of the saints and deliver them from the hand of the wicked. How do we reconcile this with Christian persecution across the globe?
9. The glorious return of Jesus is described in detail in Revelation 19. Why did God use the marriage metaphor to describe Jesus's relationship with the church?
10. Verse 12 exhorts God's people to give thanks to his holy name. How does our overflow of thanksgiving to God impact our proclamation of God to the world?

Behold His Faithfulness

PSALM 98

Main Idea: God's faithfulness to his people means we can always rely on his promises and experience peace, joy, and hope in every circumstance.

I. **What Faithfulness Means**
    A. God never forgets his people.
    B. God always keeps his promises.
II. **Why God's Faithfulness Matters**
    A. You can have peace from your past.
    B. You can have joy in the present.
    C. You can have hope for the future.

Life is full of struggles. There are physical struggles—disability, infertility, the loss of a loved one, sickness, cancer—as well as emotional, relational, and spiritual struggles. Amid all these struggles, we have all kinds of questions for God, like, Where are you in the middle of this? Are you even there? Why is this happening in my life? When will this change? Some days we just ask, "God, how do I make it through this?"

If you're asking those questions now, or if you've ever asked those questions, then you're not alone in at least two senses. First, you're not alone in that we all ask these questions at times, and it's not just those who are alive today. The Bible is filled with people who asked real, honest questions like this of God—like the prophet Habakkuk: "How long, Lord, must I call for help and you do not listen or cry out to you about violence and you do not save?" (Hab 1:2). The Bible is not a book of shallow, trite faith that pretends everything is perfect in the world. This is a book about real wrestling with the realities of sin and suffering in the world and the inevitable questions that come with that.

Second, you're not alone in your questions to God because God has not abandoned you in the middle of your questions. Amid the inevitable questions you and I wrestle with in this world, the God of the universe is faithful. Even when your faith starts to falter, God is faithful—to be with you, to help you, to uphold you, and ultimately to save you from a world of sin and suffering. That's what Psalm 98 is all about.

Psalm 98 can apply to all sorts of different occasions. The psalmist praises God for his faithfulness but doesn't identify a specific setting. Some people think this psalm is celebrating God's salvation of his people out of slavery in Egypt, while others think it is celebrating when God saved his people out of slavery in exile, bringing them back to Jerusalem.

We'll see what God's faithfulness means, and then we'll see why it matters.

What Faithfulness Means

In verse 3 the psalmist says that God has "remembered his love and faithfulness to the house of Israel." Think of God remembering. We're talking about the omniscient God of the universe, the one who knows everything in the world. How does *he* remember something? Doesn't remembering something seem to imply that he forgot it at some point? You and I may forget all kinds of important and unimportant information, but not so with God.

Although God never forgets anything, there are times when we *feel* he has forgotten to listen to us, help us, or provide for us. God's people felt this way when they were slaves in Egypt for four hundred years. We can only imagine the struggles of their faith during those years. They must have thought, *God, where are you? When is this going to end?* Yet we read this in Exodus 2:23-24 (emphasis added):

> *The Israelites groaned because of their difficult labor; and they cried out; and their cry for help because of the difficult labor ascended to God. And God heard their groaning; and God* remembered *his covenant with Abraham, with Isaac, and with Jacob.*

That phrase doesn't mean God had forgotten his people. It means that when God's people were wondering, "Does he remember us?," God's Word says he absolutely remembered them. He had not for one moment forgotten them. We read something similar in Exodus 6:2-6:

> *Then God spoke to Moses, telling him, "I am the LORD. I appeared to Abraham, Isaac, and Jacob as God Almighty, but I was not known to them by my name 'the LORD.' I also established my covenant with*

them to give them the land of Canaan, the land they lived in as
aliens. Furthermore, I have heard the groaning of the Israelites, whom
the Egyptians are forcing to work as slaves, and I have remembered
my covenant.
     "Therefore tell the Israelites: I am the LORD, and I will bring
you out from the forced labor of the Egyptians and rescue you from
slavery to them. I will redeem you with an outstretched arm and
great acts of judgment."

God heard and remembered his people, and he delivered them. This
kind of background in Israel's history helps us makes sense of Psalm 98,
for the Lord has "performed wonders; his right hand and holy arm have
won him the victory. . . . He has remembered his love and faithfulness to
the house of Israel" (vv. 1,3).

Psalm 98 also matches with the exile. For instance, after Babylon's
destruction of Jerusalem and deportation of the people of God, we
read the following in Lamentations 5:1: "LORD, remember what has
happened to us. Look, and see our disgrace! . . . Why do you continually forget us, abandon us for our entire lives?" (Lam 5:1,20). The
people felt God had forgotten them. Yet, when God spoke to his people in the midst of exile, he reminded them that what they felt was
not reality:

> *For this is what the Lord GOD says: I will deal with you according to*
> *what you have done, since you have despised the oath by breaking the*
> *covenant. But I will remember the covenant I made with you in the*
> *days of your youth, and I will establish a permanent covenant with*
> *you.* (Ezek 16:59-60)

God had not forgotten his people, and he eventually brought them
back from exile. This is why many people believe Psalm 98 was written
on that occasion. Regardless of when this psalm was written, there are
two things God's faithfulness means.

God Never Forgets His People

Even when it seems like the world is caving in around you, you don't
ever have to wonder if God has forgotten you. God is faithful, which
means he hears you in your groaning, he sees you in your suffering. He
knows you and he loves you, and he doesn't ever forget you.

God Always Keeps His Promises

Verse 3 says that God has remembered his "love" to the house of Israel. The psalmist uses the word for God's covenant love. When God called Abraham, the father of God's people Israel, God entered into a covenant with Abraham. A covenant is similar in some ways to a marriage commitment. God promised to be with Abraham and his descendants; he promised to bless them, to protect them, to preserve them, and to bring them into the promised land. So when God saved Israel from slavery in Egypt, and then from slavery in exile, God was keeping his promises. This covenant-keeping love is featured throughout the book of psalms (and throughout Scripture as a whole).

For example, Psalm 105 recounts the history of God's people, including the time when God's people were slaves in Egypt (v. 23). God sent Moses to perform all kinds of signs and send all kinds of plagues among the Egyptians (vv. 26-36), eventually bringing Israel out of Egypt (v. 37) and leading them with a cloud by day and fire by night (v. 39). God gave them bread from heaven and water from a rock (vv. 40-41). So why did God do all of this? Psalm 105:42 tells us: "For he remembered his holy promise to Abraham his servant." God never forgets his people, and God always keeps his promises.

Another place we see God's faithfulness is in the story of Christ's birth. Here's how Luke's Gospel presents God's covenant-keeping love to his people through a man named Simeon:

> There was a man in Jerusalem whose name was Simeon. This man was righteous and devout, looking forward to Israel's consolation, and the Holy Spirit was on him. It had been revealed to him by the Holy Spirit that he would not see death before he saw the Lord's Messiah. Guided by the Spirit, he entered the temple. When the parents brought in the child Jesus to perform for him what was customary under the law, Simeon took him up in his arms, praised God, and said,
>
> Now, Master, you can dismiss your servant in peace, as you promised. For my eyes have seen your salvation. You have prepared it in the presence of all peoples—a light for revelation to the Gentiles and glory to your people Israel. (Luke 2:25-32)

God's promises of a coming Messiah started centuries before Simeon, stretching all the way back to the beginning of the Bible when sin, suffering, and death first entered the world. In Genesis 3:15 God promised that he would send a seed from the woman who would crush the head of Satan. In Genesis 12:1-3 God foretold how the seed of Abraham would bring blessing to all the peoples of the earth. He would be a prophet like Moses, according to Deuteronomy 18:15. According to 2 Samuel 7:16, he would be a king from the line of David, and his throne would last forever. Isaiah explained that he would be born of a virgin (Isa 7:14) and that he would be called "Wonderful Counselor, Mighty God, Eternal Father, Prince of Peace" (Isa 9:6).

These promises were a perpetual source of comfort and consolation in the midst of massive suffering among God's people, whether it was during slavery in Egypt or when foreign nations eventually plundered them, destroyed the temple, and scattered them into exile. Yet, amid exile, God promised his people a shepherd from the line of David (Ezek 37:24-27). So even after God's people returned from exile, they were still waiting for the Messiah. Again God promised, "Look, your King is coming to you; he is righteous and victorious. . . . He will proclaim peace to the nations" (Zech 9:9-10). All the way to the last chapter of the last book of the Old Testament, God promised, "The sun of righteousness will rise with healing in its wings" (Mal 4:2). Then there was silence—for four hundred years.

Imagine generation after generation asking, "Where do we look for help? What's wrong?" Then, after centuries of silence, Simeon, who Luke says was "righteous and devout," a man who had longed and looked for Israel's consolation (Luke 2:25), walked into the temple trusting the promise of God on a day that seemed like every other day. But this day was different. The glory of God was in the temple; the consolation of Israel had come. Simeon had waited all his life; *creation* had waited for centuries. And now the *Christ*, the promised Messiah, was right in front of him. This was, and is, the greatest news in all the world: God has not forgotten his people! God has kept his promise—to bring salvation to you and me! This is why, according to Psalm 98, we respond by singing "a new song to the LORD," for "he has remembered his love and faithfulness to the house of Israel; all the ends of the earth have seen our God's victory" (vv. 1,3).

Why God's Faithfulness Matters

After seeing what God's faithfulness means, the psalmist gives us at least three reasons God's faithfulness matters for our lives.

You Can Have Peace from Your Past

Psalm 98 starts by looking back, then it looks to the present, and finally it looks to the future. Regardless of whether the psalmist is looking back to slavery in Egypt or slavery in exile, he's talking about the Lord's deliverance and salvation. How much more, on this side of the coming of Christ and his death on the cross for our sins, should we sing this "new song"?

God has saved us not just from slavery in Egypt or exile but from our sin! Despite our unfaithfulness to him, he has remained faithful to us. He has not forgotten us. He has kept his promises to us—to love us, to care for us, to keep us, to preserve us, to save us from our sin. In Jeremiah 31:34 God promises to all who trust in Jesus, "I will forgive their iniquity and never again remember their sin." Oh, Christian, let this soak in: God has saved you not only from the penalty and power of sin but also from the remembrance of it in your life altogether. He chooses not to remember *any* of it!

You Can Have Joy in the Present

In light of God's faithfulness, the psalmist exhorts the whole earth to "shout for joy" to the Lord (v. 4) and to "shout triumphantly in the presence of the LORD, our King" (v. 6). The language in these verses is loud, with "trumpets and the blast of the ram's horn" accompanying shouts and singing. In a world of sin and suffering, because of the faithfulness of God, we have a loud, triumphant song to sing.

Even in the midst of struggle, we know God has not, and will not, forget us. He will keep every single one of his promises to us—promises to strengthen us in the middle of our weakness, to give us wisdom in the middle of confusion, peace in the midst of turmoil, rest in the midst of stress, calm in the midst of anxiety, courage in the face of fear, and ultimately, hope in the face of despair. God has promised us every single one of these things, and he always keeps his promises, no matter how hard this world gets.

You Can Have Hope for the Future

The last part of this psalm is a call for all creation to celebrate the coming of the Lord. The righteousness of God will reign over the world, and everything in the world will be made right. This psalm is about something much bigger than deliverance from slavery in Egypt or from exile. It's about something much bigger than even the initial coming of Christ. This is why Isaac Watts wrote his hymn "Joy to the World." He wasn't painting a picture of the birth of Christ; he was painting a picture of the return of Christ. He wrote about the day when heaven and nature are fully united in song before Christ the King.

> No more let sins and sorrows grow,
> Nor thorns infest the ground;
> He comes to make His blessings flow
> Far as the curse is found,
> Far as the curse is found,
> Far as, far as, the curse is found.
>
> He rules the world with truth and grace
> And makes the nations prove
> The glories of His righteousness,
> And wonders of His love,
> And wonders of His love,
> And wonders, wonders, of His love. (Watts, "Joy to the World")

Watts wrote this hymn in anticipation of the day when Christ will rule the world with truth and grace, and we will *perfectly* enjoy the glories of his righteousness and the wonders of his love. Obviously, all of these things are possible because of the first coming of Christ—his life, death, and resurrection—but we're still waiting for the day when sin and suffering will be no more. We have put our hope in the faithfulness of God.

Reflect and Discuss

1. Why do times of trial and suffering cause us to doubt God's promises?
2. How would you respond to the following statement: Only unbelievers feel abandoned by God. What examples would you use from Scripture?
3. Given that God is all-knowing, why does Scripture talk about God "remembering" his promises? How is this different from our inability to recall important bits of information from the past?
4. When have you felt forgotten by God? How were you reminded of his faithfulness?
5. What episodes in Israel's history caused them to doubt God's faithfulness?
6. What are some examples of God's being faithful to Israel in the Old Testament?

7. How does Psalm 98 call us to respond to God's faithful love?
8. How is God's faithfulness demonstrated through Christ's life, death, and resurrection? Name some specific Old Testament promises that were fulfilled.
9. How should God's faithfulness affect our motivation to read, meditate on, and memorize Scripture?
10. Make a list of promises God has made to those who are in Christ so that you can memorize them.

Responding to the Otherness of God

PSALM 99

Main Idea: The exclusive holiness of God demands that we trust him to save us and make us holy.

I. **What Sets God Apart**
  A. He is sovereign (99:1-2).
  B. He is just (99:4).
  C. He is accessible (99:6-8).
II. **How We Should Respond**
  A. Trust Jesus as sovereign (99:3).
  B. Trust Jesus for salvation (99:5).
  C. Trust Jesus for sanctification (99:9).

While teaching at New Orleans Seminary, I had a humbling experience that has stuck with me. Two young Asian men were considering coming to our seminary to study, so they called to set up an appointment to discuss their journey. When they arrived for the appointment, I went out to the outer office to meet them. They greeted me with the traditional bow, we shook hands, and I invited them into my office. As I entered, I turned around to invite them to sit down. That's when I saw something I'll never forget. They were bent over, backing into my office with their faces to the ground. In my surprise I asked what they were doing. One of them responded, "This is the way we enter our professors' offices in our country. It's a sign of respect for them."

Although I thought their response to me was misplaced, that humbling experience did make me process how I act toward people who—by virtue of their person or position—deserve appropriate response from me. It especially made me process my response to God. Psalm 99 is the sixth of the royal psalms (93; 95–100), all of which magnify God's sovereign rule over the universe. After the joyful energy of the previous psalm, this song keeps our spirits in check with how exalted and holy God actually is and with the great reverence we owe him because of his personal character and positional reign.

God's holiness defines and describes this psalm. The word *holy* is used four times to describe him and his rule (Ross, Vol. 3, 175-76). The word can be defined as "separate, set apart, totally different" and has been described as that attribute of God that makes him *wholly other* (Wiersbe, *Be Exultant*, 37). It emphasizes the distance between God and man morally—as between the pure and the polluted—as well as existentially—as between the infinite and the finite. The previous psalm assures us the gulf between God and man has been bridged, but this psalm reminds us that God constructed the bridge. So the repeated cry, "He is holy," ensures that we don't act casually or tritely toward him, his holiness, or his grace (Kidner, Vol. 16, 387).

God's holiness also determines the development of this psalm. The uses of the term *holy* are all found in the thematic refrain repeated in verses 3, 5, and 9. "He is holy" is declared in the first two refrains (vv. 3,5), and then the restatement "The LORD our God is holy" is declared in the third one (v. 9). Each of these declarations is prefaced by some command to worship God, obviously in response to his holiness. The psalm essentially comprises three sequences, each containing some expression of praise to this holy God followed by the refrain calling for a suitable response to his holiness. We can easily analyze the psalm by identifying what sets God apart in each sequence and then determining from the refrains how we ought to respond to his holiness.

What Sets God Apart

We really can't know how to respond appropriately to someone unless we understand his or her nature. The Asian students I mentioned above responded the way they did to me not because of anything about me personally but because of the regard they had for my role. In their minds the nature of the role of a professor deserved a certain respect. Understanding God's nature is the key to knowing how to respond to him.

He Is Sovereign (99:1-2)

As with Psalms 93 and 97, the first sequence of this psalm opens with the declaration, "The LORD reigns!" He is not just king in Israel but sovereign over the whole planet. While God's holiness was first exhibited in his distinctive kingly authority over Israel, the entire world is destined to acknowledge it. The commands to "Let the peoples tremble. . . . Let the earth quake" suggest it would be unwise for anyone to respond to this God in any way other than fear. He is sovereign, and he is all-powerful!

This universal scope of God's reign is pictured in two ways. First, "he is enthroned between the cherubim." These angelic beings were identified with God's rule not only over Israel (80:1; cf. 1 Sam 4:4; 2 Sam 6:2; 2 Kgs 19:15; 1 Chr 13:6) but also over all creation. Contrary to much religious art, these cherubim aren't harmless, unarmed, cuddly cupids. They're mighty beings representing the whole kingdom of earthly creatures (Ezek 1:4-28; 10:1-22; Rev 4:6-11). God's throne isn't inanimate or stationary but magnificently depicted as a living, flying, fiery chariot that moves over the earth. Second, "the LORD is great in Zion." While Zion was the city of Jerusalem from which God ruled Israel, it also is the locus of his reign over the whole earth (cf. Pss 2:1-12; 110:1-7)! Both cherubim and Zion show his supreme reign!

He Is Just (99:4)

The second sequence of this psalm describes God not merely as one who exercises authority and power over everybody but also as one who does what is right and fair by everybody. He does what is right and fair because he loves what is right and fair. God *does* what he *is*. So because he is perfectly upright, faithful, and righteous in his character, he is fully just in his actions. Only in him are holiness, power, and justice perfectly united with one another. He rules justly because he is completely holy and just himself.

This attribute of God ran contrary to the ethic of most nations in the ancient world. Most kings ignored and even defied justice. They were driven by their own self-interest, regardless of who had to be manipulated or oppressed—including their own citizens. God's condemnation of foreign nations during the exodus and conquest is misunderstood at this point. It's easy to view his treatment of Egypt, the Canaanite peoples, and other nations as unfair and uncaring, as if he were playing favorites with Israel. The reality is that God was killing two birds with one stone! After many years of patience, he exercised judgment against nations who rejected justice (Gen 15:16; Dan 8:23; 1 Thess 2:16) while establishing Israel as an example of a people who reflected his values of justice, righteousness, and the proper exercise of authority.

He Is Accessible (99:6-8)

The mention of "Moses and Aaron . . . Samuel" (v. 6) at the beginning of the third sequence of this psalm is sudden. It almost seems out of place. What do these guys possibly have to do with what sets *God* apart? All three served in different capacities—Moses as deliverer at the exodus, Aaron as his priest, and Samuel as a great prophet in a later era of the early monarchy. But one role tied them together: all were mediators between God and his people (Goldingay, Vol. 3, 130)! All three were "calling on his name. . . . And he answered them" (v. 6). God "spoke to them; . . . they kept his decrees" (v. 7). They prayed to God for his people, and God taught his people through them. And through them he granted access to both his mercy and his justice.

Before Israel entered the promised land, Moses reiterated how important it was for them to have prophets who would serve as their mediators so they could have access to God (Deut 18:15-19). He reminded them how at Sinai they were right to understand this necessity in light of God's holiness, sovereignty, and justice. When God manifested his awesome power on the mountain, the Israelites trembled with fear to the point they asked Moses to mediate between them and God lest they be destroyed (Exod 20:18-19). They dared not approach this holy God! So Moses told the people God would raise up another prophet to mediate on their behalf so they could have access to him.

How We Should Respond

The recurring refrain of this song provides us with built-in application, calling us to respond to the holiness of God. The repeated declarations "He is holy" (vv. 3,5) and the companion "The LORD our God is holy" (v. 9) indicate each action is a fitting response to this God who is set apart from all others. And each response gives us a window into how our worship is realized through trust in the person of Jesus Christ. Consider three proper responses to God's holiness for those of us living on this side of the cross.

Trust Jesus as Sovereign (99:3)

The readers and singers of this psalm are first beckoned to "praise [God's] great and awe-inspiring name" (v. 3). Praise is the only suitable and natural response to one whose name—and therefore whose self—is so great and awesome that it makes people tremble and the earth shake (vv. 1-2)! Otherwise, we will find ourselves on the judgment end of God's stick. He's the distinct, supernatural, transcendent, and all-powerful God. We can choose to either tremble before him with reverential praise or tremble before him with petrified horror. The choice is ours.

How to make this choice is clear from this side of the cross. God has determined to receive his praise through Jesus. In him God's sovereignty is wed with his great and awesome name so that ultimately he might be glorified. And one day everybody in the universe will confess Jesus as sovereign, either willingly or by force. Paul said, "God highly exalted him and gave him the name that is above every name, so that at the name of Jesus every knee will bow—in heaven and on earth and under the earth—and every tongue will confess that Jesus Christ is Lord, to the glory of God the Father" (Phil 2:9-11). So we offer this holy and sovereign God the praise he is due by trusting Jesus as Lord and bowing before him in reverent obedience. God has exalted him as sovereign over the universe, and he is worthy of our praise!

Trust Jesus for Salvation (99:5)

The second response solicited by the psalmist is to "exalt the LORD our God; bow in worship at his footstool" (v. 5). To "exalt" and to "bow" convey simultaneous actions that can't be separated. The former means to lift high while the latter means to prostrate oneself. If you lift something high, you inevitably become lower. If you prostrate yourself before something, you inevitably make it high (see Ross, Vol. 3, 180-81). This synchronized action leaves the worshiper at God's "footstool." Scripture uses this term to signify several aspects of God's reign (1 Chr 28:2; Ps 132:7; Isa 60:13; 66:1; Ezek 43:7; Lam 2:1), all of which find the worshiper in a humble and submissive position—bowing at the feet of royalty. Kneeling at the feet of a God who loves and exercises justice is an incredibly vulnerable position, one that reminds us we are at his mercy!

On this side of the cross, we can see the connection these harmonized acts of exalting and worshiping have with God's love for and administration of justice (v. 4). Because sin separates us from this holy God, justice is the last thing on our wish list. So we need someone to help us worship this just God, against whose justice we can't even begin to measure up by ourselves. So God redeemed us and made us righteous through Christ's sacrificial death, "so that he would be righteous and declare righteous the one who has faith in Jesus" (Rom 3:26). God *does* what he *is*! So we offer this holy and just God praise by trusting Jesus to save us. God "presented him as an atoning sacrifice in his blood, received through faith" (Rom 3:25)! God executed justice for us in Christ!

Trust Jesus for Sanctification (99:9)

The psalmist's final call to worship repeats the partnering actions to "exalt the LORD our God; [and] bow in worship." However, this time—instead of bowing at God's footstool—worship is to be offered "at his holy mountain." In addition to being the earthly city of Jerusalem from which God ruled Israel and the nations, Mount Zion also refers to God's eternal reign in heaven (Heb 12:22; Rev 14:1). Both places are holy because God who inhabits them is holy! So this is a summons for us to come into the presence of the holy God and bring him his due worship, now and forever! But how are we as sinful and finite creatures sufficient for such a great privilege?

At the Passover in Egypt, God gave the Israelites *positional* holiness. But then he used men like Moses, Aaron, and Samuel to foster *functional* holiness in them. On this side of the cross, we need a mediator to do the same for us. We get positional holiness by faith in the "one mediator between God and humanity, the man Christ Jesus" (1 Tim 2:5); we're made right with a holy God. However, we still need access to him to get *functional* holiness. That's called sanctification, or holiness fleshed out, with skin on it! Jesus is our mediator for that work as well—for both maintaining and maturing our faith in a hostile world (see Heb 4:14-16; 7:25; 10:19-25). When that journey is over, we'll assemble with angels and Old Testament saints before God in the heavenly Mount Zion, not dreading his holy terror but rejoicing in his holy reign. So with that hope and his holiness, we trust our mediator, Jesus, to equip us to be able to offer holy lives as his acceptable worship as we await his eternal glory (Heb 12:18-29; cf. Rom 12:1-2)!

Conclusion

Recently two professional golfers in the United States went against the grain of the current trend of professional athletes who are publicly criticizing our sitting president on Twitter and other media outlets. Their reason? Both of them said they believe that—regardless of whether you agree with the president—the office deserves respect. Even when it comes to imperfect human beings, certain characteristics of age, administrative roles, and positions of authority deserve a certain response from all of us.

If that's true for humanity, then certainly the holy God of the universe—who has no flaw or sin—deserves respect, worship, and allegiance from every man, woman, boy, and girl on the planet, all of whom he created by his grace and for his glory. And as if that weren't enough, he pursued us in Christ Jesus even when we rebelled against him. Certainly the God of the gospel merits our reverential response. But instead of our having to back into his presence, he welcomes our entrance face-to-face, with open arms as the waiting father did with his prodigal son. The Holy Other has graciously invited sinful people to come home to be in relationship with him.

Reflect and Discuss

1. How does God's "otherness" impact our approach to him?
2. Should we meditate on God's holiness as we approach God's Word and prayer? Why or why not?
3. If the angels cry out "Holy, holy, holy" in their worship of God in heaven, how might we specifically consider his holiness while we worship God here?
4. How does God's sovereignty inform our worship of God and relationship with God?
5. What does the fact that God "loves justice" say to the way we relate with people in our normal day-to-day interactions with them?
6. In what ways should God's accessibility encourage us to pray and yet convict us of our times of prayerlessness?
7. How does Jesus demonstrate God's sovereignty, his holiness, and our sanctification all at the same time? In what ways does he do each?
8. What's the difference between "positional holiness" and "functional holiness"?
9. In what ways does "positional holiness" encourage our walk with the Lord?
10. What does "functional holiness" communicate to us about sanctification in our walk with the Lord?

Marks of the Church

PSALM 100

Main Idea: God is glorified in a joyful people who are eager to know him and make him known.

I. **Rejoice (100:1-2)!**
    A. The volume of worship is loud.
    B. The call to worship is global.
    C. The spirit of worship is joyful.
    D. The scope of worship is total.
II. **Know the Lord (100:3-4)!**
    A. He is God.
    B. He made us.
    C. We are his.
III. **Spread the Word (100:5)!**
    A. We take the gospel to every nation.
    B. We transfer the gospel to every generation.

What comes to mind when you think "church"? I got into a conversation recently with someone who is skeptical about Christianity. At several points his negative feelings about Christianity came through. To him Christians are ignorant and judgmental. Sadly he might have proof from his own experience to back up his evaluation.

What about you? If you had to give three verbs that capture the essence of what it is to be God's people, what would you say?

Psalm 100 is God's own answer to the question. This passage paints a picture of the church, and wherever the church in modern times bears little reflection to this passage, we have lost our way. This is the kind of community Jesus is building. The kind of people Jesus meant to unleash on the world. It doesn't say everything, but I believe we can hear three clear imperatives that point to the essence of what it means to be God's people.

Rejoice!

PSALM 100:1-2

There's a call to worship that in verse 1 goes out to the whole world. But it doesn't stay broad. In verse 3 it's clearly the community of faith that's in view. Notice four realities right there in the first two verses:

The Volume of Worship Is Loud

Growing up, how many of you would have been considered a loud child? That was me. My mom always used to say, "Matt, your voice carries." Now I know what she was talking about because we have a child like that.

When the boys were little, I chose an evening for YouTube clips of Pavarotti. I saved my favorite song for last—Pavarotti's 1994 performance of "Nessun Dorma"—and my sons were wide-eyed. That's when our second son started doing Pavarotti impressions. He was too young to pronounce Pavarotti, so he just called it his "pow-ful voice." And it was so loud. Even just recently he and I were singing at the piano in the house. It was 9:30 at night, and I was convinced our neighbors could hear my son's voice inside their houses! His voice carries!

Well, Psalm 100 speaks of the joy of the church as something *audible*—even loud. I love the way commentator Marvin Tate describes this:

> The enthusiasm of Israelite worship is illustrated
> throughout Psalms 93–100. Shouts are raised. Praises
> chanted and sung while musical instruments are played
> and horns blown. The noise of the Temple worship was
> legendary. (*Psalms 51–100*, 525)

Some places in the Psalms call for us to "be still, and know that [he is] God" (46:10 ESV), to come before him with a sense of reverent awe. And then there are psalms like this one. In verse 1 God has his hand on the volume knob, and he's cranking it up! "Shout triumphantly." Make a joyful noise! Turn it up!

The Call to Worship Is Global

As the one true God and maker of heaven and earth, God has the right to command worship from all peoples. This is where history is going. The terminal moment in history as we know it will find all of creation standing in awe of the glory of God. Those who have trusted Christ

will stand on the new earth and look out, and there will be a sea of
people from every tribe, tongue, and nation—your brothers and sisters
in faith—with one voice singing the praises of Jesus Christ.
This call to worship is meant to ring out to the farthest reaches of
the earth. And the nations will hear it. As the prophet Habakkuk wrote,
"The earth will be filled with the knowledge of the LORD's glory, as the
water covers the sea" (Hab 2:14). The Great Commission isn't wishful
thinking; it's where history is going.

The Spirit of Worship Is Joyful

In verse 1 it's not just noise; it's a triumphant shout, a "joyful noise"
(ESV). And in verse 2 it's not just serving and songs; it's "joyful songs"
and serving "with gladness." Stop and consider: Does this passage
describe you? Does it describe us? Psalm 100 isn't a passage for other
churches; it's here for every church. God means for his people to be
marked by joy.

In a popular TV show called *MythBusters* a team of science whizzes
work out various crazy experiments, often involving blowing things
up in the name of science. At the beginning of every show, they say
the same thing: "Don't try this at home. Leave it to the experts."
There's no label like that attached to Psalm 100. This *is* a "try this at
home" passage.

Yes, we acknowledge our sin in light of God's holiness. But along
with that, every Sunday we remember the good news of what God has
done about it. Jesus came, lived, and died to save us from our sin, to
claim us for God, and to bring us into God's forever family. For all who
hide in Jesus—for all who have trusted in his perfect work on the cross—
we can celebrate good news every Sunday.

If the truth of the gospel gets into our bloodstream, our worship will
have an unmistakable note of joy. Christian friend, your future couldn't
be brighter. Here's your story as a believer: "One who is righteous has
many adversities, but the LORD rescues him from them all" (Ps 34:19).
Joy will catch you in the end—joy Peter describes as "inexpressible and
glorious" (1 Pet 1:8).

The Scope of Worship Is Total

Worship lays claim to everything we do. Paul writes, "And whatever you
do, in word or in deed, do everything in the name of the Lord Jesus,

giving thanks to God the Father through him" (Col 3:17) and, "So, whether you eat or drink, or whatever you do, do everything for the glory of God" (1 Cor 10:31). For the Christian all of life is meant to be an act of worship. I love the old hymn "Take My Life and Let It Be Consecrated" because it connects worship to my lips, my hands, my feet, and how I spend my money and my time.

> Take my silver and my gold—Not a mite, would I withhold;
> Take my intellect and use Every power as Thou shalt choose.
> (Havergal, "Take My Life")

This term *serve* in verse 2 is a comprehensive term in Hebrew. It's used in the Old Testament to describe formal acts of praise in the temple, but it's also used to describe ordinary work in Genesis 2. What does this mean? It means serving the Lord with gladness isn't just about what we do when we gather. It's an all-of-life worship. What you do the other six days of the week matters to God. Paul writes, "Whatever you do, do it from the heart, as something done for the Lord and not for people, knowing that you will receive the reward of an inheritance from the Lord. You serve the Lord Christ" (Col 3:23-24). Does it change anything if you wake up tomorrow thinking, *I don't merely work for this retail store. I don't merely work for this financial institution. I'm not just rearing children, I'm not just working toward my undergraduate degree. I'm serving the Lord Christ?*

What comes to mind when you think "church"? We ask God that question in Psalm 100, and he doesn't borrow the words of the skeptic: *ignorant* and *judgmental.* Instead, *joy* looms large in God's description of and intention for his people. God has given us a reason to be glad. He wants us to be marked by joy.

Know the Lord!
PSALM 100:3-4

The CSB translates verse 3, "Acknowledge that the LORD is God." The word *acknowledge* carries the sense of recognizing something—not just mentally nodding yes but taking it on board. That's helpful. However, I love an earlier translation on this one: "Know that the LORD, he is God" (ESV). Notice three truths right here in verse 3:

He Is God

Look at how much this psalm is focused on God: "to the Lord" (v. 1); "Serve the Lord"; "Come before him" (v. 2); "Acknowledge . . . the Lord"; "He made"; "We are his"; "his people"; "his pasture" (v. 3); "his gates"; "his courts"; "to him"; "his name" (v. 4); "Lord is good"; "his faithful love"; "his faithfulness" (v. 5). It's all about him.

Think about gathered worship for a moment. The reason we want our songs and sermons to be God centered isn't because God-centeredness is trending. It's because God is at the center of the universe. There's no one better to talk about. Gathered worship is a great reminder to me that the universe doesn't orbit around me. I'm not in control. I'm not sovereign. I'm not the one the world was waiting for. As the preacher J. Vernon McGee used to say, "This is God's universe and he does things his way. You may have a better way, but you don't have a universe."

God runs the universe, and that's good. God is God, and I'm not. In one way or another, we acknowledge that and sing that truth every Sunday. He is God.

He Made Us

The road of dependence only travels in one direction. We need God. He doesn't need us. He made us. We didn't make him. We didn't make ourselves. We exist because God graciously decided we would. You're breathing right now because God is saying yes to your existence, now and now and now again.

Human history tells a story of the human thirst for transcendence. There's an insatiable desire in us to experience something way bigger than we are—to be out of our depth, to be lost in wonder. We find experiences in this world that are meant to point us further up and further in. The truth that awaits us at the core of reality is that God is the one we were made to know and experience.

This psalm isn't just restating the obvious: God made the world and everything and everyone in it. The psalmist goes on to clarify that God has claimed a people for himself.

We Are His

He uses the imagery of sheep—a flock (v. 3). In the Old Testament these descriptions fit the people of Israel. However, early in the Old Testament it becomes clear that, from the beginning, God intended to gather a multiethnic family (Gen 12:3; 22:18). God would send Messiah—Jesus Christ—to purchase a people from every nation, tribe, and tongue (Rev 7:9). Paul addresses the believers in Corinth, reminding them they are not their own, for they "were bought at a price" (1 Cor 6:20). This means Christians are twice claimed: we are debtors to our Creator who gave us life and sustains us by his providence, and we are debtors to our Redeemer who bought us with his blood and saved us from the judgment we deserve for our sin.

Think about that in relation to your life right now. We look within—at battles and turmoil of heart and mind. We look around—at suffering in friends' lives and in the world. Don't we feel that we are out of our depth? Don't we feel the need for a God of grace and power? Here is Psalm 100 telling us we've got one!

Christian friends, we don't gather to worship a souped-up version of ourselves. God is a God of sovereignty and providence. He sets the dates for the rise and fall of every kingdom in world history. Think about this in relation to your life, your struggles, your cares, and your anxious thoughts. Does the thing you fear the most—the thing that keeps you up at night—have on its resume, "Maker of heaven and earth"? This is our God. Trust him. Cast your cares on him. Be still and know that he is God. Our world has enough mirrors. What we need is a window to see out—to see God in his high and holy place.

In Psalm 100 everything is under God's authority. The gates are his. The courts are his. The songs are his. The earth is his. We are his. Gathered worship isn't an exercise in navel-gazing. It's not, "Let's all circle up and try to see the inner workings of our hearts so we can feel appropriately terrible, and maybe the guilt will motivate us to do something better with our lives." That's what church can be if we don't keep good news front and center! This is why the last word as we leave gathered worship on Sunday must not be, "Do more! Do more!" That will either crush you because you can't pull it off, or it will inflate you beyond tolerable limits because you *think* you're pulling it off.

There's a better way. The big reveal we wait to uncover every Sunday is some version of this: Jesus is the one we need! You reply, "You said that last week." Right! And we'll say it again next week! We say it again and again, until the truth of it breaks in on us—until the truth breaks through darkness, sin, addiction, boredom, suicidal thoughts, nominalism, shame, and guilt. We speak this good news—this gospel about what God has done in Christ—until it becomes our new favorite thing to hear and say.

Every Sunday as the church we're inviting one another to know the Lord. Paul prayed for the early Christians that they would know the Lord, "being rooted and built up in him" (Col 2:7), "growing in the knowledge of God" (Col 1:10). As a church, therefore, it's our business to know God better and better. The better we know him the more we love him. The more we love him the more we trust him. The more we trust him the more we obey him.

Spread the Word!
PSALM 100:5

What we're seeing here is the threefold task of the church: worship, nurture, and mission. A people praising God. A people growing in the knowledge of God. A people taking the gospel to the city and the world. We see this truth develop in at least two areas.

We Take the Gospel to Every Nation

God wants this life of rejoicing to impact the whole world. How do we know? It's where our psalm began (v. 1). Derek Kidner said that verse 1 "claims the world for God" (*Psalms 73–150*, 356). This psalm of joy is also a song that pulsates with mission. Missions is a joy project. Romans 10 is a compelling picture of missions—happy feet bringing good news to the nations. The Great Commission is joy in tennis shoes—joy on the run.

We Transfer the Gospel to Every Generation

This psalm ends with God's faithfulness being seen by generation after generation. As the church we have a passion for every nation and every generation. It's not one at the expense of the other. This is why we encourage family worship, where parents gather the children around the table or in the living room, if only briefly, to talk to God (prayer) and to hear God talk to us (Scripture).

This is why our church does kids' ministry the way we do. Our hope is to reinforce what Christian parents are doing at home, to come alongside parents in the effort to fill up our kids' hearts with love for Jesus. We want to help the next generation know the Lord.

This is why we encourage families to attend worship together. This way children grow up seeing mom and dad worshiping, singing, praying, listening to the preaching of God's Word, taking it in eagerly, giving in the offering. These are means of grace that God uses to show our children how beautiful and glorious God is—how worthy he is of everything.

In each of these, we are building a framework of understanding. We are telling our children and the nations who God is. Who they are. Why they exist. What's wrong on the inside. What's wrong with the world. And how the one true and living God, as revealed in the story of the gospel, makes all things new.

When a cynical culture hears the word *church*, all kinds of words come to mind: *ignorant, judgmental, lame, boring, rules, religion, irrelevant*. God has a different list: *joyful, gladness, songs, thanksgiving*. Nations worshiping. Children and their children's children knowing God's faithfulness. What kind of church do we want to be?

Reflect and Discuss

1. What descriptions do you most often hear when non-Christians talk about Christians? In what way does that shed light on the church's call to reflect God's character?
2. Does your approach to gathered worship include both reverent stillness and enthusiastic joy? Which one seems more prominent and why?
3. What are some ways Christians and local churches can display God's passion for all nations?
4. What kinds of unhealthy habits/ideas grow when someone neglects gathered worship?
5. What kinds of unhealthy habits/ideas grow when someone neglects all-of-life worship?
6. How would you help someone grasp worship as involving the whole of one's life?
7. How are you leveraging your time, talent, and treasure to invest the gospel in generations coming after you?
8. How are you leveraging your time, talent, and treasure to take the gospel to the nations?
9. What do you think it looks like for gathered worship to be centered on God and his glory?
10. Which of these marks of the church are most lacking in your life? On the other hand, in which area have you seen growth, by God's grace? What might be a good next step to cultivate these marks of spiritual health?

WORKS CITED

Adnan, Duraid, and Tim Arango. "Suicide Bomb Trainer in Iraq Accidentally Blows Up His Class." *New York Times.* February 10, 2014. www.nytimes.com/2014/02/11/world/middleeast/suicide-bomb-instructor-accidentally-kills-iraqi-pupils.html. Accessed July 9, 2019.

Augustine. *The Confessions,* book 1, paragraph 1. In *Basic Writings of Saint Augustine,* vol. 1. Edited by Whitney J. Oates. New York: Random House, 1948.

Barnhouse, Donald Grey. *God's Remedy: Exposition of Bible Doctrines, Taking the Epistle to the Romans as a Point of Departure,* vol. 3: *Romans 3:21–4:5.* Grand Rapids: Eerdmans, 1954.

Bartlett, John. *Familiar Quotations: A Collection of Passages, Phrases and Proverbs Traced to Their Sources in Ancient and Modern Literature,* 13th edition. Boston: Little, Brown and Co., 1955.

Boice, James Montgomery. "Monday: Dark Night of the Soul." http://www.alliancenet.org/tab/monday-the-dark-night-of-the-soul. Accessed August 20, 2019.

———. *Psalms,* vol. 2. Grand Rapids: Baker, 1986.

———. *Psalms 42–106: An Expositional Commentary.* Grand Rapids: Baker, 2005.

Brown, F., S. R. Driver, and C. A. Briggs. *A Hebrew and English Lexicon of the Old Testament.* London: Oxford University, 1906. [BDB]

Campbell, Murdoch. *From Grace to Glory: Meditations on the Book of Psalms.* Carlisle, PA: The Banner of Truth Trust, 1970.

Centers for Disease Control and Prevention. "Youth Risk Behavior Survey Data Summary and Trends Report 2007–2017." https://www.cdc.gov/healthyyouth/data/yrbs/pdf/trendsreport.pdf. Accessed July 3, 2019.

Chan, Francis, and Preston Sprinkle. *Erasing Hell: What God Said about Eternity and the Things We've Made Up.* Colorado Springs: David C. Cook, 2011.

Charnock, Stephen. *The Existence and Attributes of God.* Discourse V: On the Eternity of God, part IV, Use 2, paragraph 3. https://www.gutenberg .org/files/53527/53527-h/53527-h.htm. Accessed July 8, 2019.

Chesterton, G. K. *Orthodoxy.* 1909: repr., Wheaton: Harold Shaw, 1994.

Edwards, Jonathan. *The Works of President Edwards.* Vol. 1. New York: Robert Carter and Brothers, 1881.

Fernando, Ajith. *Crucial Questions about Hell.* Wheaton: Crossway, 1991.

Gesenius' Hebrew Grammar. Edited by E. Kautzsch, translated by A. E. Cowley. Oxford: Clarendon, 1910.

Goldingay, John. *Psalms—Volume 2: Psalms 42–89.* In Baker Commentary on the Old Testament. Grand Rapids: Baker, 2007.

———. *Psalms—Volume 3: Psalms 90–150.* In Baker Commentary on the Old Testament. Grand Rapids: Baker, 2008.

Gray, James Comper, and George M. Adams. *The Biblical Encyclopedia.* Vol. II. Cleveland, OH: F. M. Barton, 1903.

Grudem, Wayne. *Systematic Theology.* Grand Rapids: Zondervan, 1994.

Henry, Matthew. *Matthew Henry's Commentary on the Whole Bible: Complete and Unabridged in One Volume.* Peabody: Hendrickson, 1994.

Hofstadter, Richard. *America at 1750: A Social Portrait.* Vintage International series. New York: Vintage, 1973.

Hossfeld, Lothar, and Erich Zenger. *Psalms 2: A Commentary on Psalms 51–100.* Hermeneia. Minneapolis: Fortress, 2005.

Howell, Kellan. "Bill Maher: God a 'Psychotic Mass Murderer' Who 'Drowns Babies.'" *The Washington Times.* March 15, 2014. https:// www.washingtontimes.com/news/2014/mar/15/bill-maher-god -psychotic-mass-murderer-who-drowns. Accessed September 20, 2018.

Kidd, Reggie. *With One Voice: Discovering Christ's Song in Our Worship.* Grand Rapids: Baker, 2005.

Kidner, Derek. *Psalms 1–72: An Introduction and Commentary on Books I and II of the Psalms.* Tyndale Old Testament Commentaries. Downers Grove: InterVarsity, 1973.

———. *Psalms 73–150.* Downers Grove: InterVarsity Press, 1975.

Langley, James A. *The Washington Post.* March 31, 2017. Accessed Sept. 30, 2019, https://www.washingtonpost.com/opinions/who-coined -government-of-the-people-by-the-people-for-the-people/2017/03 /31/12fc465a-0fd5-11e7-aa57-2ca1b05c41b8_story.html.

Lewis, C. S. "The Weight of Glory." In *The Weight of Glory: And Other Addresses.* New York: HarperCollins, 2001.

Luther, Martin, C. M. Jacobs, C. H. Jacobs, Henry Cole, F. Bente. "Of Prayer," *The Collected Works of Martin Luther*, e-artnow (ebook). 2018.

Metzger, Will. *Tell the Truth: The Whole Gospel to the Whole Person by Whole People*. Downers Grove: IVP, 2002.

Miller, Paul E. *A Praying Life: Connecting with God in a Distracting World*. Colorado Springs: NavPress, 2017.

Moon, Gary W. *Becoming Dallas Willard*. Downers Grove: InterVarsity, 2018.

Ortlund, Raymond, Jr. *When God Comes to Church: A Biblical Model for Revival Today*. Grand Rapids: Baker, 2000.

Perowne, J. J. Stewart. *The Book of Psalms*. Cambridge: Deighton, Bell and Co., 1870.

———. *The Book of Psalms, Vol. 2*. Cambridge: Deighton, Bell and Co., 1882.

Pink, A. W. *The Doctrine of Human Depravity*. Hollis, NH: Bradford: Puritan Press, 2009.

Piper, John. "Can Christians Be Depressed?" https://www.desiringgod .org/interviews/can-christians-be-depressed. Accessed on November 1, 2018.

———. "Let the Nations Be Glad." https://www. desiringgod.org/messages /let-the-nations-be-glad. Accessed 10/31/2018.

———. *Let the Nations Be Glad! The Supremacy of God in Missions*. Grand Rapids: Baker, 1993.

———. *When I Don't Desire God: How to Fight for Joy*. Wheaton: Crossway, 2004.

———, and Justin Taylor, eds. *Suffering and the Sovereignty of God*. Wheaton: Crossway, 2006.

Platt, David. *Radical: Taking Back Your Faith from the American Dream*. Colorado Springs: Multnomah, 2010.

Ross, Allen P. *A Commentary on the Psalms, Volume 2: 42–89*. Grand Rapids: Kregel, 2013.

———. *A Commentary on the Psalms, Volume 3: 90–150*. Grand Rapids: Kregel, 2014.

Ryle, J. C. *Facts and Men*. London, William Hunt and Company, 1882.

Spurgeon, Charles. *An All-Round Ministry: Addresses to Ministers and Students*. Carlisle, PA: Banner of Truth, 1960.

———. "The Child of Light Walking in Darkness." Sermon no. 1985. *The Metropolitan Tabernacle Pulpit*, 1887, vol. 33. Pasadena: Pilgrim Publications, 1974.

———. *The Metropolitan Tabernacle Pulpit, Vol. XV.* Pasadena, Texas: Pilgrim Publications, 1984.

———. *The New Park Street Pulpit, Vol. V.* Pasadena, Texas: Pilgrim Publications, 1981.

———. "On Expectations." Sermon no. 2186. Metropolitan Tabernacle, Newington. January 15, 1891.

———. *The Quotable Spurgeon.* Wheaton: Harold Shaw, 1990.

———. "Rest as a Test." Sermon no. 2748. *The Metropolitan Tabernacle Pulpit*, 1901, vol. 47. Pasadena: Pilgrim Publications, 1977.

———. *Spurgeon on Prayer and Spiritual Warfare.* New Kensington, PA: Whitaker House, 1998.

———. *Spurgeon on the Psalms Book Two: Psalm 26 through Psalm 50.* Newberry, FL: Bridge-Logos, 2015.

———. *Spurgeon's Sermons*, vol. 28: 1882. http://www.ccel.org/ccel/spurgeon/sermons28.xlvi.html. Accessed September 18, 2019.

———. *The Treasury of David.* Three volumes. Peabody: Hendrickson, 1990.

———. "The Valley of the Shadow." Sermon no. 1595. *Metropolitan Tabernacle Pulpit*, 1881, vol. 27. Pasadena: Pilgrim Publications, 1973.

Stott, John R. W. *Christ the Conversationalist: A Study in Some Essentials of Evangelical Religion.* London: Tyndale, 1970.

———. *The Cross of Christ.* Downers Grove: InterVarsity, 1986.

Swindoll, Charles R. "Strengthening Your Grip on Prayer." *Insight for Living Ministries.* https://www.insight.org/resources/article-library/individual/strengthening-your-grip-on-prayer. Accessed September 19, 2018.

Tate, Marvin E. *Psalms 51–100.* Word Biblical Commentary, vol. 20. Dallas: Word, 1990.

Tozer, A. W. *Knowledge of the Holy: Drawing Closer to God through His Attributes.* New York: Harper & Row, 1961.

———. *Tozer on Worship and Entertainment: Selected Excerpts.* Compiled by James L. Snyder. Camp Hill, Pennsylvania: Christian Publications, 1997.

VanGemeren, Willem A. *Psalms.* Expositor's Bible Commentary, vol. 5. Edited by Frank E. Gaebelein. Grand Rapids: Zondervan, 1991.

Volf, Miroslav. *Free of Charge: Giving and Forgiving in a Culture Stripped of Grace.* Grand Rapids: Zondervan, 2009.

Wilson, Gerald H. *Psalms Volume 1.* The NIV Application Commentary. Grand Rapids: Zondervan Academic, 2014.

Wilson, Thomas. *The Works of the Right Reverend Father in God.* Vol. III.
Oxford: John Henry Parker, 1863.

SCRIPTURE INDEX

79:13 *266*
80 *269, 275*
80:1 *272, 391,*
435
80:1-2 *270*
80:1-3 *270*
80:3,7,19 *271*
80:4 *271*
80:4-7 *271*
80:5 *272*
80:7 *273, 276*
80:8 *274*
80:8-17 *270*
80:8-19 *274*
80:9 *274*
80:10-11 *274*
80:12 *274*
80:17 *274*
80:18 *274*
81 *277, 283*
81:1 *278*
81:1-2 *278*
81:1-5 *278*
81:3 *278*
81:4-5 *278*
81:5-7 *280*
81:7 *280*
81:8 *281*
81:8-12 *280*
81:9 *281*
81: 10 *282*
81:10 *281*
81:11-12 *281*
81:12 *281*
81:13 *283*
81:13-16 *283*
81:14-15 *283*
81:14-16 *285*
81:15 *283*

81:16 *283*
82 *75, 286–87*
82:1 *287–88*
82:1-7 *289*
82:2 *288*
82:3 *288*
82:3-4 *72, 290*
82:5 *288*
82:7 *287*
82:8 *289, 391*
83 *292, 295*
83:1 *293*
83:1-8 *293*
83:1-15 *297*
83:2 *293–94*
83:3 *293–94*
83:3,5 *293*
83:4 *294, 296*
83:5 *294*
83:6-8 *293*
83:9 *296*
83:9-15 *295*
83:10 *296*
83:11 *296*
83:13-15 *296*
83:16 *298*
83:16-17 *297*
83:16-18 *297*
83:18 *298–99*
84 *304–5, 311–12*
84:2 *305*
84:3 *304*
84:4 *305*
84:4-5,12 *302*
84:5 *307*
84:6 *307*
84:6-7 *302*
84:7 *307*
84:8 *306*

84:9 *312*
84:10 *303*
84:11 *306*
84:12 *308, 311*
85 *315, 318*
85:1 *317, 321*
85:1-3 *317*
85:2 *317*
85:3 *317*
85:4 *318*
85:4,6 *319*
85:4-7 *318*
85:6 *315, 319*
85:7 *319*
85:8-13 *320*
85:9 *315*
85:10 *315*
85:11 *315*
86 *323, 326*
86:1-7 *323*
86:2 *323–24*
86:3 *324*
86:3,6 *323*
86:5 *326*
86:8,10 *325*
86:8-13 *324–25*
86:9 *325–26*
86:11 *324–25*
86:14 *323,*
325–26
86:14-17 *325–26*
86:15 *325–26*
86:17 *325*
87 *328, 332,*
339–40
87:1 *329*
87:1-3 *329*
87:2 *330*
87:3 *333, 339*